Creating and Sustaining Competitive Advantage

Chandra S. Mishra

Creating and Sustaining Competitive Advantage

Management Logics, Business Models, and Entrepreneurial Rent

palgrave
macmillan

Chandra S. Mishra
Florida Atlantic University
Boca Raton, Florida, USA

ISBN 978-3-319-54539-4 ISBN 978-3-319-54540-0 (eBook)
DOI 10.1007/978-3-319-54540-0

Library of Congress Control Number: 2017940472

Printed on acid-free paper

This Palgrave Macmillan imprint is published by Springer Nature
The registered company is Springer International Publishing AG
The registered company address is: Gewerbestrasse 11, 6330 Cham, Switzerland

To my wife, Sukhdeep
To my children, Mitushi and Sachit

Contents

List of Figures

PART I

In Search of a Theory of Competitive Advantage

CHAPTER 1

Competitive Advantage Logics

Introduction

Some thirty years ago, Michael Porter (1985) published *Competitive Advantage*, in which Porter developed a framework to guide corporate executives and management consultants to formulate a company's strategy. In Porter's framework, a company's strategy is a set of value activities and the company may perform their value activities differently to achieve competitive advantage. Since then extensive research has been done in the field of strategic management. Some of these research perspectives are, however, at odds with Porter's frameworks. Moreover, the underlying process, the "black box" of competitive advantage creation, is not yet clearly understood. Our entrepreneurial logic enhances extant strategic frameworks. According to our framework, the firm's competitive advantage lies in the value creation and appropriation mechanism, which is enhanced by the entrepreneurial incentives. The entrepreneurial incentive is the proportion of uncertain performance-based compensation in the executive pay, in that the firm performance is set by an external arbiter such as the capital market. The entrepreneurial incentives enhance the firm's entrepreneurial behavior, which further enhance the value creation and appropriation mechanism wherein the competitive advantage lies.

The proposed framework is a two-stage competitive advantage creation model such that in the first stage the entrepreneurial incentives enhance the firm's entrepreneurial orientation, which further enhance management cognition, active learning, combinative capabilities, and dynamic capabilities.

C.S. Mishra, *Creating and Sustaining Competitive Advantage*,
DOI 10.1007/978-3-319-54540-0_1

In the second stage, the business model value drivers are enhanced, which further enhances the firm's competitive position. The value creation and appropriation processes that underlie the firm's competitive advantage creation is hitherto a "black box." Our theory of competitive advantage looks into and opens this black box. Further, in economics and finance literature, the processes that underlie the relation between management incentives and firm performance are also a black box. Our theory of competitive advantage, namely, the theory of entrepreneurial rent, uncovers these processes. Our theory thus explains the processes underlying how superior management incentives enhance the value creation and appropriation drivers that may ultimately result in the firm achieving superior firm performance.

The firm's entrepreneurial capacity to proactively exploit the environmental uncertainty in their favor and act on their value opportunities in a timely manner, sustaining the value creation and appropriation, is a source of competitive advantage. To seize and exploit value opportunities, the firm must regularly test and revise the management logics. The management must maintain sufficient situation awareness and focus attention on the critical aspects of the environment to recognize cognitively distant value opportunities. With sufficient entrepreneurial incentives that enhance the management logics which further enhance the management cognition and situation awareness, the manager seizes and exploits distant value opportunities in a timely manner, enhancing the firm's value creation and appropriation mechanism that provides the firm superior performance and competitive advantage. Entrepreneurial incentives provide the firm an execution advantage that enables the firm to create and sustain competitive advantage.

Entrepreneurial incentives are key to the firm's achieving superior performance. In an interview with the *Harvard Business Review*, Hatsopoulos (1995), Chairman and CEO of Thermo Electron Corporation, says: "When executives from other companies ask me what they need to do to increase new business activity, the first advice I give them is to change their organizations' basic incentive structures." Further, Holt (1995), Vice President for Research & Technology at Xerox Corporation says: "If innovation is the ability to recognize opportunity, then the essence of being an entrepreneur is being able to mobilize talent and resources quickly to seize that opportunity and turn it into a business." It is the entrepreneurial execution of the firm's value creation and appropriation mechanism wherein the firm's competitive advantage lies. The buyer value design and the business model mechanism that creates, delivers, sustains, monetizes, and appropriates the buyer value are central to the firm's competitive advantage (Mishra 2015).

The business model execution advantage enhances the firm's competitive position.

Entrepreneurial incentives enhance the management abilities to seize the opportunities today to gain competitive advantage in the future. For example, Hamel and Prahalad (1994) found that managers devoted less than three percent of their time to developing a view of the future. They urge managers to spend more time on creating the firm's future instead of spending too much time on catching up with competitors by cutting costs and improving quality. The enactment of the future empowered by powerful entrepreneurial incentives should drive the firm's current strategy and opportunities. The management should consider who their customers are today and who their customers will be in the future; who their competitors are today and who their competitors will be in the future; further, which activities and capabilities make the firm competitive today and which will make them competitive in the future.

Why are some managers more successful at identifying value opportunities that enhance the value creation and appropriation mechanism providing the firm a competitive advantage? A greater ability to recognize complex stimuli in their environment distinguishes entrepreneurial executives from their traditional counterparts. High-powered entrepreneurial incentives and the potential to earn an entrepreneurial surplus that enhance management learning and their cognitive adaptability further enhance the management logics and management cognition. Entrepreneurial incentives to earn an entrepreneurial surplus provide the firm competitive advantage and superior performance, enhancing the management cognition under dynamic competitive conditions, and timely seizing and acting on value opportunities while attending to the needs of the firm's existing operations.

Creating and Sustaining Competitive Advantage develops a comprehensive theory of competitive advantage based on entrepreneurial value creation and appropriation mechanism and explains the phenomena of competitive advantage creation in a firm with a dynamic environment. The frameworks in *Creating and Sustaining Competitive Advantage* not only reconcile and integrate the extant strategic logics but also fill the voids therein by providing a comprehensive treatment of the value creation and appropriation mechanism underlying competitive advantage creation, starting with the entrepreneurial incentives for the management to earn an entrepreneurial surplus that enhance the management logics and value opportunities, which further enhances the business model execution advantage and provides the firm superior performance. Our theory of competitive advantage, namely the theory of entrepreneurial rent, addresses following strategic issues, among others:

- How does a firm create competitive advantage in a changing environment?
- How does a firm sense and seize value opportunities in a timely manner?
- How is the value creation and appropriation mechanism configured?
- What is the role of core resources in the firm value creation?
- Why do some managers recognize superior value opportunities?
- How do the management logics change in a dynamic environment?
- Does a firm benefit by imitating a competitor's superior resources?
- What drives executive incentives to differ in organizations?
- When is the financial slack or excess free cash flow beneficial to a firm?
- How does a firm measure and enhance the value chain effectiveness?
- How does a firm measure and enhance the revenue model effectiveness?
- How does a firm measure and enhance the business model advantage?
- How does a firm adapt its business model in a changing environment?
- How does active learning in a firm enhance the business model mechanism?
- How do a firm's dynamic capabilities enable its business model mechanism?
- How do entrepreneurial incentives in the firm enhance the business model advantage?

Our theory of competitive advantage enhances extant strategic management views within an entrepreneurial value creation and appropriation framework. According to our entrepreneurial logic, the entrepreneurial incentives provide the firm an execution advantage that enhances management cognition, active learning, combinative capabilities, dynamic capabilities, and proactive adaptation to environmental uncertainty that further enhance the firm's value creation and appropriation mechanism, thereby enhancing the business model advantage and the firm's competitive advantage. Our theory of competitive advantage, namely the theory of entrepreneurial rent, is based on the entrepreneurial logic that identifies the entrepreneurial incentives that enhance the firm's value creation and appropriation drivers underlying the firm's competitive advantage creation.

The entrepreneurial incentives in the firm provides the management powerful incentives to enhance the management logics and thereby management cognition, seize cognitively distant value opportunities in a timely manner, enable dynamic capabilities that enhance the resources and activities, and enhance the business model mechanism. The competitive advantage is created and sustained in the firm's value creation and appropriation mechanism. The greater the business model execution advantage, the greater is the firm's competitive position. The business model advantage construct constitutes the business model scalability, sustainability, and adaptability.

In *Creating and Sustaining Competitive Advantage*, it is proposed that the greater the entrepreneurial incentives for the management that enhance the firm's alertness, agility, absorptivity, and proactive adaptability, the greater is the likelihood of the business model advantage and the more likely is the firm to achieve and sustain competitive advantage. The frameworks explain the interior processes underlying the creation of competitive advantage and the relations between several strategic and behavioral constructs, namely, entrepreneurial incentives, management logics, entrepreneurial orientation, management cognition, situation awareness, core resources, combinative capabilities, value opportunities, value activities, activity drivers, business model, buyer value, and firm value, among others.

One of the most studied theories of strategic management in the last thirty years is the resource-based theory. The resource-based theory claims that a firm's strategic resource, that is valuable, rare, imperfectly imitable, and imperfectly substitutable, is a source of competitive advantage for the firm. But the resource-based theory does not explain the interior processes of how a strategic resource may create competitive advantage in a firm. Our theory of competitive advantage, namely the theory of entrepreneurial rent, addresses that void. Another problem with the resource-based theory is that its logic is tautological, in that a strategic resource is defined and identified as a resource that is valuable or that enhances firm performance, and the outcome or competitive advantage is defined in terms of firm performance. The resource-based logic is not helpful because of its failure to explain the underlying processes of competitive advantage creation; and further, the resource-based logic assumes that the firm's value creation and appropriation mechanism will always deliver superior performance when a strategic resource is present.

The resource-based theory thus assumes that the firm's activity implementation and value appropriation processes will deliver competitive advantage when a strategic resource is present. In contrast, our theory of competitive advantage explains the interior processes of value creation and appropriation underlying the firm's competitive advantage. However, we view the role of the strategic resources in enhancing the business model mechanism and hence the firm value when the management is empowered with the entrepreneurial incentives that enhance the management cognition and identification of value opportunities. Further, it is how successful an organization is in executing their value creation and appropriation processes that ultimately determines whether the firm can achieve competitive advantage.

It is indeed the value creation and appropriation processes or the firm's business model mechanism that underlies their competitive advantage. For example, many startups do not have strategic resources but they do successfully compete with established market leaders. Therefore, a strategic resource is not a prerequisite or a guarantee for a firm to attain competitive advantage. Entrepreneurial organizations are resource constrained but they proactively and quickly learn and build resources, and exploit value opportunities in an uncertain environment; whereas traditional organizations, consistent with the resource-based theory, build on their existing resources. In contrast, entrepreneurial organizations are alert, agile, absorptive, proactively adaptive, and opportunity driven.

Further, the extant resource-based views ignore the firm's product market conditions and competitive forces in explaining the competitive advantage. Porter's (1985) positioning view, on the other hand, ignores the effects of strategic resources when explaining the value activities that create competitive advantage. Furthermore, the value creation and appropriation mechanism or the implementation processes linking a firm's strategic resources to the competitive advantage and firm performance are currently absent. In the absence of a comprehensive theory that relates the firm's strategic resources to their effective implementation using the business model that sustains value creation and appropriation, it is difficult to test the firm resource-performance relationship. Further, in the absence of a framework explaining value creation and appropriation mechanism underlying the competitive advantage, not only is it difficult to test the resource-based theory but the extant findings are also subject to misinterpretation.

Most current empirical studies verify whether a resource that meets the strategic resource criteria provides superior firm performance. The problem with such a test design is that since the strategic resource by definition is valuable, the strategic resource chosen by the researcher has a priori positive resource-performance relationship. That is, the researcher chooses a resource that enhances the firm's revenues or lowers the costs. Thus when the result is that the firm's strategic resource increases the firm performance, it only means that the resource a priori increasing the firm's revenues or lowering the costs does increase the firm's performance, which is rather an obvious result. Thus, a positive relation found in the extant resource-performance studies only means that a strategic resource identified that enhances the firm's revenues or lowers costs does increase firm performance, a trivial result indeed. The interior process of value creation with the strategic resource must be clearly identified and controlled for to test the resource-based theory.

Since the underlying processes of competitive advantage creation are not known, it is difficult to estimate the relative contribution of a strategic resource to the firm's competitive advantage. Further, the resource-based theory does not explain the conditions under which a strategic resource may provide the competitive advantage. Our theory of competitive advantage explains the interior processes linking firm resources and activities to firm performance and competitive advantage.

In terms of normative implications of the resource-based theory, Barney (2001) suggests that the resource-based theory can guide managers to identify the firm's strategic resources that provide the competitive advantage. Strategic resources are valuable, rare, imperfectly imitable, and imperfectly substitutable (Barney 1991). In practice, the firm's intangible resources are identified as strategic resources. However, by their nature all intangible resources are imperfectly imitable and imperfectly substitutable. Further, a strategic resource is valuable when it enhances the firm's revenues or lowers its costs. However, all resources the firm employs either directly or indirectly potentially enhance the revenues or lower the costs. Thus, all intangible resources meet the criteria of imperfectly imitable, imperfectly substitutable, and potentially valuable.

The only strategic resource criterion remaining for managers to confirm a resource as a potential source of competitive advantage is to determine whether there is limited competition for the rare strategic resource. However, enhanced competition, not limited competition, in the resource market indeed ensures that firms appropriate the value they create (McDoland and Ryall 2004). Thus, limited competition for a strategic resource will inhibit value appropriation and hence the firm will not realize superior performance and competitive advantage. Therefore, the resource-based theory does not provide helpful criteria for managers to identify the sources of competitive advantage.

McDoland and Ryall further show that the strategic resource criteria, namely, valuable, rare, imperfectly imitable, and imperfectly substitutable, are neither necessary nor sufficient for a resource to provide the firm a competitive advantage. The resource-based logic does not provide the conditions under which a strategic resource may provide the firm a competitive advantage. Our framework identifies such conditions, namely the presence of entrepreneurial incentives that enhance the business model execution in an organization, which enhance the firm's value creation and appropriation that underlies the competitive advantage.

Second, Barney (2001) suggests that managers may employ the resource-based theory to identify the strategic resources that the firm is lacking which the competitors may have and then the firm may imitate such resources. However, resource deployment in the competitor's value creation and appropriation mechanism is causally ambiguous. Further, the value creation and appropriation mechanism is a black box in the resource-based theory. Without an understanding of the value creation and appropriation mechanism of the competitor, it is not possible to know the conditions when the strategic resource of the competitor might enhance the imitating firm's value.

Assuming that the strategic resource identified is a source of competitive advantage for the imitator, the bigger problem with the imitation prescription is that it is not always incentive compatible for all firms to imitate a resource employed by a competitor. It is thus not incentive compatible for all organizations to imitate a high-ability competitor's strategic resources since the incentives of low-ability managers are not compatible with the deployment of some resources found in competitive organizations. Powerful incentives can be designed and offered to enhance the incentives of the low-performing managers so that a high-performing competitor's strategic resource may be imitated; however, some managers may not choose such high-powered incentives since that will impose excessive risk on the managers in the uncertain environment. The compensation choice of a manager is an incentive signal of their managerial ability. Furthermore, a firm's strategic resource choice is an incentive signal by the management of their managerial ability in our framework.

However, the incentive compatibility can be enhanced by firing the firm's low-ability managers, but that is not always the case with the firms that undergo strategic change. Thus, it is not always possible to imitate a competitor's strategic resource even if it is possible in rare cases to identify such a resource given that strategic resource deployments are causally ambiguous. Moreover, in firms undergoing strategic change, the management logics determine the strategic resources that are compatible with the firm's value creation and appropriation mechanism.

For example, Grinyer et al. (1988) examine whether a strategic change in an organization requires a change in top management. The authors found that in 45 percent of the sample firms undergoing a strategic reorganization, there was no change of top management. New CEO was recruited in some cases but even in those cases the change in firm performance was not fully explained by the change in the CEO. Further, Grinyer et al. found that performance improvements in firms undergoing radical reorganization were the result of the change in the management logics that enabled the managers to reconfigure the firm's value activities.

None of the current strategic management books provides a comprehensive treatment of implementation or value creation processes underlying creation and sustainability of competitive advantage. None of these books looks into the "black box" or interior processes explaining how a firm may achieve competitive advantage. For example, some books focus on resource selection strategies. However, when selected resources fail to create the buyer value or the firm may not have an effective value appropriation mechanism, such resources then may not provide the firm with competitive advantage. Similarly, some books focus on the firm's dynamic capabilities and organizational routines explaining the role of dynamic capabilities in reconfiguring a firm's resources. Further, there is no consensus on the definition of dynamic capabilities, nor can they guide which resources are reconfigured. The business model mechanism captures the interior processes of value creation and appropriation, as illustrated in our framework. The competitive advantage lies in the business model execution.

Competitive advantage is the rationale underlying a firm's superior performance relative to its competitors. Extant strategic logics clash because the interior processes underlying a firm's competitive advantage creation are missing. Our theory of competitive advantage, namely the theory of entrepreneurial rent, provides a comprehensive treatment of interior value creation and appropriation processes underlying the creation and sustainability of competitive advantage in a firm. The theory of entrepreneurial rent argues that entrepreneurial incentives enhance the firm's entrepreneurial behavior, which further enhances and sustains the firm's value creation and appropriation mechanism wherein the competitive advantage lies. In the following we explain extant strategic logics, namely, resource-based logic and positioning logic. Further, we present our entrepreneurial logic that underlies our theory of competitive advantage, namely the theory of entrepreneurial rent. The entrepreneurial logic premises the creation of competitive advantage on the entrepreneurial incentives that enhance the business model mechanism in the firm, which further enhances the firm value creation and appropriation mechanism wherein the competitive advantage lies. The entrepreneurial incentives enable the management to earn an entrepreneurial surplus.

Resource-Based Logic

The resource-based logic of competitive advantage claims that strategic resources underlie the firm's competitive advantage. Barney (1991) identifies the characteristics of strategic resources. Strategic resources are valuable, rare, imperfectly imitable, and nonsubstitutable. According to the resource-based view, the strategic resources underlie the firm's competitive advantage. Firms develop and nurture strategic resources to achieve and sustain competitive advantage.

Penrose (1959) was one of the first proponents of the resource-based logic. She proposes that a firm's growth is constrained by its resource position, not by the product market conditions. However, in her theory of the growth of the firm, she assumes that the product market provides unlimited opportunities, and managers are always aware of these opportunities and they can seize and exploit the opportunities in a timely manner. Thus, in Penrose's theory of the growth of the firm, the only constraint is the resource constraint inhibiting the firm growth. In particular, she emphasizes the managerial capacity as the major resource limitation constraining the firm's growth. Penrose did not distinguish strategic resources from the other productive resources of the firm. Indeed, Penrose's theory is more in line with our entrepreneurial logic in that her emphasis was on the entrepreneurial capacity of managers. For instance, she argues that enterprising managers can achieve and sustain firm growth. Penrose's theory of the growth is thus consistent with the entrepreneurial behavior of the firm; in particular, she emphasizes the importance of the entrepreneurial abilities of managers. It is the absence of enterprising management that limits the firm's growth.

Wernerfelt (1984) first coined the term, resource-based view. He defines resources as the firm's strengths and weaknesses. He argues that there are two ways to analyze a firm, namely, resource perspective and product perspective. "For the firm, resources and products are two sides of the same coin" (Wernefelt 1984: 171). Wernerfelt emphasizes the resource perspective for formulating a firm's strategy. By analyzing a firm's products, one infers the minimum resource requirements; conversely, by identifying the firm's resource position, one can understand the firm's product market strategy. The resource position of the firm is analyzed using the firm's strengths and weaknesses.

Wernerfelt claims that both resource and product perspectives yield the same insights; however, analyzing a firm's resource perspective is easier. Wernerfelt proposes that a firm can identify types of resources that can lead to high profits. The firm's strategy is to strike a balance between the exploitation of existing resources and the development of new ones. Wernerfelt compares market entry barriers that provide a firm competitive advantage under the product market perspective to the firm's resource position barriers as potential sources of competitive advantage. Wernerfelt identifies strategic resources as attractive resources. He argues that "what a firm wants is to create a situation where its own resource position directly or indirectly makes it more difficult for others to catch up" (Wernerfelt 1984: 173). In the resource-based view, resource position barriers are analogous to market entry barriers, and thus a firm can achieve competitive advantage by creating resource position barriers.

In a stable and predictable environment, it may be possible to identify and build resource position barriers to provide a firm with competitive advantage. In a dynamic environment, however, it is difficult to determine a resource position barrier that will not become irrelevant when the firm's environmental conditions change. Thus, a resource position barrier providing a firm competitive advantage may erode quickly. Competitive advantage obtained with resource position barriers is only transitory. Further, Rumelt (1984) identifies the firm's resource position barriers as isolating mechanisms. Thus, isolating mechanisms provide the firm the barriers to competitive imitation and therefore help the firm sustain their competitive advantage.

Isolating mechanisms make it increasingly difficult for competitors to imitate a firm's competitive advantage. Lippman and Rumelt (1982) provide the conditions for the imperfect imitability of a firm's competitive advantage, primarily due to the causal ambiguity associated with isolating mechanisms. Isolating mechanisms are causally ambiguous. Causal ambiguity with strategic resources prevents competitors from knowing which resources to imitate or how the resources exactly drive a firm's superior performance. Isolating mechanisms include knowledge assets, buyer switching costs and search costs, channel crowding, reputation, property rights, information advantage, among others. The imperfect imitability of a strategic resource by a competitor is central to the resource-based theory. Imperfect imitability and causal ambiguity with strategic resources prevent rent dissipation and thus sustains the firm's competitive advantage.

Peteraf (1993) offers four conditions under which a strategic resource provides a firm competitive advantage, namely, resource scarcity, imperfect imitability, imperfect mobility, and limited competition. A resource must meet all four conditions to be a source of competitive advantage. First, resource scarcity implies that strategic resources are in limited supply. Strategic resources are heterogeneously distributed across firms in an industry. With a limited supply of strategic resources, firms who own strategic resources will thus earn Ricardian rent (excess profits) or scarcity rent. Second, the imperfect imitability of a strategic resource or the causal ambiguity underlying the relation between firm performance and strategic resources constrains competitive imitation.

Causal ambiguity makes it difficult for a competitor to implement a strategic resource, thus making the firm's resource imperfectly imitable. The imperfect imitability of a strategic resource sustains the firm's economic rent. Third, imperfect mobility implies that a strategic resource is difficult to trade. Strategic resources are firm-specific and thus earn quasi rents. That is, strategic resources lose value in their next best use. Specialized and co-specialized resources of a firm are imperfectly mobile. Finally, imperfect competition in strategic factor markets implies that there is limited knowledge of a strategic resource which limits the competition for the resource. Limited competition provides the firm with a strategic resource monopoly rent. Peteraf (1993) thus provides the conditions under which a firm can earn excess profits through Ricardian rent, quasi rent, and monopoly rent.

However, enhanced competition, not limited competition, ensures that firms appropriate the rent they create. Thus the rent created may not be appropriated when the competition for the resource is limited. McDonald and Ryall (2004) examine how the market competition influences the firm value appropriation. According to resource-based view, a resource that is valuable, rare, imperfectly imitable, and nonsubstitutable is a source of competitive advantage for the firm (Barney 1991). However, McDoland and Ryall show that strategic resource criteria, namely, valuable, scarcity, imperfectly imitability, and nonsubstitutability, are neither necessary nor sufficient for a firm to achieve competitive advantage. A firm appropriates the value it creates when, and only when, the firm's failing to do so would unleash competitive forces that could never be satisfied unless the firm appropriates the value it has created. Enhanced competition ensures that the firm appropriates the value it creates. The strategic resource enhances the value appropriability but not because of the limited competition. It is rather enhanced competition, not limited competition, which stimulates the firm's value appropriation, increasing the odds of the firm achieving competitive advantage.

In a stable and predictable environment, when a resource meets these conditions, namely, resource scarcity, imperfect imitability, imperfect mobility, and limited competition, the resource may provide a firm competitive advantage. These conditions assume that the resource identified is strategically relevant for the firm. In a dynamic environment, however, the resource relevance is lost when the rules of competition change. By our entrepreneurial logic, however, the entrepreneurial behavior of a firm does not lose relevance in a changing environment; indeed, the entrepreneurial behavior of the firm becomes even more relevant in a dynamic environment. The entrepreneurial behavior of an organization meets the conditions of the source of competitive advantage, namely, scarcity, imperfect imitability, and imperfect mobility. Entrepreneurial behavior in organizations is scarce, imperfectly imitable, and imperfectly mobile. Further, entrepreneurial behavior driven by the desire of the management to earn an entrepreneurial surplus ensures value appropriation by the firm. The entrepreneurial behavior of an organization provides competitive advantage in both stable and dynamic environments. The entrepreneurial behavior of a firm thus creates and sustains competitive advantage according to our theory of competitive advantage.

Strategic resources are nontradable or costly to trade. Dierickx and Cool (1989) identify the conditions under which a firm may accumulate strategic resources over time especially when these resources cannot be obtained in the strategic factor markets. The conditions under which a strategic resource may be accumulated in a firm include time compression diseconomies, asset mass economies, asset interconnectedness, asset erosion, and causal ambiguity. It takes time to accumulate a strategic resource as time compression diseconomies suggest. Without asset mass or initial asset endowment, it is difficult for a firm to accumulate or replicate a strategic resource. That is, without sufficient prior knowledge, it is difficult for a firm to accumulate or imitate a strategic asset of a competitor.

Asset interconnectedness implies that for a strategic asset to be accumulated, the firm must have complementary assets and capabilities. Thus a competitor attempting to replicate a strategic asset may not have access to the necessary complementary assets. Asset erosion implies that strategic assets depreciate or become obsolete over time. If a strategic resource has a shorter half-life, then it is hard for a competitor to have time to accumulate the resource before it has lost relevance in the changing competitive environment. Finally, the strategic asset accumulation process is causally ambiguous and therefore it is hard for a competitor to accumulate another firm's strategic asset. Strategic assets are imperfectly imitable and hard to replicate.

Entrepreneurial behavior of a firm is difficult to trade unless the firm is bought. However, the entrepreneurial behavior of a firm may not meet the conditions of strategic assets. For example, startup firms are entrepreneurial from the inception and thus a firm's entrepreneurial behavior does not meet the condition of time compression diseconomies. Further, the entrepreneurial behavior of a firm does not erode; in fact, it only strengthens over time. The entrepreneurial behavior of a firm does not require asset interconnectedness complementary assets. Further, entrepreneurial behavior is not contingent on the firm's current resource position; in fact, most entrepreneurial firms are generally resource constrained. The only condition the entrepreneurial behavior of a firm meets is causal ambiguity. Indeed, the firm's entrepreneurial culture is causally ambiguous. Thus, entrepreneurial behavior of a firm is not a strategic asset.

Our theory of competitive advantage, namely, the theory of entrepreneurial rent, is not a resource-based view. In the theory of entrepreneurial rent, the entrepreneurial incentives that provide the management the potential to earn an entrepreneurial surplus enhance the firm's value creation and appropriation mechanism wherein the firm's competitive advantage lies. Entrepreneurial behavior enhances the management logics and enables the firm's decision makers to overcome traditional behavioral bounds. Entrepreneurial organizations are alert, agile, adaptive, absorptive, proactive, and opportunity driven. The entrepreneurial orientation or behaviour of a firm varies across firms in an industry. The firm's entrepreneurial orientation is thus enhanced by the presence of entrepreneurial incentives.

The resource-based theory thus emphasizes scarcity, imperfect mobility, and imperfect imitability to help a firm identify strategic resources that provide competitive advantage, where competitive advantage is the rationale underlying a firm's superior performance. According to the resource-based theory, this rationale is a strategic resource. However, it is not clear what defines a resource in the resource-based theory. In the resource-based theory, resources include anything and everything associated with a firm. In that case a firm's competitive advantage attribute or rationale is also a resource, which is meaningless.

Thus, a firm's resource needs a clear definition. Anything and everything that is related to a firm is not a resource. Many definitions of resources are rather vague. For example, Wernerfelt (1984) defines a firm's resources as their strengths and weaknesses. Penrose (1959) defines a resource as a firm's productive resource. Barney (1991) defines a resource as anything having to do with a firm, including assets, processes, capabilities, or any and all attributes of the firm. Further, resources must be defined without a reference to firm performance; and as a result, the resource-performance relationship can then be examined. In our framework, we define resources as factor inputs to the firm's value creation and appropriation mechanism. In this definition, a resource in and of itself may not provide superior performance, certainly not by its definition. Our definition of resource solves the tautology associated with the resource-based theory, since in our framework, resources are valuable a priori only if the firm's opportunity options, embodied in the resource, are explicitly identified and shown to be valuable.

In our entrepreneurial logic, the firm's strategic resources are potentially valuable a priori in that the strategic resources may embody valuable opportunity options for the firm. The greater the uncertainty associated with the underlying opportunity, the more time left for the opportunity to expire, the greater the present value of the opportunity, or the lower the investment required to exploit the opportunity, the more valuable is the opportunity option. For a strategic asset to be valuable for the firm, the strategic asset must reduce the risk of loss for the firm in pursuing the opportunity underlying the opportunity option associated with the strategic asset, extend the opportunity's time to expiration, enhance the present value of cash flows from the opportunity, or reduce the investment required to exploit the opportunity.

To assess that a strategic resource is valuable a priori for the firm, the firm's opportunity options embodied in the strategic resource must be explicitly identified and it must be shown that these opportunity options have not expired or been preempted by competitors. The opportunity options must be valuable for the strategic resource to be valuable a priori. However, it is difficult to spot the firm's opportunity options a priori so it is difficult to know whether the strategic asset is valuable a priori. When testing the resource-performance relation, it is easier to see ex-post whether the firm with a strategic asset has seized and exploited opportunity options that were embodied in the strategic asset. Thus, a strategic asset is valuable a priori only if the firm with the strategic asset has greater performance with the underlying opportunity than without the opportunity. Thus, the resource-performance relationship with a strategic asset must be tested in conjuction with the underlying opportunities available to a firm. Further, a strategic resource that is valuable a priori does not imply that the strategic resource is a source of competitive advantage. That is, to show ex-post that the firm resource-performance relation is enhanced with the opportunities associated with the strategic resource is not a test of competitive advantage.

To test that a strategic resource is a source of competitive advantage for a firm, a control sample must be gathered in that the competitors included in the control sample pursued similar opportunities to those pursued by that the focal firm with the identified strategic asset. Further, the competitors in the control sample, however, did not have the strategic asset the focal firm had. Thus, it must be shown that the focal firm with the strategic asset enhanced the firm performance by pursuing the opportunities underlying the opportunity options associated with the strategic asset better than the competitors did without the strategic asset over a reasonable time span, for example, after a five to ten-year period.

To meaningfully test the resource-based logic in that a strategic resource is a source of competitive advantage for the firm, the test regression must be longitudinal over a period of five to ten years, not cross-sectional at a given time period or over a short period. Further, to select the control sample of competitors, the researcher must explicitly recognize a focal firm's opportunity options associated with the strategic resource. Further, these opportunities must be controlled in the regression when comparing the performance of the focal firm with that of the competitors. Thus, a strategic resource provides superior performance or competitive advantage only if the focal firm had exploited the underlying opportunities with the strategic resource better than its competitors exploited similar opportunities without the identified strategic resource. Thus, the interior process of firm value creation mechanism must be explicitly recognized and controlled when empirically testing the resource-based theory in that whether a firm's strategic resource identified by the criteria prescribed by the resource-based theory is a source of competitive advantage for the firm.

Strategic resources are factor inputs that meet the criteria prescribed by the resource-based view, namely, valuable, scarcity, imperfectly imitability, imperfectly mobility, and hard to accumulate. Strategic resources cannot be defined valuable a priori unless the firm's opportunity options are explicitly identified and found to be valuable with the strategic resource than without. Further, enhanced competition in the resource market is necessary to ensure a firm appropriates the value created. The empirical resource-performance relation will then show whether and when a strategic resource is valuable.

Commitment theory is consistent with the resource-based view in that the firm's current resources determine the likelihood of their achieving competitive advantage. Ghemawat (1991) defines commitment as the tendency of an organization to persist with a given strategy. Thus, by locking in a strategy the firm may lose flexibility to adapt to new opportunities which will thus create core rigidity and organizational inertia. However, entrepreneurial organizations seeking competitive advantage are proactively adaptive and are not constrained by their prior strategy or the current resources. The strategy and resources of proactively adaptive entrepreneurial organizations are emergent and evolve with the changing competitive conditions.

Commitment theory is premised on that resources are largely irreversible investments and that a new strategic investment must take sunk costs or prior resources into account. In modern finance theory, sunk costs are irrelevant when considering new strategic investments. In contrast, commitment theory argues that sunk costs are relevant in determining new investments. Sunk costs, in modern finance theory, however, may enter indirectly in investment decisions through the effect on the real options embedded in the firm's prior resources. Prior resources may contain flexibility and growth options that may influence the cash flows accruing from new investments.

Further, the dynamic capabilities are the firm's capacity to orchestrate their resources to adapt to changing competitive conditions. In our framework, the firm's dynamic capabilities are enhanced with the entrepreneurial incentives. When a firm is entrepreneurial, it is alert, agile, absorptive, and proactively adaptive, and its dynamic capabilities are high. An entrepreneurial organization thus has superior dynamic capabilities. Dynamic capabilities sustain the firm's business model mechanism and enhance the value chain effectiveness in our framework. There are, however, some problems with how the dynamic capabilities are identified. Teece (2007) argues that the firm's dynamic capabilities are firm-specific and situated with the management; whereas Eisenhardt and Martin (2000) argue that the dynamic capabilities include industry best practices. Further, Teece views the dynamic capabilities as the firm's strategic capabilities, whereas Eisenhardt and Martin include the firm's operational capabilities in the dynamic capabilities.

Dynamic capabilities require a clear definition in order to test the dynamic capabilities theory. By viewing dynamic capabilities as the firm's ability to adapt proactively, the dynamic capabilities may include the firm's strategic and operational capabilities. However, industry best practices only help a firm to catch up with their competition and enhance preactive adaptation, not proactive adaptation (see Chapter 3). Thus the industry best practices may not be included in proactive dynamic capabilities.

Adaptation occurs when a firm responds to reduce an increased gap between their potential performance and actual performance. Active adaptation occurs when "the instance of adaptation is triggered by an increase in the potentiality without any change in the actual performance, and when the system increases its actual performance, thus seizing the new opportunity" (Sachs and Meditz 1979: 1087). Active adaptation may be proactive or preactive. In both cases, organization responds to an increased gap between their potential performance and the actual performance. The difference between the two active adaptations is that in proactive adaptation the stimulus of an increase in potential performance comes from within the organization, whereas in preactive adaptation the stimulus of an increase in potential performance comes from outside the organization. Further, in passive adaptation the firm responds to a drop in their actual performance; however, the firm's potential performance remains unchanged.

Thus, to test the dynamic capabilities theory, one may examine the relation between the firm's proactive adaptability or entrepreneurial orientation and value chain effectiveness. The value chain effectiveness is the ratio of the buyer value added to the firm's cost to serve (see Chapter 5). Further, when a firm has greater dynamic capabilities, the relation between the firm's proactiveness or entrepreneurial orientation and the value chain effectiveness will be enhanced. Furthermore, the firm's dynamic capabilities are enhanced by the entrepreneurial incentives. One may examine the relation between the firm's dynamic capabilities and executive incentives. Thus, the firm's proactive dynamic capabilities construct may be proxied by the firm's entrepreneurial orientation. The firm's entrepreneurial orientation construct constitutes the firm's alertness, agility, proactive adaptability, absorptivity, and opportunity focus (see Chapter 3).

Positioning Logic

The positioning logic attributes the rationale underlying a firm's competitive advantage to the firm's strategic position and value activities. It is the value activities that a firm does differently that enhance the buyer value, which creates and sustains the firm's competitive advantage. The buyer value and the firm's value-creating activities are central to the positioning logic. Value activities are a firm's activities that increase the buyer value. Competitive heterogeneity arises when firms employ different activity configurations to achieve a strategic position. The source of competitive advantage lies in the activity system and activity drivers (Porter 1996). However, the positioning view assumes that managers will always seize and act on attractive strategic positions in a timely manner. In contrast, our entrepreneurial logic argues that a firm seizes an attractive strategic position and optimally adapts its activity system when the entrepreneurial incentives are present.

It is the not the firm resource heterogeneity or scarcity, but the activity differentiation that drives the firm's superior performance, according to the positioning logic. That is, different firms may choose different value activities even though they have similar resource bundles. Activity differentiation may enhance the buyer value or lower the activity cost. When a firm's value chain or activity system provides superior buyer value, the firm has a differentiation advantage; and when the activity system lowers the firm's cost to serve, the firm has a cost advantage relative to its competitors. The value activities are chosen to be consistent with the firm's strategic position.

Further, the activities are complementary to each other such that the value created by one activity does not destroy the value of another. The positioning logic explains the firm's strategic position choice and buyer value creation underlying the business model mechanism. The activity system implements the firm's competitive strategy. According to entrepreneurial logic, entrepreneurial incentives that enhance proactive adaptation further enhance the firm's strategic position and value activities, which may create and sustain the competitive advantage. Thus, the entrepreneurial logic enhances the positioning logic.

In the positioning logic, the firm value is enhanced when the buyer value increases or the activity cost decreases. The activity drivers that influence the buyer value or activity cost are the sources of competitive advantage (Porter 1996). The firm's activity system is differentiated from another firm by their value activities and the linkages between the value activities. The firm's value activities and activity linkages may change over time in a dynamic environment. The firm adapts its activity system and the activity drivers to changing competitive conditions. The firm's activity system has properties of a complex adaptive system (see Chapter 5). In changing competitive conditions the firm's activity system is emergent and self-organizing, when the managers are empowered with the entrepreneurial incentives, according to our entrepreneurial logic. Furthermore, the complexity, tacitness, and interrelatedness of an activity system sustain the firm's competitive advantage since it is difficult for a competitor to imitate the firm's activity system.

The activity system is configured consistent with the firm's strategic position. Further, the firm's competitive success is a function of the attractiveness of its industry and its relative strategic position in that industry (Porter 1985). The firm performance can be decomposed into an industry component and a positioning component. Further, the firm's actions can influence the industry structure and profitability. Porter suggests that an ideal strategic position for a firm is such that the firm's actions trigger a response by rivals which improves the industry performance and at the same time favors the firm. Such a positioning strategy is called "shaping" (see Chapter 4). Organizations often employ shaping strategies in hypercompetitive industries.

Porter (1980) offers a five-force framework to analyze industry structure and its relative attractiveness. The five competitive forces that drive industry profitability include bargaining power of customers, bargaining power of suppliers, threat of new entrants, threat of substitutes, and rivalry among current competitors. A five-force industry structure analysis identifies the opportunities and threats for a firm competing in the industry such that the firm may choose a profitable strategic position at a given time. The industry structure is dynamic and thus the firm must adapt its strategic position and value activities. The industry structure is also influenced by the actions of incumbent firms. To achieve competitive advantage the firm must understand its industry, where it competes and how it must compete, so that the firm may choose an attractive strategic position and optimize its value activities. The analysis and understanding of the industry structure is central to the firm's choice of strategic position and thus for the configuration of its value activities.

The firm can obtain competitive advantage or achieve superior performance relative to its competitors either through lower activity costs or with a differentiated product that enhances the buyer value, or by both. A differentiated product may thus command a price premium, thereby enhancing the firm's revenues. Further, lowering activity costs lowers the firm's cost to serve. Thus, a firm achieves competitive advantage when it enhances the revenues or lowers the costs greater than the competitors can. In positioning logic, a firm may choose a low cost position or a product differentiation position, or both. Firms may choose both a low cost and a differentiation position, but it is infrequent since the activity drivers for these two strategic positions can be very different even in the same industry.

Competitive advantage results from a firm's ability to perform the value activities at a lower cost relative to its rivals, or perform some activities in unique ways that enhance the buyer value and thus allow the firm to command a price premium (Porter 1996). For a given strategic position, several activity configurations are possible for the firm to choose to differentiate itself from the competitors. The firm may choose an activity configuration and drivers that provide the firm competitive advantage. An activity system comprised of discrete value activities is enabled by firm resources and capabilities, the economies of which determine firm performance and the likelihood of the firm achieving competitive advantage.

Performing activities require tangible and intangible resources. Thus, the resource-based logic and the positioning logic are complementary. Further, within our theory of entrepreneurial rent, the firm's value activities enable organizational learning and enhance the knowledge assets such as the human capital, social capital, technology assets, and management systems. The organization's knowledge assets are the firm's core resources that accumulate over time. The firm's value activities also create organizational assets external to the firm such as firm reputation, relationships, contracts, and networks. To maintain and enhance the firm's internal and external organizational assets the firm must make continuing investments in its value activities. However, all activities do not create organizational assets. Indeed the activities that are performed poorly or those inconsistent with the buyer value create liabilities for the firm.

The firm's tangible and intangible resources are not valuable in and of themselves (as opposed to the resource-based view). For example, when the firm's strategic resources are used to perform activities that are inconsistent with the buyer needs, those resources are not valuable. The buyer value is enhanced by activities when a firm lowers the buyer cost or raises the buyer performance. Activity drivers determine whether a firm is able to perform activities at a lower cost or in ways that enhance the buyer value greater than the competitors can. Activity drivers thus determine whether the firm can achieve competitive advantage.

Activity drivers vary with the firm's business model choice, within our entrepreneurial logic. Further, the competitive advantage lies in the firm's business model implementation. Most activity drivers are generic to a firm's industry and thus available to all firms in the industry. Therefore, the activity drivers or the sources of competitive advantage are not necessarily firm-specific in the positioning logic. However, within the entrepreneurial logic, the choice of activity drivers is firm-specific since they vary with the business model implementation. Further, it is the activity system that differentiates one firm from another within the positioning logic. The sustainability of competitive advantage depends on the complexity and tacitness of the activity system.

The question is then why some firms conceive and implement superior activity systems or find attractive strategic positions in an industry. Porter (1996) admits that the answer lies in superior managerial choices, consistent with our entrepreneurial logic. Thus, an organization with entrepreneurial incentives, according to our theory of entrepreneurial rent, is more likely to find an attractive strategic position or choose a superior activity system. Porter recognizes that the firm's current resource position gives the firm an advantage with its value activities; however, he argues that it is the choices made by management that underlie the firm's current resource position. Porter thus advocates the managerial choice over the resource-based view. Thus, the entrepreneurial incentives that enhance the managerial choice are key to the firm's competitive advantage creation according to our entrepreneurial logic. Further, the positioning logic is strengthened with our entrepreneurial logic that emphasizes the entrepreneurial behavior and managerial choice in an organization.

The entrepreneurial logic argues that superior execution of the business model is the key to the superior performance. Superior execution of the business model enables the firm to lower their cost to serve or enhance the buyer value, or both, more effectively than the competitors can. In our theory of entrepreneurial rent, the entrepreneurial incentives that enhance and sustain the firm's entrepreneurial behavior further enhance the business model mechanism constituting the value activities, revenue drivers, cost drivers, and value opportunities. The entrepreneurial incentives that enhance the business model drivers are the source of competitive advantage under our entrepreneurial logic.

In contrast to the resource-based logic, Porter (1996) advocates that creative managerial choices made by management and their ability to utilize imagination are more important than the firm's current resource position. The entrepreneurial logic argues that entrepreneurial incentives induce managerial creative choices of activities and resources. Porter argues:

> Simply having pools of skills, knowledge, or other resources is not in and of itself a guarantee of success ... If managers can understand their competitive environment and the sources of competitive advantage, they can better search creatively for favorable positions that are different from competitors',

assemble the needed skills and assets, configure the value chain appropriately, and put in place supportive organizational routines and a culture which reinforces the required internal behavior. The most successful firms are notable in employing imagination to define a *new* position, or find *new* value in whatever starting position [current resource position] they have (Porter 1996: 106).

Entrepreneurial Logic

The entrepreneurial logic argues that the source of competitive advantage lies in the firm's value creation and appropriation mechanism enhanced by the entrepreneurial behavior sustained by the entrepreneurial incentives in the firm. Further, the entrepreneurial incentive in a firm is the level of uncertain performance-based compensation in the executive pay mix, in that the performance is set by an external arbiter such as the capital market. For example, many startup firms that are resource constrained win over resource rich organizations, consistent with the entrepreneurial logic. Entrepreneurial organizations are constantly seeking value opportunities to build and renew their competitive advantage. Managers empowered by powerful entrepreneurial incentives think and act creatively and proactively, and thus behave entrepreneurially.

Traditional organizations build on resources, whereas entrepreneurial organizations build resources. Entrepreneurial organizations are alert, agile, proactive, adaptive, absorptive, and opportunity driven. Further, entrepreneurial organizations continually learn and enhance the core resources and management logics. In entrepreneurial organizations, managers are motivated by powerful entrepreneurial incentives to earn an entrepreneurial surplus for bearing excess firm-specific risk. Entrepreneurial organizations have a business model execution advantage over traditional organizations in effectively executing the business model mechanism wherein lies the competitive advantage.

It is not the firm's strategic resources or strategic position per se but the entrepreneurial execution of the business model mechanism that provides the firm with competitive advantage. The greater the entrepreneurial incentives, the greater is the entrepreneurial leverage and the greater is the likelihood of the firm achieving competitive advantage. Our entrepreneurial logic is consistent with the emerging behavioral logic in that it is the entrepreneurial behavior of decision makers that overcomes traditional behavioral constraints, thereby enabling the firm to achieve superior performance. The emerging behavioral logic differs from conventional behavioral logic that emphasized bounded rationality and local search. The emerging behavioral school emphasizes the possibility of more distant searches where more profitable value opportunities may lie. In addition to distant value opportunities the entrepreneurial logic further emphasizes the business model mechanism that sustains the firm's value creation and appropriation where the competitive advantage lies.

Further, strategic leadership logic is consistent but different from the entrepreneurial logic. Strategic leadership theory is an extension of the upper-echelons theory (Hambrick and Mason 1984). Strategic leadership logic emphasizes the leadership traits of top management in explaining a firm's superior performance. The entrepreneurial logic, however, emphasizes the entrepreneurial incentives that induce the entrepreneurial behavior, not necessarily the traits of top management as emphasized by the strategic leadership logic. However, management plays a crucial role in the entrepreneurial logic as well by facilitating the entrepreneurial behavior in the organization. Entrepreneurial organizations are alert, agile, proactive, adaptive, absorptive, and opportunity driven.

Conventional behavioral logic is based on the behavioral theory of the firm proposed by Cyert and March (1963). Conventional behavioral logic is premised on three core ideas, namely, bounded rationality, local search, and unresolved conflict. First, bounded rationality recognizes the cognitive limitations of human actors and suggests that managers seek a satisficing solution rather than an optimized solution. Bounded rationality is assumed because decision makers have limited information and computational ability when making a decision. Thus decision makers follow simple rules and standard operating procedures. Second, decision makers when making a decision employ a local search and their search is path-dependent. Third, unresolved conflicts may exist in an organization because conflicting interests among individuals cannot be entirely alleviated. Individuals and groups in an organization continuously negotiate and renegotiate, which influences organizational actions.

Cyert and March (1963) suggest four behavioral concepts which underlie organizational actions, namely, quasi-resolution of conflicts, uncertainty avoidance, organizational learning, and problemistic search (Gavetti et al. 2012). The quasi-resolution of conflicts addresses conflicting interests of individuals within an organization in that they resolve their conflicts partially through forming temporary coalitions. Temporary coalitions involve tradeoffs between conflicting goals of individuals leading to mutually acceptable solutions. A complete resolution of conflicts cannot be achieved within an organization. An organization attempts to create a negotiated environment through coordination with interdependent actors.

Further, uncertainty avoidance is possible through the organization's short-run responses that require little forecasting ability. Furthermore, a problemistic search is motivated when the firm performance falls below the firm's aspiration level. Thus the firm's failure to achieve a satisfactory performance triggers a problemistic search. The search stops when an alternative is found that is satisfactory, but not necessarily optimizing. The problemistic search is incremental and path-dependent. In our entrepreneurial logic, however, managers empowered with powerful entrepreneurial incentives do not avoid uncertainty; rather they actively exploit the uncertainty to favor the firm. Finally, in conventional behavioral logic, organizational learning occurs through cycles of search and adaptation resulting in improvements in the organizational goals, rules, and procedures.

In conventional behavioral logic, thus, a search driven by the organization's conservative expectation is biased more toward a local, incremental search. This search is based on imperfect environmental matching and the limited foresight of managers. The search for distantly situated opportunities is largely absent in conventional behavioral theory. However, emerging behavioral logic argues that superior opportunities lie in the distant regions of the competitive landscape. Thus to spot superior opportunities requires a distant search. According to the entrepreneurial logic, it is possible to search distant regions for superior opportunities when the management is empowered with entrepreneurial incentives that enhance management cognitive adaptability, and thus the management logics are continually updated through active learning and experimentation in the organization. In the emerging behavioral logic, management cognition continually adapts in a dynamic environment, and the search strategy is driven by proactive entrepreneurial behavior, not by conservative static expectations.

Gavetti and Levinthal (2000) argue that the bounded rationality of managers does not prevent them from coarsely foreseeing distant opportunities. Coarse foresight is possible when the agents actively learn and update their mental models. Managers with entrepreneurial incentives have coarse foresight and they can search distant regions in the environment to spot superior opportunities. Entrepreneurial logic allows decision makers to search distant regions for superior opportunities. Managers with entrepreneurial incentives learn continually and actively update their management logics, which enables them to search distant regions (see Chapter 2).

Gavetti (2012) offers an emerging behavioral theory that emphasizes management's superior abilities to sense, seize, and shape distant opportunities. Gavetti's emerging behavioral logic focuses on opportunity identification and selection processes. Our entrepreneurial logic is consistent with Gavetti's emerging behavioral theory. The management logics are enhanced by powerful entrepreneurial incentives in organizations. Gavetti identifies three behavioral drivers of superior firm performance, namely, the ability of a firm to identify superior opportunities, the ability of the firm to act on them, and the ability of the firm to shape the opportunities.

In the emerging behavioral logic, the firm's superior performance lies in the managerial abilities to overcome cognitive bounds. The cognitive constraints of decision makers are central to the conventional behavioral theory. The source of competitive advantage for a firm lies in distant opportunities according to the emerging behavioral logic. Entrepreneurial logic further argues that entrepreneurial decision makers supported by powerful entrepreneurial incentives can sense and seize cognitively distant opportunities in a timely manner. Thus the managers who can overcome certain behavioral bounds to pursue cognitively distant opportunities achieve superior performance. Our entrepreneurial logic is consistent with the emerging behavioral logic in that it emphasizes the role of decision makers in sensing and seizing cognitively distant superior value opportunities. Further, our entrepreneurial logic emphasizes the superior execution of the firm's business model mechanism. Superior opportunities are cognitively distant and as a result they are not easily competed away; since they are difficult to spot by managers with traditional behavioral bounds, superior value opportunities are source of competitive advantage. In the entrepreneurial logic, high-powered entrepreneurial incentives empower the managers to sense and seize the cognitively distant opportunities in a timely manner.

Proximate opportunities are visible to most managers and thus proximate opportunities may not provide the firm superior performance. Superior opportunities are not proximate to the firm and may not be found through a problemistic, local, incremental search as employed in the conventional behavioral logic. The source of competitive advantage lies in superior, cognitively distant opportunities. Furthermore, the emerging behavioral logic identifies three key abilities of decision makers, namely, the ability to identify opportunities, the ability to act on opportunities, and the ability to shape opportunities. The more distant the opportunities, the more pronounced are the behavioral bounds. To identify, act on, and shape the value opportunities, organizations must continually test and revise their mental models. Thus entrepreneurial cognitive adaptability underlies the superior management logics of entrepreneurial organizations.

The emerging behavioral logic emphasizes the superior cognitive abilities of management as the source of the firm's competitive advantage. Accordingly, decision makers with traditional cognitive bounds cannot spot cognitively distant superior opportunities. In the entrepreneurial logic, however, it is the superior entrepreneurial incentives that empower managers to seize the superior opportunities and provide the firm competitive advantage. It is thus the high-powered incentives that enhance the management cognition enabling them to spot cognitively distant opportunities that drive the firm's value creation and appropriation mechanism where the competitive advantage lies.

Cognitively distant opportunities are less contested than more proximate ones. More distant opportunities are Schumpeterian (Schumpeter 1934) as opposed to Kirzerian (Kirzner 1997). Schumpeterian opportunities are industry shaping opportunities (creative destruction) that alter the industry rules of competition, and these opportunities are difficult to spot and act upon. In contrast, proximate opportunities are Kirzerian, which are incremental in nature and easier to spot and act upon. Kirzerian opportunities arise when the product and resource markets are in temporary disequilibrium. Market disequilibrium arises when there is either an excess demand or a shortage of supply in a good or resource. Managers with traditional behavioral bounds may spot Kirzerian proximate opportunities, although few may act upon them in a timely manner without adequate incentives.

Furthermore, exploiting Kirzerian opportunities restores the market equilibrium, whereas exploiting Schumpeterian opportunities disrupt the market equilibrium. Kirzerian opportunities can be found with a local search. Kirzerian search is thus consistent with conventional behavioral logic. Schumpeterian opportunities are cognitively distant for managers and likely to enhance the firm's competitive advantage, which, however, require a distant search strategy possible through enhanced cognitive adaptability of the management driven by the entrepreneurial incentives, according to our entrepreneurial logic. Entrepreneurial organizations continually seek cognitively distant opportunities to build or renew competitive advantage (see Chapter 4).

Management logics, when proactively adapted in a dynamic environment, can overcome the traditional behavioral bounds of managers and enable them to identify, act upon, and shape cognitively distant opportunities. Entrepreneurial organizations who seek cognitively distant opportunities are more likely to achieve the competitive advantage. Entrepreneurial incentives propelling management action to identify, shape, and exploit cognitively distant opportunities underlie a firm's competitive advantage. Cognitively distant opportunities enhance the buyer value added or lower the firm's cost to serve to be greater than that which the competitors can achieve.

To spot cognitively distant opportunities in a dynamic environment, organizations must have sufficient situation awareness or coarse foresight. With coarse foresight a manager has sufficient situation awareness to overcome traditional rationality constraints. Coarse foresight enhances the managerial ability to spot and project current trends the potential of which is not yet fully realized, but not necessarily the managerial ability to forecast future trends. To recognize distant opportunities does not require perfect foresight. Entrepreneurial incentives help managers overcome organizational inertia and propel firm growth. Thus it is not enough to spot cognitively distant opportunities to build competitive advantage. The firm must be also agile to seize the opportunities and proactively adaptive with its business model to exploit such value opportunities. Entrepreneurial organizations are alert, agile, proactive, adaptive, absorptive, and opportunity driven.

Organizations must be agile to seize and act upon the value opportunities in a timely manner before it is too late, so that competitors do not preempt the opportunities. Absence of agility enhances organizational inertia. Further, absence of adaptability enhances core rigidity. Entrepreneurial organizations overcome organizational inertia, and seek value opportunities to avoid competency traps. However, organizations face less internal resistance when acting on incremental opportunities. With cognitively distant opportunities, there is likely to be more resistance within the organization. Managers with superior incentives and execution skills can overcome such resistance and exploit the value opportunities in a timely manner to build competitive advantage.

The more entrepreneurial the organization, the less inert or the more agile and proactive is the organization, and the likelier it is to sense and exploit cognitively distant opportunities. Organizations not only must recognize cognitively distant opportunities but they also must have superior dynamic capabilities to reconfigure their activities to exploit the value opportunities. Entrepreneurial incentives enhance the dynamic capabilities in that managers have the superior ability to lead and shape the social cognitive processes within an organization such that multiple parties can be persuaded and the resources are gathered quickly to configure the value activities to exploit the value opportunities.

Figure 1.1 illustrates the entrepreneurial logic. Entrepreneurial incentives enhance the firm's entrepreneurial orientation that further enhances active learning and core resources, management cognition and value opportunities, and proactive adaptation and value activities. Entrepreneurial incentives provide the firm an entrepreneurial advantage that further enhances the firm's value creation and appropriation mechanism. Competitive advantage is achieved and renewed as the firm's value creation and appropriation is sustained (see Fig. 1.1). The firm's core resources, value opportunities, and value activities enhance the business model mechanism wherein the competitive advantage is created and sustained.

The entrepreneurial logic explains the entrepreneurial value creation and appropriation mechanism underlying the competitive advantage creation. The value creation and appropriation mechanism underlies the firm's competitive advantage, and the entrepreneurial incentives in the firm enhance the value creation and appropriation mechanism. Entrepreneurial logic underlies the theory of entrepreneurial rent, which explains competitive advantage creation. The extant logics fail to explain competitive advantage phenomena because they presume the firm's value creation and appropriation mechanism always delivers superior performance when a strategic resource is present or an attractive market position is found. The firm's

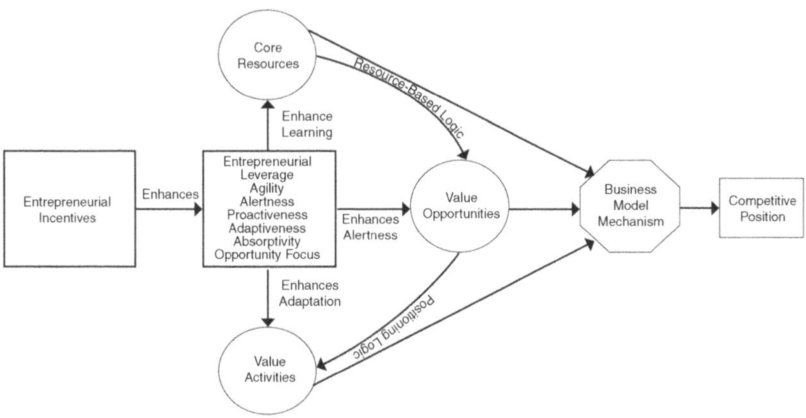

Fig. 1.1 Entrepreneurial logic

value creation and appropriation mechanism enhanced by the entrepreneurial behavior is central to our theory of competitive advantage.

Resource-based logic explains the role of core resources. The firm's core resources are sources of competitive advantage within the resource-based logic. Within resource-based logic, firms accumulate core resources and seek value opportunities to leverage the core resources to build competitive advantage (see Fig. 1.1). In Fig. 1.1, core resources are thus linked to value opportunities consistent with the resource-based logic. However, entrepreneurial organizations continually build and enhance their core resources. Furthermore, entrepreneurial organizations identify, act on, and shape value (cognitively distant) opportunities (see Chapter 4). The core resources in and of themselves do not provide competitive advantage in the absence of superior entrepreneurial incentives. Further, in the absence superior execution of the business model, the core resources and value opportunities do not provide the firm competitive advantage.

According to positioning logic, the source of competitive advantage lies in the firm's activity system or value activities. The activity system is optimized consistent with the firm's choice of strategic position. The firm seeks value opportunities consistent with its strategic position. In Fig. 1.1, value opportunities are thus linked to value activities consistent with the positioning logic. The entrepreneurial incentives enhance the firm's entrepreneurial orientation and provide the firm an execution advantage. Further, when a firm is more entrepreneurial, managers earn an entrepreneurial surplus (see Chapter 3). Entrepreneurial organizations with managers sufficiently incentivized thus choose attractive strategic positions and proactively adapt the firm's value activities and value opportunities in changing competitive conditions.

Active learning in the organization enhances the core resources. Entrepreneurial logic argues that the firm's active learning capability is enhanced by the entrepreneurial behavior. Active learning enhances the combinative capabilities that further enhance the knowledge resources and management logics. The management logics enhance the firm's management cognition, dynamic capabilities, and value activities, which enhance the value creation and appropriation mechanism wherein the competitive advantage lies. Entrepreneurial incentives further enhance the management logics, which helps the firm to effectively overcome core rigidity and competency traps in a dynamic environment. Further, the management logics bind the loosely coupled value activities. Organizational and individual knowledge capital are enhanced by the active learning and combinative capabilities, namely, the firm's absorptive capacity, that include the knowledge externalization, internalization, socialization, and combination.

Entrepreneurial incentives enhance the firm's dynamic capabilities. Entrepreneurial organizations build resources, combine and recombine resources, configure value activities, to exploit the value opportunities. Proactive dynamic capabilities are enhanced by the firm's active learning, namely, the knowledge generation and integration. Entrepreneurial organizations are agile, absorptive, and proactively adaptive. Proactive adaptation enhances the firm's value activities. The management logics enhanced by active learning support proactive dynamic capabilities that further enhance the firm's value activities and business model advantage.

Entrepreneurial logic explains how powerful entrepreneurial incentives enhance the firm's entrepreneurial behavior that enhances the active learning, management cognition, and proactive adaptation, which further enhance the core resources, value opportunities, and value activities, thereby enhancing and sustaining the value creation and appropriation mechanism wherein the firm's competitive advantage lies (see Fig. 1.1). Extant strategic logics address some of these competitive advantage drivers separately but presume the firm value creation and appropriation mechanism always delivers competitive advantage. The entrepreneurial incentives enhance the value creation and appropriation mechanism that underlies the firm's competitive advantage, according to our theory of entrepreneurial rent.

Entrepreneurial organizations continually learn and actively adapt their management logics. Entrepreneurial organizations have superior execution abilities, and the entrepreneurial incentives underlie their execution success. The greater the entrepreneurial incentives or the more entrepreneurial the firm, the superior are the management logics and the greater is the advantage of their value creation and appropriation mechanism, and the greater is the likelihood of the firm achieving competitive advantage.

The next two parts of the book develop our theory of competitive advantage, namely the theory of entrepreneurial rent. Entrepreneurial logic underlies the theory of entrepreneurial rent. Part II develops core concepts underlying the entrepreneurial logic, namely, management logics, management cognition, cognitive adaptability, value opportunities, entrepreneurial orientation, combinative capabilities, organizational agility, proactive adaptation, absorptive capacity, active learning, entrepreneurial agency, value appropriation, and business model mechanism.

The entrepreneurial incentives that promote entrepreneurial behavior in an organization and enhance the firm's value creation and appropriation mechanism are at the heart of our theory of entrepreneurial rent. Entrepreneurial incentives enhance the management logics which further enhance the management's recognition of distant value opportunities. Entrepreneurially oriented organizations are constantly seeking superior value opportunities to build and sustain competitive advantage.

Part III proposes two theories built on the entrepreneurial logic, namely the theory of entrepreneurial rent and the theory of franchising. The entrepreneurial logic explains two major strategic phenomena, namely, how firms can create and sustain competitive advantage, and when and why firms franchise. The theory of franchising proposes that franchising business model enhances the firm's value creation and appropriation. The theory of franchising explains when and why firms franchise. The theory of franchising develops firm-specific and location-specific conditions in explaining the franchising phenomena. The franchising mechanism enhances the business model advantage.

The theory of entrepreneurial rent proposes that the entrepreneurial incentives enhance the value creation and appropriation mechanism wherein lies the firm's competitive advantage. Our theory of competitive advantage, namely, the theory of entrepreneurial rent, explains how the value creation and appropriation mechanism underlying the competitive advantage is enhanced by the entrepreneurial incentives. Further, entrepreneurial incentives enhance the management logics that further enhance the management cognition, value opportunities, dynamic capabilities, core resources, and activity drivers, which further enhance the value creation and appropriation mechanism and the likelihood of the firm achieving and sustaining competitive advantage.

PART II

Entrepreneurial Logic: Enhancing Value Creation and Appropriation

CHAPTER 2

Management Logics

Introduction

Management logics constitute management mental models and theories of how their business works and how the firm value is created and appropriated. Management logics thus constitute declarative and procedural knowledge containing schemas (causal structures), decision scripts (heuristics), and business model assumptions (theories and beliefs). Management logics are the basis the management employs when sensing value opportunities, building and configuring resources, selecting strategic positions, configuring value drivers and value activities, and understanding unexpected events and challenges. The management logics in an organization are enhanced by active learning, which is further enhanced by the entrepreneurial incentives. The entrepreneurial incentive is the uncertain performance-based compensation in the executive pay, in that the firm performance is set and evaluated by an external arbiter such as the capital market. Entrepreneurial incentives provide the firm an entrepreneurial leverage. Further, entrepreneurial orientation of a firm varies across firms in an industry.

Management logics constitute management mental models and espoused theories. A mental model is a hypothetical construct to account for human behavior in processing information and making decisions (Wickens 1984). The mental model is an individual's view of the system and its domain, what it looks like, how it operates, and how it may change. Furthermore, the mental model shapes how the individual perceives, reasons, and predicts their environment and its impact on the system. Mental models are updated

C.S. Mishra, *Creating and Sustaining Competitive Advantage*,
DOI 10.1007/978-3-319-54540-0_2

when the individual learns or acquires new information and acts on it (Rouse and Morris 1986). Mental models support an individual's cognition, that is, how they perceive the environment, how they interpret and comprehend information, and how they project and extrapolate the environmental variables that impact their action. Mental models may change over time with the individual's work experience and learning.

Management logics contain schemas, scripts, theories, beliefs, and assumptions that underlie management decisions and activities. Management logics influence an organization's strategy, value opportunities, resource allocation, competencies, business model configuration, value activities, and strategic and operating decisions. Further, management attentional capacity is limited; however, enhanced management logics reduce the load on the management attention. Managers spend most of their time absorbing, processing, and disseminating information about the organization's strategies, opportunities, challenges, and problems (Walsh 1995). Managers employ the management logics to understand the strategic issues, make decisions and solve problems. Entrepreneurial incentives in an organization enhance active learning that further enhances management cognitive adaptability and the management logics. Moreover, stagnant management logics can lead to organizational inertia and core rigidity.

Built on the management's past experience and accumulated over time in an information environment, management logics are knowledge and belief structures consisting of declarative and procedural knowledge and espoused theories including problem-solving scripts and causal relationships between the system elements. Stagnant management logics can inhibit management cognition. Management logics provide a basis for understanding a task environment; but as the knowledge and beliefs in the management logics are incomplete and potentially inaccurate, they can inhibit cognition in a dynamic environment unless the management logics are enhanced and updated through management learning.

Furthermore, management logics are shared mental models and theories of a management team; thus, some information overlap between team members' mental models is, however, necessary for the effective coordination of the team member mental models. Team members update the shared elements of their mental models with a just-sufficient level of communication among them. For example, Mosier and Childester (1991) found that better-performing teams actually communicate less than poorly performing ones.

The term, dominant logics, or the mental maps of the dominant coalition, was introduced by Prahalad and Bettis (1986). Dominant logics are top management's assumptions and beliefs of how their business works and the relation of the business with the environment. Prahalad and Bettis argue that dominant logics are information filters in that management employs dominant logics to selectively perceive information in the environment. However, the role of the dominant logics is much greater than just information filters. Management employs the dominant logics to understand strategic issues, make decisions, select opportunities, allocate resources, configure value activities, and solve problems.

Further, the assumptions and understandings on which a business is built comprise the theory of the business (Drucker 1994). Management logics include management theories and assumptions of how the business works and how the value is created and appropriated. Drucker explains that an organization's theory of business consists of three sets of assumptions, namely, environmental assumptions, customer value assumptions, and core competency assumptions. "These are the assumptions that shape any organization's behavior, dictate its decisions about what to do and what not to do, and define what the organization considers meaningful results" (Drucker 1994: 95).

In explaining why a company with superior performance in the past finds itself stagnating and possibly in trouble, Drucker attributes the root cause to lie in the inadequacy of the theory of the business (i.e., management logics), in that the assumptions on which the business is built are no longer valid. The assumptions held by management are about the markets and customers and their changing behavior, changing technologies and their influence on the nature of competition in the industry, and whether the organization's management logics still fit the changed rules of competition. The theory of the business of an organization (management logics) needs to be continually examined and updated in a dynamic environment.

Management logics are not always accurate. Management logics or management mental models may include incorrect beliefs and scripts. Management mental models may "fill data gaps with typical but perhaps inaccurate information; prompt one to ignore discrepant and possibly important information; discourage disconfirmation of the existing knowledge structure; and inhibit creative problem solving" (Walsh 1995: 282). Further, management mental models and theories are often incomplete, ambiguous, and inconsistent over time. Mental models in general are simplistic representations of how a system works. The individual's mental model includes their internal conceptual representation of causal interrelations among the elements comprising the system. Mental models constitute the individual's schemas, scripts, beliefs, and theories that the individual uses to understand specific situations or to solve a specific problem.

It is not that a management has choice whether or not to use the management mental models; the management logics or mental models are rather the basis for management decision making. Stagnant management logics, however, can inhibit the management cognition and situation awareness. Entrepreneurial incentives prevent the management logics from becoming stagnant. Furthermore, entrepreneurial incentives enhance management learning and cognitive adaptability that further enhance the management logics, which enhance the management cognition. Entrepreneurial incentives that provide the management an opportunity to earn an entrepreneurial surplus enhance the management learning and thus the management logics are updated when the competitive conditions change in an industry. Entrepreneurial incentives empower managers to learn proactively and continually. Thus in entrepreneurial organizations, the management logics are regularly surfaced, examined, and updated, and consequently entrepreneurial organizations have high management cognition. Entrepreneurial incentives enhance the management learning and management cognitive adaptability.

In a dynamic environment, management must continually question and improve their mental models and theories. Senge (1992) explains: "The problems with mental models lie not in whether they are right or wrong – by definition all models are simplifications. The problems with mental models arise when the models are tacit – when they exist below the level of awareness" [5]. Often managers are unaware of their mental models; and as they are unaware, management mental models remain unexamined and unchanged, which results in an increasing gap between reality and management actions.

Organizations must detect when the organization's strategic actions begin to lead or lag their current strategic intent (Burgelman and Grove 1996). The divergence between the firm's strategic actions and the strategic intent is a sign of strategic dissonance which requires a shift in the organization's strategy and a change in their strategic intent. Strategic dissonance signals a strategic inflection for the organization. Entrepreneurial incentives enhance the management's ability to detect strategic dissonance early. Burgelman and Grove provide a framework to detect strategic dissonance in an organization. First, the management should utilize the competitive force analysis (Porter 1980) to identify the current trends in the market environment and understand the basis of competition in their industry. Second, the management should reexamine their management logics that have made the company successful.

The management should thus reexamine the management logics, or their beliefs and assumptions about the competitive environment and the schemas and scripts they use in their opportunity selections and resource allocation decisions including the cultural elements that comprise the internal selection environment. The internal selection environment and management logics mediate the link between the firm's competencies and the basis of industry competition. The management should look at what the company is actually doing and compare the firm's actions with their espoused theory. When these drivers, namely the basis of industry competition, the firm's current resources and competencies, the management logics and theories, and the firm's internal selection environment, are not in harmony with each other, there are signs of strategic dissonance in the organization and the management must quickly act. Organizations with high-powered entrepreneurial incentives are more likely to detect and act on strategic dissonance early.

Senge (1992) argues that many of the best ideas in the industry are known to managers yet these ideas are never put into practice. The lack of implementation in practice is not the result of poor management skills, but rather because the new ideas are at great variance with the management logics. However, the entrepreneurial incentives will enhance the likelihood of the management revising their beliefs and theories, thus enhancing the management logics and increasing the likelihood of implementation of best ideas that enhance the business model execution and the firm's value creation and appropriation mechanism wherein the competitive advantage lies. Management logics thus should be regularly reexamined and revised through actively surfacing, testing, and improving the management assumptions and espoused theories of the business and its environment. The management logics enhance the management's implementation and execution of the businesss model comprising value opportunities, core resources, and value activities, where the firm's competitive advantage truly lies.

Mental Models and Theories

The use of the phrase, mental models, is ubiquitous but their meanings and applications are varied in the contexts they are used. In cognitive psychology, the focus of mental models is on the way humans understand systems and their workings. The definitions of mental models range from messy and incomplete belief structures to specific detailed processes and knowledge structures regarding how the systems operate.

In human control system theory, " a mental model includes knowledge about the system to be controlled, knowledge about the properties of disturbances likely to act on the system, and knowledge about the criteria, strategies, and so forth associated with the control task" (Rouse and Morris 1986: 350). In human control function, the individual's role is monitoring operating processes to detect, diagnose, and compensate for system failures. Mental models serve as assumptions and a knowledge base that allow an estimation of the expected performance of an organization.

Within cognitive psychology, the use of mental models is to predict and explain the system behavior, to formulate plans and goals, and to translate goals into strategies and actions (Wickens 1984). Rasmussen (1979) uses mental models for predicting future events, finding causes of observed events, and determining appropriate actions to cause changes, including performing thought experiments. The themes underlying the use of mental models in psychology are describing what a system looks like, explaining how the system operates and what it is currently doing, and predicting how the system will behave in the near future. Rouse and Morris (1986) define "mental models as mechanisms whereby humans are able to generate descriptions of system purpose and form, explanations of system functioning and observed system states, and prediction of future system states."

Mental models and theories are used by individuals for everyday reasoning. People use mental models for mental simulation and thought experiments. For example, if people are shown a device, they often mentally simulate the working of the device. Mental models are not always accurate, and they are, moreover, incomplete simplifications. Further, individuals may hold two or more inconsistent mental models at the same time in the same domain. Reasoning using mental models often relies on qualitative relations, not generally on quantitative relations. It is easier to reason one value is less than another without involving their numerical values. People use mental models not only to describe a situation but also to understand what is going on and predict how the situation might change. Mental models facilitate problem solving in a task environment and may yield incorrect or correct results.

Gentner (2002) suggests qualitative process (QP) theory can be used to represent mental models. QP theory was originated in artificial intelligence in computer science to help develop expert systems. QP theory captures representations and reasoning that underlie human reasoning in a manner that is sufficiently precise to permit computer simulations. The premise of QP theory is that human reasoning relies on qualitative relations, whether one value is greater than another, with or without knowing their numerical values. Using QP theory, a mental model is represented in terms of (a) the elements in a domain, (b) qualitative relations between values of the elements, (c) the processes that create change in the values, and (d) the predictions that must hold for the processes to operate to effect the change in the elements (Gentner 2002).

QP theory uses ordinal relationships between variables without using their numerical values. Instead of using exact equations to describe a process of change, QP theory employs qualitative mathematics to provide a causal linkage to describe partial relationships between the system elements. For example, people may know that greater force leads to greater acceleration, without knowing the mathematical equations that describe the relation or the numerical values of the two variables. QP theory thus allows researchers to describe mental models of individuals in explaining what is happening in a situation, how the system is changing, and what changes might occur. Mental models support and enhance an individual's cognitive activities.

A mental model that emulates the process of how environmental states change helps the individual to perceive and interpret the environmental information. The internalization of this process is the individual's mental model. The individual's mental model facilitates their learning of a situation; for example, what is happening in a situation and what changes might occur in the near future. For the mental model to be effective, the individual must have the ability to extract the cues from the environment. To effectively extract and interpret the environment cues, the individual employs their attentional resources as well as their current goals.

The individual's mental models, directed by their attention and goals driven by incentives, influence how the individual will explain, reason, and predict the environmental cues. The individual's goals can reduce the workload on the individual's attentional resources necessary to extract and interpret the environmental cues. Further, an individual's conceptualization of how a system works or the mental model is influenced by their attentional resources and goals.

Further, when identifying the causes of the suboptimal performance of an individual's mental models, one should avoid confounding the individual's information processing capacity (or their executive memory and cognitive capacity) with their selection of inappropriate or incomplete cues (Rouse and Morris 1986). Cue selection and utilization differs between experts and novices. Experts are not unduly influenced by superficial cues. An important attribute of expertise is the ability to select the most useful features of problems and available information.

Mental models of experts fundamentally differ from those of novices. Experts obviously know more about the environment than novices, but mental models of experts are more than just elaborate knowledge structures. Evidence further suggests that mental models of experts are fundamentally different from those of novices (Rouse and Morris 1986). A shift away from a novice's mental models to an expert's is not merely a refinement of the novice's perspective; rather it involves a conceptual change, a shift from a merely representational model to a more abstract model. Chase and Simon (1973) describe expertise as highly developed repertoires of pattern-oriented representations.

Rouse and Morris (1986) describe the superior organization of knowledge structures as the key to the individual's expertise. Experts thus tend to have conceptually more abstract and organized mental models than novices do. Learning enhances an individual's mental models by enriching the knowledge structures and scripts to be more organized and abstract, which further enhances the individual's cognition and information processing capacity. Furthermore, the abstractness, complexity, and organization of the management logics of decision makers enable them to overcome traditional behavioral bounds assumed in conventional behavioral theory of the firm.

Management Attention

Management attention is critical to the effectiveness of managerial cognition and situation awareness. Attention at the management level is scarce (Simon 1947). The more enhanced the management attention, the greater is the management cognition and situation awareness. Management attention is a process of intentional, conscious, sustained allocation of managerial cognitive resources to guide the managerial activities (Ocasio 2011). Further, Helfat and Peteraf (2015) define management attention as a mental activity that focuses management alertness on a subset of information in the environment. Dijksterhuis and Aarts (2010) further define management attention as a managerial cognitive resource that selects and biases managerial mental and physical activities.

Simon (1947) emphasizes that management attention is the chief bottleneck in organizational activity. Further, Penrose (1959) emphasizes that management attentional capacity is a constraining factor in the growth of the firm. Penrose further suggests that as certain management activities are routinized, attentional resources are freed, which are then available for management to attend to the firm growth. Stinchcombe (1968) identifies three organizational dimensions that influence management attention, namely, spatial, temporal, and procedural. The spatial dimension of the organization regulates the availability of organizational knowledge including management logics when addressing specific issues. Second, the temporal dimension regulates the amount of time management has when responding to the issues. Third, the procedural dimension regulates the distribution of management attention to the issues and initiatives selected by the management. Together these three organizational dimensions regulate the managerial attentional resources. Procedural and communication channels in the organization significantly impact the distribution of management attention.

Ocasio and Joseph (2005) link managerial attentional capacity to organizational channels of decision making, namely the operating and governance channels. These channels regulate and focus management attention. Management uses operating channels in gathering and processing information available in the environment, and in configuring organizational resources and value activities, which consume significant management attention. Operating and governance channels are used for organizational and management processes; for example, processes for monitoring firm performance, establishing and managing the employee reward system, and aligning the operations with business strategy. The management of organizational processes requires the top management's attention, which is regulated and shaped by the organizational procedural and communication channels.

Management attention is largely determined by management goals and incentives. Management goals and incentives guide management behavior through the regulation of their attention (Dijksterhuis and Aarts 2010). Management goals are mental representations determining management behavior and behavioral outcomes. One of the primary roles of the management attention is to translate management goals into management behavior. The content of management attention at a given time is regulated by the management goals at the time. Management attention not only orients and alerts management to goal-relevant information in the environment, management attention also plays a regulating role in translating their goals into behavior. Further, the entrepreneurial incentives enhance the management goals that guide the management actions.

Dijksterhuis and Aarts (2010) argue that management goals modulate the management attention irrespective of the conscious or unconscious nature of their goals. Further, Dijksterhuis and Aarts claim that management goals are part of their mental models. Conscious processing of information is usually dependent on an individual's attention. Management attention regulates the management cognition, agility, and situation awareness, which are enhanced with the entrepreneurial incentives. Further, management cognition, agility, proactive adaptiveness, absorptivity, and situation awareness are critical for an organization to actively adapt to a changing environment. Agility is the organization's ability to respond quickly and effectively to a changing circumstance, whereas the situation awareness is the manager's ability to know what is going on and to keep the information active. Management attention is critical to achieving organizational agility and sufficient situation awareness. Further, the management goals and logics reduce the load on the management attention in enhancing the organizational agility and situation awareness.

Ocasio and Joseph (2005) propose that management attention is regulated and distributed by the operational and governance channels of an organization. The operational and governance channels focus, situate, and distribute management attention. Such channels include executive meetings, board of directors meetings, board committee meetings, annual performance reviews, strategic planning meetings, personnel evaluations, and other managerial actions and governance activities. The attentional channels also include strategic corporate activities such as mergers, acquisitions, strategic alliances, corporate restructuring, regular meetings with security analysts, and interactions with external constituencies. Operating and governance channels are the firm's decision-making channels that regulate and focus management attention.

Ocasio (1997) offers an attention-based view of the firm, which suggests that the firm behavior is the result of how firms channel and distribute the attention of their decision makers. Further, firms are heterogeneous in terms of specific aspects of the environment their decision makers attend to, and the specific aspects of the environment the management attends to are regulated by the management goals and management logics. Thus, management attention is largely determined by the management goals and management logics. Management attention enhances or constrains management cognition necessary for attaining sufficient situation awareness. Management logics and goals that enhance the management attention thus further enhance the management cognition and situation awareness.

The attention-based view of the firm postulates the principles of regulating management attention, namely, the principle of selective attention, the principle of situated attention, and the principle of distribution of attention. The principle of selective attention states that decision makers will be selective with regard to the specific issues and initiatives they will attend to at a given time (Ocasio 1997). Management attention is the scarcest resource in an organization, so management cannot attend to all issues at any one time. Management attentional resources are taxed significantly in a dynamic environment in which a greater amount of conscious processing of information is required.

The principle of situational attention states that the focus of management attention depends on the situational context or the situation the management is in when making decisions. Accordingly, the focus of attention will vary with the characteristics of decision contexts or the situations. Management attention adapts to a novel situation in light of the management goals. Further, the principle of the distribution of attention states that the focus of management attention depends on the organizational decision-making channels, namely the procedural and communication channels, which distribute and regulate the organization's issues, initiatives, and procedures (Ocasio 1997).

The distributed nature of attentional resources in an organization was first proposed by Simon (1947). Simon emphasizes that the organization's distribution of decision-making functions and processes influences the utilization of management attention. Decision-making channels are formal and informal meetings, and administrative protocols, among others. The form and organization of decision-making channels significantly impact when, whether, and how decision makers focus their attention on the specific aspects of the environment and the issues at hand (Ocasio 1997). The attention-based view can explain why and how management cognition varies across firms in an industry. Entrepreneurial organizations are agile and have speedy procedural and communication channels which focus their management attention and enhance the situation awareness. Enhanced situation awareness enables decision makers to overcome traditional behavioral bounds and seize cognitively distant value opportunities in entrepreneurial organizations.

Management attention is critical for management cognition including their conscious and automatic information processing, albeit less attentional resources are necessary for automatic processing. In a hypercompetitive environment, significant management attention is necessary for achieving sufficient situation awareness. Managers adapt their attention to the demand of environments. Management attentional capacity is a primary bottleneck in achieving sufficient situation awareness. Management attention is crucial to the effectiveness of business strategy and management decision making, and to the execution of the value creating and appropriating activities. Management with greater attentional capacity can overcome core rigidities and organizational inertia. Further, with enhanced managerial attentional capacity and sufficient situation awareness, entrepreneurial organizations have low organizational inertia, as these organizations proactively adapt to changing competitive conditions without getting stuck in competency traps.

Attentional engagement involves the conscious managerial processing of information, although the automatic processing of information requires some minimal level of management attention. Attentional engagement links conscious top-down (goal driven) and bottom-up (data driven) information processing activities to obtain sufficient situation awareness, and further revise the management logics and goals, in a dynamic environment. Thus, adequate attentional engagement or effective allocation of management attention is necessary to process weak signals in a changing environment where the signals are often fuzzy, and in the management's ability to sense distant opportunities and threats.

Managerial attentional engagement and the distribution of management attention in an organization determine the availability and exploitation of value opportunities in an organization. Seizing and exploiting value opportunities in a timely manner is crucial for a firm to achieve competitive advantage (see Chapter 4). Entrepreneurial organizations are constantly seeking value opportunities to gain and sustain competitive advantage. As management is preoccupied with ongoing activities and current operations, they have less attentional capacity left to perceive and exploit new opportunities for growth (Penrose 1959). Management could give more attention to pursuing growth opportunities, but that leaves less attentional capacity for ongoing operations. This implies a possible opportunity cost to the firm for pursuing growth, which depends on how valuable the firm considers the current operations.

Gifford (1992) examines the allocation of management attention between sustaining the firm's current operations and pursuing new value opportunities. The allocation of management attention is determined between the current operations and the pursuit of new opportunities, thus determining the effectiveness of the organization's ambidexterity. Management attention is critical to an organization's ambidexterity or its capacity to sustain the current advantage and at the same time pursue and develop a new advantage.

Gifford evaluates the distribution of management attention to two choices, namely, allocating attention to enhance the profits from current operations or to pursue new opportunities. Both activities require significant management attention. The information on sustaining the profitability of current operations as well as the information on finding and evaluating new opportunities can be gathered by allocating sufficient management attention to each activity. Furthermore, the profitability outcomes of each activity are uncertain. The expected value and the uncertainty of the payoff of pursuing an alternative is a function of the amount of attention the management allocates to that alternative. Thus, a new value opportunity can be evaluated and developed only at the expense of the management attentional neglect of the current operations.

The relative importance between the current operations and exploring new opportunities depends on the sustainability of current operations. When the cash flows and current advantages are more sustainable, the value of current operations is high enough to justify a greater allocation of management attention to maintaining the current operations and resources, which as a result reduces the firm's innovation and growth efforts (Gifford 1992). However, when the firm's current advantage is temporary or the current cash flows are less sustainable (e.g., a firm in a hypercompetitive environment), then the management may find growth activities more lucrative than trying to improve current operations. Thus, in a dynamic environment, the management may allocate more attention to seeking and exploiting new value opportunities. Further, when technological opportunities are high, even though the profits from current operations and the current advantages are sustainable, the management may choose to allocate greater attention to identifying and exploiting new value opportunities.

Management Cognition

Individual cognition is an individual competence (cognitive capacity) independent of situations. Learning enhances an individual's knowledge of solutions to a class of problems and improves their actions in a given situation. Individual cognition is independent of situations in which the individual learns but they improve with active learning. Management cognition constitutes the management's perception of the information elements in the environment, the comprehension and interpretation of the information, and the projection of the critical variables in the near future. Cognitive activities are an individual's mental activities that acquire, evaluate, store, transform, reduce, elaborate, or use knowledge. Active learning enhances the management cognition.

Stagnant management logics can inhibit the management cognition, whereas enhancing the management logics through active learning can enhance the management cognition. In top-down information processing, management goals determine the management's reasoning and interpretation of the environmental cues. In bottom-up information processing, the management formulates an interpretation of the situation from the environmental cues or the data pattern observed. In practice, however, management may use both top-down and bottom-up information processing simultaneously to more effectively evaluate and interpret a situation. Managers differ in their cognitive capabilities and information processing capacities; and thus they differ in their abilities to recognize and evaluate potential value opportunities and competitive threats in the environment.

Endsley (1988) identifies several factors that may explain the differences in individual cognition capabilities. An individual's training and work experience affect their cognition in a given situation. An individual's experience in a task environment improves their cognition through several mechanisms (Endsley and Bolstad 1994). First, the cognition of individuals can be based on their pattern matching abilities derived from previous situational experiences that are stored in their mental models. Increased situational learning in a specified task environment can lead to more accurate mental models of individuals, which helps the individual to achieve a higher level cognition.

Further, increased training and experience leads to richer mental models as the individual learns to organize the complexity and multiplicity of elements in a task environment. Richer mental models enhance the understanding of the relations between the environmental elements, their functioning and cause-and-effects information, allowing a more accurate interpretation and projection of the environmental state variables and their impact on firm performance. With training and experience, and thereby with richer mental models, individual attention is enhanced and important environmental cues that signify relevant information are identified, which further enhances the information processing capacity and environmental matching abilities of the individual, enabling the individual to overcome traditional behavioral bounds as assumed in behavioral theory. Experience and learning thus improves individual cognition by reducing the amount of attention necessary for physical tasks, thereby freeing up attentional resources for cognitive or mental activities leading to a higher level of individual cognition.

Endsley (1988) identifies certain cognitive factors that relate to differences in individual cognition, namely, attention, mental models, perception, cognitive style, field independence, and locus of control. In the previous sections, we have discussed management attention and mental models that are critical to managerial cognitive activities. Attentional resources are important to achieving a higher level of management cognition and situation awareness. The distribution of management attention across multiple, competing tasks is a significant challenge for managers. Management attentional engagement is also called upon a great deal when dealing with a hypercompetitive environment. Management attention constrains management cognition and situation awareness.

Management attention is required when managers try to perceive selected environmental information, integrate information from multiple sources, compare and reason this information with the schemas stored in their mental models and reconcile the information with the goals of the organization, and project future scenarios and trends and their impact on firm performance. Management attention is further taxed by simultaneous decision-making and operating activities. Mental models, schemas and scripts, may reduce the load on management attention. Experience also increases the automaticity of physical tasks, freeing up management attention further to improve the management cognition. Training is useful in structuring and focusing a manager's experience, enhancing management cognition further. When designing training programs to improve management cognition and situation awareness, the focus should be on the tasks the managers perform that consume maximum attentional resources.

Management attention and executive working memory capacity are primary bottlenecks to the management achieving sufficient situation awareness. The management attention is the manager's capacity to focus attention on specific information elements in the environment. The executive working memory holds the available information active for transient processing. Thus, the executive working memory is a temporary storage of information held for further processing. The situation awareness denotes the state of the manager's knowledge of the environment or what is going on. In our framework, management cognition is a process variable and situation awareness is a state variable. The management cognition constitutes managerial cognitive activities, namely, management perception, comprehension, and projection. Further, the entrepreneurial incentives enhance the management goals and thereby reduce the load on the management attentional capacity and executive working memory capacity, further enhancing the management cognition and their situation awareness.

Management cognition relies first upon the management accurately perceiving necessary and complete information. Managers with superior perceptual abilities have a slight edge over others. Pattern matching skills are frequently called upon to enhance management perception. Perceptual speed or the ability to quickly perceive information, encoding speed or the ability to encode the information, and vigiling speed or the ability to remain vigilant to weak or infrequent signals are important when managers are dealing with dynamic environments (Endsley and Bolstad 1994). Perceptual speed, encoding speed, and vigiling speed enhance organizational agility, proactive adaptation, situation awareness, opportunity focus, and absorptive capacity, the key attributes of entrepreneurial organizations (see Chapter 3).

Certain higher order cognitive functions, such as cognitive style, locus of control, and field independence also determine the level of individual cognition (Endsley and Bolstad 1994). Cognitive style ranks individuals into groups ranging from more concrete (high adaptiveness) to more abstract (high innovativeness). Concrete individuals are real-world oriented, quick to act, pragmatic, flexible, and identify highly with social status positions; whereas abstract individuals base their responses upon their internal values and beliefs. Entrepreneurs are more concrete in their cognitive style, whereas inventors are more abstract. Cognitive style is correlated with the individual's approach to problem solving. Further, entrepreneurs are field-independent. Field independence is an ability to perceive objectives distinct from their context and provide a new organization to an unstructured context. Field-dependent individuals are constrained by the prevailing representation of a problem.

Finally, locus of control is an important determinant in how likely it is that the individual will take a proactive role in cognition. Individuals with an internal locus of control believe that a successful outcome is due to their own behavior; whereas individuals with an external locus of control believe that a successful outcome is due to luck, chance, or an external factor. Thus, with internal locus of control, the individual is more proactive. Entrepreneurial incentives enhance the executive's concrete cognitive style, field-independence, and internal locus of control.

Management cognition is management's cognitive capability, that is, their information processing capability. Management cognition and situation awareness are enhanced by active learning, management logics, management attention, and management goals and incentives. Management cognition perceives and processes available information. The entrepreneurial incentives enhance and sustain the management logics, management goals, and management attention, which further enhance the management cognition (see Fig. 2.1). The entrepreneurial incentive is provided through the uncertain performance based compensation in executive pay, and the firm performance is set and evaluated by an external arbiter. Through cognitive activities empowered by entrepreneurial incentives, management senses and evaluates available information in the environment, enhancing managerial abilities to recognize the firm's value opportunities and competitive threats in a timely manner. Further, superior value opportunities are cognitively distant. While value opportunities are situations of potential value to the firm, competitive threats are situations of potential loss to the firm.

Managers with entrepreneurial incentives have a promotional focus mildly tempered with prevention focus; thus they can recognize superior opportunities that traditional managers may miss. Management cognition is shaped by the management logics, management attention, and

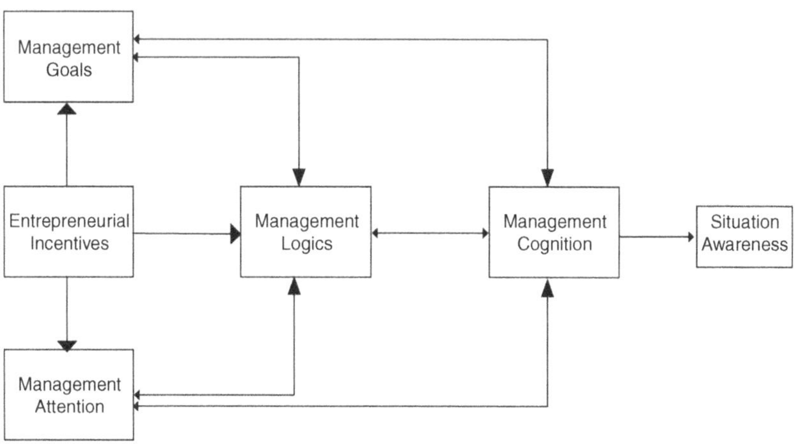

Fig. 2.1 Management cognition

management goals and incentives. Entrepreneurial incentives by providing the management an opportunity to earn entrepreneurial surplus, enhances the management goals and their mental model (management logics) that further enhance the management cognition enabling the management to sense and seize distant value opportunities in a timely manner (see Chapter 3). Entrepreneurial incentives that enhance the management learning and their cognitive adaptability (metacognition) further enhance the management cognition and situation awareness, thereby surfacing, testing, and improving the management logics. Enhanced management logics further enhance the management cognition.

Management learning and their cognitive adaptability enhance the management logics, enhancing the management cognition. Entrepreneurial incentives thus enhance management learning and management cognitive adaptability, further enhancing the management logics and situation awareness. Further, management attention is enhanced by improving the organization's operating and governance channels, enhancing the information processing capacity of management. Furthermore, the organization's transactive memory (i.e., who knows what in an organization) enhances active learning and situation awareness in the organization, which further enhances the management logics and value opportunities. The organizational transactive memory is high in an organization with entrepreneurial incentives. However, with high transactive memory, the situation awareness is distributed within an organization, thus requiring an effective coordination by the top management, a more effective management system design, and efficient operating and governance procedural and communication channels. Transactive memory enhances the management cognition and situation awareness, although it must be effectively managed and leveraged requiring top management attention.

Enhancing and maintaining management cognition and situation awareness, and continually updating the status of several key environmental variables, is essential in a dynamic environment. To build and sustain competitive advantage it is critical that an organization must sense and seize cognitively distant value opportunities in a timely manner. The environmental information may change rapidly and in complex ways in a dynamic environment. Managers empowered by entrepreneurial incentives continually learn, proactively adapt, and maintain their cognition as they are driven by powerful entrepreneurial incentives and a desire to earn an entrepreneurial surplus. Furthermore, management cognition activities involve much more than environmental scanning and scenario exercises that are part of traditional strategic planning. Management must have the abilities to integrate the information they perceive, drawing on the management logics and in light of the management goals and incentives, and to project key environmental variables that impact the firm performance in the near future.

Our framework of management cognition draws on the theory of situation awareness in a dynamic environment (Endsley 1995). As Endsley points out, a good situational model "should explain dynamic goal selection, attention to appropriate critical cues [in the dynamic environment], expectancies regarding future states of the situation and the tie between situation knowledge and typical [management] actions" [34]. Situation awareness is crucial to the organization's ability for opportunity selection and development, resource allocation and activity configuration, and thus to the value creation and appropriation mechanism that underlie the competitive advantage. Helfat and Peteraf (2015) describe the management cognition as the organization's dynamic managerial capabilities that enhance organizational dynamic capabilities; that is, the dynamic capabilities for sensing and seizing opportunities and reconfiguring firm resources (Teece 2007).

Several cognitive factors influence the management cognition, namely their cognitive style, field independence, and locus of control. Prior experience in a particular domain also influences the level of management cognition. In addition, the environmental complexity and information overload affect management cognition. The organization's procedural and communication channels and information system interfaces regulating the management attention also affect management cognition. Moreover, active learning and distributed knowledge in the organization (i.e., transactive memory) affect management cognition. The management logics and goals support management cognition. Sartar and Woods (1991) note that "adequate mental models are one of the prerequisites for achieving situation awareness" [49].

Further, management cognition is a management capability independent of a situation, whereas situation awareness refers to the knowledge of a given situation. The management cognition resides in the management and enables their situation awareness. The situation awareness is the management's snapshot of the state of the environment at a given moment, generated and enhanced by management cognition. The goal of managerial cognitive activities is "coming to know what must be known in order to behave in accord with the mandates of the arbiter of performance" (Smith and Hancock 1995: 141). The management attention directs management cognition to focus on available information in the environment, which enhances the situation awareness. Situation awareness is the core that links the management attention to management goals to available information.

Management cognition includes managerial cognitive activities including management perception, interpretation, reasoning, problem-solving, projection, communication, and social cognition. Management attention is crucial to management cognition capabilities. Helfat and Peteraf (2015) define individual perception as an individual's mental activities that help them organize information and interpret it. Problem-solving is defined as a means of finding a way around an obstacle or a problem, while reasoning refers to the evaluation of information gathered to draw a conclusion. Management projection refers to extrapolating a current trend in the environment and examining its impact on the firm performance in the near future. Projection is different from anticipation or forecasting in that the anticipation is a forecast of an unknown future (rather a difficult task), whereas projection is the ability to extrapolate a known trend that has potential value the impact of which is not yet fully realized. Further, communication includes the abilities of verbal and nonverbal expression of ideas. Social cognition further includes the mental activities that influence social interactions in an organization.

Management Perception

Perception is different from sensing (Gazzaniga et al. 2010). Sensing is feeling, a subjective experience; and the essence of sensing is information detection. The essence of perception is encoding the useful and meaningful information available in an environment. Thus, perception involves the abilities of pattern recognition and information organization. Management logics containing management schemas, scripts and theories guide the management perception. Experts differ from novices in perceptual capabilities. Pattern recognition facilitates early recognition of critical cues indicating emerging value opportunities and competitive threats. Further, repeated experience in an environment helps the individual to form and store patterns and prototypes that can be compared to make sense of the available information (see Chapter 4).

Schemas, scripts, and beliefs stored in the management logics influence the speed and accuracy of management perception. Management logics and goals play a key role in organizing the perceived information into known categories. The information categorization occurs immediately after sensing the information and is typically a deterministic process. With enhanced management logics, very fine categorization is possible. More refined classification of available information enables managers to retrieve the appropriate schemas and scripts stored in mental models for the subsequent processing of information for comprehension and projection. Effective cue utilization in information categorization is important for management cognition and information processing. Experts develop the knowledge of critical cues or the key indicators in their environmental domains to enable them to make a fine categorization of the available information.

Dutton and Jackson (1987) discuss how categorizing available information influences the subsequent information processing activities as well as the motivations of the decision makers. Different organizations may categorize the same information differently and as a result these organizations may respond differently to similar events in the environment. "Individuals rely on categorization because it reduces the complexity of the stimulus world by organizing objects into meaningful groups" (Dutton and Jackson 1987: 78). Categorization of available information can be fine grained ranging from superordinate levels to basic levels to subordinate levels, depending on the organization's goals, management incentives, internal selection environment, and management logics. Information attributes that serve to differentiate the categories are said to have cue validity. Categorization enhances the management cognition and situation awareness: (1) categorized information is easier to recall than noncategorical information; (2) categorization helps fill information gaps when incomplete information is available; and (3) noise or ambiguity in perceived information is reduced (Dutton and Jackson 1987).

Threats and opportunities are the organization's fundamental categories of environmental information since these categories have distinct attributes. Further, in a traditional organization, an opportunity implies a positive situation in which a gain is likely and upon which one has more control; whereas a threat implies a negative situation in which a loss is likely and over which the organization has little control (Dutton and Jackson 1987). However, threats are viewed as latent opportunities in entrepreneurial organizations. Further, organizations view competitive threats as challenges, thus implying a greater controllability. Small amounts of threats actually enhance the management goals and cognition; however, greater competitive threats tax the management attention impairing the management cognition. Three attributes of information, namely, a positive or negative event, a financial gain or loss, and more or less controllability, often describe an organization's opportunities and threats, respectively. Positive tone, likelihood of gain, and controllability go together, as do negative tone, likelihood of loss, and uncontrollability. The categorization of information enhances the management cognition and situation awareness.

Categorizing an event or information as a threat or an opportunity influences the speed and magnitude of management response, which may vary with the level of management incentives. Furthermore, once an event is categorized, it is easier for the management to communicate the issue and share the relevant information with others in the organization. When the information is categorized as opportunities or challenges, as is the case in entrepreneurial organizations, the management tends to be proactive and externally directed; whereas when the information is categorized as a threat, as is often the case in some traditional organizations, the management tends to be more reactive and focuses their attention on the internal processes and resources.

In most organizations, threat categorization is also followed by major strategic changes, whereas opportunities are often followed by incremental changes in traditional organizations. However, entrepreneurial organizations pursue cognitive distant opportunities that require major strategic response and organizational ambidexterity. The categorization of information is thus important in how the management views and acts on the available information. Furthermore, management can manipulate the categorization of available information to elicit a certain type of response from the organization.

As described in the previous sections, management attention is critical to their perception of the available information. Management attention determines which information is recognized and which is ignored. Management attention for the purpose of management perception has three major functions, namely, detecting the signals for subsequent processing, orientation to sensory events, and holding information active in the executive working memory for further processing (Posner and Petersen 1990). Management can enhance their attention to sensory stimuli through automatic mental activities. Conscious mental activities require a greater utilization of attentional resources. Further, automaticity of mental activities is developed through an individual's work experience and training in a given environment. Automatic processing tends to be fast, effortless, and requires little to no attention. However, it seems empirically a minimum level of attention is needed in automatic mental activities (automaticity). Further, automaticity of certain managerial mental activities greatly enhances the management cognition without requiring a great deal of attentional resources including executive working memory. Executive working memory is an executive's mental capacity to transiently hold information active for further processing. The organization's transactive memory reduces the load on the executive working memory.

However, with the automaticity of mental activities a great deal of cognitive activities occurs below one's consciousness. Then the question arises as to what extent an individual who engages in automatic mental activities has good cognition. The automaticity of mental activities may reduce the individual's need for greater attention, but it may come at the cost of reduced cognition. However, with automatic information processing, an individual is conscious of some information elements that trigger an automatic retrieval of the schemas, scripts, or beliefs from one's mental models to help information processing, but the individual may not be aware of the mechanisms used in their action selection. That is, the individual knows *the what*, but not *the how* the decision is reached (Endsley 1995). The information content is still available with the automaticity but the decision process is occluded. The individual, if asked to explain their action after the fact, would typically try to reconstruct the steps leading to their action. However, one's capacity or the extent of automatic mental activities without any attention is questioned in the literature.

Thus, a minimum level of attention is required for all automatic mental activities in order to retrieve appropriate schemas and scripts from the mental models, but the individual may not be aware of the detailed procedures. The major implications of the automatic cognitive processing of information are the enhanced cognition of the individual with minimal attention but at the same time a greater unreliability and inaccuracy of the cognitive processes leading to the individual's actions after the fact (Endsley 1995).

The primary hazard with automaticity of cognitive activities is the management inertia in a dynamic environment; that is, the management being less responsive to novel stimuli in a changing environment, as automatic processing occurs with limited use of feedback. Thus, poor management response may result with automaticity of managerial cognitive activities, thereby decreasing decision timeliness and effectiveness. In traditional organizations, managers use more automaticity and heuristics through decision rules and scripts, and thus the management cognition can be insufficient in traditional organizations. The path-dependency with automaticity exacerbates the problem of inadequate and delayed response by management to a rapidly changing environment.

Managers must spot early signals when market signals are just a glimmer, before the signals are readily apparent to everyone. Managers should pay close attention to at least three trends in the market, namely, a looming growth gap, signs of overshooting, and an emergence of disruption in adjacent and substitute markets (Anthony 2005). A looming growth gap is the difference between a company's strategic goal and where the company is actually heading, a sign that the company needs to shift their current strategy. Further, managers should spot the signs of overshooting in that the company has overshot the segments of its core business. In times of overshooting, the company's current customers are no longer valuing the current products the way once they did.

Anthony (2005) recommends a number of signals a company may track, including the market greeting its new product introductions with a collective yawn, the company's salesforce complaining about price, the company ceding a market segment to a low cost competitor, and their declining gross margins in a product market segment. Finally, a company should give heed to the signs of emerging competition in adjacent and substitute markets. Disruptive competitors in adjacent markets seem inoffensive at first, but as these competitors grow and improve, they often pose serious competitive threats.

Management Comprehension

Management comprehension is the management's synthesis of disparate elements of available information in light of the management goals, constructing a holistic picture of the significant information elements and events. The manager actively constructs and reasons cause-effect relations between the significant information elements. Kiesler and Sproull (1982) describe five principles related to management comprehension, namely, the augmentation principle, the discounting principle, illusory correlation, illusory causation, and automatic scanning. These fundamental principles drive the management's choice of which disparate elements of available information to incorporate when constructing a holistic picture of the environment in light of the management goals. Further, prior to management comprehension, the management has perceived salient cues in the environment and categorized the events as opportunities or threats, or into some meaningful categories. In this stage of management cognition, the disparate elements of information are integrated to construct a comprehensive picture of what is going on (i.e., situation awareness). Further, management reasoning and problem-solving activities are also important at this stage.

The augmentation principle states that "if for a given effect, both a plausible *inhibiting* cause and a plausible *facilitative* cause are present, the role of the facilitative cause in producing the effect will be judged greater than if it alone were present" (Kelley 1971: 12). The principle thus implies that decision makers tend to overestimate the influence of a plausible cause (Kiesler and Sproull 1982). Second, the discounting principle suggests that when there is one powerful facilitative cause, other plausible causes in general will seem to be less significant. The principle thus suggests that decision makers tend to focus on the most powerful facilitative cause among all plausible causes in interpreting an event (Kelley 1971).

Third, the illusory correlation between two events is their fortuitous association, their mutual infrequent occurrence, or their share of a common cause (Kiesler and Sproull 1982). Illusory correlations are thus psychological spurious correlations of events that are fortuitously linked. Fourth, illusory causation is the premature or inappropriate conclusion of causality through the false association of events with the prominent individuals or organizations that may draw attention (e.g., an association with a prominent individual or organization). Finally, automatic scanning is the automaticity of information processing such that the individual reaches a conclusion but they are not completely aware of the steps that led them to the conclusion. If the individual is asked to explain how they reached the conclusion, they will try to recall the steps that have led them to reach the conclusion.

Management logics influence the management's reasoning processes. Management may call upon schemas, scripts, or theories stored in the management logics. Decision heuristics (e.g., simple rules) and routines stored in the management logics are retrieved when the management is working through ill-defined or complex problems. The schemas or causal knowledge structures stored in the management logics are invoked for management reasoning and problem solving, for evaluating the available information or arguments to draw a conclusion. Further, certain prototypes and patterns considered salient stored as schemas in the management logics may erroneously order the cause-effect relationships leading to illusory causation or correlation. An incidental similarity of the events with those stored in mental models may thus lead to false reasoning.

For effective reasoning and management comprehension, management attentional capacity and executive working memory capacity are critical.

The executive working memory resource is a core executive resource that is responsible for the transient holding and processing of information. Reasoning and problem solving would not be possible without the executive working memory. The new information available is combined with the manager's existing knowledge structures recalled from the management logics to form a comprehensive picture of the emerging events. Further, a heavy load is generally imposed on the management attention and executive working memory for comprehending the situation, finding solutions, and carrying out subsequent actions. Management attentional capacity and executive working memory constitute the main bottlenecks to achieving sufficient situation awareness. The workload on the management attentions is reduced in the goal-driven top-down information processing that employs the management goals to guide the management comprehension.

Thus, management goals and motivations influence the manager's reasoning and problem solving processes. Managers choose to incorporate the information that is personally enhancing when reasoning an event. Managers differ in their goals and motives, and their cognition is linked to their goals and motives (Kiesler and Sproull 1982). Managerial incentives are further linked to management goals and motives. For example, management goals and motives are different in entrepreneurial organizations than those in traditional organizations, in opportunity focused organizations versus resource focused organizations. Entrepreneurial incentives drive managerial motives to earn an entrepreneurial surplus, which influences the management comprehension and reasoning (see Chapter 3). Managers with entrepreneurial incentives thus may incorporate the available information and comprehend an event differently.

The biases of decision makers, linked to their goals and motives, reflect in their problem formulation approach and reasoning processes. The motivationally driven cognitive processes apply whether the motives are held by an individual or a group to which the individual belongs. Thus, when mangers are heavily vested in their current strategy and encounter new information that contradicts their current beliefs, that is inconsistent with their current goals, or that is not personally enhancing, they may not incorporate the new information in their reasoning activities (Kiesler and Sproull 1982).

Managers are not just passive recipients of information from the environment. In most environments, especially in entrepreneurial organizations, managers actively seek information in light of their goals. Management cognition is thus fundamentally linked to management goals. In top-down information processing, management goals guide which aspects of the information are attended to by managers in developing management comprehension. However, simultaneous with top-down processing, bottom-up information processing occurs in which data patterns in the information are recognized to develop management comprehension; and further, the current management goals are revised or the new goals are put into place. Top-down and bottom-up information processing together allows a manager to be more effective in attending to the salient information in the environment and integrating the new information in light of the revised goals. The information processing and management comprehension in a dynamic environment is more meaningful when viewed in the context of the manager's revised goals. Further, simultaneous top-down and bottom-up processing enriches the organization of the management logics and enhances the situation awareness, which further enhances the firm's value opportunities.

The management logics in light of the management goals and attention determine what information is to be attended to in an environment in interpreting an event and developing the management comprehension. Further, the management's recognition of new data patterns and novel stimuli in the information perceived enrich the management logics and revise management goals. The absorption of new information and revision of the management logics depend on the management learning or managerial absorptive capacity. The prior knowledge and experience of the management in a given task environment stored in the management logics enhances the managerial absorptive capacity, thus enhancing the management reasoning and comprehension. Further, management learning is enhanced by the managerial absorptive capacity. The managerial absorptive capacity is high in entrepreneurial organizations.

Management Projection

Management projection is the ability of management to extrapolate current trends to forge a coherent relationship between the firm's present and future. Projection is not forecast of new trends. Projection is the extrapolation of current trends that have an ongoing impact the full potential of which is not yet realized. Projection is a process of "planned learning" (Vecchiato 2015). Management projection requires that the management has gathered sufficient information and has sufficient comprehension of the current environment.

Projection is not forecasting. "A key feature of strategic foresight is the premise that the future is neither predictable nor predetermined, but it might be influenced by the present choices of the organization" (Vecchiato 2015). Forecasts are accurate statements of future events, but forecasting is difficult; whereas projections are general trend statements of the ongoing events. For example, smartphone sales reaching 3 billion in 2020 is a forecast, but smartphone sales continuing to grow in the near future is a projection (Vecchiato 2015).

Projection gives the management a timing advantage on when to act on an opportunity or mitigate a threat. Projection enhances the management logics, and evaluates and revises the management goals. Projection enhances the situation awareness, assess the impact of the critical environmental variables on the firm performance, and provides sufficient foresight enabling managers to recognize cognitively distant opportunities. Projection is the manager's ability to cope with the future. It is not about acting in the future, but rather enacting the future; that is, projection necessarily means management acts in the present to enact a future. It is not fortune telling, speculation, or prophesizing. Projection is the capability to enact the future in the present, and extrapolate current trends and act upon them.

Projection is an entrepreneurial ability that gives the management a comparative advantage to spot opportunity options and seize value opportunities in a timely fashion, to respond proactively to potential threats in a changing environment, and to enable management to act on faint signals in the market before the signals are apparent to everyone. Entrepreneurial incentives empower managers to proactively manage the firm's present to compete for the future. Projection ability is crucial to a firm trying to build and sustain competitive advantage. Projection further requires the management to have achieved sufficient perception and comprehension of their environment. Moreover, projection shapes the management logics and revises the management goals. Further, projection ability requires a great deal of management attention and executive working memory. Projection capability of the management is enhanced with sufficient management incentives. Thus, organizations with high-powered entrepreneurial incentives have superior management projection capabilities.

Strategic foresight literature describes projection not as forecasting but as the "memories of the future"; that is, the management acts in the present with an eye on the future (Vecchiato 2015). Management is foresightful when, through their actions in the present, they can forge a coherent relationship between the firm's past, present, and future. Projection enables management to spot fresh developments in the present and the departures from the past. Thus, management projection is not the management ability to forecast what will happen in the future, but the ability to engage in the firm's present. Foresight is acting on the current trends, which creates alternative pathways to the firm's future. Sensing weak signals early, evaluating them, comprehending their potential impacts on the firm performance, and projecting in the present to enact a future are essential to thrive in a dynamic environment. Entrepreneurial incentives for the management induce high projection abilities.

Hamel and Prahalad (1994) found that managers devoted less than three percent of their time to developing a view of the future. They urge managers to spend more time on creating the firm's future instead of spending too much time on catching up with competitors by cutting costs and improving quality. The enactment of the future should then drive the firm's current strategy and opportunities. The management should consider who their customers are today and who their customers will be in the future; who their competitors are today and who their competitors will be in the future; further, what capabilities make the firm competitive today and what will make them competitive in the future. To enact a future, management should project how their industry will be shaped in the near future, determine which value opportunities they must seize now and how to exploit the uncertainty associated with the value opportunities to resolve in the firm's favor to be competitive in the future, and determine which organizational capabilities they need to support the opportunities. Entrepreneurial incentives enhance the management ability to sense and seize the opportunities today to gain advantage in the future.

Why are some managers more successful at identifying value opportunities that enhance the value creation and appropriation mechanism providing the firm competitive advantage? A greater ability to recognize complex stimuli in their environment distinguishes entrepreneurial executives from traditional counterparts. High-powered entrepreneurial incentives that enhance management learning and cognitive adaptability further enhance the management logics and situation awareness. Thus, entrepreneurial incentives enable the management to proactively adapt the management logics under dynamic competitive conditions, and to seize and act on new value opportunities in a timely manner while attending to the needs of the firm's operations.

Management cognition may vary in range from (1) weak perception, (2) inability to discern the current state of the environment, (3) clarity about the current environment but no foresight, (4) limited foresight, to (5) enhanced foresight. Level 1 managers have weak perception and encoding abilities. Level 2 managers have a high level of perception but weak comprehension abilities. Further, Level 3 managers have a high level of perception and comprehension but weak projection abilities. Level 4 managers have a high level of perception and comprehension abilities but moderate projection abilities. Level 5 managers have high level of perception, comprehension, and projection capabilities. However, Level 5 managers are rare. Entrepreneurial executives have enhanced cognitive capabilities driven by their desire to earn an entrepreneurial surplus. Level 5 managers are visionary leaders and entrepreneurs.

To summarize, management cognition includes management perception, comprehension, and projection abilities. Management cognition is constrained by the management attention and executive working memory capacity. The management logics and transactive memory reduce the load on the executive working memory and management attention, which further enhance the management cognition. Management goals guide the management attention, further enhancing the management cognition. Furthermore, management learning and cognitive adaptability enhances the management logics, which further enhance the management cognition and situation awareness. High-powered entrepreneurial incentives enhance managerial learning that further enhances the management logics, providing the firm with sufficient situation awareness. Management cognition can be enhanced by the automaticity of cognitive activities. However, the automaticity of managerial cognitive activities may leave the firm vulnerable to the impact of novel stimuli in a dynamic environment.

Management goals further reduce the load on management attention and thus enhance management cognition. Management cognitive activities enhance the management logics and revise the management goals. Management cognition can vary widely across firms in an industry ranging from weak perception to enhanced foresight. Level 5 managers are rare. The managerial abilities to spot weak and distant signals early before they are apparent to others and to recognize cognitively distant value opportunities require enhanced management cognition. Entrepreneurial incentives enhance the management cognition.

Management Team Situation Awareness

Situation awareness is a team awareness of the environment. Situation awareness is a shared awareness among the management team members. Situation awareness is thus the team's shared understanding of the environment at a point in time. Team awareness constitutes the awareness of team members with overlapping information elements. Each member's awareness requirement is determined by their responsibilities as defined by the organization. Some overlap between member awareness requirements is required for effective team awareness and the overlapping information elements must be managed and resolved by a top executive (e.g., chief executive). Furthermore, team awareness is enhanced through team protocols, verbal exchange, and some duplication in information processing.

The shared information elements of team member awareness determine the effectiveness of the team awareness. The team awareness is the degree to which every team member possesses the awareness required by their responsibilities. The degree to which each team member has sufficient situation awareness on the shared elements determines the level of team coordination. Every team member must have sufficient awareness for a team to have sufficient situation awareness; otherwise the member with low awareness becomes the weakest link, making the situation awareness insufficient.

It is not adequate for some team members to have sufficient awareness and the others to have insufficient awareness. This will weaken the team awareness. Each team member must achieve sufficient situation awareness without much demand on the team for communication. Thus, shared elements are present in the team awareness when the team members address the same environment. The demand on team communication must be minimal in meeting each member's awareness needs. Transactive memory (i.e., who knows what in the organization) enhances team awareness. The operating and governance channels that distribute management attention enhance team awareness. Thus, the design of the decision-making channels in an organization are critical for achieving sufficient situation awareness. Moreover, Mosier and Childester (1991) found that better-performing teams actually communicated less than poorly performing teams.

In team awareness, every team member does not need to know everything but each member needs sufficient situation awareness concerning their functional responsibilities with some minimal overlapping elements. Furthermore, each team member must know what other team members need to know; that is, each team member has access to the organization's transactive memory (Wegner 1986). The transactive memory is the knowledge of who knows what in the organization. Transactive memory enhances the team awareness and management logics. Further, transactive memory enhances team coordination and provides each team member with access to more information than each individual member can acquire on their own. Transactive memory enhances each individual executive's working memory capacity and thus enhances individual cognition. Executive working memory is one of the primary bottlenecks in management cognition. Transactive memory enhances the executive working memory capacity of the management team.

Argote and Ren (2012) identify three indicators of the existence of transactive memory in an organization, namely, knowledge specialization, task credibility, and task coordination. With knowledge specialization, each team member develops specialized and complementary expertise; task credibility depends on how much team members trust each other's knowledge; and the task coordination is the ability of the management team to work together. Transactive memory allows each member of the management team to specialize in a particular function. Further, transactive memory is more valuable in a dynamic environment. Management teams with active transactive memory are more alert, agile, absorptive, and proactive (thus more entrepreneurial) as the team members are able to combine their knowledge in new ways to develop creative solutions and solve complex problems. Entrepreneurial organizations have active transactive memory.

Inadequate Situation Awareness

Situation awareness is the outcome of a managerial cognitive process in which the managerial mental models and management goals interact with the environment aided by the managerial attentional resources. Management cognition enables their situation awareness and is a crucial management capability in that a higher level of management cognition and sufficient situation awareness enable the management to sense and seize the cognitively distant superior value opportunities in a timely manner, which enhance the firm's value creation and appropriation mechanism wherein the firm's competitive advantage lies. Superior firm performance is possible when the managers with sufficient situation awareness seize cognitively distant opportunities and act in a timely manner.

Moreover, when the firm performance is strong, the management team receives credit for perceiving the opportunities and threats in a timely fashion, for making correct predictions, and for taking appropriate actions. However, when the firm performance is poor, the management gets blamed for perceiving the situation erroneously, for making mistakes in comprehending actual problems, for making poor predictions, and for taking inappropriate or delayed actions. However, it is the management's situation awareness which is at the root of the firm's poor financial performance. The management team may be very strategic and the firm may own or control several strategic resources, but when their situation awareness is insufficient, the firm performance suffers and the firm will not achieve competitive advantage.

Further, the firm may have a great strategy, own strategic resources, and have sufficient situation awareness, but if the management team does not have sufficient incentives to act on the value opportunities in a timely manner and exploit the uncertainty associated with the opportunities in the firm's favor, then the firm performance still suffers. Situation awareness that is crucial to strategic decisions and business model execution, might be incomplete or inaccurate, or both. Management team's situation awareness is incomplete when the management team has the knowledge of only some of the key environmental elements; and the situation awareness is inaccurate when the management team has erroneous knowledge of the environmental variables that affect the firm performance.

Management cognition may break down at different stages of the cognitive process. At the perception stage of management cognition, an executive or a team may simply fail to detect certain key information in the environment, leading to an incomplete awareness. This may result from a lack of detectability or discriminability of critical cues or signals, or the failure of information channels or attentional resources to make the information available to management in a timely fashion. Or the management may miss early warning signs, or spot them too late, in which case the signals are discernible but the management has failed to perceive them when the information is relevant in making their decisions.

Complex environments present an abundance of information, and further, in a dynamic environment the information changes rapidly. The available information may be sampled incorrectly or inadequately, or the statistical properties of the data are misinterpreted, resulting in the omission of key environmental variables. In addition to incomplete situation awareness, an inaccurate perception of the signals can occur. Distortions in management perception can occur when the management logics are incomplete or inaccurate, when the management goals and incentives are inconsistent, when the information is categorized incorrectly, when the attentional resources are lacking, or when the management finds the information is not personally enhancing.

Further, some individuals are better than others at dividing their attention across tasks (Damos and Wickens 1980). Even though the environment is sampled effectively, the firm's procedural and communication channels that distribute the management attention may be poorly designed, which can lead to incomplete awareness. Attentional problems are further compounded when environmental complexity and ambiguity are present as in a rapidly changing environment. Attentional capacity constraints brought on by competitive stress and environmental complexity can lead to incomplete awareness. With attentional limits, management wants to be certain that they are attending to what is the most important information but there is no way to test it without knowing the value of the missing information. Management attentional constraint can lead to a serious inadequacy in situation awareness.

Inadequate situation awareness is most often due to the management's inability to properly integrate and comprehend the meaning of perceived information in light of their goals. The management logics may not have the appropriate schemas and scripts necessary to properly comprehend and integrate the incoming information. In the absence of good mental models, the team must accept low situation awareness (Endsley 1995). Moreover, the management logics may fail to adapt to a changing environment and novel stimuli, especially when the managerial cognitive adaptability is low. Entrepreneurial organizations are agile, adaptive, proactive, and absorptive; and furthermore, the entrepreneurial incentives enhance the management cognitive adaptability. However, traditional organizations may not have sufficient management cognitive adaptability. Low management cognitive adaptability is often associated with organizational inertia and core rigidity.

In some situations, the management may choose the wrong schema based on a subset of existent cues and use that schema to interpret all related data. Moreover, to realize that a wrong schema is active can be very difficult because the new information is interpreted by the active schema. The management may also choose a schema which will interpret the information to be personally benefitting, which will result in a confirmation bias (Fracker 1988). Furthermore, an incorrect schema may be chosen because of a cognitive bias such as the representativeness, availability, and other biases.

Even if a correct schema is selected to interpret and comprehend the incoming data, certain aspects of the data may not match the prototype in the selected schema, resulting in a failure to recognize a prototypical situation. Inadequate situation awareness can also occur from overreliance on default values in the selected schema. When novel situations or stimuli are encountered for which the default values of a schema are not appropriate, the schema is modified to incorporate the new information. It is also difficult to know when to modify a schema stored in the management logics. Before the current schemas are modified even when the management has high cognitive adaptability, significant inadequacy in situation awareness has occurred by incorrectly assuming the defaults for some of the variables in the new information.

Inadequate situation awareness can also occur when some habitual scripts or routines are activated while automatic cognitive processing is in effect, but a change in the routine or rule is needed to accommodate a new management goal. In this situation, while habitual scripts are still processing, the new goal (possibly an emergent one) will be suppressed and the management may not be receptive to the relevant signals appropriate for the new goal. Then the appropriate schemas to recognize the information relevant for the new goal may not be retrieved or may be retrieved with a time delay from the management logics.

Further, inadequate situation awareness can occur not because the manager relies on automatic processing or habitual scripts such as simple rules, but when the manager fails to recognize the presence of conditions in which they must switch from automatic processing mode to conscious processing or active thinking mode. Furthermore, Louis and Sutton (1991) identify three conditions that will help a manager to sense the need for switching from automatic script to conscious thinking requiring attentional engagement: (1) when the manager experiences an unusual or novel situation, (2) when there are significant disruptions in the environment, or (3) when deliberate efforts are called for either initiated by the manager or asked for by others.

Often the management lacks projection abilities or it may be difficult to project correctly in a rapidly changing environment. Management projection or extrapolation of certain current trends is rather difficult without well-developed management logics and high managerial absorptive capacity. The lack of well-developed and continually updated management logics, insufficient managerial absorptive capacity, managerial attentional capacity constraints, weak transactive memory, and the firm's information processing constraints account for most of the weaknesses in managerial comprehension and projection abilities, leading to incomplete or inadequate situation awareness.

A real challenge is in how the management team can know when their situation awareness is inadequate. Often the management is completely unaware of how much they do not know. The main clue to inadequate situation awareness is when the management perceives some new data that do not fit their expectations. This is typically resolved by adopting a new mental model, revising the existing model, or revising the management goals to accommodate the new information. But an inappropriate choice can impair the situation awareness for some time. Moreover, as stated earlier, the management is often not aware of their mental models since the mental models are tacit and exist below the level of situation awareness (Senge 1992). Thus it is even more difficult to revise a mental model when the management is not even aware of their existing models. In the next section, we present a meta-recognition framework to enable managers to adapt the management logics and enhance the situation awareness when they encounter novel stimuli or unusual situations.

Another common problem for management in light of new data is whether to continue to revise the existing mental model or adopt an alternate model. To adopt an alternate mental model, something in the data must flag that a different situation is present requiring a new model or theory; otherwise the data will continue to be misread by the management's existing incorrect model (Endsley 1995). Moreover, even when the inadequacy of an existing management mental model or theory is recognized but no appropriate new model or theory is immediately available, a significant deficiency in situation awareness can occur while the new mental model is being tested and developed.

In summary, inadequate situation awareness may result when the management logics are not well-developed; managerial absorptive capacity is insufficient; management cognitive adaptability is limited; management attentional capacity is limited; the firm's information processing capacity is limited; a wrong schema is retrieved; the environment is too complex or rapidly changing; certain simple rules and habitual scripts are in effect but the management goals or the environment have changed; the schemas and scripts are combined with erroneous expectations; or the schemas and scripts are personally benefiting the management but not the organization, especially when the management incentives are weak. Inadequate situation awareness also results from the choice of incorrect schemas and scripts in light of the management's cognitive biases such as confirmation bias, familiarity bias, availability bias, representativeness bias, and overestimation and underestimation biases, among others.

Management Cognitive Adaptability

Situation awareness exists at the interface between the management and their environment; thus situation awareness is externally directed consciousness. The situation awareness specifies what must be known to solve a class of problems or issues in a dynamic environment. Management cognition is the management's knowledge generating behavior and cognitive activities that can be intentionally manipulated by the management goals and incentives. To enhance management awareness, executives "must have developed a level of [cognitive] adaptive capability sufficient to match the specification of task goals and the criteria for assessing performance variables" (Smith and Hancock 1995: 139). Cognitive adaptation is a process by which the management can channel their knowledge and behavior to attain the task goals and meet the performance criteria set by an external arbiter such as the capital market or product market (Holland 1992).

Entrepreneurial incentives enhance the management cognitive adaptive capability that further enhance the management cognition. The performance criteria for the firm must reside in the external environment, or the firm performance criteria may be set a priori by the management. An organization "first must intend its goals, beliefs, and knowledge to match the task and performance specified by dicta from its environment" (Smith and Hancock 1995: 139). Entrepreneurial organizations are proactively adaptive in that the stimulus to increase the gap between the target performance and their actual performance comes from within the organization (see Chapter 3). Management learning stimulated by the entrepreneurial incentives provide the internal stimulus to increase the target performance.

Cohen et al. (1996) suggest a meta-recognition framework that outlines metacognitive processes that management may use to adapt proactively and handle a rapidly changing dynamic environment. Management logics contain stored patterns and prototypes that enable the management to focus their attention on selected cues and elements in the environment. However, there are novel situations in changing environments when the stored patterns and prototypes do not match the environmental elements, or there are conflicts between competing schemas in the management logics in recognizing the data patterns. How do managers then handle these situations? How do managers choose to give more attention to a given situation or to act immediately? How do managers adapt their mental models in a changing environment?

Metacognitive processes enhance and regulate the management cognition. Metacognitive processes improve the effectiveness of pattern recognition and comprehension in novel and uncertain situations. Metacognition is a set of cognitive skills that include going beyond pattern matching in order to create plausible stories for novel situations; noticing conflicts between observations and a conclusion; elaborating on a story to explain a conflicting cue rather than simply disregarding or discounting the cue; having sensitivity to problems in explaining away too much conflicting data; attempting to generate alternative coherent stories to account for the data; and having a refined ability to estimate the time available for decision making (Cohen et al. 1996).

With metacognitive abilities, management can effectively adapt their mental models to novel stimuli in a dynamic environment. Furthermore, management incentives can regulate and adapt attentional resources and management goals. Cohen et al. (1996) extend metacognition processes to develop meta-recognition processes for an individual's understanding and making sense of a dynamic, uncertain situation. Meta-recognition skills include critiquing (or evaluation) skills and regulating (or correcting) skills. Evaluation skills involve questioning the causal logics, whereas regulating skills involve examining the sources of information, assessing and constructing cause-effect explanations, and comparing the explanations with certain criteria and standards (justification standards) to evaluate whether the explanations are adequate.

A third set of skills included in meta-recognition is known as "quick test," the ability of individuals to determine whether the current choice is adequate to stop the meta-recognition processes and to act on the choice. In a changing environment where the patterns and prototypes stored in the management logics prove to be inadequate, the managers draw on more abstract structures (in the form of stories) for organizing the incoming information in light of the management goals. The stories constructed using meta-recognition processes enable the mangers to identify and fill gaps where important pieces of explanatory structures may be missing in the management logics (Cohen et al. 1996).

Pennington and Hastie (1993) suggest a framework for constructing stories or causal models from the available data. Decision makers, as they become familiar with an environment, acquire abstract knowledge in the domain on different types of events and relationships among the events. In novel situations, managers use their acquired abstract knowledge to fill the information gaps and then integrate the new information into a plausible story. Managers then subject their story to repeated inquiry, reflection, and modification. Pennington and Hastie show how a story can be used in comprehending a novel situation. Story construction thus consists of selecting events *that evoke* the management goals *which motivate* the management action *that results in* the performance consequences. Central to the story construction process is the management intent that is applied to make sense of the possible causes leading to an observed event and to make sense of the consequences of the event. Entrepreneurial incentives enhance the management intent that is central to the story construction processes employed in the management meta-recognition.

Figure 2.2 illustrates meta-recognition processes to enable management to adapt to a changing environment. In Fig. 2.2, management cognitive adaptability results in enhanced management cognition and situation awareness. Management cognition processes include attention, perception, comprehension, and projection. The management logics influence the management cognition and the level of situation awareness, a level of understanding of what is going on in the firm's environment. As shown in Fig. 2.2, the management's situation awareness or their knowledge of the environment is quickly tested to determine whether the management knowledge is adequate to proceed to the management action, whether the management can wait before they may commit to an action, whether there is a low probability of cognitive biases, whether the management's beliefs and assumptions are valid; and whether the situation encountered is atypical or novel (Cohen et al. 1996).

If there is not enough time left before a decision must be made by the management, the likelihood of cognitive biases of the management is low, and the situation is not atypical, the management then proceeds to take action (see Fig. 2.2). However, if the aforesaid conditions do not hold, the management then determines whether the current causal explanation meets the justification standards or needs to be further revised, using the external criteria set by an external arbiter (e.g., the basis of industry competition set by the product market structure) or using criteria set a priori by the management. When there is no significant deviation with the

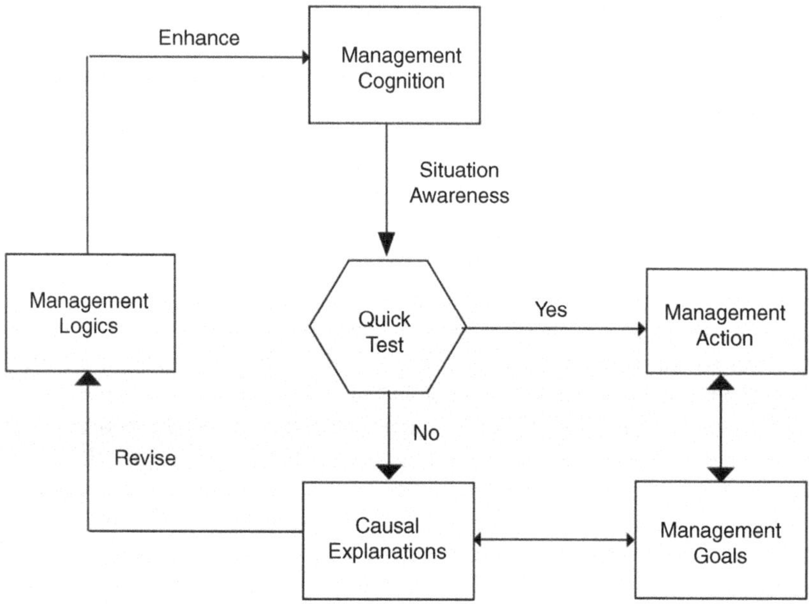

Fig. 2.2 Cognitive adaptability

firm's internal selection criteria or justification standards, the management proceeds to taking action.

However, when the quick test fails and the causal explanation needs to be revised, the management uses story construction techniques to come up with novel explanations. Further, management intent or goals influence the construction of causal explanations. Then the revised explanations are incorporated and the management logics are updated. The situation awareness is reassessed with the modified management logics and thus the situation awareness is enhanced. The quick tests are applied again to determine whether the revised explanations are adequate to take action or repeat the meta-recognition processes (see Fig. 2.2).

Hypercompetitive Environments

Hypercompetitive environments are more dynamic. The rules of competition are evolving in a hypercompetitive environment; thus, an advantage a firm may have today will become irrelevant in a short period. In such an environment, firms are constantly seeking new value opportunities to develop new competitive advantages. Entrepreneurial organizations thrive in hypercompetitive environments. Agility, alertness, absorptivity, proactiveness, and adaptiveness are key behavioral characteristics of entrepreneurial organizations. The state of competition rapidly escalates in these environments, in which firms can expect to have reduced periods of competitive advantage.

Hypercompetitive environments are different from the temporary hyper turbulence associated with an industry shock or introduction of a major technology. In hypercompetitive environments, the environment is in a perpetual state of ferment (Bogner and Barr 2000). But it is not chaotic or in complete disorder either. A hypercompetitive environment can change rapidly in a complex way. The environmental variables are emergent, as are the firms and their business models in the hypercompetitive environment. Competitive advantages when possible to create are transitory.

In hypercompetitive environments, managements have limited abilities to comprehend and project the environmental state variables; that is, the situation awareness is impaired and they have limited foresight at best. Management logics need to be continually tested and adapted in such environments. Management mental models soon become obsolete. Managers must actively learn to surface, test, and adapt their mental models to operate in these environments.

In a hypercompetitive environment, a continual occurrence of triggering events such as major regulatory changes, technological changes, aggressive new entrants, and changes in the rules of competition radically undermine a firm's existing management logics. The changes are large in scale and scope, of a longer-lasting duration. Firms in hypercompetitive industries are unable to commit to developing competencies since the rules of industry competition are uncertain and emergent. Management will not know a priori which of their investments will win. However, entrepreneurial behavior, namely, agility, awareness, learning, flexibility, proactiveness, and adaptiveness help an organization to survive and thrive in a hypercompetitive environment. Firms may pursue multiple opportunities at the same time since they are uncertain which ones will win and create advantage for them.

Nevertheless, it is an expensive proposition for a firm to pursue multiple opportunities simultaneously. Further, the value opportunities available to a firm will have a shorter window. Management must be quick to seize the value opportunities in a timely manner when they are ripe. Current resource advantages quickly may become a liability for the firm. Firms quickly need to reconfigure the resources and build new competencies, but it is difficult for firms to predict which capabilities to pursue in order to win the competition. Managers will have difficulty in articulating the attributes of new products since it is difficult to predict which product attributes will be important to their buyers (Bogner and Barr 2000). Consumers will not be knowledgeable about upcoming product innovations and it is difficult to assess market demand. Firms cannot afford to wait until the demand uncertainty is completely resolved, by which time the window of opportunity for the firm might have been closed.

The challenge to managers is not simply that they need to make new interpretations of changing environmental stimuli, but also their accumulated knowledge (path-dependent) may be rendered ineffective (Bogner and Barr 2000). Managers need to adapt their mental models and theories, or the management logics, continually and update their situation awareness regularly. Not only do managers need to gather more data to comprehend a hypercompetitive environment but they must also adapt their mental models quickly and proactively to interpret and project the environmental variables in a meaningful and timely fashion. Managers try to revamp their mental models and management logics at the same time they use the models to try to make sense of the environment.

The management logics and the situation awareness are enhanced through the firm developing management mental model complexity, implementing rapid decision-making capabilities, and taking experimental actions (Bogner and Barr 2000). Moreover, entrepreneurial incentives in an organization enhance management mental model complexity, organizational agility and rapid decision-making, and learning and experimentation that further enable the managers to overcome traditional behavioral bounds. Managers actively learn and have high cognitive adaptability with entrepreneurial incentives. The management logics in the presence of entrepreneurial incentives are continually tested and revised. Management cognition and situation awareness are high.

Mental model complexity refers to the number of concepts and interacting links present in the management logics. The greater the number of concepts and links, the greater is the mental model complexity. Further, the greater the complexity of the management logics, the greater is the number of situations to which the organization can respond in changing environmental conditions, and the greater is the environmental fitness of the management logics. The richer and more complex management logics are environmentally fit to respond effectively to a rapidly changing environment.

The greater complexity of management logics allows managers to notice more complex stimuli in a changing environment and respond more effectively. Furthermore, the mental models of a diverse management team are richer and more complex than those of a chief executive. A management team with diverse cognitive perspectives can enhance the situation awareness in a dynamic environment. The management team should continually learn by actively identifying their theories and assumptions of how their business works, and testing them to enhance the management mental model complexity. Management team members with different functional backgrounds and industry experiences can enrich the complexity of the management logics. Further, shared elements in individual executive mental models are necessary for effective coordination and consensus among the management team members.

Second, as competition escalates in an environment, managers tend to use more real-time information and make faster decisions. Eisenhardt (1989) found that in high-velocity environments more successful firms made decisions faster than less successful ones. Further, rapidly changing environments undermine the effectiveness of more deliberate considerations of the decision alternatives. "We might expect that speed, rather than a 'consistent close look,' would dominate whenever anyone has to adapt to complex cue patterns" (Weick 1995: 58).

The way the information is processed in hypercompetitive environments is different from that in predictable environments. In a hypercompetitive environment, top-down (goal driven) and bottom-up (data driven) information processing occur simultaneously. Moreover, as competition escalates, managers make use of more informal, face-to-face sources of information. The management attentional resources utilized in hypercompetitive environments are thus different from those in predictable environments. Through a greater reliance on faster automatic scanning and faster decision making, management is able to reduce the load on the management attention and update their mental models and logics more quickly by incorporating richer cues and faster feedbacks.

In hypercompetitive environments, historical information of industry structure, customer preferences, and competitor competencies are largely unhelpful (Bogner and Barr 2000). Real time information is mostly relevant in hypercompetitive environments. Fast decision making gives little time for management to deliberate on decision choices. Further, the management logics are inherently inaccurate and incomplete in hypercompetitive environments; thus, through active learning management continually must adapt their mental models and theories to changing situations. Continual disruptions triggered by rapid changes in a hypercompetitive environment do not allow consistency in feedbacks that managers receive across time periods. Further, the rapid changes in the environment lessen the useful life of recent information.

In hypercompetitive environments, managers actively learn by undertaking experimental actions. The motivation to experiment in a hypercompetitive environment results from the fact that such environments are essentially unknowable. Management learning follows from quick action and experimentation (Bogner and Barr 2000). Thus, in hypercompetitive industries, the firm's absorptive capacity or the ability of organizations to actively learn, that is, to continually enhance and integrate organizational knowledge is a source of advantage for firms. Entrepreneurial incentives enhance the organization's actively learning and combinative capabilities to continually integrate knowledge within the organization (see Chapter 3). The pursuit of knowledge creation and integration is the path to superior performance in a dynamic hypercompetitive environment. Further, experimental actions firms undertake in a hypercompetitive environment are either not repeated (due to novel and changing situations) or may be repeated but they might result in different outcomes.

Gavetti and Levinthal (2000) examine how management logics influence experimental actions undertaken by management. In their study, the search using experimentation is viewed as an on-line search for decision choices, whereas the search using mental models is viewed as an off-line search (e.g., strategic planning exercises). In on-line experimentation, a modest number of alternatives are examined, whereas in an off-line search, multiple alternatives may be explored simultaneously. Further, experimentation explores alternatives in the neighborhood of the current activities of the firm. Off-line searches, however, can explore multiple local and distant choices. In practice, however, organizations may use both off-line and on-line searches in decision making.

Gavetti and Levinthal (2000) found that superior decisions result when both on-line and off-line search strategies are combined, in that management use on-line experimentation and revise their off-line mental models in a changing environment. The richer and more complex the firm's management logics are, the more effective was the strategy of combining the on-line with off-line search. Gavetti and Levinthal also explored the factors that determine the frequency of change in management logics. The firm performance improved when management mental models were revised in response to a drop in the performance level below a threshold measured relative to the competition.

Although a new management mental model captures a changed competitive landscape more effectively, the experiential wisdom accumulated in the previous mental model is lost as a result of adopting the new mental model. Gavetti and Levinthal (2000) simulated a competitive environment that perturbs every five years. They found that the firm performance relative to the leading organizations in their domain improved when the management revised the management logics in response to a change in the competitive landscape. However, subsequent to a shift in the competitive landscape, during the brief stable period, the performances of organizations shifting the mental models continually and the ones using fixed mental models converged, which indicates that changes in the management logics may be beneficial when there is a major shift in the firm's competitive landscape. However, in hypercompetitive industries, a firm's competitive landscape is constantly in flux, suggesting a continual adaptation of the management logics and the portfolio of opportunity options by the management. Further studies are needed to test the need for actively adapting management logics in dynamic environments.

Managerial Absorptive Capacity

Management learning is a cognitive process that specifies what must be known to solve a class of problems in given a task environment. The management learning process is purposeful and can be intentionally manipulated by management incentives. Entrepreneurial incentives can stimulate active learning in the organization and enhance the managerial absorptive capacity. Management learning is a situational learning capability. Situational learning ability is an individual's capacity to direct their consciousness to generate solutions to a problem in a given situation. Situational learning activities can be intentionally manipulated by the individual. The outcome of situational learning results in solutions to a problem at hand or to an impending challenge or task in a given situation. Further, situational learning is dynamic in that the same learning activities may not be repeated in a subsequent situation or learning cycle.

Situational learning capability requires an understanding of the individual-environment relationship. Situational learning is enhanced when the individual is experienced in the environment and multiple courses of action are available to the individual.

Metacognitive skills enhance management learning such as the skills of reflection and the skills of advocacy and inquiry. Management mental models and theories are surfaced and enhanced with management learning. Management learning occurs when management employs double-loop learning in that the management assumptions are surfaced and the management logics are revised. Management logics, if not updated regularly, can inhibit management cognition. Further, strategic planning exercises including analyzing industry scenarios and trends enable managers to question their current mental models and theories. Scenario exercises employed in traditional strategic planning processes can unfreeze the management logics, a benefit of the planning process, even when a strategic plan itself may not be of much value in a rapidly changing environment. Furthermore, strategic planning processes need not produce perfect plans, but they do enhance management learning (Senge 1992).

The long-term success of a firm depends on continual management learning that helps the managers change their current management mental models and assumptions about the firm's business model, markets, customers, and competitors. Senge (1992) groups management learning into two broad management activities, namely, skills of reflection and skills of advocacy and inquiry. The skills of reflection include thought experiments for managers to become aware of their mental models and the ways the mental models influence their actions. Further, the skills of advocacy and inquiry enable the management team to question and adjust their mental models and theories in face-to-face interactions, especially when dealing with novel patterns or situations. Further, management learning closes the gap between the management's espoused theory and the theory-in-use implied in management actions.

Managers become aware of their mental models by recognizing "leaps of abstraction" (Senge 1992). Recognizing leaps of abstraction and being willing to question their premises can help managers unfreeze the management logics and accelerate management learning. A similar process is used in lean startups when entrepreneurs formulate and test their initial hypotheses to test and understand their environment and enhance their mental models and theories. The management assumptions and beliefs, namely, environmental assumptions, customer value assumptions, and core competency assumptions, are especially important for a management to surface and test them regularly. The theory of the business should be tested and updated periodically, and the gap between the espoused theory and the theory-in-use should be closed regularly through enhanced management learning.

Managers often act based on their leaps of abstraction. For example, the first-to-market often is considered as an advantage, but as we know first mover advantages are not available in all situations or in all industries. Senge (1992) recommends managers examine their leaps of abstraction by asking what they believe about the way their business works and challenge the data on which their beliefs are based. Managers should be open to possibilities that the premises and assumptions in the management logics can be inaccurate and incomplete. Managers should test their assumptions and logics directly when possible. Management learning enables managers to effectively test and improve their assumptions and theories.

To be effective with the skills of inquiry, managers should be open to learning from each other rather than advocating only their solutions to others. Managers as they gather experience and rise to senior positions tend to develop advocacy skills which can be counterproductive to management learning. Instead, management should promote collaborative learning and tap the insights of others especially when solving complex problems or facing novel situations. Thus advocacy without inquiry leads to rigidity in the management logics. The snowball effects of management advocacy can be prevented if management asks some simple questions such as what has led to their current positions on the issues, and based on what data (Senge 1992).

However, inquiry skills only are not as effective for management learning as a balanced approach of advocacy and inquiry. Management learning, however, is limited unless managers can combine both advocacy and inquiry skills. Simply asking a lot of questions can inhibit individual learning by hiding their views behind a wall of questions (Senge 1992). A more effective way to learn is when managers combine advocacy and inquiry skills, that is, when their advocacy and inquiry skills are balanced. One should not only inquire into others' views but also should state their own views in a way that reveals their own assumptions (Senge 1992). When using a balanced approach of advocacy and inquiry, one's goal is not winning an argument but finding alternative solutions to the problem at hand. Further, managers must try to disconfirm their assumptions rather than confirm them using advocacy skills. Successful entrepreneurs have the skills to test and disconfirm their initial assumptions when designing and testing a new venture idea.

The discipline of balancing advocacy with inquiry is challenging to learn but is crucial to unfreeze the management logics and improve them. Management should be open to revising their mental models and theories continually; otherwise the rigidity of their mental models will impair their decision-making abilities and the performance of the organization will suffer. Further, the management logics and how the management acts are based on the theory-in-use, not on the management's espoused theories. Espoused theories are part of an organization's mission and vision, but often not a part of management actions. Management actions are consistent with the theory-in-use in an organization. Thus the management in trying to unfreeze and improve their mental models should question the theory-in-use, not their espoused theories.

Management learning occurs when the gap between the management's espoused theory and the management actions is surfaced consciously and bridged. The gap once surfaced and recognized in an organization holds the potential for improving the management logics. Management learning skills, that is, the skills of reflection, advocacy, and inquiry, can improve management logics. Management learning starts with management identifying and unfreezing the leaps of abstraction or their beliefs and assumptions contained in their current management logics (see Fig. 2.3).

The management's leaps of abstractions are surfaced by questioning the management assumptions and theories contained in the management logics determining how the firm's business model works and how the firm value is created and appropriated. The management further uses active advocacy and inquiry skills to facilitate collaborative learning in the organization. The advocacy and inquiry learning results in the management actions that further enhance the management logics (see Fig. 2.3). The management learning cycle illustrated in Fig. 2.3 repeats as the management learning applies to another situation, thus further enhancing the management logics. Management learning cycles through the learning activities involving new opportunities or challenges, enhancing the management experience and management logics, as illustrated in Fig. 2.3. Management learning thus enhances the managerial human capital and organizational social capital. Management learning is high in organizations when powerful entrepreneurial incentives drive the management learning. Without continual management learning, the management

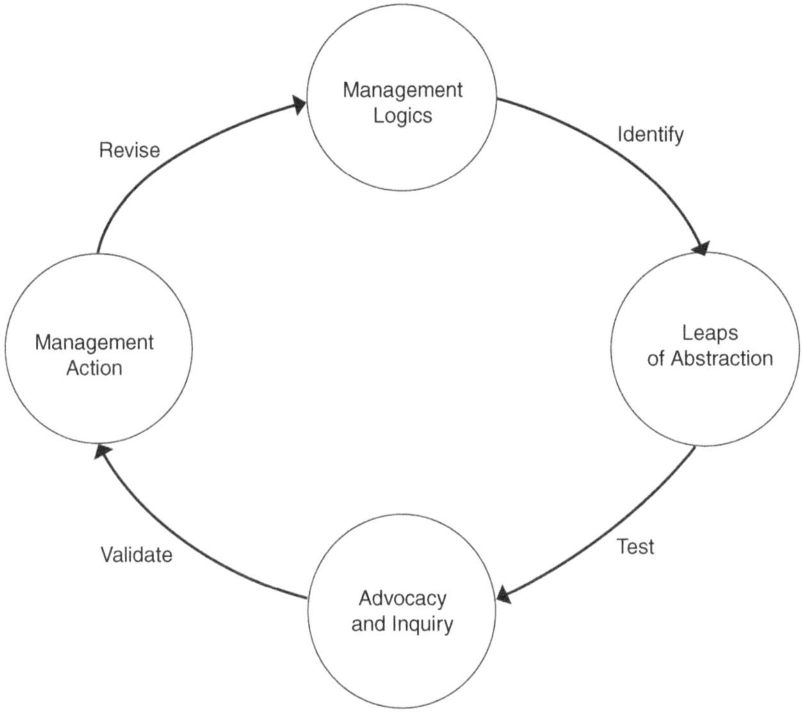

Fig. 2.3 Management learning

logics become quickly stagnant, thereby inhibiting the management cognition and lowering the situation awareness.

However, there are several obstacles at each stage of the management learning cycle shown in Fig. 2.3, inhibiting management learning. Above we described how the leaps of abstraction are surfaced and tested, how management balances inquiry with advocacy, and how they try to close the gap between their actions and their espoused theories. Each stage in the learning cycle is challenging and difficult to learn; moreover, it varies from situation to situation. Each situation evokes new challenges for management. Further, managers empowered by high-powered entrepreneurial incentives engage in an active management learning cycle regularly.

Management learning activities continually revise and enhance the management logics. The managerial learning capacity is the managerial ability to evaluate, acquire, and assimilate available information. Management cognition and situation awareness are further enhanced with managerial learning. Further, management cognitive adaptability is enhanced with managerial learning. The entrepreneurial incentives further enhance the management learning and cognitive adaptability, enhancing the management logics, thus enhancing the management cognition, and enabling the organization to seize cognitively distant value opportunities and reconfigure the resources and value activities to enhance the value creation and appropriation mechanism wherein the firm's competitive advantage is created and sustained.

Management learning in a given task environment requires a specification of the task and the criteria to evaluate the individual's performance. With cognitive adaptability, the individual is capable of manipulating and adapting their learning strategy to match the task at hand. The task performance criteria, however, must reside in the task environment, not with the individual (not in their mental models). Learning to be effective requires an external arbiter, such as the product market or capital market. Management learning is thus tempered by the external market conditions. The task performance criteria must be external to the manager; otherwise situational learning will be always perfect since whatever solution is reached by the manager always meets their performance criteria (manipulated ex-post).

The task performance criteria are set externally by the competitive forces in the firm's product market domain. However, a manager may set their performance criteria a priori. Further, management learning effectiveness can be assessed using an external arbiter and is continually improved upon in each repetition of the learning cycle (see Fig. 2.3). Management learning generates management action and enhances the managerial human capital and managerial ability given the task specification and externally set performance criteria.

Management learning thus tests and improves the management assumptions and theories contained in the management logics. Further, the balanced scorecard measures when set a priori by the management can be used to enhance the management learning (Kaplan and Norton 1992). The balanced scorecard includes financial and nonfinancial performance perspectives. The balanced scorecard can be used to examine the business model assumptions and value drivers that can be tested and improved through management learning (see Chapter 5). Management learning powered by entrepreneurial incentives enhance the management logics, which further enhance the business model configuration and the firm value creation and appropriation mechanism, where the firm's competitive advantage lies.

Summary

Management logics constitute management mental models and theories of how the firm's business model works and how the firm value is created and appropriated. Management logics contain managerial schemas, scripts, theories, beliefs, and assumptions about how their business works. Entrepreneurial incentives enhance continual management learning (managerial absorptive capacity) and thus update the management logics regularly. The management logics supported by powerful entrepreneurial incentives enhance management cognition and situation awareness and thus enable the managers to seize cognitively distant value opportunities and reconfigure the firm's resources and activities in a timely manner. The management goals are further enhanced by entrepreneurial incentives. In a dynamic environment, management must continually question, test, and learn to improve the management logics and goals. Often the management is unaware of their mental models and theories. The management goals based on the management's espoused theory can be inconsistent with the organizations's theory-in-use and management actions. As the management is often unaware, their mental models remain unexamined and unchanged, creating an increasing gap between reality and the actions of management. Furthermore, unexamined and unchanged management logics increase the gap between management actions and their espoused theory in that the organizational actions will not be consistent with the management's espoused theory.

Management logics must be continually updated through surfacing, questioning, testing, validating, and improving the management assumptions of their task environment (Senge 1992). Management logics when stagnant can inhibit management cognition; however, management logics when surfaced, tested, and adapted in a dynamic environment, enhance the management cognition and situation awareness. Entrepreneurial incentives enhance management cognitive adaptability that further enhances management cognition and situation awareness. Scenario analysis employed in strategic planning exercises help the management unfreeze and improve the management logics, a benefit of the strategic planning process even when the plans themselves may not be of much value in a rapidly changing environment.

Management learning enhances the management logics. Management learning includes two learning skills, namely, the skills of reflection and skills of advocacy and inquiry. The skills of reflection include thought experiments for the managers to become aware of their mental models and the ways their mental models influence their actions. The skills of advocacy and inquiry enable the management to question and adjust their mental models and theories using face-to-face interactions with colleagues. The management learning cycle closes the gap between the management's espoused theory and their actions, and thus enhances the management logics.

Management logics must be continually examined and revised in a dynamic environment. Management learning is a crucial capability when operating in hypercompetitive environments. Three strategies help managers to continually adapt the management logics in a changing environment, namely, by developing mental model complexity, implementing rapid decision making, and taking experimental actions. In a changing environment, entrepreneurial incentives empower managers to adapt the management logics and improve their situation awareness using meta-recognition capabilities. Enhanced complexity and organization of the management logics not only enhances the management cognition to enable managers to sense and seize cognitively distant opportunities but also enhances the management ability to respond to more states and situations in a changing environment.

The entrepreneurial incentives enhance the management's attentional engagement, which further enhances management cognition, namely, management perception, comprehension, and projection. Management cognition determines the situation awareness to what is going on and thus further improves the management logics. Situation awareness is a management team's externally directed consciousness. Furthermore, the situation awareness is a shared awareness in an organization. Entrepreneurial incentives enhance the situation awareness that further enhances the organization's agility, adaptiveness, proactiveness, and opportunity focus (see Chapter 3). The organizational decision-making channels situate scarce management attentional resources on the critical aspects of the environment in light of their goals. Transactive memory in the organization (i.e., who knows what) further enhances management cognition and thus the situation awareness.

Management attention is critical to effective management cognition and achieving sufficient situation awareness. Management attention is a scarce resource in an organization. Managerial attentional capacity is enhanced in an organization when the entrepreneurial incentives are high. Entrepreneurial incentives thus enhance management's attentional engagement and enhance the situation awareness. Penrose (1959) posits that management attentional capacity limitation constrains the firm growth. Entrepreneurial incentives that enhance the management attentional capacity thus enhance the firm growth. Further, the management goals and incentives guide management actions by regulating the management attention. The organizational operating and governance channels distribute the management attention. Ocasio (1997) argues that firm behavior is driven by how attentional resources in a firm channel and distribute the management attention.

Management perception is how available information in the environment is encoded and organized. Perception involves pattern recognition and information organization. Management goals and logics guide management perception. Further, management attention influences the speed and accuracy of the encoding and categorization of the available information, which determines the management response and effectiveness. Entrepreneurial incentives enhance the manager's ability to spot market signals early when the signals are just a glimmer, before the signals are readily apparent to everyone. Market signals may be perceived as opportunities or threats for a firm depending on whether there is a potential gain or loss, whether the event is a positive or negative situation, and whether the firm has more or less control over the situation. Entrepreneurial incentives enhance management cognitive adaptability enabling managers to recognize novel stimuli and complex patterns in the environment.

Management comprehension is the management's synthesis of disparate information elements in the environment in light of the management goals. Management constructs cause-and-effect relations between the information elements. The principles that determine which information elements the management will incorporate in management comprehension and that govern management comprehension are the augmentation principle, the discounting principle, illusory correlation, illusory causation, and automatic scanning, which further guide the management in determining which cues they choose to incorporate in the construction of a holistic view of the environment. The management logics and goals enhanced by the management incentives guide management comprehension.

Management comprehension employs top-down and bottom-up information processing and reasoning. The automaticity of managerial cognitive activities enhances comprehension but the manager is slow to respond with the automaticity when the management goals change or novel situations are encountered. Further, with automaticity of information processing, there is less load on executive working memory and management attention, thus enhancing the speed of management cognition, but the manager's reasoning steps leading to reaching a conclusion are occluded and thus the accuracy of situation awareness suffers. Executive working memory and management attention are primary bottlenecks in management comprehension. Transactive memory reduces the load on the executive working memory, and thus enhances the situation awareness.

Management projection is the ability of management to extrapolate current trends and project their impact on the near-term firm performance. Projection is not the forecasting of new trends. Rather projection is an extrapolation of current trends that have an ongoing impact, the potential of which is not yet realized. Management projects a future by acting in the present. The management is foresightful when, through their choice of actions in the present, they forge a coherent relationship between the firm's present and future. Projection is not predicting what will happen in the firm's future but whether the management has the ability to proactively engage in the present in that the management projection enacts alternative pathways in the present to the firm's future. Entrepreneurial incentives enhance management projection that enables managers to spot weak market signals before the signals are readily apparent to everyone. Management projection is enhanced by the managerial cognitive adaptability, which is further enhanced by entrepreneurial incentives.

Management cognition can vary from weak perception (Level 1), inability to discern the current state of the environment (Level 2), clarity about the current environment but no foresight (Level 3), limited foresight (Level 4), to enhanced foresight (Level 5). However, Level 5 cognition is rare. Entrepreneurial incentives enhance management learning and cognitive adaptability, thus enhance the management cognition. The situation awareness and management logics are further enhanced when the management has high cognitive adaptability. Enhanced situation awareness enables the managers to seize cognitively distant value opportunities in a timely manner, which enhances the firm's value creation and appropriation mechanism wherein the firm's competitive advantage is created and sustained.

CHAPTER 3

Entrepreneurial Orientation

Introduction

An organization is entrepreneurial when it is alert, agile, proactively adaptive, absorptive, and opportunity driven. The greater the alertness, agility, proactiveness, adaptability, absorptivity, and opportunity focus of the firm, the more entrepreneurial is the firm and the greater is its entrepreneurial orientation. Executive in entrepreneurial organizations are empowered by high-powered entrepreneurial incentives to earn an entrepreneurial surplus. Entrepreneurial organizations are constantly seeking value opportunities to enhance and sustain the firm's competitive advantage. The entrepreneurial incentive is provided through the uncertain performance-based compensation in the executive pay, in that the firm performance is set by an external arbiter such as the capital market. Entrepreneurial incentives provide the executives an entrepreneurial surplus. Entrepreneurial surplus is the excess compensation for the executives when the firm-specific risk exceeds the industry average. Entrepreneurial value creation processes should be the core of strategic management (Drucker 1970). Entrepreneurial incentives enhance the firm's management logics, situation awareness, value opportunities, active learning, dynamic capabilities, core resources, and the firm's value creation and appropriation mechanism.

Further, entrepreneurial organizations can be resource constrained but their ability to create competitive advantage implies that the presence of a superior resource is not a prerequisite for a firm to achieve competitive advantage. Entrepreneurial value creation processes are the key to the firm's

C.S. Mishra, *Creating and Sustaining Competitive Advantage*,
DOI 10.1007/978-3-319-54540-0_3

building and sustaining competitive advantage. Entrepreneurial organizations have enhanced situation awareness, opportunity focus, absorptive capacity, dynamic capabilities, empowered by entrepreneurial incentives. Entrepreneurial organizations are alert, agile, proactive, adaptive, absorptive, and opportunity driven. Thus, entrepreneurial organizations are more successful in identifying superior value opportunities, and are timely in responding to the opportunities and changes in the environment. Entrepreneurial organizations actively learn and adapt proactively, enhancing the firm's human capital, social capital, and knowledge capital that constitute the firm's core resources and support growth opportunities and value activities. Entrepreneurial organizations build resources, whereas traditional organizations build on the resources.

Entrepreneurial organizations are innovative or innovatively imitative. Entrepreneurial organizations are proactively adaptive and situationally alert. They balance efficiency with flexibility. They are adaptive in dynamic environments. They are efficient in stable environments. They have emergent properties associated with complex adaptive systems (see Chapter 5). They thrive in hypercompetitive environments. Entrepreneurial organizations are found in all industries and environments. Further, entrepreneurial behavior is the key to building or sustaining the firm's competitive advantage. "Entrepreneurship is thus central to the function, work and performance of the executive in business. His behavior, his actions, his values must be seen and analyzed in relation to economic performance and entrepreneurial action" (Drucker 1970: 3).

Competitive advantage is the rationale underlying a firm's superior performance relative to its competitors. The greater the entrepreneurial orientation of the firm is relative to its competitors, the more likely the firm is to achieve competitive advantage. Entrepreneurial incentives create and sustain the firm's entrepreneurial orientation and nurture an entrepreneurial culture in the organization. Entrepreneurial incentive is provided through the uncertain performance based compensation in the executive pay, such that the firm performance is set and evaluated by an external arbiter such as the capital market or product market. The likelihood of a firm building competitive advantage is high when the firm has high entrepreneurial incentives. Entrepreneurial incentives enhance active learning and management logics, and enable decision makers to overcome traditional behavioral bounds assumed in conventional behavioral logic. Management logics are management mental models and theories that constitute declarative and procedural knowledge of how the business works. Further, the management logics must be continually tested and updated in a dynamic environment. Further, sufficient situation awareness (i.e., knowing what is going on) is crucial for the firm to respond to environmental changes, seek value opportunities, and enhance core resources. Combinative capabilities supported by active learning enhance and align the firm's core capabilities or the knowledge capital. Entrepreneurial behavior is essential for a firm to survive and thrive in a dynamic environment.

Entrepreneurial incentives enhance the business model advantage. Entrepreneurial firms are alert, agile, proactive, adaptive, absorptive, and opportunity driven. The more entrepreneurial the firm or the greater the entrepreneurial incentives in the firm, the greater is the likelihood of the firm achieving competitive advantage. The competitive advantage creation may be viewed in a two-stage framework; in that in the first stage, the entrepreneurial incentives enhance the firm's active learning, combinative capabilities, absorptive capacity, management cognition, and dynamic capabilities. In the second stage, the firm's value creation and appropriation mechanism is enhanced, in that the business model configuration constituting management logics, value opportunities, core resources, and value activities proactively adapts to the changing competitive conditions, which further enhances the business model advantage and the firm's competitive position.

The entrepreneurial tasks in an organization include articulating the firm's theory of the business, creating tomorrow's business, configuring the business model to make it more effective, and identifying and realizing the business's full potential (Drucker 1970). First, management should be aware of and continually update their theory of the business. The theory of the business is the management's assumptions and mental models of how the business works both inside and outside the organization. The theory of the business of an organization in practice (i.e., the theory-in-use) often is different from the espoused theory. The management should be aware of the theory-in-use by analyzing their actions, and close the gap between their actions and their espoused theory. The management logics include the management mental models and theories of how and why the business works today and how and why the business will work in the future.

The entrepreneurial incentives enhance the management's awareness of the management logics and enable the management to question whether the theory of the business is the right one in the current environment and to ensure that the entire organization share the same theory. These tasks require active learning, sufficient alertness, and cognitive adaptability on the part of the management. "But even the clearest and most effective 'theory of the business' needs constant pretesting and reformulation"

(Drucker 1970: 9). In a dynamic environment, the manager's cognitive adaptability enhances their ability to continually adapt the management logics. With entrepreneurial incentives, the management logics are not stagnant. Entrepreneurial incentives enhance management learning, which further enhances their cognitive adaptability that enables the managers to proactively adapt to changing competitive conditions.

Management logics are continually tested and reshaped in entrepreneurial organizations. Active learning is crucial to effectively adapt the management logics in a changing environment. The business may not change outwardly with a change in the theory of the business, but the management behavior may change greatly. Organizational inertia is caused by stagnant management logics, which results in competency traps and core rigidity. Soon these organizations lose their competitive advantage. Entrepreneurial behavior helps a firm prevent core rigidity and organizational inertia.

Second, creating tomorrow's business is a crucial entrepreneurial task of management. "The approach towards creating tomorrow's business starts out with the conviction that it will be and must be different, but it also starts out-of-necessity-with the business of today" (Drucker 1970: 7). Thus, it is not the organization's innovative ability to create a new future but to make the current business capable of achieving a vision. Management must have the ability to project a future. Drucker differentiates "projection" from "forecasting," in that forecasting is to know what is likely to happen in the future and projection is what is happening today that has an ongoing impact.

Drucker (1970) argues that "few of us can imagine what we have not already seen" [8]. Foresight or the ability to forecast the future accurately is not necessary for an entrepreneurial organization to create tomorrow's business. What is needed is an ability of the management to project what is happening today when the impact is not fully realized. Management projection enhances the situation awareness (see Chapter 2). Drucker cautions managers against relying too much on popular scenario forecasting, a part of traditional strategic planning process. However, one key benefit of strategic planning process is that it helps the management to continually examine and update their business model assumptions and the management logics.

Third, another entrepreneurial function of management is to identify the business's full potential and bring the business a little closer to the realization of its potential. "Even the most successful business works at a low coefficient of performance as measured against its potential" (Drucker 1970: 6). Drucker differentiates this from innovation in that identifying and realizing a business's potential is not about innovation but rather the management knowing what is going on inside and outside the business and what factors can be inhibiting the business from reaching its full potential. Management should figure out, for example, "what *relatively minor changes* in product, technology, process, market and so on, would significantly improve or alter the economic characteristics and results of this business" (Drucker 1970: 7).

Drucker does not rule out innovations by entrepreneurial firms. Many entrepreneurial firms innovatively imitate rather than strictly innovate. Innovations and creative imitations take place not only with new products and technologies but with markets, business models, and firm capabilities as well. Moreover, innovations and creative imitations do not always require perfect foresight on the part of the management. Instead the management should be situationally alert to what is going on and what factors are inhibiting the organization from realizing its full economic potential. Situation awareness is enhanced by the entrepreneurial incentives.

An entrepreneurial challenge is to have the ability to convert what everyone considers a threat into an opportunity. Management should further identify the areas that others neglect today and reexamine their own assumptions. They should be constantly seeking opportunities to enhance the firm performance and exploit the opportunities in a timely manner. The organization should build a portfolio of opportunity options which should be exercised in a timely manner. Opportunity options are unrealized value potential and they are embodied in the knowledge assets of the firm (see Chapter 4). Management must identify the firm's opportunities and exploit them in a timely manner. Further, when the opportunities are exploited, the firm builds new knowledge assets that further enhance the portfolio of opportunities.

Fourth, another entrepreneurial task is to increase the business effectiveness, not merely the efficiency. Managements typically focus on cost improvements and process efficiency. The entrepreneurial approach is, however, to focus on value opportunities. Entrepreneurial organizations are opportunity focused. The focus should be "on opportunities to produce revenue, to create markets and to change the economic characteristics of existing products and markets" (Drucker 1970: 6). Efficiency concerns the operational effectiveness of organizational resources and activities, whereas the business model effectiveness is based on the fact that "10 or 15 percent of the phenomena – such as products, orders, customers, markets, or people – produce 80 to 90 percent of the results" (Drucker 1970: 6). The other 85 to 90 percent of the organization, no matter how efficiently managed, produces nothing but costs. The entrepreneurial challenge is to identify the critical 10 or 15 percent of the value activities and make them more effective to achieve extraordinary economic results.

An entrepreneurial organization requires a focus on opportunities, not on problems; and a focus on customers and competitors, not on operational efficiency. The entrepreneurial manager "looks at everything that is today as in the *process of obsolescence*. The entrepreneur knows that the moment a product or process is ready for the market, its ageing has begun" (Drucker 1970: 11). Entrepreneurial organizations are aware that rather than competitors making their products or processes obsolete, they will proactively make the changes in their products or processes in a timely manner to stay ahead of the Red Queen race (see Chapter 5).

Entrepreneurial organizations do not spend much time on solving operational problems since solving problems always implies an attempt to do what is being already done, better. Problem solving concerns operating efficiency rather than organizational competitiveness. Entrepreneurial organizations focus on opportunities, the areas of extraordinary value creation potential for their customers and shareholders. Seizing and exploiting opportunities in a timely manner to improve organizational competitiveness rather than focusing on costs and operational efficiency separates entrepreneurial organizations from traditional counterparts.

Entrepreneurial organizations are constantly seeking cognitively distant value opportunities to enhance their competitive position. Entrepreneurship is opportunity-focused value creation and appropriation processes that sustain superior firm performance. Entrepreneurial processes are a means for promoting the firm's competitive advantage. However, there are significant ambiguities and inconsistencies among researchers on how the firm's entrepreneurial orientation construct is operationalized (Covin and Miles 1999), a problem partly due to lack of a coherent theory of the entrepreneurial processes (Mishra and Zachary 2014, 2015). Different researchers conceptualize "entrepreneurs" differently and identify certain behavioral attributes and labeled them as entrepreneurial. For example, most studies of entrepreneurial orientation used Miller's (1983) conceptualization of the entrepreneurial behavior consisting of innovation, proactiveness, and aggressive risk taking.

However, it is not that entrepreneurial organizations are aggressive risk takers, but their ability to proactively exploit the environmental uncertainty in the firm's favor is remarkable. That is, successful entrepreneurs are effective risk managers in that they manage excess firm-specific risk and earn an entrepreneurial surplus (reward) (Mishra 2015). Entrepreneurial surplus is the excess compensation the management earns when the management is empowered with the entrepreneurial incentives. Entrepreneurial organizations are proactive but it is not necessary that they are always first movers. Moreover, first mover advantages are not always present in all industries or businesses. Entrepreneurial organizations exploit value opportunities in a timely manner. They are proactive not in anticipating the future but in exploiting the current trends that have an ongoing impact, the potential of which is not yet realized. They actively learn and are proactively adaptive under changing competitive conditions. Entrepreneurial incentives enhance the firm's alertness, agility, absorptivity, proactive adaptability, and opportunity focus; enable decision makers to overcome traditional behavioral bounds assumed in conventional behavioral logic; and seize cognitively distant Schumpeterian type value opportunities to enhance the competitive advantage. Entrepreneurial incentives thus stimulate and nurture entrepreneurial behavior in organizations, which enhances the firm's value creation and appropriation mechanism.

Entrepreneurial Incentives

The entrepreneurial incentive is provided through the uncertain performance-based compensation in the executive pay. Entrepreneurial incentives provide the executives an opportunity to earn an entrepreneurial surplus. Entrepreneurial surplus is the excess compensation for the executives when the firm-specific risk exceeds the industry average. Entrepreneurial incentives promote entrepreneurial behavior in an organization in that the entrepreneurial behavior constitutes the firm's alertness, agility, proactiveness, adaptability, absorptivity, and an opportunity focus. The more entrepreneurial the firm, the greater is the likelihood of achieving competitive advantage. Entrepreneurial incentives provide the managers a potential for earning an entrepreneurial surplus for bearing and managing excess firm-specific risk. The firm-specific risk is higher when the firm exploits cognitively distant value opportunities. The entrepreneurial behavior provides the firm an entrepreneurial rent, a part of it is distributed to the management as entrepreneurial surplus.

Adverse managerial incentives and agency costs associated with strategic investments and capital market adverse selection are discussed in Chapter 4. In particular, we have discussed managerial overinvestment, underinvestment, overconfidence, and overcommitment problems associated with a firm's strategic investments. When agency costs of free cash flow are present, that is, when low-growth organizations have excess free cash flow, managers overinvest in negative net present value opportunities. Free cash flow in a firm increases the financial slack, where the financial slack includes cash on hand, unused debt capacity, and marketable securities. Jensen (1986) suggests that firms with potential agency costs of free cash flow may use more debt to discipline the managers. However, as we have argued, debt financing constrains the firm's growth, that is, a "debt overhang" effect. Debt financing causes an underinvestment in superior value opportunities in high-growth firms. Further, excess debt lowers the value of the firm's knowledge assets.

In this section, we discuss agency and incentive problems associated with management moral hazard and adverse selection in organizations. Agency costs arise in organizations because of information asymmetry between firms and capital market. Asymmetric information causes moral hazard and adverse selection problems. Moral hazard particularly arises because the manger's effort is unobservable and their contribution to the value of the firm is difficult to verify. It is difficult and costly to monitor management effort and align their interests with those of the shareholders. Typically a proxy variable is used in lieu of the unobservable managerial effort to compensate management, where the proxy variable is an objective or subjective measure of firm performance. However, often proxy performance measures are manipulated by the management.

Further, firm performance measures are noisy and imperfect proxies of value contribution by the management. The performance-based variable compensation component thus imposes a risk on management when the noise distorts the firm's true unknown performance. Management pay includes a fixed salary and a variable incentive compensation based on several performance measures to capture the manager's contribution to firm value. A simple compensation contract is: $c = a + bx$; where c is the executive's total compensation, a is the fixed compensation, bx is the variable compensation, b is an incentive vector, and x is the firm performance proxy vector. The higher the b is, the greater is the incentive component of the compensation mix, and the greater is the entrepreneurial incentive. The vector b can be multidimensional and nonlinear in x.

However, incentive compensation is not the only mechanism to address agency problems and correct adverse managerial incentives. The market for corporate control and corporate governance are alternative mechanisms to monitor the management performance and replace an incompetent management team when necessary. Reputation in the managerial labor market is a self-reinforcing mechanism to correct managerial adverse incentives. Managers can be replaced by an active board of directors or through a hostile takeover in the market for corporate control. However, these are imperfect and insufficient monitoring devices to discipline an incompetent management.

The board of directors is often dominated by management-friendly directors who are reluctant to fire an incompetent management team even when the board may have a greater percentage of legally defined independent directors. Further, a chief executive officer (CEO) is often the chairman of the board at the same time. The chairman presides over the board of directors; thus it is difficult to fire the CEO. Thus, the board-of-directors governance mechanism to monitor and discipline an incompetent management is generally ineffective and inadequate.

The market for corporate control can be more effective in disciplining an incompetent management, but most corporate charters include antitakeover provisions such as poison pills and golden parachutes to protect incumbent management and discourage potential bidders from making hostile bids. Further, offers to buy the firm must be approved by management-friendly directors who often support the management's position. However, in monitoring and disciplining incompetent management, the market for corporate control is more effective than the corporate governance mechanism, and therefore the market for corporate control imposes a credible threat of the dismissal of an incompetent management team.

Shareholder proxy fights initiated by activist shareholders can be another mechanism to discipline an incompetent management destroying firm value. However, proxy fights often fail since most of a company's shares are owned by large financial institutions who on behalf of individual shareholders vote in the management's favor. Further, the market for corporate control and proxy fights are costly processes to replace an incompetent management team and can also potentially destroy firm value. Thus, in addition to the market for corporate control and corporate governance, incentive compensation contracts are often used to align the interests of the mangers with those of the shareholders.

Another agency problem is the adverse selection in the capital market in that shareholders are uncertain about the management ability. Management often chooses to share more favorable information about the company with their shareholders. The shareholders thus have incomplete and imperfect information to evaluate the management ability. Firm valuation is often made by equity analysts based on the management forecasts. The greater are the firm's growth opportunities, the greater is the adverse selection and the greater is the uncertainty about the management ability. The firm value measure is often based on the firm's past successes and failures; but in a changing environment, it is less certain that a management that has performed well in the past will continue to perform well in a changed competitive environment. The more dynamic and uncertain an environment and the greater are the firm's growth opportunities, the worse is the adverse selection problem and the greater is the uncertainty concerning the management ability.

The capital market adverse selection (uncertainty about the management ability) exacerbates the moral hazard or executive performance monitoring problem. Adverse selection in the capital market makes executive performance monitoring and incentive alignment even more difficult. The management incentive compensation may not be as effective in eliciting high performance from the management since it is difficult for the shareholders to evaluate the firm performance with the incomplete and imperfect information the management provides. Further, the inability of shareholders to fully evaluate the management ability makes it difficult to replace an incompetent management team. Furthermore, managers may need a greater flexibility in a dynamic environment and a different compensation mix than those in a stable and predictable environment. With adverse selection it is difficult to determine the management's true contribution to the firm value. Thus, the adverse selection exacerbates the executive moral hazard and complicates the executive incentive compensation design. Furthermore, in hypercompetitive industries where the adverse selection is worse, it can be difficult to incentivize a management team.

The greater the equity-linked compensation, the less severe is the moral hazard problem as a low-ability manager who wants more certainty in their compensation will not accept compensation with a greater proportion of equity-linked variable compensation. The manager's equity-linked compensation thus provides an incentive signal that mitigates the adverse selection in part and helps shareholders separate high-ability from low-ability managers. Managers with entrepreneurial incentives will prefer a greater equity in their compensation mix such that they can earn an entrepreneurial surplus, whereas low-ability managers will prefer a lower proportion of equity in their compensation.

High-ability managers will accept their incentive compensation linked to the firm's stock performance, whereas low- to average-ability managers prefer their compensation to be based on more predictable accounting measures. Low- to average-ability managers need more predictable components in their compensation mix. Further, when management human capital is high as in the case of entrepreneurial organizations, the moral hazard is worse since it is more difficult to monitor the performance of the management team in a more dynamic environment. High-ability managers with superior human capital and cognitive abilities will need high-powered entrepreneurial incentives that provide an opportunity to earn entrepreneurial surplus, and thus they will be willing to accept a more uncertain, risky equity-linked entrepreneurial incentive than would traditional low- to average-ability managers. High-ability managers thus choose high entrepreneurial incentives or a high proportion of equity-linked variable compensation in their pay.

Entrepreneurial Surplus

Castanias and Helfat (1991, 2001) have developed managerial rents theory within the confines of the resource-based theory in that managerial resources are valuable, scarce, imperfectly imitable, and nonsubstitutable; and thus managerial resources are sources of competitive advantage and earn excess rents. Management is a key resource of the firm. Managerial human capital, a core resource, generates competitive advantage according to the resource-based theory. However, according to our entrepreneurial logic, for managerial human capital to be a source of competitive advantage, high-ability managers must be adequately incentivized through the provision of entrepreneurial incentives that provide the management an opportunity to earn an entrepreneurial surplus.

Managerial human capital is thus a rent generating resource but under certain conditions, where the rent is the above-average return from a resource. Executives need an entrepreneurial surplus or an excess compensation relative to their peers in the industry for their superior human capital. Entrepreneurial surplus is therefore the excess compensation earned by high-ability executives empowered by entrepreneurial incentives for their above-average managerial human capital. Further, the opportunity to earn an entrepreneurial surplus provides powerful incentives to managers to seize cognitively distant value opportunities and build competitive advantage.

The economic rent generated by scarce entrepreneurial human capital includes Ricardian rent (or scarcity rent) and quasi-rent (or asset specificity rent). Ricardian rents are excess profits from the use of a resource that is relatively scarce. Quasi-rents are excess profits earned by a resource in its first-best use relative to its next-best use. Superior managerial skills such as entrepreneurial skills are relatively scarce; thus these resources may earn a Ricardian rent. Thus, high-ability executives must earn an excess compensation or an entrepreneurial surplus in order to be adequately incentivized.

Further, a firm-specific resource can be a source of quasi-rents. Firm-specific managerial human capital thus can earn quasi rents. Thus, a specialized or co-specialized firm resource when used in another firm, especially with a different business model mechanism, may generate less return. The business model mechanism constitutes the management logics, value opportunities, core resources, and value activities. The core resources include managerial human capital and social capital in addition to technology assets and management information systems. Entrepreneurial managerial human capital is more firm specific; therefore entrepreneurial organizations earn a quasi-rent too. Entrepreneurial managerial human capital as it is business model specific is also causally ambiguous; thus the excess profits for the firm or the entrepreneurial rent are sustainable, making the entrepreneurial surplus for managers achievable and thus providing the management adequate incentives in a dynamic environment.

Castanias and Helfat (1991) describe three types of managerial human capital, namely, generic, industry-related, and firm-specific human capital. Firm-specific human capital can earn quasi-rents, whereas all three types of managerial human capital can earn Ricardian rents. Thus, a manager with superior ability has high generic, industry-related, and firm-specific human and social capital. The greater the managerial ability, the greater is the potential for entrepreneurial surplus. Entrepreneurial surplus is potentially sustainable since the managerial human capital is largely tacit and causally ambiguous. It is often difficult to codify tacit managerial knowledge. Furthermore, managerial human capital becomes more tacit and firm-specific with managerial learning and their work experience.

In the theory of entrepreneurial rent, shareholders and managers jointly solve the firm value maximization problem in that they together maximize their return (or their utilities), which is different from the traditional agency theory in which the principal or shareholders maximize their return subject to a manager's incentive compatibility and participation constraints. Shareholders provide investment capital and must earn a competitive, risk-adjusted rate of return. Similarly, management provides human capital and must earn a competitive rate of return. The greater the risk of the investment capital, the greater must be the return for shareholders. The more superior the managerial human capital, the greater must be the management compensation. Further, the joint value maximization ensures that shareholders and managers maximize their compensations for their contributions to the firm value; not that one party maximizes their value subject to the other party meets their opportunity cost as is normally assumed in the traditional agency theory.

Further, shareholders should be compensated for the firm's systematic risk (i.e., the stock beta) since shareholders diversify away the firm-specific or unsystematic risk by investing in diversified portfolios. An individual shareholder may hold a diversified portfolio of stocks of several companies or invest in an institutional fund that is diversified. Thus, shareholders need not be rewarded for the unsystematic, firm-specific risk. Further, managers bear and manage the firm-specific or unsystematic risk, and thus management should be compensated for the firm's unsystematic risk in addition to the systematic risk. As a result, management should be then compensated for their human capital contribution with a return commensurate with the firm's total risk, the sum of systematic and unsystematic risks. Further, the firm's shareholders since they bear the systematic risk should be compensated for providing the investment capital with a return commensurate with the firm's systematic risk or stock beta.

In Fig. 3.1, the management pay is on the vertical axis and the firm performance is on the horizontal axis. Management pay includes the total compensation of the manager including fixed and variable components. The variable compensation is uncertain and may be based on the firm's objective or subjective performance measures. For managers with low-to-average ability, their choice is consistent with management pay that increases either at a low rate or fixed rate with the firm performance. The slope of the line shown in Fig. 3.1 is the management pay-performance sensitivity, determined by the proportion of the variable compensation in the management pay.

For low- to average-ability managers, the pay-performance sensitivity is low-to-moderate with respect to the firm performance. For low-ability managers, the pay-performance sensitivity or the slope of the line may be close to zero as low-ability managers prefer their compensation in fixed salary or they may accept their pay tied to more predictable firm performance measures. For high-ability managers, the slope or the pay-performance sensitivity increases at an increasing rate with managerial ability and stabilizes at a certain high-performance level (see Fig. 3.1).

More able managers will accept greater pay-performance sensitivity since they can earn greater compensation or an entrepreneurial surplus when the firm performance is higher than industry average. More able managers expect the firm performance to be high and they prefer more of their pay to be variable and tied to the uncertain firm performance. More

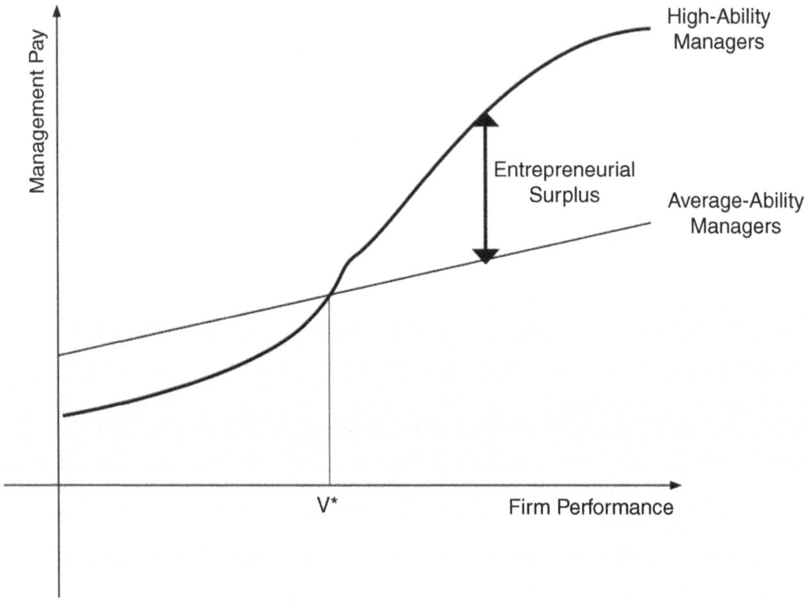

Fig. 3.1 Entrepreneurial surplus

able managers thus choose more entrepreneurial incentives. However, an average-ability manager is uncertain whether the firm performance will be high or low; thus they will prefer less of their compensation to be variable or tied to an uncertain firm performance. Low to average ability managers thus accept less uncertain compensation in their pay.

A manager's choice of compensation mix provides an incentive signal to shareholders about their managerial ability and human capital. More able managers will thus choose a pay mix with pay-performance sensitivity greater than their industry peers. Further, if a low- to average-ability manager accepts a pay mix with high pay-performance sensitivity, they will earn less since they may fail to deliver superior performance unless by luck the firm performance turns out to be high. Therefore, a low- to average-ability manager will not accept high pay-performance sensitivity.

As shown in Fig. 3.1, a low- to average-ability manager, if they choose a pay mix with increasing pay-performance sensitivity, will earn less when the firm performance falls below V^*; therefore, low- to average-ability managers will not accept such a pay mix. It is possible for overconfident or overly optimistic managers to choose a more variable pay in a rapidly changing competitive environment but these managers may not deliver superior performance and will earn less. Therefore, a low- to average-ability manager anticipating such a possibility will choose a pay mix with lower pay-performance sensitivity. Thus, an executive pay mix with higher uncertain compensation or higher management pay-performance sensitivity is associated with superior managerial ability and thus appropriate for entrepreneurial organizations. Managerial pay mix is an incentive signal of the managerial ability or managerial human capital.

A high-ability manager is also accepting the possibility that they will earn less if they fail to deliver firm performance equal to or above the level V^* (see Fig. 3.1). However, for a high-ability manager, the likelihood of achieving superior firm performance is high and if they were to choose to lower pay-performance sensitivity, they would certainly earn less. Therefore, to maximize their compensation and earn an entrepreneurial surplus, high-ability managers will prefer a pay mix with greater pay-performance sensitivity. Further, the pay-performance sensitivity increases with their managerial ability (see Fig. 3.1). High-ability managers therefore are expected to extract greater entrepreneurial surplus to be adequately incentivized. Thus the pay mix of a high-ability manager will include a greater proportion of stock options, restricted stock, and long-term stock-based performance plans, and a lower fixed salary. Some high-ability managers get 70 to 80 percent of their compensation in stock-based pay such as stock options and restricted stock.

Beck and Zorn (1982) show that managerial human capital should earn a higher rate of return than the shareholder's investment capital. Beck and Zorn show that shareholders should sell shares to management at a discount to compensate for their value-added human capital. The excess return to the management in terms of receiving restricted shares at a discount may be viewed as an entrepreneurial surplus. Further, the share price discount or the entrepreneurial incentives must increase with the managerial ability or human capital. The managerial equity-linked awards are thus an incentive signal of the managerial ability.

The higher the ability of manager, the greater is the likelihood that the manager will accept a pay mix with a greater proportion of their pay in stock-based compensation, and it is more likely the firm will provide the stock options to the manager at a greater discount. Firms will pay their high-ability managers an entrepreneurial surplus. Executives with superior human capital may not be incentivized adequately without the potential for them to earn an entrepreneurial surplus. Entrepreneurial incentives must be provided to high-ability executives for a firm to achieve superior performance even in the presence of corporate control mechanisms such as the market for corporate control, proxy fights, and corporate governance.

Environmental Dynamism

In an uncertain and dynamic environment the managerial task is more complex. The greater the task complexity, the more flexibility or discretion the management needs in their strategic and operating decisions. Thus, the greater the task complexity and the more dynamic the environment, the greater is the need for different compensation mix and pay-performance sensitivity. Further, the greater the task uncertainty or the more dynamic the environment, the more difficult it is to assess the ability of the management since the adverse selection problem is worse.

In a dynamic and uncertain task environment, performance-based variable compensation imposes a greater risk on the manager. Therefore a risk-averse manager will demand a greater risk premium, and the risk premium makes performance-based incentive compensation more costly to the firm and shareholders. The pay-performance sensitivity is thus lower for a risk-averse manager in a dynamic environment, and the predictable component of managerial pay should be greater. On the other hand, in a dynamic environment, there are greater opportunities and high-ability executives can earn an entrepreneurial surplus with higher pay-performance sensitivity. Consistent with our theory of entrepreneurial rent, the entrepreneurial abilities of managers are even more valuable in a dynamic and uncertain environment. Thus, high-ability executives see a greater opportunity to earn an entrepreneurial surplus in a dynamic environment.

Superior-ability managers in general prefer greater pay-performance sensitivity as shown in Fig. 3.1. Further, the task complexity theory within the theory of entrepreneurship (Mishra and Zachary 2014, 2015) also suggests that greater equity-based compensation is chosen by more able entrepreneurs when the task complexity is high since entrepreneurs need greater flexibility, and less constraints and control from their investors. Rigid performance-based milestones will not be appropriate for entrepreneurs in a more uncertain task environment. High-ability executives will want less corporate governance and monitoring and more flexibility in decision making, and therefore will accept greater variable compensation in a dynamic environment. High-ability executives thus signal their superior ability to the capital market by choosing a greater proportion of their pay in equity, vested over a longer period of time, thus increasing their pay-performance sensitivity.

Furthermore, in a more dynamic environment in which the firm performance is more uncertain, since the firm's equity is a call option on the firm value, the option value of equity-based compensation is higher. Thus the equity-linked incentive compensation will provide a greater entrepreneurial surplus to managers in a dynamic environment. However, low-ability managers will not accept a more variable compensation in a dynamic environment as the risk imposed by uncertain compensation is high on low-ability managers, and therefore they will not receive an entrepreneurial surplus. Low-ability managers are thereby sorted out in a dynamic environment. The restricted stock (with vesting conditions) and stock options when included in the managerial compensation package increases a manager's pay-performance sensitivity and are more valuable in a more dynamic and uncertain environment to high-ability managers.

High-ability executives would thus choose a greater proportion of their pay package in stock-based compensation and accept greater pay-performance sensitivity in a more dynamic and uncertain environment, sending an incentive signal of their entrepreneurial ability to capital market investors. Low-ability managers are more likely to lose compensation with greater pay-performance sensitivity in a dynamic environment and therefore they will accept a smaller portion of their pay package in stock-based compensation.

Thus, managers who choose lower pay-performance sensitivity are more likely to be low-ability managers and thus they are less likely to achieve superior performance in a dynamic and uncertain environment. High-ability executives must be paid an entrepreneurial surplus in a more dynamic environment. As the level of competition and market dynamism increases, we will see an increase in the level of executive compensation and a greater percentage of equity-linked pay in an industry.

Pendergast (2002) argues that when the task environment is less uncertain, managerial effort is less difficult to monitor, and thus the monitoring mechanisms such as the market for corporate control and the corporate governance are more effective in a more stable environment. The market for corporate control and the board-of-directors monitoring provide credible threats of dismissal of incompetent managers in a less uncertain and stable environment, when there is less noise in firm performance measures. A lower level of pay-performance sensitivity may thus be sufficient in a less dynamic environment. Managerial incentives through the threat of possible dismissal are not effective in a dynamic and uncertain environment. Monitoring the management in a dynamic environment is more difficult and less effective, thus requiring a higher level of managerial pay-performance sensitivity (entrepreneurial incentives).

Furthermore, in a more dynamic environment, management needs more discretion and flexibility in the firm's strategy and operations. More stringent corporate control and board monitoring mechanisms would be short-sighted and will hamper management effort to enhance the firm's long-run competitiveness. Furthermore, short-term strategic investments in building temporary competitive advantage may fail in the long term, which may further waste the firm's resources. Traditional organizations strive for temporary advantages in a dynamic environment, whereas entrepreneurial organizations that provide greater equity compensation to their managers strive for developing longer term advantages. There exists a critical level of environmental uncertainty beyond which the performance monitoring is less effective and thus entrepreneurial incentives through higher management pay-performance sensitivity is more desirable.

Executive Tournament

Do executive tournaments (i.e., large pay dispersion among senior executives in an organization) provide effective incentives in entrepreneurial organizations? The tournament theory explains why large pay gaps exist among executives in an organization. In particular, the tournament theory is based on the premise that when it is difficult to measure an executive's contribution to the firm, the compensation of the executive may be based on the rank of the executive in the organization. Further, the larger the pay gap between the ranks of executives, the greater is the managerial incentive in that a lower ranked executive is incentivized to get promoted to a higher rank that has substantially higher pay. However, when the executives have to work in a team and team interdependence is critical to the organization's success, large pay dispersion among the team members may be harmful to the team performance and thus the firm performance may suffer.

In an entrepreneurial organization in a dynamic environment, task interdependence among management team members is critical to the success of the organization. Galbraith (1973) argues that executive team interdependence is a function of the level of uncertainty in the task environment. Environmental uncertainty creates task interdependence that necessitates coordination and collaboration among executives. When the environmental uncertainty is dynamic and pronounced, there is thus a greater need of team interdependence and collaboration among the members of the management team. Large pay dispersion among top management team members is found to be negatively related to the firm performance in high-technology industries where the task environment is more dynamic. Thus in a dynamic environment, executive pay dispersions should be smaller. Furthermore, the executive pay levels are generally tied to the chief executive officer's pay.

Fredrickson et al. (2010) found that the larger the pay dispersion among the members of top management team, the lower was the firm performance. Further, the negative effects of large pay dispersion among management team members on firm performance were more pronounced in firms whose stock prices were more volatile (greater uncertainty). Lazear (1989) argues that small pay dispersions are actually more efficient when large pay dispersions among senior executives could create dysfunctional incentives among management team members.

Lazear (1989) extends their tournament model (Lazear and Rosen 1981) by allowing individuals in a team to use two kinds of actions in attempting to win a tournament, namely, effort (as was modeled in their original paper, which is often cited in support of tournament incentives) and sabotage (a new variable they introduced in their model). Thus, a big prize for winning a tournament requires not only a great deal of effort but also a great deal of sabotage (Gibbons 1998). Thus when sabotage is possible, such as within a top management team where finger pointing is common if the firm performance is below expectation, the pay dispersion among the team members should be smaller compared to a situation where only effort is needed to win the tournament. Large pay variations within top management team members are detrimental to the firm performance in a more dynamic environment such as in an entrepreneurial organization.

In entrepreneurial organizations, sabotage among management team members will hurt firm performance since greater team interdependence and collaboration are necessary to seize and execute superior value opportunities in a timely manner. The business model mechanism is more complex in a dynamic environment where the competitive conditions are regularly changing (see Chapter 5), and team interdependence is critical to execute the business successfully. The task uncertainty is high in entrepreneurial organizations and there is a greater need for team effort to achieve the organization's success. Tournament incentives that engender sabotage among team members will hurt firm performance when the task environment is dynamic; and without the team effort, entrepreneurial organizations may not achieve superior performance. In entrepreneurial organizations, pay-performance sensitivities are higher but pay dispersions among management team members are lower. Thus, tournament incentives are not appropriate as entrepreneurial incentives to incentivize management team members.

Entrepreneurial incentives enable organizations identify and seize cognitively distant value opportunities in a timely manner, configure available resources creatively, secure and leverage outside resources, manage the risk exposure by proactively adapting to environmental changes, and actively learn and continually update the management logics. Entrepreneurial incentives enhance the firm's value creation and appropriation mechanism and improve the odds of the organization gaining and sustaining competitive advantage in a changing environment. Moreover, entrepreneurial incentives enable organizations to figure out complex patterns of stimuli to recognize superior value opportunities, exploit the opportunities creatively and efficiently in a timely manner with the limited available resources, and compete effectively with resource-rich market leaders in a dynamic environment.

Entrepreneurial Agility

Entrepreneurial organizations practice a different religion; they are opportunity focused. They are quick to respond to an opportunity. "Hustle is their style and their strategy" (Bhide 1986: 59). Hustle and energy is what counts for entrepreneurial organizations to compete effectively with their resource-rich counterparts. Entrepreneurial agility allows an organization to quickly adapt to environmental change and enhances the organization's adaptability, learning, and cognition. Agility enhances the organization's opportunity focus and overcomes resource barriers. Alertness, agility, adaptability, absorptivity, proactiveness, and opportunity focus are hallmarks of entrepreneurial organizations.

Entry barriers in the market are often ignored by entrepreneurial organizations. Innovations are often quickly imitated or become obsolete in a dynamic market. Further, entrepreneurial organizations do not have much faith in long term strategic plans nor are they obsessed with managing costs and efficiency. "Ask yourself, if all your competitors gave their strategic plans to each other, would it really make a difference" (Bhide 1986: 59). Traditional strategic plans call for firms erecting massive entry barriers or developing strategic resources, which Bhide calls the big-play theory. Putting too much faith in the big-play theory has not been rewarding for many organizations. Such strategies rarely yield sustainable competitive advantages.

Conventional strategy suggests that without entry barriers and superior resources firms earn only a low to average return. However, consider the financial services industry. The economic rewards in financial services are often huge; but there are practically no proprietary products or processes. All firms serve similar customers with similar products. Bhide (1986) says that these high profits come mostly from the superior execution abilities of the individuals who are entrepreneurial in their approach to business. Not all financial service firms make huge profits but those who are more entrepreneurial get most of the business.

Bhide (1986) compares an entrepreneurial strategy to that of poker, not of chess. Bhide argues, "While it is important to understand and anticipate your opponent's actions, instead of devising a consistent and long-term strategy for the match, you play each hand as it is dealt and quickly vary tactics to suit conditions" [62]. The key to achieving superior performance is how a firm hustles and takes advantage of the available value opportunities in a timely manner. Agility determines how often and consistently a firm wins. Organizational agility is more important than long term strategic plans.

Stevenson and Gumpert (1985) compare the strategy making process of entrepreneurial organizations with that of nonentrepreneurial ones. A traditional organization uses a process of determining what resources they control, what factors influence the relationship between the organizational factors and the market, how they can minimize the impact of others on the firm performance, and then select the appropriate existent opportunities. In contrast, entrepreneurial organizations recognize and seize the opportunities in a timely manner, and determine how they can capitalize the available opportunities, what resources they would need, and how they can gain control of the resources. Entrepreneurial organizations are opportunity driven without regard to their current resource position, whereas most traditional organizations are resource driven. Entrepreneurial organizations continually learn and build resources actively to exploit available opportunities, whereas traditional firms select their opportunities dictated by the resources and competencies they control. Entrepreneurial organizations constantly seek opportunities to build resources and gain competitive advantage.

Entrepreneurial organizations are opportunity driven without regard to their current resource position. They are situationally alert and attuned to environmental changes. They are excellent at sensing and seizing value opportunities and quickly acquiring the resources to capitalize on those opportunities. They see challenges as opportunities. Many organizations would resist uncertainty and would rather play it safe, but entrepreneurial organizations welcome uncertainty and actively exploit it in the firm's favor. Further, traditional organizations take comfort in organizational routines and prefer predictable environments. Entrepreneurial organizations actively learn and adapt to environmental changes and build new routines and competencies in the process of exploiting available opportunities.

Entrepreneurial organizations spot opportunities early and exploit them in a timely manner. They move quickly past the opportunity recognition to its development and value creation. Traditional organizations lock into long-term commitment (Ghemawat 1991), but agile entrepreneurial organizations know their environment well to get into and out of a strategy quickly if necessary. Entrepreneurial organizations are alert, agile, absorptive, proactive, and flexible.

Entrepreneurial organizations excel at risk management and actively exploit the environmental uncertainty in their favor. They are not averse to risk and rather welcome changes since there are more value opportunities in a more dynamic environment. Entrepreneurial organizations manage their risk exposure and commit resources in several stages, and are quick to abandon an opportunity when the stage outcomes are unfavorable. They actively learn and experiment before they commit large resources. Entrepreneurial managers regularly test and update the management logics of how their business works. Empowered by entrepreneurial incentives, entrepreneurial organizations with regularly updated management logics actively learn and proactively adapt their strategies to environmental changes.

Entrepreneurial organizations pursue opportunities not constrained by the firm's current resources. Stevenson and Gumpert (1985) defines entrepreneurship as a process by which individuals pursue value opportunities without regard to the resources they currently control. Stevenson and Gumpert argue that firm performance is unrelated to the size of the resource commitments. Entrepreneurial organizations have superior resource orchestration capabilities enabled by a series of real options resulting from the exercising of firm's opportunity options (see Chapter 4). The combinative capabilities enable organizational knowledge integration that enhance the core resources that enable the dynamic capabilities. Further, entrepreneurial organizations are more creative at configuring new products with better user interfaces to increase consumer acceptance of their products.

Entrepreneurial organizations make imaginative uses of their limited resources when competing with their resource-rich counterparts. Entrepreneurial organizations never have enough resources, let alone superior resources. Startup organizations, for example, with very limited resources compete with giant established corporations that control superior resources and have deep pockets. An entrepreneurial organization considers itself as a collection of startup business units in that each unit is constantly seeking value opportunities and continually building competitive advantage. Large organizations commit too many resources at the outset to a given opportunity, whereas an entrepreneurial organization commits the resources in several stages such that their risk exposure is minimized and their learning is maximized (Mishra 2015).

The timing of each stage commitment is crucial to effectively manage the firm risk exposure. Exercising the firm's opportunity options and seizing the value opportunities creates a series of real options that give the organization the right, but not an obligation, to invest in real assets in several stages (see Chapter 4). The timing of the exercise of the real options and investments in the real assets is critical to proactively exploiting uncertainty in the firm's favor. Stevenson and Gumpert (1985) argue that "commitments in stages foster the most effective response to new competitors, markets, and technologies" [7]. Furthermore, a multistage commitment to an opportunity enhances management responsiveness, whereas a one time commitment creates unnecessary risk. However, multistage investments might escalate a manager's commitment to a failing opportunity under certain conditions (see Chapter 4).

Traditional managers try to limit their risk exposure by committing large resources at the outset when pursuing an opportunity. The focus of firm resources for success is consistent with the resource-based view of strategic management. It is possible to commit large resources at the outset when the environment is stable and predictable. When the environment is dynamic and the task complexity is high, a resource committed at the outset may be found irrelevant in midcourse; then the resource is not only wasted but it also might lower the chances of success with the opportunity.

Venture capitalists when investing in startups invest resources in several stages. Further, they learn in each stage and enhance their human capital. Entrepreneurial organizations embrace venture capital investment discipline in their resource management strategies. Further, entrepreneurial organizations leverage external resources at the outset when exploiting a value opportunity through strategic alliances and partnerships while keeping their options open to bring the resources in-house when and if necessary in order to lower the cost of operations and achieve scale economies. Agility, alertness, flexibility, absorptivity, proactiveness, and opportunity focus are hallmarks of entrepreneurial organizations.

Entrepreneurial organizations are quick to sense new opportunities and act on them in a timely manner without regard to their current competencies. They welcome environmental uncertainty and actively exploit the uncertainty in their favor. They often disrupt and reshape the rules of competition. In contrast, traditional managers are either complacent with their current success or react only when they spot a threat in the environment. Entrepreneurial organizations actively learn and proactively adapt their strategy to a changing environment. They are situationally alert, agile, proactively adaptive, and absorptive. They continually test and enhance the management logics that enable managers to overcome traditional behavioral bounds and seize cognitively distant opportunities. Entrepreneurial organizations are successful in finding and leveraging necessary resources and using their limited resources creatively to exploit a value opportunity. The presence of a superior resource relative to competitors is not critical to their success.

An opportunity is a situation of potential value to the firm, such as an increase in market demand, a shortage of supply, a superior technology for a new product or process, a new trend in the socioeconomic environment, and so on. Entrepreneurial organizations see environmental changes and threats as opportunities to create value for their organization. They actively manage their risk exposure in the firm's favor when pursuing new opportunities. They are more proactively adaptive and absorptive in managing and exploiting uncertainty than traditional managers. Thus, managers who "make a conscious effort to lessen negative consequences of failure when opportunity is pursued will exhibit a higher degree of entrepreneurial behavior" (Stevenson and Jarillo 1990: 24).

Three attributes critical to the entrepreneurial behavior of an organization are "detection of the opportunity, willingness to pursue it, and confidence and the possibilities of succeeding" (Stevenson and Jarillo 1990; 25). Entrepreneurial incentives must be viewed differently from traditional management incentives in that entrepreneurial organizations with their opportunity focus provide their managers to earn an entrepreneurial surplus to help the firm build and sustain competitive advantage.

Entrepreneurial organizations engage in "entrepreneurial judo" when competing with resource rich organizations (Drucker 1985). Entrepreneurial judo is opportunity driven regardless of the firm's resource constraints. Three key elements of an entrepreneurial judo strategy are agility, flexibility, and leverage. Drucker notes three situations where entrepreneurial judo may work best, namely, in a rapidly changing environment, in a situation where a market leader may not find an opportunity worthwhile, or in a situation where the market leader refuses to make their current products or processes obsolete or refuses to creatively destroy existing competencies and construct new ones. Entrepreneurial judo enables firms with limited resources to compete with established market leaders. "Hits them where they ain't" (Drucker 1985: 24); that is, an entrepreneurial judo hits the competitors in their weak areas before the competitors become aware of their competitive challenges.

Fast and flexible entrepreneurial organizations take on market leaders not only in high-tech sectors such as computer hardware and software but also in traditional, low-tech sectors such as retail. They do so using entrepreneurial judo. In judo, a combatant uses the weight and strength of his opponent to his own advantage. Moreover, judo is different from "sumo" matches in that in a sumo match, competitors compete using their strengths (or resources) against each other; whereas in a judo match, resources do not decide the winner, and competitors compete with agility, flexibility, creativity, and opportunity leverage. Thus, a sumo competition is resource driven, whereas judo is opportunity driven. In a sumo match, resource constrained entrepreneurial organizations will lose to resource rich market leaders who control superior resources.

The three principal elements of a judo competition are agility, flexibility, and creativity. A firm with greater entrepreneurial orientation will thus employ a judo strategy and win the competition. Agility requires entrepreneurial organizations to move rapidly to new markets by establishing beachheads that established market leaders either do not defend at all or defend halfheartedly (Drucker 1985); and this allows entrepreneurial organizations to avoid a head-to-head sumo match with market leaders. Flexibility requires an organization to give way to superior force when squarely attacked, in that an entrepreneurial organization embraces competitors' smart moves and makes quick adjustments in their own tactics. Entrepreneurial organizations are creative and use the weight and strength of their competitors and complementors by forging alliances with them.

Entrepreneurial organizations avoid a head-to-head sumo match with market leaders by avoiding competition on resources that the resource-based theory may prescribe to build competitive advantage. Rather, they are opportunity focused and seek opportunities to forge strategic alliances with competitors. Entrepreneurial organizations compete on superior opportunities, not on resources. Furthermore, entrepreneurial organizations never escalate an unwinnable war such as a price competition. By yielding to superior force rather than resisting it, a resource constrained firm can enhance its chances for survival). Agility, proactive adaptability, creativity, and opportunity leverage are hallmarks of entrepreneurial judo. Entrepreneurial judo provides a resource constrained firm an advantage to win over competitors' superior resources.

Absorptive Capacity

The absorptive capacity is the firm's knowledge generating and integration capacity. The firm's absorptive capacity requires two complementary investments, the development of knowledge (active learning) and the integration of knowledge (combinative capabilities). Learning is defined as knowledge acquisition and assimilation by an individual, a group, or an organization. Active learning enhances the firm's human capital, social capital, technology assets, and management systems. Entrepreneurial organizations are learning organizations. The tools and systems to gather and analyze the data in a timely manner as well as to effectively disseminate and use the results within the organization are necessary to benefit from active learning.

Active learning enhances and aligns the organization's core resources, which further enhances active learning. The returns to investments in learning and experimentation may vary over time as the returns are higher in the early stages of product development or process setups. Organizational and individual knowledge are enhanced by the active learning and combinative capabilities, namely the firm's absorptive capacity. The firm's absorptive capacity enhances the dynamic capabilities and value activities, and the management logics and value opportunities.

Nonaka (1994) examines knowledge generation in an organization. Learning takes place at the individual level. Further, individual learning enhances the knowledge of the organization. The organizational knowledge is further internalized by the individuals and groups. Individual knowledge may be tacit or explicit. Individual tacit knowledge is codified to enhance the organization's explicit knowledge (externalization); and further, the organizational explicit knowledge is internalized by the individuals and groups (internalization), enhancing the organization's human and social capital. Externalization and internalization processes continually enhance the firm's core resources. The core resources constitute the organization's human capital, social capital, knowledge capital, and management systems.

Knowledge creation requires developing both explicit knowledge and tacit knowledge. Explicit knowledge and tacit knowledge reinforce each other, enhancing the organization's core resources. The externalization of individual knowledge is the process of "learning-by-sharing"; whereas the internalization of organizational knowledge is "learning-by-doing" (Nonaka 1994). Learning occurs at the individual level and is a purposeful activity; therefore the individual's motivation and attention are critical to active learning and building knowledge resources in organizations. Thus, the entrepreneurial incentives are critical to enhance active learning at the individual executive level in the organization. Further, executive goals driven by the management's desire to earn an entrepreneurial surplus determine the speed and effectiveness of active learning. Furthermore, management attentional capacity and organizational attentional resources such as procedural and communication channels facilitate active learning in the organization.

Organizational knowledge is created at the individual level in that individuals accumulate knowledge through direct experience (i.e., experiential learning). The quality of experience and the commitment to learning through individual's goals and incentives affect the quality of the knowledge created in the organization. Interaction of the individual with their task environment is fundamental to their learning activity. The individual's reflection of their action and experience enhances the effectiveness of their learning. Further, social interaction with external participants such as customers, suppliers, and security analysts enhances organizational knowledge.

Individuals through social interaction contribute to the team knowledge creation. Teams drive organizational knowledge creation. Teams create organizational knowledge through two processes, namely, experience sharing and creative dialogues. Creative dialogues conceptualize individuals' perspectives. For creative dialogues to occur, some redundant information must exist within a team. Team leaders must take responsibility to facilitate interactions within team members. The two active learning processes are sharing of individual experience through social interactions in an organization and conceptualization of individual perspectives through creative dialogues (Nonaka 1994).

The two active learning processes, individual experience sharing and creative dialogues, occur simultaneously in a team. The team perspective is thus created when one individual with redundant information enters another individual's functional area and gives advice, a process called "learning by intrusion" (Nonaka 1994). The degree of information redundancy in a team determines the degree of knowledge diffusion in a team. Further, advocacy and inquiry by team members enhance the team's conceptualization of knowledge. The team's knowledge created is then crystalized into some concrete form such as a new product, process, strategy, etc. Further, the conceptualization employs experimentation and the validation of concepts developed by a team, a social process that occurs at the collective level.

Active learning is a continuous knowledge creation process in an organization. Nonaka (1994) defines organizational knowledge as justified beliefs. Thus the knowledge created by an organization is evaluated by the organization's justification standards to determine whether the created knowledge is considered as worthwhile for the organization to retain. The evaluation standards may be qualitative or quantitative such as profit margin, or unit cost, etc., which are determined a priori by the management. Justification standards are periodically revised to reflect the organization's evolving priorities and competitive strategy. Management logics enhance the justification standards in organizations, which further enhance the firm's absorptive capacity.

Active learning is a continuous, circular process that occurs within the organization and at the interfaces between the organization and its environment. The environment is a continual source of stimuli enhancing organizational knowledge. Further, for efficient knowledge creation to occur, organizational members should be aware of who owns what information (organizational transactive memory), and no member should be overloaded with more information than necessary for their functional needs. Entrepreneurial incentives enhance the organization's active learning in that the organization acquires, creates, exploits, and accumulates knowledge capital continuously through interactive processes between teams and individuals, between the organization and teams, and between the organization and external stakeholders.

Figure 3.2 illustrates the active learning cycle in an organization. An individual's learning cycle comprises of four learning activities, namely, experience, assess, design, and implement. Actions enhance the individual experience, and individuals consciously or unconsciously assess their actions or experience. Individuals conceptualize or design an appropriate response. And then individuals test and implement their response, which leads to a new concrete experience for them. Individuals thus repeat the active learning cycle continually. The active learning cycle enhances individual and organizational knowledge (see Fig. 3.2). Further, individual learning cycle is more effective when the individuals learn through a double-loop learning process (see Chapter 2), in which an individual's assumptions and mental models are tested and updated.

Organizations learn through learning-by-sharing. Organizations use double-loop learning in that the organizational assumptions are surfaced, questioned, tested, and challenged at the group and organizational levels. Individual knowledge and organizational knowledge reinforce each other

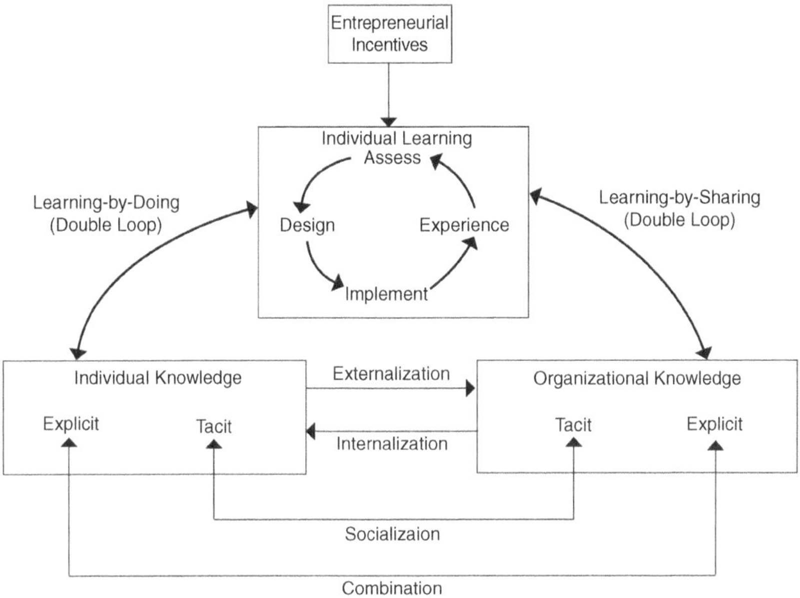

Fig. 3.2 Active learning

in their active learning, enhancing the knowledge of the individuals, groups, and the organization. Knowledge consists of tacit and explicit components. The firm's absorptive capacity constitutes active learning and combinative capabilities. The combinative capabilities or the knowledge integration activities constitute knowledge externalization, internalization, socialization, and combination. Knowledge externalization and socialization transform individual knowledge into organizational knowledge; and knowledge internalization and integration further transform organizational knowledge into individual knowledge. Thus, knowledge socialization enhances organizational tacit knowledge; and knowledge combination enhances organizational explicit knowledge (see Fig. 3.2).

Organizational members also should look outside their immediate environment such as suppliers, customers, competitors, and complementors, to gain new insights and perspectives, including learning from industry best practices. Knowledge generated from external learning should be rapidly and widely integrated within the organization. Entrepreneurial organizations empowered by entrepreneurial incentives and the management's desire to earn an entrepreneurial surplus have high active learning and knowledge absorption capacity.

Knowledge generated through the active learning cycle (see Fig. 3.2) is assessed using the organization's justification standards, and if the knowledge is considered as worthwhile to the organization, it is retained. Active learning enhances the firm's core resources. The core resources constitute the human capital, social capital, technology assets, and management systems. The core resources are the firm's knowledge resources. The firm's absorptive capacity that enhances the core resources and embedded value opportunities is further enhanced by the entrepreneurial incentives and management goals. The active learning cycle (see Fig. 3.2) enables the firm's combinative capabilities, and the combinative capabilities further enhance the firm's core resources, management logics, value opportunities, and value activities, thus enhancing the firm's value creation and appropriation mechanism. The combinative capabilities or the firm's knowledge integrative capabilities constitute the firm's knowledge externalization, internalization, socialization, and combination.

Active learning includes generative learning such as experimentation and problem-solving in an organization, as well as adaptive learning in integrating existing knowledge into new product and process applications. British Petroleum's CEO John Browne, in an interview, stressed that active learning "is the key to being able both to identify opportunities that others might not see and to exploit those opportunities rapidly and fully" (Prokesch 1997). Active learning and combinative capabilities are enhanced by the entrepreneurial incentives in an organization.

The entrepreneurial incentives enhance continually active learning in an organization, and their accumulated knowledge enables them to create new resources and capabilities. Entrepreneurial organizations are thus learning organizations; they are more effective at continually creating, acquiring, and integrating organizational knowledge, enabling the organization to proactively adapt to a changing environment. "A learning organization is an organization skilled at creating, acquiring, and transferring knowledge, and at modifying its behavior to reflect new knowledge and insights" (Garvin 1993: 3).

Garvin (1993) suggests five learning activities to transform an organization into an active learning organization, namely, solving problems systematically, learning by experimenting, learning from past experience, learning from others, and transferring knowledge throughout the organization. Garvin suggests managers should develop systematic methods to solve problems, not always use their gut instincts. Learning-by-experimentation involves small investments in testing new ideas and generating incremental knowledge. Individuals in organizations learn from theirs and others' past experiences by reviewing organizational successes and failures.

Managers have difficulty in transferring an organization into a learning organization. Building a learning organization requires developing and managing active learning processes facilitated by a supportive top management who, empowered by entrepreneurial incentives, reinforces learning and integrates knowledge throughout the organization. In building a supportive environment, employees must feel safe when disagreeing with others, take risks in exploiting the unknown, and recognize the value of opposing ideas. Active learning includes the formal processes of gathering intelligence on competitors, markets, customers, new technologies, and environmental trends, among others; processes for interpreting the gathered intelligence and sharing the information with colleagues and superiors; programs for developing employee skills; processes for identifying and solving problems; and experimentation with new ideas and products (Garvin et al. 2008). More importantly, managers must entertain and promote alternative viewpoints, allow employees to spend time on problem identification and solution, and actively inquire and listen to their colleagues.

Senior managers should practice the discipline of enhancing and regularly updating their mental models and theories (see Chapter 2). Senge (1992) argues that many brilliant ideas or strategies in the organization are never implemented because the new ideas are at odds with the existing management logics. Management logics are management mental models and espoused theories, or generalizations of how the business works, and they shape how the managers act. Managers with different mental models also learn differently. Management logics focus management attention on information elements that are consistent with the management logics and incentives. More importantly, management is often unaware of their mental models since mental models are tacit and exist below the level of awareness. In a changing environment, managers must constantly question their business assumptions or their theory of the business, and actively learn and continually update the management logics for the firm to remain competitive.

Active learning is an entrepreneurial capability. To promote and foster active learning in an organization, the management team, both at the corporate and divisional levels, must lead the learning activities. Active learning enhances the firm's core resources that enhance the value activities, and the value activities further enhance the active learning that further enhances the core resources. Knowledge accumulates through the value activities, which enhances the firm's core resources and value opportunities. A firm's outsourced activities may not provide as many learning opportunities as the firm's internal activities (Itami and Nishimo 2010). External partners, however, accumulate learning benefits from the firm's outsourced activities. The firm's value activities enhance active learning in an organization. However, the learning implied in the firm's value chain design is more subtle.

In many organizations, managers do not understand their business model nor are they aware of the assumptions underlying the business model or how their business works. Often the management's espoused theory of how the business works is different from how the business is actually carried out in an organization. Active learning further helps to bridge the gap between the management's espoused theory and the theory-in-use. Active learning supported by the management logics and entrepreneurial incentives enhances the firm's value creation and appropriation drivers. In organizations powered by entrepreneurial incentives, managers continually surface, test, validate, learn, and revise the business model assumptions and continually enhance the management logics. Thus, the entrepreneurial incentives help transform an organization into a learning organization.

Combinative Capabilities

The combinative capabilities include the firm's knowledge sharing and absorption activities such as knowledge externalization, socialization, internalization, and combination. The active learning cycle enhances the firm's knowledge base that is further enhanced by the combinative capabilities. Individual knowledge enhances the organizational knowledge through knowledge externalization, combination and socialization, while the organizational knowledge further enhances the individual knowledge through knowledge internalization and integration. The combinative capabilities enhance the core resources and value opportunities that help reconfigure and align the firm's organizational capabilities with the value opportunities. The firm's core resources and organizational capabilities enable the value activities enabling the execution of the business model mechanism. The business model mechanism constitutes the value creation and appropriation drivers. Thus, the combinative capabilities enhance the firm's value creation and appropriation.

Further, Grant (1996) proposes that the primary role of an organization is the effective integration and utilization of acquired or generated knowledge. The entrepreneurial incentives enhance the firm's knowledge generation and integration, namely, the absorptive capacity constituting active learning and combinative capabilities. The combinative capabilities enable the firm to leverage and enhance their knowledge resources to generate new products and processes. The firm's active learning enhances the combinative capabilities that further enhance the value opportunities and value activities. Further, active learning is enhanced by the value activities.

The combinative capabilities further enhance the firm capabilities through the processes of substitution, evolution, and transformation (Lavie 2006). Capability reconfiguration occurs in two stages. In the first stage, the firm's situation awareness enhanced by active learning such that the management logics alerts the management to emerging value opportunities and the management estimates the capability requirements to exploit the value opportunities. In this stage, the cognitive biases in the management logics updated through the firm's active learning may explain the heterogeneity in the firm capabilities in an industry (Levinthal and March 1993).

In the second stage, the firm's combinative capabilities enable the reconfiguration of the firm capabilities according to the management's estimate of the capabilities required to exploit the opportunities. In this stage, the differences in the firms' combinative capabilities may explain the differences in the firm capabilities in the industry. The entrepreneurial incentives enhance the firm's absorptive capacity that constitutes the firm's active learning cycle (stage-one basis of firm capability heterogeneity) and the combinative capabilities (stage-two basis of capability heterogeneity). Thus the differences in the absorptive capacity powered by the entrepreneurial incentives may explain the capability differences across firms in an industry.

The firm's value opportunities influence the firm's resource orchestration capabilities since the new opportunities may require new configurations of the capabilities and processes. Further, the actions of incumbent organizations in an industry alter the level of environmental uncertainty, the intensity of competition, the structural conditions such as entry and mobility barriers, and the customer preferences and market demand. The nature of value opportunities available to a firm thus influences the evolution of the firm's organizational capabilities. The management logics, value opportunities, and organizational capabilities also support the activity drivers that underlie the firm's value activities. The intensity of competition in an industry depends on how and when incumbent firms in an industry reconfigure their organizational capabilities in response to the value opportunities.

The firm's value opportunities can be competence-enhancing (i.e., enhancing the firm's existing competencies) or competence-destroying (i.e., making the firm's existing competencies obsolete) (Tushman and Anderson 1986). Often competence-destroying value opportunities are seized by new entrants who are not subject to existing competency traps or core rigidities, whereas competence-enhancing value opportunities are generally seized by incumbent organizations in an industry. Furthermore, entrepreneurially oriented organizations that are alert, agile, absorptive, proactively adaptive, and opportunity driven are less likely subject to competency traps and thus they are more likely to seize competence-destroying value opportunities. Organizations seizing competence-destroying (Schumpeterian creative destruction) value opportunities require high entrepreneurial incentives.

The environmental uncertainty and product market dynamism also determine how an organization proactively adapts to the environmental uncertainty and exploits a value opportunity. When the environment is fast paced and less predictable, that is, when the rules of competition are ambiguous and rapidly changing, entrepreneurial organizations pursue competence-destroying value opportunities. However, when the level of uncertainty and market dynamism is low-to-moderate, that is, when the management is more certain of the industry structure and competitive conditions, they may pursue competence-enhancing value opportunities. Further, with competence-enhancing value opportunities, the firm's capabilities evolve slowly. Entrepreneurial organizations may pursue more competence-destroying Schumpeterian opportunities. However, when pursuing competence-destroying opportunities, the organizations will require high absorptive capacity including continually active learning and superior knowledge integration or combinative capabilities that are powered by the entrepreneurial incentives.

Kogut and Zander (1992) view the investments in knowledge assets of the firm (the core resources, in our framework, constituting the firm's human capital, social capital, technology assets, and management systems) as the opportunity-embedding platform (see Chapter 4). New investments in knowledge assets serve as platform investments embodying the firm's opportunity options. The firm's knowledge resources enhanced by the active learning cycle and combinative capabilities are socially constructed and embedded in the firm's core resources, namely the human capital, social capital, technology assets, and management systems.

The knowledge assets or core resources enable the resource coordination mechanisms or the dynamic capabilities within a firm. The knowledge base of the firm enables the management to coordinate the resources when pursuing new opportunities. Grant (1996) views the firm as serving the role of an integrator of specialized and co-specialized resources that reside in the firm. The knowledge assets or core resources that enhance the dynamic capabilities further enhance the coordination of value activities and organizational capabilities. The firm's dynamic capabilities thus serve as resource coordinator and orchestrator. The dynamic capabilities are enhanced by the firm's active learning and combinative capabilities, namely the firm's absorptive capacity. Knowledge integration is facilitated by the shared knowledge among the individuals, enabling the further development of organizational capabilities. For example, American Express's customer billing system is dependent on their "ability to harness and integrate the knowledge of many individual specialists" (Grant 1996: 116). In developing a firm's distinctive competencies, Grant considers "the extent to which a capability is 'distinctive' depends upon the firm accessing and integrating the specialized knowledge of its employees" [116].

Entrepreneurial organizations learn faster and better than their competitors; and they are more effective in integrating their acquired knowledge throughout the organization faster and more widely than their competitors. Entrepreneurial organizations thus have enhanced active learning and combinative capabilities. "No matter where the knowledge comes from, the key to reaping a big return is to leverage that knowledge by replicating it throughout the company so that each unit is not learning in isolation and reinventing the wheel again and again" (CEO John Browne in an interview; see Prokesch 1997). Thus the firm's combinative capabilities are central to the business model execution advantage that sustains the firm's competitive advantage or superior performance in the industry. Active learning and combinative capabilities, which enhance the knowledge generation and integration in an organization, enhance the business model value creation and appropriation mechanism which is further enhanced and sustained by powerful entrepreneurial incentives. Organizational members continually learn from their experience and interactions, from customers and suppliers, and from their competitors and complementors. Entrepreneurial organizations have enhanced absorptive capacity for learning and knowledge assimilation that further enhances the firm's business model mechanism and the superior execution of the business model mechanism builds and sustains the firm's competitive advantage.

The broader the knowledge base underlying an organizational capability, the greater is the causal ambiguity associated with the capability and the more difficult it is for a competitor to imitate the firm's capabilities. Knowledge assets are both inputs and outputs of the combinative capabilities. The knowledge resources are combined and recombined to enhance the organizational knowledge base underlying the firm's capabilities. Grant (1996) describes the organizational processes by which the knowledge capital residing in the firm's core resources can be combined and recombined to support and reconfigure the firm's capabilities.

Further, organizational knowledge enhances the firm's dynamic capabilities. The firm's dynamic capabilities are defined as "the firm's ability to integrate, build, and reconfigure internal and external competencies to address rapidly changing environments" (Teece et al. 1997: 516). Eisenhardt and Martin (2000) further define the dynamic capabilities as the firm's "processes to integrate, reconfigure, gain and release resources – to match and even create market change" [1107]. Both definitions emphasize the importance of organizational learning and knowledge integration underlying the firm's dynamic capabilities.

The firm's combinative capabilities enhance the dynamic capabilities that reconfigure the firm's activity system and organizational capabilities. Thus the collective knowledge base of the individuals in an organization embedded in the core resources enables the coordination of the value activities and the configuration of the firm resources. Moreover, the firm's operating and governance channels that regulate the management attention enhance the dynamic capabilities. The entrepreneurial incentives that enhance the firm's absorptive capacity further enhance the knowledge base underlying the activity drivers that enable the firm's value activities. The activity drivers are enhanced by the firm's absorptive capacity and regenerated by the dynamic capabilities.

Entrepreneurial organizations are constantly seeking value opportunities to enhance their competitive advantage. Entrepreneurial organizations pursue opportunities regardless of their current resource position. Thus, a firm's current resource position, contrary to what the resource-based views may suggest, neither is sufficient nor does it constrain the firm's potential to achieve competitive advantage. In the absence of entrepreneurial incentives, the strategic resources will not be leveraged to enhance the firm's value creation and appropriation mechanism wherein the competitive advantage lies.

The absence of entrepreneurial incentives will limit a firm's absorptive capacity, namely, active learning and combinative capabilities, thus constraining the knowledge base underlying the organizational capabilities that support the activity drivers and the linkages between the firm's value chain and the buyer value drivers; and thus the firm will fail to enhance and appropriate the added value and thus will fail to achieve competitive advantage. Furthermore, the core resources (the firm's knowledge base) enhance the dynamic capabilities that enable the firm's proactive adaptation of the value activities to exploit the environmental uncertainty in the firm's favor. Entrepreneurial organizations with their opportunity focus continually learn and proactively adapt in a changing environment, enhancing the firm's business model drivers constituting the management logics, core resources, value opportunities, and value activities, linked to the buyer value drivers, thereby enhancing the firm's value creation and appropriation engine wherein the firm's competitive advantage is created and sustained.

Core Resources

Active learning and combinative capabilities enhance the firm's core resources. The firm's core resources are the human capital, social capital, knowledge capital resources, and management systems. The knowledge capital is embedded in the firm's core resources. The core resources strengthen the activity drivers and enhance the linkages between the firm's value chain and the buyer value chain (see Chapter 5). The core resources embody the firm's opportunity options (see Chapter 4). Core resources are further enhanced through value activities that enhance the active learning within and outside the organization. The entrepreneurial incentives enhance the firm's core resources, value opportunities and value activities through active learning and combinative capabilities. The firm's knowledge resources are also known as the core capabilities (Leonard-Barton 1992). Itami (1987) refers the firm's knowledge resources as "invisible assets"; Prahalad and Hamel (1990) refer them as the core competencies.

Prahalad and Hamel (1990) describe the core competencies as "the collective learning in the organization, especially how to coordinate diverse production skills and integrate multiple streams of technologies" [4]. Core competencies are thus the firm's collective knowledge. For example, NEC leveraged their core competencies to discover emerging opportunities and to coordinate their diverse technologies and resources to exploit those opportunities. The core competencies enhance the firm's combinative or knowledge integrative capabilities. Further, the firm's core competencies are enhanced by the entrepreneurial incentives, according to our theory of entrepreneurial rent.

The more entrepreneurial the organization, the more enhanced and sustainable are their core competencies.

Prahalad and Hamel (1990) propose that the core competencies underlie the firm's competitive advantage. "The real sources of advantage are to be found in management's ability to consolidate corporate wide technologies and production skills into competencies that empower individual businesses to adapt quickly to changing opportunities" (Prahalad and Hamel 1990: 4). The core competencies coalesce around the individuals in a firm; that is, the core competencies or the collective knowledge in the organization embed in the human capital, social capital, and technology assets. The core competencies "are the glue that binds existing businesses… and [drives] the engine for new business development" (Prahalad and Hamel 1990: 6).

Core resources embody the knowledge capital or "invisible assets" that do not depreciate (Itami 1987). The core resources indeed appreciate when they are employed and shared within an organization. The firm's technology assets, however, must be enhanced continually through active learning since technology knowledge can rapidly become obsolete unless it is continually enhanced. Active learning and knowledge integration are high in entrepreneurial organizations and thus the knowledge resources are continually renewed in these organizations. Invisible knowledge assets enable a firm to achieve and sustain competitive advantage. Itami (1987) asserts that: "Invisible assets are the real source of competitive power and the key factor in corporate adaptability for three reasons: they are hard to accumulate, they are capable of simultaneous multiple uses, and they are both inputs and outputs of business activities" [12].

It is impossible to separate the core resources from the individuals in the organization since the invisible assets are embedded in the firm's human capital and social capital. "People are important assets of the firm, but they are important because much of the invisible assets of the firm are embodied in people" (Itami 1987: 14). Some invisible assets may situate outside the organization, which are included in the firm's social capital. Further, the invisible assets can be simultaneously used in several functional applications. The invisible assets are accumulated when the individuals engage in transactions within the organization (internal learning) or with outside parties (external learning). Active learning by individuals in an organization enhances and renews the organization's core resources. Internal learning originates and terminates within the firm, enhancing the firm's core resources. External learning occurs in the environment as the external information flows from the environment to the firm and is assimilated within the firm.

Itami (1987) stresses the importance of the firm's operating and communication channels in the accumulation of the invisible assets. The procedural and communication channels are critical for situating and enhancing management attention (Ocasio 1997). The greater the firm's communication channel capacity, the more enhanced the management attention, and the more enhanced are the core resources in the firm. The greater the management attention, the higher is the situation awareness and the higher is the likelihood of the firm seizing distant opportunities that provide superior performance. The entrepreneurial incentives enhance the communication channel capacity and hence the management attention and alertness, which further enables the firm to seize superior value opportunities and sustain competitive advantage.

Leonard-Barton (1992) defines the core capabilities constituting the knowledge assets of the firm. The core capabilities unless renewed and aligned continually will lead to organizational inertia and core rigidity. The core capabilities include employee knowledge and skills, social values and norms, and managerial and technical systems. Employee knowledge and skills include firm-specific human capital as well as generic and industry-related human capital. Technical systems include the information systems and the procedural knowledge. Managerial systems include the reporting structures that control the flow of information and thus affect the accumulation of knowledge. The social values are the values and priorities that the individuals in the organization value. Further, the social values and norms influence the interpretation of the organizational knowledge.

Blyler and Coff (2003) show how a firm's social capital supports the firm's dynamic capabilities. The social capital is embedded in the individuals and groups by virtue of their membership in the organization or a network. Blyler and Coff suggest that the social capital is essential for the firm to acquire, integrate, recombine, and release their resources. Furthermore, external social capital including strategic alliances is essential in acquiring the resources the firm does not have. Social capital within a firm, including the values and norms, support the resource reconfiguration activities.

Proactive Adaptation

Entrepreneurial incentives enhance the organization's ability to seek value opportunities and proactively adapt in an uncertain and dynamic environment to build and sustain competitive advantage. Proactive adaptation requires enhanced management logics. Adaptation occurs when an organization responds to reduce an increased gap between their potential performance and actual performance. Active adaptation occurs "when the instance of adaptation is triggered by an increase in the potentiality without any change in the actual performance, and when the system increases its actual performance, thus seizing the new opportunity" (Sachs and Meditz 1979: 1087).

Active adaptation may be proactive or preactive. In both situations, organization responds to an increased gap between their potential performance and actual performance. The difference between the proactive and preactive adaptations is that in proactive adaptation the stimulus of an increase in potential performance comes from within the organization, whereas in preactive adaptation the stimulus of an increase in potential firm performance comes from outside the organization. Furthermore, in passive adaptation the organization responds to a drop in their actual performance; however, the firm's potential performance remains unchanged.

Standard strategic tools can be used by a firm to develop a strategic plan in a predictable and stable environment. Traditional strategic planning yields meager benefits for firms. As the future unfolds and the ensuing events fail to fit into the planned scenarios, the strategies become irrelevant and are discarded. The benefit of strategic plans, however, is in the planning process that hopefully surfaces, tests, and updates the management logics (see Chapter 2). The difficult part of strategy, however, is how firms cope with an uncertain environment. In the traditional method of planning, managers try to get a handle on future events using forecasting and scenario tools, scanning procedures, surveys and market research, and judgmental prediction methods such as Delphi and cross-impact matrices. In a less dynamic environment, some future scenarios may be predictable and some current trends might continue into the near future (see Chapter 4). In a more dynamic environment, however, the future events often unfold not as expected by the firm and the plan recommendations are discarded.

In the traditional method of planning, uncertainty is dealt with by making assumptions about future events and preparing contingency plans around the variations of these assumptions. Unexpected events, however, make these strategies irrelevant, notwithstanding the resources and technologies devoted to sophisticated forecasting techniques. In a dynamic environment, when changes in the environment occur faster than an organization has the ability to act, traditional strategic planning often fails.

Allaire and Firsirotu (1989) describe two types of adaptation in a dynamic environment, namely, the power adaptation of enacting a future through influencing the sources of uncertainty and the structural adaptation of building the firm's capacity for a flexible response to whatever may happen. The power method to actively adapt in an uncertain environment is when managers don't forecast a future but shape it. The power adaptation is opportunity driven. The organization thus reduces their vulnerability to future uncertainty by proactively shaping their environment by investing in new opportunities before the future events unfold and thus shifting the competition in their favor. For example, corporate restructuring activities such as mergers, acquisitions, and divestitures change the firm's competitive landscape and may give the firm a dominant position in the competitive landscape. Other proactive power methods are to shift the uncertainty to partners in the supply chain using long-term contracts, contingent prices, cost-plus contracts, and minimum volume commitments, among others. These power actions enable the firm to influence and shape the future events.

Proactive adapters shape the competitive environment in their favor. Proactive adapters use the power method to drive the competitive environment into a new shape of their devising. Shaping strategies include setting new standards and stimulating market demand, etc. Shapers play a dominant or leadership role in the industry. Shapers try to control the direction in which the market may evolve. Shapers rewrite the rules of competition in an industry as they discard their preconceived notions of the nature of the market and the current way business is being done. Further, shapers rewrite the rules shifting the competition in their favor, thus surprising the competitors. In the process of shaping the rules of competition, new value opportunities and new markets emerge. The rules of competition in an industry evolve, and the market leaders soon find themselves with lost advantages.

When shifting the rules of competition, a proactively adaptive firm, rather than waiting for the competitive battle to come to them, will choose the battlefield and the manner and timing of the conflict (Buaron 1981). The proactive firm actively chooses what the rules will be, where the new rules will be most potent, and how it might bring about the change. The firm may choose to attack across the entire market or focus their efforts on one or some market segments where the competitors are especially vulnerable.

In a dynamic environment, imitating a competitor's advantage is merely preactive, not proactive adaptation. Moreover, preactive adaptation only gives the firm competitive parity. To achieve competitive advantage the firm needs to be proactively adaptive and continually explore new opportunities for how the current rules of competition can be shifted in the firm's favor. A proactively adaptive firm should seek and seize value opportunities that were not previously considered competitively important, thereby taking the competitors by surprise.

Shaping strategies can be developed for the entire market or for specific segments. In one type, an across-the-board game, a proactively adaptive firm rewrites the rules of competition for an entire market or industry, although it is often difficult to do that. However, it may be possible to shape the rules of an entire industry when the market is in temporary turbulence. In a second type of shaping, a selective game, the firm may carve out a slice of the market by redefining a segment to suit the firm's unique way of doing business.

To the extent the firm succeeds in modifying the rules of competition, possibly in their favor, the firm may establish a new set of key success factors in the market. The existing market leaders find themselves with lost competitive advantages. The firm that successfully shaped the rules will find themselves with a competitive advantage which may, however, be transitory. The competitors facing the choice of losing market shares soon learn how to play by the new rules and try to shift the rules in their favor. The actions and reactions of competitors escalate the competition leading to a hypercompetitive environment. Competitive actions by proactively adaptive firms create a hypercompetitive environment in which the competitive advantages created are often transitory. Proactively adaptive firms thus must continually seek opportunities to create the next advantage before the current ones become obsolete. Another method of proactive adaptation is the firm's reserving-the-right-to-play strategy, in which the firm makes small investments now to stay in the game. The firm learns and waits until the uncertainty is mostly resolved before making a major investment in an opportunity. By making small upfront investments the firm reserves the right to take advantage of opportunities in the future as they may arise in changing market conditions.

Another method of active adaptation is the structural adaptation response by the firm such that the firm is ready for any possible future event. The structural response method calls for investing in new opportunities and building resources that enhance the firm's flexibility. For example, a firm may broaden the scope of its products or markets by investing in its product innovation capability. Another structural adaptation response is to set up strategic alliances and joint ventures to share the risks and resources. Structural methods require a firm to preadapt to absorb future uncertainties that they cannot control. Structural methods take the evolution of the industry structure as a given and exploit the value opportunities the market offers. Structural adaptation strategies are predicated on the firm's accumulated resources. Firms in low-to-moderate dynamic environments may preadapt using structural solutions. Preadaptation thus makes the firms largely impervious to changing environmental conditions. In rapidly changing environments, however, a combination of power actions and structural adaptation will be more effective.

In a hypercompetitive environment, in which markets, products, and technologies are largely unpredictable and uncontrollable, a corporation should view itself as a collection of entrepreneurial business units. Each entrepreneurial business unit actively monitors their value opportunities in their market space, and seizes and exploits the value opportunities in a timely manner to remain viable and competitive. The organization is continually shaped and reshaped by the actions of their entrepreneurial business units as they proactively adjust to a fast-changing and unpredictable environment. To support the entrepreneurial units within the corporation, top management must foster an active learning environment within the organization. Management must be agile and flexible to quickly switch the firm resources around in the organization to take advantage of the value opportunities across the business units.

Dynamic Capabilities

The firm capabilities to proactively adapt in an uncertain and dynamic environment are the dynamic capabilities. Proactive adaptation involves the firm proactively seeking value opportunities and configuring firm resources to exploit the opportunities. The difference between proactive and preactive adaptation can reconcile the difference between the two views of dynamic capabilities in the literature. In Teece's (2007) view of dynamic capabilities, the firm's dynamic capabilities enable proactive adaptation, in that a stimulus to adapt originates from within the firm, and when the firm seizes an opportunity, the gap between the potential performance and actual performance is widened. Proactive adaptation is thus opportunity driven. However, in Eisenhardt and Martin's (2000) view of dynamic capabilities, the stimulus to adapt arises external to the organization as the firm uses competitive benchmarking and industry best practices to adapt preactively to catch up with the performance of competitors. Thus, preactive adaptation is resource or competency driven. Teece's description of dynamic capabilities is consistent with entrepreneurial proactive adaptation, whereas Eisenhardt and Martin's description is consistent with preactive adaptation.

Entrepreneurial organizations seek and leverage value opportunities to adapt and compete proactively. In contrast, traditional organizations seek and leverage superior resources to adapt preactively. Entrepreneurial organizations adapt proactively and exploit value opportunities to build resources; whereas traditional resource-focused organizations build on the resources and adapt preactively to restore competitive parity. Value opportunities increase with environmental uncertainty; thus entrepreneurial organizations will choose to compete in a more uncertain environment in that they are more likely to find cognitively distant Schumpeterian opportunities to achieve competitive advantage.

Baldwin and Clark (1992) describe the dynamic capabilities firms employ to proactively adapt to a dynamic environment. The firm's dynamic capabilities include external integration, internal integration, operational flexibility, and self-cannibalization. External integration enables a firm to integrate customer knowledge and market intelligence with product design and development activities to improve product quality and consumer acceptance. External integration capabilities consist of market research and external learning capabilities such as probe and learn methods to understand customer needs and preferences. External integration also includes the firm's internal routines and processes that translate and assimilate external information into product outcomes. Further, entrepreneurial organizations develop products that not only match the customer needs but often surpass their expectations. Entrepreneurial organizations thus have superior external integration abilities.

Information about customers and the way they use the products must be gathered and analyzed through the organization's sales and marketing departments; and the knowledge of customer needs and preferences must be translated into specific product outcomes. By probing the market periodically, the data on customer usage of the products and their preferences can be gathered and analyzed. Product testing by simulating customer usage can confirm whether the new product design meets customer requirements. Investments are required to enhance both the sales and service capabilities and the product design and development systems to improve the firm's external integration capabilities. Two critical investments, namely, the gathering of customer knowledge and linking the customer knowledge to the product outcomes, are required to enhance the firm's external integration capabilities. Entrepreneurial organizations have superior external integration capabilities. The returns to investments in external integration capabilities are likely to be higher for firms with differentiated products than for those with commodity products.

Second, internal integration capabilities enable a firm to be more efficient. Internal integration is achieved when the firm's functional areas are tightly connected such that decisions in one functional area take into account the concerns of other functional areas. Tight integration across functional areas enhances the speed and efficiency of the organizational processes. Cross-functional integration requires investments in specialized human capital and communication channels to facilitate cross-functional collaborations and interactions. Appropriate incentives and rewards, training programs, and human resource development are necessary to facilitate cross-functional interactions and internal integration.

The primary benefits derived from investments in internal integration capabilities are organizational efficiency and agility. Organizational agility enables firms to move in a timely manner to seize value opportunities and adapt to changing competitive conditions. Efficiency provides the scale advantage that lowers the firm's cost to serve and increases the market share. Cross-functional interactions also facilitate active learning in the organization. Efficiency, scale, learning, and speed are thus the primary benefits from internal integration.

Third, investments in enhancing operational flexibility should be weighed against the benefits from flexibility. Product flexibility affords a quick change in the product mix on short notice and enhances the ability of the firm to introduce new products quickly. Process flexibility allows for rapid and easy changeovers in process setups. For example, modular design enhances product flexibility such that product components and sub-components can be quickly assembled, which increases product variety. Flexibility enables firms to adapt to rapidly changing market conditions. However, flexibility must be balanced against the firm's efficiency needs. Further, since flexibility is costly to the firm, so investments in flexibility should be weighed against the organization's needs and benefits.

Active learning enhances the firm's core resources or knowledge assets to support the value activities. The firm's knowledge assets enhance the activity drivers and strengthen the linkages between the firm's value chain and the buyer value chain. The core resources further enhance the firm's proactive adaptation and thus the dynamic capabilities. For example, knowledge of the customers and markets enhances the firm's external integration capability. Knowledge of processes, specialized human capital, management systems, and social capital enhances the internal integration and operational flexibility.

Finally, a company self-cannibalizes when it replaces existing products and processes with new products and processes. Often companies are reluctant to self-cannibalize their existing products or processes because self-cannibalization would reduce the current profits and thus their market value. The unwillingness to self-cannibalize the firm's existing products or processes means that established firms are less likely to introduce new generation products. Consequently, in the long run, established firms cannot stay competitive and eventually are forced to exit the industry. Self-cannibalization is the best strategy if a company wants to sustain competitiveness and prevent competitors from entering their market space. For established firms, self-cannibalization is time inconsistent in that when it is time to introduce a new product or process, it will not be in the company's best financial interests to do so. The firm's self-cannibalization capability cannot be justified if managers are to maximize the financial performance of the firm at all times. The traditional capital budgeting systems and standard cash flow valuation models discourage self-cannibalization.

There are two parts to the self-cannibalization capability, namely, the ability to explore and recognize value opportunities (see Chapter 4), and the ability to implement and exploit the opportunities while phasing out the old products or processes (see Chapter 5). To identify value opportunities and seize them in a timely manner, the managers must have enhanced management logics and sufficient situation awareness, which are enhanced by active learning powered by the entrepreneurial incentives (see Chapter 2). The organization must cultivate opportunity options at low cost before committing major resources to the opportunities. The firm may pursue multiple opportunity options simultaneously while it is busy with managing and supporting its existing product lines and processes (i.e., organizational ambidexterity). The firm's support activities also include incremental improvements to the current products and processes while the new products and processes are being developed.

In the second part of the self-cannibalization capability, managers must have the ability to follow through with the implementation of new products or processes while gradually phasing out the old. Organizational ambidexterity is crucial to the management of self-cannibalization. Further, an organization focused on supporting existing product lines will have built-in inertia to strongly resist the changes involved with the implementation of new products or processes. Therefore, the firm's internal procedures and systems for existing products and processes must include built-in procedures for anticipating the need for and implementation of new products and processes.

The entrepreneurial incentives enhance the firm's self-cannibalization capabilities, what Schumepeter (1934) called "creative destruction." Thus, established organizations who do not self-cannibalize in a timely manner fail to proactively adapt, and these organizations will either fail to introduce new products or processes to remain competitive, or they will implement new products and processes with a delay, take inappropriate actions, and make costly mistakes and thereby lose market share and competitiveness.

Entrepreneurial Leverage

The greater are the entrepreneurial incentives, the more entrepreneurial is the firm and the greater is the firm's entrepreneurial orientation. The entrepreneurial incentives thus provide the firm an entrepreneurial leverage that further enhances the firm's absorptive capacity, management logics, management cognition, value opportunities, core resources, dynamic capabilities, and the value creation and appropriation mechanism underlying the competitive advantage. Entrepreneurial leverage provides the firm an entrepreneurial rent and enhances the firm's competitive position. Entrepreneurial leverage provides the management the opportunity to earn entrepreneurial surplus. Further, the greater the firm's entrepreneurial orientation, the greater is the entrepreneurial leverage. Thus the firm's entrepreneurial orientation is enhanced when the entrepreneurial incentives are high. Zahra and Covin (1995) found a positive relation between a firm's entrepreneurial orientation and its financial performance. The greater the firm's entrepreneurial orientation, the greater the likelihood of the firm achieving superior performance.

The theory of entrepreneurship explains the impact of the firm's entrepreneurial leverage on the firm performance (Mishra and Zachary 2014, 2015). The theory of entrepreneurship, namely the entrepreneurial value creation theory, is a comprehensive theory of entrepreneurial processes of value creation and appropriation led by the entrepreneur powered by entrepreneurial aspiration. Entrepreneurial incentives thus provide the management the entrepreneurial intent or an opportunity to earn entrepreneurial reward (surplus). The theory of entrepreneurship describes the interiors of the entrepreneurial processes in sufficient detail. The entrepreneurial value creation process is a two-stage process. In stage one of value creation, the entrepreneur recognizes an opportunity stimulus and further develops the opportunity. In the second stage of value creation, the entrepreneur acquires complementary dynamic capabilities and configures the firm resources that enable the business model mechanism where the firm value is created and appropriated.

The resource acquisition and development by the entrepreneur occurs under adverse selection conditions, in that the entrepreneurial ability is unknown and the venture value is difficult to assess. Successful entrepreneurs use incentive signals to attract investment capital to acquire the necessary resources and capabilities to enhance the business model mechanism. The business model mechanism sustains entrepreneurial value creation and appropriation, creates and sustains the firm's competitive advantage, and generates an entrepreneurial reward or surplus for the entrepreneur.

Figure 3.3 illustrates the stage-one processes of competitive advantage creation, in which the entrepreneurial incentives enhance the absorptive capacity, management logics, management cognition, situation awareness, and dynamic capabilities. Enhanced management logics enable the management to overcome traditional behavioral bounds and thus enable them to sense and seize cognitively distant opportunities. Further, active learning enhances the

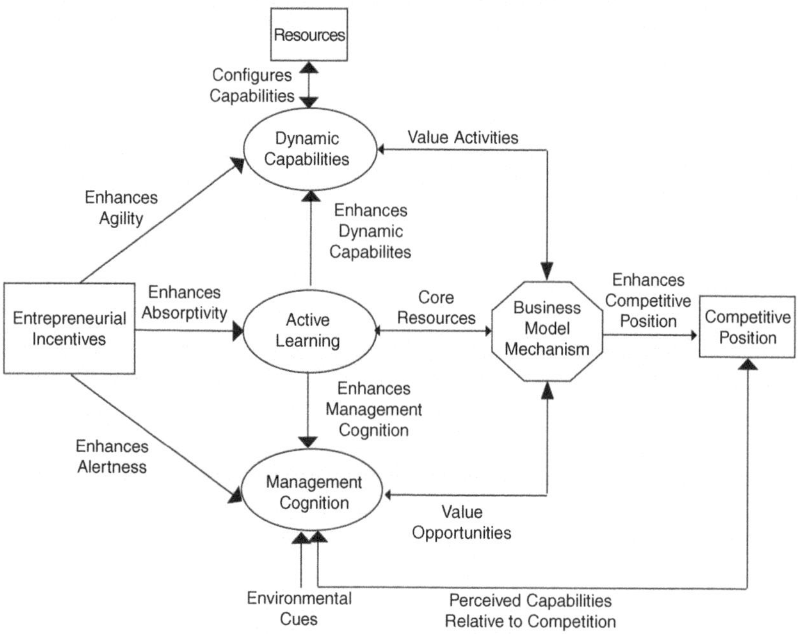

Fig. 3.3 Entrepreneurial leverage

management logics that further enhance the firm's execution of the value creation and appropriation mechanism. Furthermore, the combinative capabilities integrate the knowledge generated or acquired by the firm and enhance the core resources and value opportunities. The dynamic capabilities reconfigure the organizational capabilities that support the value activities. The entrepreneurial incentives thus enhance the firm's management logics, value opportunities, core resources, organizational capabilities, and value activities that enhance the business model mechanism. The business model constitutes the firm's value creation and appropriation mechanism wherein the firm's competitive advantage is created and sustained.

Further, the entrepreneurial incentives enhance the management cognitive adaptability and management logics enabling the management to overcome traditional behavioral bounds, which further enhances the management cognition and situation awareness. The entrepreneurial incentives provide the ignition and the value opportunities the fuel for the value creation and appropriation mechanism that creates and sustains the firm's competitive advantage, according to our theory of entrepreneurial rent. The value creation and appropriation mechanism and its superior execution underlies the firm's competitive advantage. The entrepreneurial incentives stimulate active learning that enhances the management logics and the value creation and appropriation mechanism. The entrepreneurial incentives are central to the firm's value creation and appropriation mechanism and hence to the creation and sustainability of the firm's competitive advantage.

The greater the entrepreneurial incentives, the greater the entrepreneurial leverage of the firm and the greater is the likelihood of the firm achieving and sustaining competitive advantage through superior execution of the firm's business model mechanism. The firm's competitive advantage or the rationale underlying the firm's superior performance is sustained by the value creation and appropriation mechanism enhanced by the entrepreneurial incentives. The business model mechanism sustains the firm value creation and appropriation. The entrepreneurial incentives enhance the firm's absorptive capacity that further enhances the management logics, value opportunities, and core resources which configure the value activities and activity drivers that further enhance the firm's value creation and appropriation, thereby enhancing the business model advantage and the firm's competitive position. The core resources, or the firm's human capital, social capital, management systems, and technology assets, enhance and are enhanced by the firm's active learning and combinative capabilities. The management logics and core resources enhance the linkages between the firm's value chain and the buyer value chain, which further enhance and sustain the buyer value added. The core resources thus enhance the firm's value creation and appropriation mechanism when the entrepreneurial incentives are high.

The firm's dynamic capabilities configure the value activities and firm resources to exploit the value opportunities. The management logics further influence the firm's opportunity selection and resource allocation decisions. The firm's resources are enhanced and recombined by the dynamic capabilities and supported by the firm's knowledge generation and integration (active learning and combinative capabilities). Further, the firm's absorptive capacity is enhanced and sustained by the entrepreneurial incentives.

The firm's core resources, value opportunities, and value activities co-evolve with the firm's business model and thus the firm's competitive position is effectuated. Standard effectuation theory (Sarasvathy 2001) argues that the entrepreneur, given their resource position, in that their resources are fixed, effectuates an opportunity that can be exploited with the given resources. In our framework, however, the entrepreneurial organization powered by entrepreneurial incentives learns actively, renews the management logics, and accumulates core resources; and thus the management logics, value opportunities, core resources, and value activities morph simultaneously as the business model mechanism is effectuated. The firm's management logics, core resources, value opportunities, and value activities are effectuated and configured simultaneously; that is, the management logics, core resources, value activities, and value opportunities are emergent along with the business model configuration under the conditions that the management is provided with the entrepreneurial incentives that provide the management the opportunity to earn an entrepreneurial surplus and the firm an entrepreneurial rent. Thus, the firm's business model configuration is effectuated in our framework, not the opportunity alone, in that the business model mechanism co-evolves with its constituents, namely, the management logics and value opportunities, core resources and organizational capabilities, and activity drivers and value activities (see Chapter 5).

The firm capabilities and opportunities are reconfigured and developed further through the staged exercise of the real options resulting from the exercise of the opportunity options (see Chapter 4). Thus, active learning and the exercise of real options associated with the opportunity options explain the simultaneous effectuation of the firm's value opportunities and firm resources. The staged exercise of real options enables the firm's dynamic capabilities that enhance the firm's resource configuration.

The management logics enable the exercise of the staged real options. Further, the entrepreneurial incentives enhance the firm's active learning and combinative capabilities that further enhance the management logics (see Fig. 3.3). The management logics include management mental models, beliefs, theories, knowledge structures, procedural scripts, heuristics, and assumptions of how the business model works and how the value is created and appropriated (see Chapter 2).

The entrepreneurial incentives that enhance active learning enable the business model effectuation including continuous morphing of the management logics, core resources, organizational capabilities, value opportunities, and value activities. The firm's business model mechanism employs the emergent opportunities, resources and activities to create and sustain firm value, thus resulting in an emerging competitive advantage. Thus, the first stage of the entrepreneurial rent creation processes involve an effectuation of the firm's management logics, core resources, and value opportunities enhanced by the firm's active learning sustained by the entrepreneurial incentivese. Further, the emergent business model configuration with the activity drivers and value activities drives the second-stage entrepreneurial rent creation processes that constitute the value creation and appropriation mechanism that enhances the business model advantage and the firm's competitive position. The entrepreneurial incentives thus enhance the firm's value creation and appropriation mechanism that generates entrepreneurial rent and thus creates and sustains the firm's competitive advantage.

Summary

Entrepreneurial organizations are alert, agile, proactively adaptive, absorptive, and opportunity driven. Further, the greater a firm's alertness, agility, proactiveness, adaptability, absorptivity, and opportunity focus, the more entrepreneurial is the firm and the greater is the likelihood of the firm achieving competitive advantage. The theory of entrepreneurial rent states that the greater the entrepreneurial incentives, the more entrepreneurial the firm, and the greater is the likelihood of the firm achieving competitive advantage. The entrepreneurial incentive is provided through the uncertain performance-based compensation in the executive pay, in that the firm performance is set by an external arbiter such as the capital market. Entrepreneurial incentives enhance the absorptive capacity, management logics, active learning, management cognitive adaptability, management cognition, and value creation and appropriation mechanism. Entrepreneurial incentives enhance the firm's business model drivers that further enhance the value creation and appropriation mechanism wherein the firm's competitive advantage lies, according to our theory of entrepreneurial rent.

The entrepreneurial incentives thus enhance the firm's absorptive capacity, namely active learning and combinative capabilities, which further enhance management cognitive adaptability and management cognition, management logics and value opportunities, dynamic capabilities and organizational capabilities, and the value creation and appropriation mechanism that generates an entrepreneurial rent and enhances the firm's competitive position, and provides the management with an entrepreneurial surplus. The more entrepreneurial the firm, the greater is the firm's capacity for superior execution of the value creation and appropriation mechanism and the greater is the business model advantage. The firm's management logics, core resources, value opportunities, and value activities are enhanced by the entrepreneurial incentives. Further, the entrepreneurial incentives enhance the firm's absorptive capacity constituting active learning and combinative capabilities.

Entrepreneurial incentives enhance the management cognition that enables the managers to actively seek cognitively distant value opportunities to help build and sustain the competitive advantage. Competitive advantage is the rationale underlying the firm's superior performance. Entrepreneurial incentives enhance the likelihood of a firm achieving competitive advantage. Entrepreneurial organizations are often resource constrained; thus their ability to build competitive advantage implies that the presence of a superior resource is not necessary for a firm to achieve competitive advantage. Entrepreneurial organizations are not discouraged by their current resource position relative to the competitors when pursuing superior opportunities.

Entrepreneurial functions in an organization include the management articulating and enhancing management logics, acting in the present to enact tomorrow's business, configuring the business model to increase its effectiveness, and identifying and realizing the business's full potential. Management should regularly examine the management logics and their actions, and thereby surface and update the management logics, and close the gap between the theory-in-use and espoused theory. Entrepreneurial organizations employ entrepreneurial judo when competing with resource-rich market leaders. Judo match is different from sumo matches in that in a sumo match, competitors compete on their strengths (resources); but in a judo match, agility, flexibility, and opportunity leverage matter. Agility, flexibility, active learning, and opportunity focus are hallmarks of entrepreneurial organizations. Entrepreneurial organizations avoid a head-to-head sumo match with resource-rich competitors and thus ignore traditional market entry barriers and resource position barriers when pursuing value opportunities.

Entrepreneurial organizations are opportunity focused, whereas traditional organizations are resource focused. Traditional organizations determine what resources they control or have access to, what factors influence the relationship between the organization and the market, how they can minimize the impact of others on the firm performance, and then select appropriate opportunities. In contrast, entrepreneurial organizations recognize superior opportunities and then determine how they can capitalize on the opportunities, what resources they will need, and how they may gain control of these resources. Entrepreneurial organizations build resources, whereas traditional organizations build on the resources. Entrepreneurial organizations excel at identifying superior value opportunities and quickly gathering the resources to capitalize on the opportunities.

Entrepreneurship is a process in which individuals pursue opportunities without regard to the resources they currently control or their current resource position. Entrepreneurial organizations have an execution advantage. Entrepreneurial organizations execute the value creation and appropriation mechanism more effectively than traditional organizations can. Further, to build and sustain competitive advantage entrepreneurial managers must be incentivized differently than traditional managers. Traditional managers may choose low pay-performance sensitivity in a dynamic and uncertain environment, since environmental dynamism imposes a greater risk on traditional managers when the executive pay-performance sensitivity is high. However, in a dynamic environment, high-ability executives prefer high pay-performance sensitivity and thus they have a potential to earn an entrepreneurial surplus. Environment dynamism provides greater opportunities and hence greater potential to earn an entrepreneurial surplus. Entrepreneurial surplus is the excess compensation earned by executives for bearing excess firm-specific risk. Managerial human capital earns a return commensurate with the firm's total risk, whereas the shareholder's investment capital earns a return commensurate with the firm's systematic risk.

The greater the managerial ability, the higher pay-performance sensitivity the manager may choose. Thus, the managerial compensation, that is, the mix of uncertain and predictable components of the management pay, is an incentive signal of the managerial ability. Average-ability managers will choose a pay mix that has a higher proportion of predictable pay components. Predictable pay components include fixed salary, expected bonus, and predictable accounting-performance based incentive compensation. More uncertain pay includes stock-based incentive compensation, stock options, and restricted stock. Stock-based pay is more uncertain and less predictable, often preferred by high-ability managers, which provides the managers an entrepreneurial surplus.

High-ability managers provide superior managerial human capital and cultivate high social capital in an organization. Further, high-ability executives are incentivized when their compensation package provides an entrepreneurial surplus in the event the firm generates excess profits or entrepreneurial rent. Entrepreneurial surplus is the manager's excess compensation for bearing excess firm-specific risk. Managers with entrepreneurial incentives thus have the potential to earn excess compensation when the firm achieves and sustains superior performance. High-ability managers must earn more than their peers; thus an entrepreneurial surplus is necessary to align the manager's interests with those of the shareholders when the competitive advantage is desired.

Shareholders provide investment capital and bear the firm's systematic risk. Since the firm's shareholders are diversified investors (i.e., holding a diversified portfolio of securities or investing in diversified institutional funds), they bear the systematic risk (i.e., measured by the stock's beta). The shareholder should then be compensated for the firm's systematic risk, not for the unsystematic or firm-specific risk which is borne by the manager. Managers thus bear the firm's unsystematic or firm-specific risk that is actively exploited and managed with managerial human capital. Shareholders are thus compensated for providing investment capital with a risk premium commensurate with the firm's systematic risk; whereas managers are compensated for providing human capital with a risk premium commensurate with the firm's total risk (the sum of systematic and firm-specific risks).

Tournament incentives (or large pay dispersions among executives in an organization) may provide powerful incentives in traditional organizations. The tournament theory suggests that when it is difficult to measure a manager's contribution to firm performance, the manager's compensation may be based on their rank in the organization. According to the tournament theory, the larger the pay gap between the ranks of managers in an organization, the more effective is the managerial incentive alignment. However, when the members need greater team collaboration and interdependence, tournament incentives break down and the firm performance suffers. With tournament incentives, the firm's managers may engage in a great deal of effort, but at the same time the team performance suffers as a great deal of sabotage is expected to occur between management team members. Team interdependence is crucial to the success of entrepreneurial organizations. Tournament incentives thus have detrimental effects on firm performance in entrepreneurial organizations. In entrepreneurial organizations, the task environment is dynamic and complex; thus there is a need for greater team interdependence and team collaboration, and therefore the tournament incentives are detrimental.

The entrepreneurial incentives enhance active learning and combinative capabilities that further enhance the management logics and enable the management to overcome traditional behavioral bounds. The entrepreneurial incentives enhance the firm's value activities and core resources that exploit the value opportunities in a timely manner, sustaining the value creation and appropriation mechanism wherein the firm's competitive advantage lies. The organization's competitive advantage creation process may be viewed as occurring in two stages. In stage one, the entrepreneurial incentives enhance active learning and combinative capabilities, which further enhance the management logics, cognitive adaptability, and situation awareness. The firm's core resources and value opportunities are enhanced. Organizations seize and exploit cognitively distant value opportunities in a timely manner. The entrepreneurial incentives enhance the management logics that further enhance the firm's proactive exploitation of the environmental uncertainty to resolve in the firm's favor. The core resources embody the firm's opportunity options that enable the management to proactively adapt their business model to changing competitive conditions.

In stage two, the business model mechanism driven by the firm's management logics, value opportunities, core resources, and value activities enhance the firm value creation and appropriation, which further enhances the business model advantage and the competitive position. Entrepreneurial incentives enhance the dynamic capabilities that further enhance the business model scalability, sustainability, and adaptability. The greater the business model advantage, the greater is the firm's competitive position. The entrepreneurial incentives enhance and sustain the business model advantage that provide the firm an entrepreneurial rent and the management an entrepreneurial surplus. The greater are the entrepreneurial incentives, the more entrepreneurial is the firm and the greater is the likelihood of the firm achieving competitive advantage.

CHAPTER 4

Seizing Value Opportunities

Introduction

Managers empowered by entrepreneurial incentives are not limited by prevailing logics in their industry. They actively seek value opportunities to disrupt the prevailing logics in their favor. In a dynamic environment, a firm's competitive advantage is not secure. When industry rules shift, a firm's competitive advantage can become their liability. Managers therefore must constantly seek new value opportunities to renew the firm's competitive advantage. At the same time they must be alert to the actions of competitors who are also planning to disrupt the industry rules. It is not a question of whether the firm's competitive advantage will be eroded but rather how soon it will happen and what the firm can do now (MacMillan 1988). The firm should be constantly seeking fresh opportunities and laying the groundwork for an upcoming advantage even as the firm benefits from their current advantage.

Entrepreneurial organizations continually seek cognitively distant opportunities to build and renew the competitive advantage. The greater the entrepreneurial incentive in the executive pay, the more entrepreneurial is the firm. The entrepreneurial incentive is provided through the uncertain performance-based compensation in the executive pay, in that the firm performance is set by an external arbiter such as the capital market. Proximate opportunities are visible to most managers and may not provide the firm with superior performance. Superior opportunities

C.S. Mishra, *Creating and Sustaining Competitive Advantage*,
DOI 10.1007/978-3-319-54540-0_4

are not proximate to a firm and thus may not be found by a local, incremental search as assumed by conventional behavioral logic.

Further, emerging behavioral logic identifies three entrepreneurial abilities of decision makers, namely, the ability to identify opportunities, the ability to act on the opportunities in a timely manner, and the ability to shape the opportunities. Entrepreneurial incentives are consistent with emerging behavioral logic. Entrepreneurial incentives enable managers to overcome traditional behavioral bounds. The more distant the opportunities, the more pronounced are the behavioral bounds of decision makers. To identify, act on, and shape the cognitively distant opportunities, managers must actively learn and continually revise the management logics. Traditional managers with a resource focus may not spot cognitively distant value opportunities. Furthermore, entrepreneurial incentives enhance the organization's entrepreneurial orientation and opportunity focus.

Cognitively distant opportunities are less contested than more proximate opportunities. More distant opportunities are thus Schumpeterian (Schumpeter 1934) as opposed to Kirzerian (Kirzner 1997). Schumpeterian opportunities are innovative and innovatively imitative opportunities (i.e., creative destruction) that change the rules of industry competition, and these opportunities are difficult to spot and act upon. In contrast, proximate incremental opportunities are Kirzerian, which arise when the markets are in temporary disequilibrium. Kirzerian opportunities are relatively easier to spot. Market disequilibrium arises when there is an excess demand or a shortage of supply in a good or service. Most managers with traditional behavioral bounds can spot Kirzerian proximate opportunities, although few may act upon them in a timely manner without adequate incentives. Furthermore, exploiting Kirzerian opportunities restores the market equilibrium, whereas exploiting Schumpeterian opportunities continually disrupts the market equilibrium. Kirzerian opportunities can be found with a local search. However, a more distant search is necessary to spot cognitively distant Schumpeterian value opportunities. According to our entrepreneurial logic, Schumpeterian opportunities are sources of competitive advantage.

In a dynamic environment entrepreneurial organizations are constantly seeking distant value opportunities to build competitive advantages. An uncertain and dynamic environment provides a large number of opportunities for established firms and new entrants. However, the management cognition varies across firms in an industry. Accordingly, managers may sense value opportunities differently; may seize them too soon, too late, or not at all; or may or may not succeed in shaping the opportunities for exploitation. Thus traditional managers may or may not succeed in seizing and exploiting the value opportunities available to the firm in a timely manner. The theory of entrepreneurial rent predicts that entrepreneurial organizations are more likely to sense and seize cognitively distant value opportunities, act on them in a timely manner, and exploit the uncertainty associated with the opportunity successfully in the firm's favor; consequently, our entrepreneurial logic predicts that entrepreneurial organizations are more likely to build and sustain competitive advantage.

Competitive advantage is the rationale underlying the firm's superior performance. This underlying rationale is termed as a "resource" in the resource-based view (Barney 1991) and as an attractive strategic position in the positioning view (Porter 1985). However, firm resources and strategic positions may not provide competitive advantage when the management does not seize and exploit the opportunities in a timely manner. Further, in resource-based views as well as in positioning views, it is assumed that management will act rationally and timely to sense, seize, and exploit valuable opportunities. However, the management may fail to recognize a valuable opportunity and act upon it in a timely manner even when the firm owns a strategic resource. Our theory of entrepreneurial rent argues that entrepreneurial incentives empower the management to recognize cognitively distant value opportunities and act on them in a timely manner. Thus, our theory of entrepreneurial rent enhances extant resource-based and positioning views of competitive advantage.

Management's ability for sensing, seizing, and acting on a value opportunity in a timely manner is a source of competitive advantage. To seize and exploit value opportunities in a timely manner, the firm must regularly test and update the management logics. The management must maintain sufficient situation awareness and focus their attention on the critical aspects of the environment to recognize cognitively distant value opportunities. With entrepreneurial incentives, managers seize and exploit value opportunities in a timely manner, which enhances the firm's value creation and appropriation mechanism and provides the firm competitive advantage. The competitive advantage lies in the firm's value creation and appropriation mechanism which is enhanced by high-powered entrepreneurial incentives. The entrepreneurial incentives enable the firm to create and sustain competitive advantage.

Entrepreneurial organizations view an uncertain and dynamic environment as a source of value opportunities, rather than a source of threats. Entrepreneurial organizations are alert, agile, active learners, proactively adaptive, and opportunity driven. The entrepreneurial incentives in an organization empower the management to timely seize and successfully exploit superior value opportunities that yields an entrepreneurial surplus. Entrepreneurial organizations thus have an advantage in seizing and exploiting value opportunities more effectively and timely. Managers empowered with entrepreneurial incentives constantly seek value opportunities without being constrained by their resource position. Contrary to resource-based views that suggest a firm with resource advantage is more likely to achieve competitive advantage, entrepreneurial incentives empower organizations to build competitive advantage notwithstanding their current resource disadvantages.

A firm should be viewed not only as a collection of entrepreneurial business units but each unit should be also viewed as a series of startups in that each startup is expected to create competitive advantage that may last a short duration. The long-term strategy of a business unit should be thus viewed as a series of startup opportunities with a plan to transition effectively from one startup opportunity to another. Such a dynamic long-term strategy needs an entrepreneurial organization that is constantly seeking and shaping value opportunities to build new competitive advantages to sustain superior performance. The firm's entrepreneurial capacity to proactively adapt and exploit the environmental uncertainty in their favor and act on the value opportunities in a timely manner is a source of competitive advantage.

Value opportunities seized and exploited in the presence of entrepreneurial incentives are sources of superior performance. Value opportunities must meet three conditions, namely, (1) the opportunity has the potential to enhance the economic value of the firm, (2) the potential value is commensurate with the risk and investment undertaken, and (3) the potential value created is appropriable by the firm. Thus, a value opportunity is an opportunity that has the potential for the firm to enhance the buyer value and the value added must commensurate with the opportunity risk and investment. The risk and reward of value opportunities must be worthwhile for a firm to act on them. The net present value of a value opportunity must exceed a critical positive value for the firm, where the critical value is determined by the uncertainty associated with the opportunity.

A value opportunity must satisfy the condition: $V \cdot (1 - \pi) > I$, where V is the present value of the cash flow from the opportunity, π is the firm's risk of investment loss with the opportunity, and I is the present value of investment outlays. The traditional net present value rule (i.e., $V > I$) is not sufficient for value opportunities. The value opportunity condition can be easily derived from the venture delta equation presented in Mishra (2015). The value opportunity condition should apply not only to new ventures but must apply to all value opportunities to be considered as worthwhile for firms to pursue. The risk of investment loss (π) is the uncertainty associated with the value opportunity underlying the opportunity option and a function of the product demand uncertainty, price uncertainty, and cost uncertainty. The estimates of *V, I, and* π of an opportunity can change over time as management monitors the opportunity options and gathers more information.

The value opportunities do not have to be strictly innovative to be a potential source of superior performance. The value opportunities may be innovatively imitative. Levitt (1966: 63) notes: "Imitation is not only more abundant than innovation, but actually a much more prevalent road to business growth and profits." Innovation sparks waves of imitations, in that some of which are innovatively imitative and some are just mere imitations. Innovation occurs when something created is entirely new and has never been done before. However, when competitors in the same industry or firms in another industry copy an innovation, it is not innovation even though the idea is new for the company or the industry. Rather, it is innovative imitation.

In Miles and Snow's (2003) typology, prospectors pursue innovative opportunities and analyzers pursue innovatively imitative opportunities. Prospectors as well as analyzers are entrepreneurial organizations. They are alert, agile, proactive, absorptive, and opportunity driven. Thus, prospectors and analyzers both can have high entrepreneurial orientation. Levitt (1966) further warns managers to recognize the impossibility of sustaining innovation leadership. "No single company, regardless of its determination, energy, imagination, or resources, is big enough or solvent enough to do all the productive first things that will ever occur in its industry and to always beat its competitors to all the innovations emanating from the industry" (Levitt 1966: 65).

Imitation is often perceived to be less risky than innovation. However, imitation does not necessarily reduce the risk; it simply changes the character of the risk (Levitt 1966). Innovators may face the risk of not finding ready markets, but imitators face the risk of entering a market that is glutted. With innovation as well as imitation opportunities, the market timing is always critical. Successful imitation requires the imitator to enter the market when competitors are still few and the margins are still attractive. In some industries, imitations are more rampant because of the low capital requirements and the relative ease of copying an innovation. Imitation should not be a merely reactive or occasional response by a firm; imitation indeed requires careful planning and a great deal of management attention. Successful imitations require no less attention and formal planning than innovations.

Value opportunities may be classified along two primary dimensions, namely, how the opportunities affect the firm competencies that impact operational effectiveness and the product market linkages that impact the buyer value added (Abernathy and Clark 1985). The operational competencies include technology design, production systems, personnel skills, information technology, raw materials used, capital equipment used, and managerial knowledge and experience. The firm's product market linkages include customer relationship, customer needs and preferences, distribution channels, customer and market knowledge, and modes of marketing communication. Thus, a value opportunity is classified according to its potential to enhance the firm's operational competencies or the potential to enhance the product market linkages, or both.

Value opportunities enhance the firm value by enhancing the buyer value and the firm's operational effectiveness. The value opportunities may enhance the firm's existing competencies, or render them obsolete and create new competencies. The latter case is referred to as "creative destruction" (Schumpeter 1934). Schumpeter argues that the processes of creative destruction of existing firm competencies and the creation of new competencies are led by entrepreneurs who drive the engine of economic growth. Furthermore, value opportunities may enhance the firm's existing markets or create entirely new markets.

Value opportunities that enhance the firm value may be classified under four categories, namely, architectural opportunities, niche opportunities, regular opportunities, and revolutionary opportunities (Abernathy and Clark 1985). Architectural opportunities create new competencies and new markets; niche opportunities enhance the firm's existing competencies while creating new markets; regular opportunities incrementally enhance the firm's existing competencies and markets; and revolutionary opportunities strengthen the firm's existing markets while creating new competencies.

Architectural opportunities shape the industry architecture and the rules of competition. These opportunities reform existing markets and create new ones. Three themes define these opportunities: the durability of their economic impact, the role of new knowledge, and the importance of breaking the grip of the existing industry structure. Architectural opportunities emerge in user environments latent with needs. Architectural opportunities arise when firms proactively seek value opportunities to develop new competencies in response to previously unanticipated user needs.

While finding new markets and building new competencies describes architectural opportunities, opening up new markets with the firm's existing competencies describes niche opportunities. Niche opportunities may, however, involve incremental changes in the firm's existing competencies. New market segments are identified to leverage the firm's existing competencies with or without minor changes in the competencies. Niche opportunities appear with new product introductions, competition based on product differentiation, and technical enhancements. Existing firm competencies are refined, improved, or changed in a way that will support new marketing linkages and drive sales growth. However, market share gains are not durable as competitors can quickly copy innovations with improved product differentiation strategies. Niche opportunities may provide temporary competitive gains. Long-term advantage requires a firm introduce a sequence of new products to counter competitor moves. The market timing and entrepreneurial agility are critical to the success of niche opportunities. For example, startup firms often exploit niche opportunities to enter new markets.

Regular opportunities are value opportunities associated with continuous improvements of the firm's existing products and processes. Continuous innovations are incremental in nature and often are invisible. However, the cumulative effect of a series of continuous improvements can alter the firm's competitive significance. Regular opportunities thus involve incremental enhancements in the firm's existing competencies to enhance their existing markets. Continuous improvements raise the firm productivity, enhance the economies of scale, and increase process capacity. Continuous innovations can have dramatic cumulative effects on the firm's product cost and process performance.

Revolutionary opportunities disrupt the firm's existing competencies and render them obsolete while strengthening the existing market linkages. New competencies and technologies emerge out of revolutionary opportunities. The industry rules of competition are altered with the emergence of new firm competencies. These value opportunities are generally technology driven and are risky as they might fail if they are ill timed. Thus, with revolutionary opportunities, the timing of a new product launch is critical. Firms with fewer resources may suffer a disadvantage while resource-rich firms may succeed with revolutionary opportunities. Close collaboration between engineers and marketing executives is essential to successfully exploit revolutionary opportunities.

Opportunity Recognition

Why are some firms more successful at identifying and exploiting value opportunities? A greater ability to recognize complex environmental stimuli distinguishes managers with entrepreneurial incentives. Enhanced management logics to spot cognitively distant opportunities and the timely acting on new opportunities while attending to the needs of existing operations are hallmarks of entrepreneurial organizations. Entrepreneurial organizations are ambidextrous.

Baron (2004) explains cognitive activities associated with an individual's opportunity recognition. Entrepreneurial incentives enhance the odds of the manager recognizing the firm's potential value opportunities. Entrepreneurial executives are more likely to perceive the complex pattern of stimuli associated with value opportunities. The pattern recognition ability of the individual enhances the opportunity recognition. Opportunities, at some level (even latently), exist in an environment. The environment is in a state of disequilibrium and it moves from one state of disequilibrium to another. The opportunities are available continually in the environment. Firms seize the opportunities and act on them, which changes the state of the environment into another state of disequilibrium. Further, unrelated opportunities share recognizable patterns and the nature of patterns of stimuli can help individuals discover potential opportunities (Baron 2004). Opportunity recognition and development are central to the entrepreneurial rent creation and appropriation processes that underlie a firm's competitive advantage.

Individuals recognize patterns of stimuli. Pattern recognition models include feature-analysis models and prototype models, among others (Baron and Ensley 2006). Feature-analysis models suggest that patterns are identified by their distinctive features (Baron 2004). Past patterns identified by individuals are stored in their mental models (see Chapter 2). When new patterns are observed, they are compared with the features of the stored patterns. The stored patterns in managers' mental models define what they might perceive as viable opportunities. Managers analyze observed stimuli and patterns, and if the observed patterns meet the distinctive features of the stored patterns considered in the past as viable opportunities, then such patterns will be recognized as indications of potential value opportunities.

An alternative to feature-analysis models for recognizing stimuli in the environment are prototype models. Managers construct prototypes of viable opportunities considered in the past and the prototypes are stored in the management logics. Prototype models of pattern recognition apply to more complex patterns related to innovative opportunities. An opportunity prototype contains the essential nature of an object or a pattern – that is, the cues that are most frequently observed with a group of opportunities – not necessarily the distinctive features of cues suggested by feature-analysis models. Managers may employ opportunity prototypes stored in their mental models to identify new value opportunities and analyze their viability.

Pattern recognition models assume that individuals consider observed patterns of stimuli as worthwhile when analyzing opportunities. Managers with entrepreneurial incentives are more likely to evaluate complex patterns in the environment to identify novel opportunities than nonentrepreneurial counterparts. Two theories, namely, signal detection theory and regulatory focus theory, may explain this phenomenon. Signal detection theory explains four possible situations related to cues for potential opportunities in an environment (Baron 2004): (1) an opportunity cue indeed exists and the manager categorizes the cue as an opportunity (considered as a "hit"); (2) an opportunity cue does exist but the manager fails to recognize the cue (considered as a "miss"); (3) the opportunity cue does not exist but the manager may conclude that the cue signals an opportunity (considered as a "false alarm"); and (4) the opportunity cue does not exist and the manager concludes that the cue is not an opportunity (a correct rejection and again a "hit").

Signal detection theory predicts the relative rate at which individuals may experience hits, misses, and false alarms in a given situation. Signal detection is based on several factors including the properties of cues (e.g., strong vs. weak signals), individual mental models, their cognitive capabilities (see Chapter 2), and the signal evaluation criteria (set by external arbiter or a priori by individual). Some managers in some situations may employ weak criteria to qualify a signal as an opportunity, while others in different situations may not qualify the same signals as opportunities. Whether an observed signal in the environment is to be considered as worthwhile as an opportunity cue depends on the executive attention and the evaluation criteria applied to a situation.

Regulatory focus theory suggests that managers, in regulating their attention focus, adopt one of two perspectives, namely, promotion focus or prevention focus, in that with a promotion focus a manager seeks a positive outcome but with a prevention focus the manager seeks to mitigate a negative outcome (Baron 2004). Regulatory focus theory predicts that an individual, when using a promotion focus, will generate several options and explore all possible means to reach the desired goal (Baron 2004). However, when the individual is using a prevention focus, they will generate fewer options and focus primarily on avoiding mistakes. Individuals may habitually differ in their attention focus or may adapt their focus to situational factors. Some individuals may employ a combination focus with different levels of prevention and promotion.

Regulatory focus theory, when combined with signal detection theory, offers a powerful explanation of why managers with entrepreneurial incentives are more likely to recognize value opportunities than their nonentrepreneurial counterparts. Signal detection and regulatory focus theories combined predict that managers when adopting a promotion focus are likely to get more hits (or they recognize an opportunity when it is present) and avoid misses (or they do not miss an opportunity when it is indeed present). When managers adopt a prevention focus, they are likely to make correct rejections (or they conclude that an opportunity does not exist when it is indeed absent) and avoid false alarms (or they do not conclude falsely that an opportunity exists when it does not).

Managers who adopt a promotion focus are more likely to examine more combinations of patterns in an environment and thus are more likely to identify cognitively distant opportunities. These managers are also likely to use less stringent criteria for observed patterns to qualify as value opportunities. However, in such situations, false alarms can occur but the odds of finding superior opportunities are higher. Thus, the greater a manager's chronic disposition is to adopt a promotion focus, the more likely are they not to miss new opportunities. Further, entrepreneurial incentives enhance a manager's promotion focus.

With prevention focus, managers are more vigilant to make correct rejections and avoid false alarms. They use more stringent criteria for a signal to be qualified as an opportunity and thus they may qualify fewer patterns as opportunities in the environment. As a result, they are likely to miss more opportunities. When they do identify opportunities, these opportunities are likely to be of high quality. When managers adopt primarily a promotion focus with a mildly tempered prevention focus, they are more likely to find value opportunities and avoid false alarms, thus increasing the odds of seizing the value opportunities in a timely manner.

Managers with entrepreneurial incentives have a habitual disposition of promotion focus tempered with a mild prevention focus and are more likely to recognize cognitively distant value opportunities. In contrast, most investors (e.g., venture capitalists) have a habitual disposition of prevention focus with a mild promotion focus; so venture investors are less likely to recognize the opportunities in the first place, but because they have a prevention focus, the investors may use more stringent criteria to screen the opportunities identified by entrepreneurs, and thus the opportunities selected by investors are of higher quality. However, it is entrepreneurs who in the first place recognize value opportunities, whereas venture capital investors with a predominantly prevention focus only vet those opportunities. Furthermore, in the absence of entrepreneurial incentives, executives are more disposed to a prevention focus, and thus these executives may miss most value opportunities or recognize them too late.

Environmental changes may have a dramatic impact on the competitive landscape of an industry, but more importantly the industry is shaped by the actions and reactions of incumbent organizations. Environmental changes and the actions of incumbent organizations create more opportunities in an industry. Entrepreneurial organizations seek opportunities to disrupt the rules of competition in an industry and turn them in their favor. Managers seeking new opportunities should be aware of the rules and roles that govern their industry; the emerging technologies and regulations that might shift the rules of competition; competitor actions and reactions that have created opportunities in the industry; the resources that stand to gain from an environmental shock; potential changes in the rules of competition in an industry that is in turbulence; and assets that can cause bottlenecks in the industry supply chain.

Buaron (1981) lists several cues in an environment for managers to spot opportunities. Some of the cues include: the emergence of a new technology in the same or closely related industry; a head-on battle between major competitors; shifts in economic, regulatory, social, and political environments; shifts in market forces; the emergence of substitute technologies; major changes in raw materials; overcommitment by a market leader to a particular resource and thus loss of flexibility; industry in turbulence; new regulatory standards affecting the suppliers and customers; and long-term stability in an industry with little or no change.

Sources of Opportunities

Value opportunities may arise from unexpected occurrences in an organization, incongruities in industry practices, process needs, industry and market changes, demographic changes, changes in people's perception and preferences, and changes in technologies, among others (Drucker 1998). The value opportunities may differ in their risk, difficulty, and complexity. Unexpected successes or failures experienced by a firm often can be a source of value opportunities. A product aimed for one market may find opportunities unexpectedly in other markets. For example, computers were originally designed for scientific research but were found to have successful applications in business.

An unexpected failure with a new product can be a source of opportunity for the firm. Drucker (1998) cites the example of Ford's Edsel model, a new car model that failed but later became the foundation for much of Ford's success. Unexpected failures are productive sources of value opportunities but are often dismissed by management. Drucker advises that a company's monthly and quarterly reports should contain not only current problems and challenges but also a list of opportunities currently available to the organization. Further, managers should spend equal time in solving problems and developing new opportunities.

Product features, product consumption, and business model assumptions often contain product or process incongruities or inconsistencies that may suggest further value opportunities. For example, Alcon labs discovered an enzyme for cataract surgery by exploiting an incongruity or patient pain point in the cataract surgical procedure (Drucker 1998). Furthermore, often there are incongruities in a company's financials or in the economics of an industry that could be a source of value opportunities. For example, an industry that is steadily growing but the profit margin remains low can be exploited. Incongruities may be also found in industry best practices and competitor financials.

Incongruity between the management's expectations and the organization's performance may open up new opportunities. Management should continually examine their assumptions about how their business works. The change in management assumptions regarding how the business works or incongruities in management assumptions can produce new opportunities. Business models and technologies employed in one industry can be a source of value opportunities in other industries, in that the successful business models and technologies can be profitably adapted by entrepreneurial organizations.

Industry structures and competitive forces periodically change (in some industries and environments, more quickly), which can provide a firm with tremendous opportunities. A rapidly changing and uncertain environment is a source of numerous value opportunities. Environmental uncertainty and market dynamism are not enemies but the friends of entrepreneurial managers. The more proactively adaptive organizations are in a given industry or the more dynamic that industry is, the greater is the number of value opportunities available in the industry. Drucker (1998) provides the example of the health care industry in which ongoing changes have resulted in numerous opportunities for managers and entrepreneurs.

Drucker observes that when an industry's growth is in the neighborhood of 40 percent in ten years or less, the industry has already undergone structural changes and the rules of competition have changed. Market leaders are often complacent with their successes and miss the changes in the industry structure. The agile and alert new entrants take advantage of the changes in the rules of competition and make inroads into the industry. Entrepreneurial organizations actively adapt to uncertain environments and exploit available value opportunities.

Demographic changes are the most reliable sources of value opportunities. For example, Japanese companies pay greater attention to demographic changes than American companies. Drucker (1998) explains that Japanese leadership in the robotics field came about because of their advantage in anticipating demographic changes. Many managers know that demographic changes matter but they believe these changes are rather slow. In a dynamic global economy, demographic changes such as consumer income, education, occupations, age distribution, and geographic mobility have been changing rapidly. Demographic changes thus lead to "the most rewarding and least risky of entrepreneurial pursuits" (Drucker 1998: 6).

Changes in consumer perception can be a source of value opportunities. Drucker (1998) provides an example. The progress in modern medicine has greatly improved the longevity of human life. Rather than rejoicing in the positive aspects of the progress made in the longevity of life, people all over the world have become more health conscious and are more worried for their health. Perceptual changes in consumer preferences have created value opportunities in health care, nutrition, and fitness industries. Alert managers with entrepreneurial incentives anticipate and continually revise their assumptions about consumer perceptions, and quickly respond to exploit available opportunities. Drucker (1998) notes: "A change in perception does not alter facts. It changes their meaning though – and very quickly" [6].

New knowledge, be it scientific, technical, or social, often creates massive opportunities. Knowledge-based opportunities differ from other value opportunities in that they are more risky; they require a long lead time to develop into useful products, processes, or services; they are more challenging for companies to manage; their acceptance by consumers is rather slow and uncertain; and they often require complementary technologies and resources a company may or may not have. For example, computer hardware products would not have been successful without software technologies. Thus the developments of several technologies and knowledge areas must converge for a knowledge-based value opportunity to be successfully exploited. Drucker (1998) argues that knowledge-based value opportunities are more market timing dependent than other value opportunities. Therefore, market timing is critical to the success of knowledge-based opportunities. Furthermore, knowledge-based value opportunities require the firm to have access to complementary assets such as process technologies, production systems, and marketing capabilities to profitably exploit value opportunities (Teece 1986).

Innovative Opportunities

Creative processes to shape value opportunities include conceptual combinations, analogies, and problem formulation strategies, among others. Creative processes manipulate the existing knowledge base of a firm to create novel ideas for new products or technologies. Conceptual combination involves combining two or more previously separate concepts into a single concept with novel properties that were not present in earlier separate concepts. Analogy is a mapping of knowledge from a familiar domain onto a less familiar one. The problem formulation approach can be abstract or concrete, and the abstract approach to problem formulation can generate superior opportunities.

Conceptual combination is mentally merging previously separate concepts to form a new concept, be it a new product or a new process. Especially effective is combining two or more contrasting ideas. Novel ideas are generated by merging opposing ideas. For example, a new product, "nonalcoholic beer," is potentially more appealing to health conscious individuals. Similarly, one may consider the opposing wants of consumers (e.g., excitement and tranquility, comfort and ruggedness, etc.) to develop novel product opportunities.

Combining two separate concepts can have emergent features that can be novel). Even simple combinations of ideas can create emergent novel opportunities. When the concepts are opposing, the emergent features of the combination is especially novel. Diverse needs of consumers may be combined to generate novel ideas for new products. Similarly, diverse market segments can be combined to create new market segments. Further, elements of separate business models can be combined to create innovative business models.

Another creative process to configure value opportunities is to use analogical reasoning, a process of projecting knowledge from a familiar domain to a less familiar one. Good analogies connect a familiar domain to a less familiar domain at a deeper level, but not superficially. Further, the distance between the two domains mapped determines how distant or close an analogy is. Distant analogies generate more innovative value opportunities but they can be more risky.

Another way to configure novel opportunities is how one defines and formulates the problem. The premise of this approach is that the way people conceptualize a problem strongly influences the likelihood of generating novel solutions. A problem formulation approach that can generate more options increases the likelihood of finding a novel product solution. Existing knowledge is necessary for problem solving but the way one retrieves that knowledge can have a major effect on the novelty of the solution. There may be external constraints on how existing knowledge can be accessed within an organization. Individual mental models can also enhance or constrain their approach to problem formulation, resulting in more or fewer novel solutions. Novel value opportunities can be generated using an abstract or conceptual approach to problem formulation.

Opportunity Options

An opportunity option gives the firm a right but not an obligation to act on an underlying value opportunity. The firm's knowledge resources embody opportunity options available to the firm. The firm's knowledge resources are embodied in the firm's human capital, social capital, technology assets, and management systems. The knowledge capital is the firm's "invisible assets," continually enhanced with active learning and combinative capabilities. Furthermore, entrepreneurial organizations have a greater learning capacity that enhances their knowledge resources continually and with their promotion focus more opportunity options are available to these organizations. The exercise of the opportunity options results in the series of real options that enable the firm's resource orchestration.

Bowman and Hurry (1993) view organizational resources and capabilities embedding opportunity options as potential future opportunities available to the firm. Opportunity options are unrealized value potential for the organization and are embodied in the knowledge resources. An opportunity option gives the firm preferential access to a future value opportunity. With the firm's opportunity options, the firm's knowledge resources are valuable. The opportunity options are valuable unless the underlying opportunities have expired or not been preempted by competitors. However, without exercising and exploiting the valuable opportunity options in a timely manner, the knowledge resources may not enhance the firm performance.

The firm's opportunity options are valuable as long as the options have positive time value (i.e., there is time left before the underlying opportunities expire). When the window of an opportunity underlying an opportunity option shuts, the opportunity option expires and the value of the option drops to zero. The more uncertain an underlying value opportunity, the greater is the value of the opportunity option. The firrm's knowledge resources are valuable a priori when the embedded opportunity options have not expired or not been preempted by competitors.

Opportunity options are often difficult to recognize. The firm's opportunity options are the options on available value opportunities, in that an opportunity option gives the firm the right to seize a future value opportunity with the risk of losing only a small cost of experimentation. Further, the investment in an opportunity option is minimal since the investment cost of experimentation is staged over time, and the option can be abandoned if the learning outcomes are not favorable. Thus a full commitment is not made to a value opportunity at the beginning when the opportunity option is recognized. Opportunity options when exercised, that is, when the value opportunities are seized, result in a sequence of real options to acquire tangible and intangible assets. Thus the exercise of the real options requires a series of future investments by the firm and a reconfiguration of the firm's resources and capabilities. The firm's opportunity options are thus compound options (i.e., the options on real options).

The firm's core resources that embody knowledge capital embed bundles of opportunity options; and as the firm acquires new knowledge, their opportunity option portfolio is enhanced. The cost of learning and experimentation is the cost of the opportunity options. The firm's portfolio of opportunity options is enhanced by the firm's active learning and absorptive capacity. However, the firm's opportunity options are often difficult to spot. It is the management's job to recognize and exercise valuable opportunity options in a timely manner. In general, resource focused traditional managers may not recognize the firm's opportunity options, or recognize them too late. However, the entrepreneurial incentives enhance the entrepreneurial orientation of the firm and hence their opportunity focus, which enhances the manager's ability to spot the firm's opportunity options before the options expire and the exploitation of the value opportunities underlying the options in a timely manner providing the manager an entrepreneurial surplus and the firm an entrepreneurial rent. The entrepreneurial rent is the excess profit for the firm and the entrepreneurial surplus is the excess compensation for the manager relative to their peers for pursuing cognitively distant value opportunities that may carry excess firm-specific risk.

Pattern recognition models described earlier can help managers identify cognitively distant value opportunities and opportunity options. Managers with entrepreneurial incentives have a greater promotion focus and are more likely to recognize the firm's opportunity options. Furthermore, exercising an opportunity option, that is, seizing a value opportunity may create additional opportunity options. When an opportunity option is exercised and the underlying opportunity is seized by the firm, a sequence of real options is acquired by the firm to invest in assets resulting in a new configuration of the firm capabilities.

Further, exercising the firm's opportunity options enhances the business model (see Chapter 5). The business model is the firm's value creation and appropriation mechanism. The entrepreneurial incentives and the resultant entrepreneurial culture nurtured in a firm increase the likelihood of recognizing and exercising of the firm's opportunity options in a timely manner and thus enhance the business model value creation and appropriation. Active learning that enhances the firm's core resources further enhances the firm's bundle of opportunity options. The option creation cycle enhances the firm's business model advantage as the exercise of the opportunity options triggers the acquisition and exercise of the real options, enhancing the firm's opportunity portfolio and core resources. The firm's opportunity set and capabilities are thus reconfigured simultaneously as the business model adapts to changing competitive conditions (see Chapter 5). Active learning enhances the firm's opportunity options. Further, enhanced situation awareness determines when to exercise the existing opportunity options. Active learning enhances the firm's dynamic capabilities that reconfigure the organizational capabilities and value activities. Active learning enhances the firm's opportunity options and organizational capabilities.

The management logics and management's attentional engagement also influence the recognition and exercise of the firm's opportunity options. Further, sufficient situation awareness is necessary for timing the exercise of the firm's opportunity options. The management logics and the management goals enhance the situation awareness (see Chapter 2). However, management logics when not tested and updated regularly in a dynamic environment may inhibit recognition of the firm's opportunity options. Insufficient management attention resulting from the firm's poorly designed operating and governance channels can inhibit the management's recognition of the firm's opportunity options.

Barnett (2008) examines how managers attend to and act on the firm's opportunity options. The firm may have abundant opportunity options available, but the management when preoccupied with the current operations may fail to recognize or exercise the opportunity options in a timely manner. Gifford (1992) examines the conditions under which a management may allocate their attention between the firm's current operations and cultivating new value opportunities. As the management is preoccupied with the firm's ongoing activities, they have less attention available to sense and shape new opportunities for growth (Pensrose 1959). Management could give more attention to pursuing new opportunities, but that will require giving less attention to the ongoing operations. This implies a possible opportunity cost to the firm for pursuing new opportunities in that the opportunity cost of a new opportunity depends on how valuable the current operations are.

Gifford (1992) models allocation of management attention between sustaining current operations and pursuing growth opportunities. The model determines the optimal allocation of management attention and predicts the firm's innovation rate and growth rate. Gifford evaluates management attention based on two choices, namely, allocating attention to enhancing profits from the current operations or pursuing new value opportunities. Both activities require significant management attention. Information on the profitability of the firm's current operations as well as that of new opportunities can be acquired by allocating sufficient management attention. Furthermore, the profitability outcomes are uncertain. The expected value and uncertainty of the payoff from each alternative is a function of the amount of attention management allocates to the evaluation of the alternative. A new opportunity option can be evaluated only at the expense of neglecting the firm's current operations.

The relative importance between current operations and new opportunities depends on the sustainability of current operations. When the cash flows and current advantages are more sustainable, the value of the current operations is high enough to justify the allocation of more management attention to maintaining the current operations and resources, which results in a reduction in the firm's innovative efforts (Gifford 1992). When the firm's current advantages and sustainability of the current cash flows are temporary (e.g., in hypercompetitive environments), then the management may find exploring new value opportunities more lucrative than trying to improve the current operations. Further, when the new opportunities are more valuable, even though the profits from current operations and the firm's current advantages are sustainable, the management may still choose to allocate more attention to developing innovative opportunities. The firm will be more likely ambidextrous when the opportunity options are more valuable. The opportunity option is more valuable when the opportunity's present value-to-investment ratio is higher than the critical positive value warranted by the uncertainty associated with the given opportunity.

Williams and Mitchell (2004) found that organizational channels that control the flow of information in the organization and regulate the management attention, determine how managers attend to new opportunities. According to the attention-based view of the firm, the procedural and communication channels of the firm situate and distribute the management attention (Ocasio 1997). Management goals guide the management attention and hence the management incentives that situate management goals influence the management's ability to identify and exercise the firm's opportunity options.

Management attention is a scarce resource in a firm, and the management acts on the stimuli they attend to. Bowman and Hurry (1993) recognize the difficulties the management may have in identifying and correctly timing the exercise of the opportunity options. It is difficult for the management to recognize the triggering stimuli in the environment without their sufficient situation awareness. The situation awareness thus regulates the timing of the exercise of the opportunity options. Further, Busby and Pitts (1997) found that management's behavioral considerations could prevent a firm from exercising the opportunity options. Real option theory does not consider the management motives; thus adverse incentives can prevent the management from exercising the firm's opportunity options and real options in a timely manner. The entrepreneurial incentives thus enhance the firm's recognition and exercise of the opportunity options in a timely manner, enhancing the firm's value creation and appropriation mechanism.

Entrepreneurial organizations with their opportunity focus are more likely to recognize and exercise opportunity options in a timely manner and thus are more likely to achieve growth and competitive advantage. Entrepreneurial organizations have enhanced and regularly updated management logics that provide the managers sufficient situation awareness to spot cognitively distant value opportunities, according to our entrepreneurial logic. Therefore entrepreneurially oriented organizations are more opportunity focused and are likely to recognize and exercise the opportunity options in a timely manner. Further, proactive and opportunity driven managers with the entrepreneurial incentives are effective risk managers in that they proactively exploit the environmental uncertainty in the firm's favor; thus these managers do not necessarily abhor the high uncertainty associated with the cognitively distant value opportunities. Moreover, the opportunity focused managers understand that there are more valuable opportunity options in a more uncertain environment. Furthermore, the firm's environmental uncertainty increases the range of possible future values resulting from an opportunity, making it more likely that an opportunity option will be in the money and will be exercised.

Entrepreneurial organizations proactively exploit the environmental uncertainty in their favor by creating a portfolio of opportunity options through active learning and experimentation. Upon the resolution of the high uncertainty associated with the underlying opportunities, some opportunity options cultivated by the firm become worthwhile to be exercised. Some opportunity options will be left unexercised and discarded.

Furthermore, "organizations that hold options during unstable periods and strike options in stable periods will show superior long-term growth and profit performance" (Bowman and Hurry 1993: 767). To identify and exercise the firm's opportunity options in a timely manner, the management must have sufficient situation awareness, which is possible with entrepreneurial incentives that enhance management logics (see Chapter 2). As the management achieves greater situation awareness of their environment, they are more likely spot and exercise more opportunity options in a timely manner. With enhanced management logics and situation awareness, the management spends less time on opportunity exploration and more on opportunity exploitation. The entrepreneurial incentives enhance the management learning that further enhances the management logics and situation awareness.

Small investments in experimentation with and exploration of opportunity options and the timely exercise of opportunity options enhance the firm's core resources that further enhance the portfolio of opportunities available to the firm. Opportunity options expire when the window of opportunity underlying the opportunity option closes, usually through a preemptive action by competitors. Bowman and Hurry (1993) suggest that two trigger signals are important to a timely exercise of opportunity options. One signal is for the management to know when an opportunity option should be exercised; and the other signal is for the management to be alert to actions of competitors such that the opportunity is preempted and thus the opportunity option has expired. Trigger signals may include, among others, changes in customer preferences, technologies, rules of competition, and competitor actions.

Opportunity Timing

The portfolio of opportunity options of an entrepreneurial organization may be compared to an active gardener's tomato garden. Luehrman (1998: 90) observes: "a garden of tomatoes in an unpredictable climate. Walk into the garden on a given day in August, and you will find some tomatoes are ripe and perfect. Any gardener would know to pick and eat them immediately." The ripe tomatoes may be obvious in a tomato garden to a gardener's eyes but a firm's high value opportunity options are not as obvious to most managers. Further, the gardener discards rotten tomatoes (i.e., expired opportunity options), and tomatoes not yet ripe have varying prospects. "Some are edible and could be picked now but would benefit from more time on the vine. The experienced gardener picks them early on if squirrels or other competitors are likely to get them. Other tomatoes are not yet edible, and there is no point picking them now, even if the squirrels do get them" (Leuhrman 1998: 90). Some tomatoes are sufficiently far along, and when there is enough time left in the season, they might ripen. Some look less promising and will not make it.

A firm's portfolio of opportunity options is like a garden of tomatoes with varying prospects. Some opportunity options can be exercised now, some may be later, some are to be discarded (by stopping experimentation and abandoning opportunities), and some are to be cultivated further with investments in experimentation and learning before final considerations may be made. An active gardener is able to classify the prospects of the tomatoes in their garden; similarly a manager with enhanced management logics and sufficient situation awareness can classify the firm's opportunity options into different categories based on their readiness to be exercised at a given time. Good gardeners also understand how the garden changes over time, so do managers with entrepreneurial incentives, who proactively exploit the competitive landscape.

What does a gardener do in the meantime when waiting for tomatoes to ripen? Leuhrman (1998) describes how different gardeners act. A weekend gardener visits the garden frequently and picks ripe tomatoes before they go bad or squirrels get them. A passive gardener would visit the garden the last day of the season and pick the ripe ones they can find. In the meantime, some tomatoes have gone bad or squirrels have stolen most of them. However, active gardeners do much more. They are not only watching as the tomatoes grow, they also actively cultivate the tomatoes by watering, fertilizing, weeding, and trying to grow more of them before the season runs out. The weather is always an issue for the gardener. Not all tomatoes are expected to make it. At the end of the season, active gardeners will collect more tomatoes than passive gardeners. Similarly, opportunity focused entrepreneurial organizations, like active gardeners, recognize and cultivate superior value opportunities than the organizations that are less entrepreneurial.

A manager powered by entrepreneurial incentives is like an active gardener, actively cultivating the environmental uncertainty and tending to the value opportunities underlying the firm's opportunity options by making small and incremental investments in experimentation to enhance the odds that the opportunity options will be worthwhile when exercised in a timely manner before the options expire or preempted by competitors. Further, just as active gardeners make more than simple pick or not-pick decisions, proactive managers make more than mere exercise or not-exercise decisions with the firm's opportunity options. They actively exploit the environmental uncertainty such that the firm's opportunity options will be more valuable for the firm.

Entrepreneurial organizations invest in experimentation and active learning to resolve the uncertainty associated with the underlying value opportunities in the firm's favor resulting in enhanced firm capabilities that improves the value-to-investment ratio of the opportunities. Entrepreneurial organizations thus proactively manage the uncertainty associated with the underlying opportunities; and further, they nurture the opportunity options such that the opportunity value can be enhanced and the cost of investment reduced, thereby improving the opportunity's value-to-investment ratio and the odds of exercising the opportunity options. Like active gardeners, entrepreneurial organizations don't allow "weather" or "squirrels" to determine the fate of the underlying value opportunities; instead, they proactively cultivate a portfolio of opportunity options, adapting to weather conditions and keeping squirrels away from the garden.

Consider the opportunity space shown in Fig. 4.1, adapted and modified from the one presented by Leuhrman (1998). The opportunity space is divided into five regions. In the tomato garden metaphor, region 1 contains ripe tomatoes; region 2, imperfectly ripe tomatoes; region 3, promising green tomatoes; region 4, late blossoms; and region 5, rotten tomatoes to be discarded. The vertical axis in Fig. 4.1 measures the firm's risk of cash flow loss with the opportunity. The risk of cash flow loss with an opportunity can be estimated with the cash flow uncertainty associated with the opportunity's market demand uncertainty, product price uncertainty, or activity cost uncertainty. The numerical value is not as important as the direction of change in the uncertainty. However, managerial perception and estimation of the risk of loss will vary across firms and managers. Thus, a value opportunity for one firm may not be as valuable for another firm.

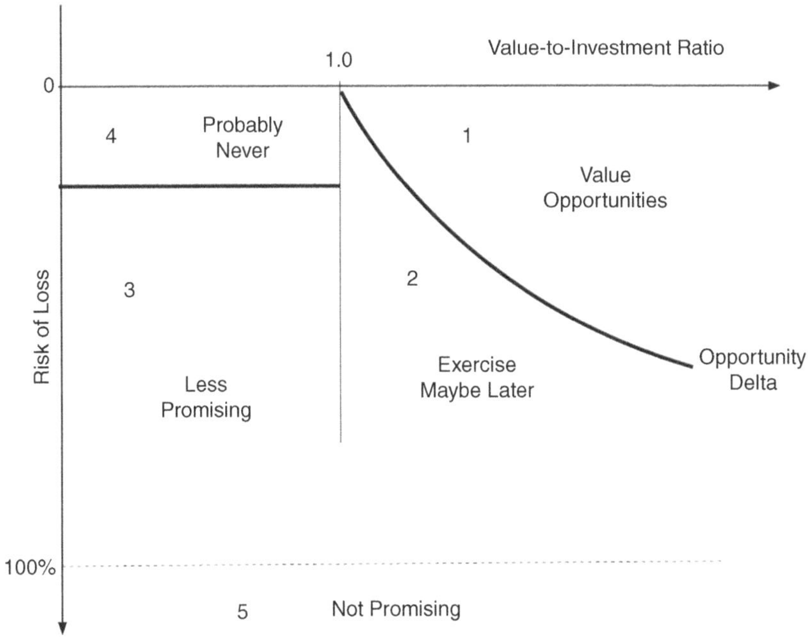

Fig. 4.1 Opportunity space (Adapted from Leuhrman 1998)

The horizontal axis in Fig. 4.1 is the value-to-investment ratio of the opportunity. The investment in an opportunity is the cost of the resources and activities if the opportunity option is exercised and the underlying opportunity is seized. The firm's cost estimate of the resources and activities to exploit an opportunity is improved as the firm gathers more information about the opportunity through learning and experimentation. The value of the opportunity is the present value of the expected cash flows from the opportunity including the time value of the options associated with the opportunity. The estimates improve with information and experimentation. Note that the value of an opportunity option cannot be negative as the value of an option is positive or zero. Further, the net present value of the opportunity underlying an opportunity option is negative when the opportunity value-to-investment ratio is less than one, but is positive when its value-to-investment ratio is greater than one. The value of an opportunity option is positive, because of the option's positive time value, as long as the underlying opportunity has not expired.

With positive risk of loss with an opportunity, the value-to-investment ratio for an opportunity must exceed one. The uncertainty is the firm's risk of loss with the opportunity. In an efficient market, however, the cost of an investment in an opportunity equals the value of cash inflows; thus, in an efficient market with no information asymmetry, the value-to-investment ratio of an opportunity is one. However, with market inefficiencies and imperfect information (adverse selection), the critical value-to-investment ratio for a firm to qualify a value opportunity rises at an increasing rate with the firm's risk of loss since shareholders expect an increasingly higher rate of return with greater uncertainty (risk of loss) associated with the firm's value opportunities.

The opportunity may have synergistic effects on other products or processes of the firm. The synergistic cash flows should be also considered. The cost of investment is the present value of investment outlays required to exploit the opportunity. The investments include the product or process development costs including capital investment expenditures. Financing costs should be included in the cost of investments. The cash flows and investment cost estimates may be revised as management evaluates the opportunities and gathers more information. Firms actively nurture the opportunity options to resolve the uncertainty in the firm's favor, as they actively learn and develop organizational knowledge that supports multiple opportunities. Active learning improves the management's value-to-investment ratio and the risk of loss estimates. The firm's cost of capital may be employed to discount future cash flows and investment outlays. Instead of using single-point estimates, managers may use a range of values for the estimates that can be obtained with simulation software such as Oracle's Crystal Ball (Mishra 2015). Mishra also shows how the risk of loss with an opportunity can be estimated using Crystal Ball.

An opportunity option is a compound option since exercising an opportunity option creates a sequence of real options for the firm to invest in future assets. When an opportunity option is exercised, an investment is made, and the investment creates a set of real options, such as the option to abandon the opportunity if the experimentation results are not favorable, the option to switch to another opportunity, or the option to defer a future investment, among others. The real options associated with an underlying opportunity should be identified and valued using a decision tree tool. At least major real options must be included in valuing the opportunity as these options are likely to influence the value of the cash flows associated with the opportunity. The cash flows in the decision tree model provide a probabilistic estimate of the value of an opportunity. The precision in numerical estimates is not as important as the direction of change in their values as the management monitors and evaluates the opportunities. As long as the same models are applied consistently when considering the movement of an opportunity from one region to another in the opportunity space (see Fig. 4.1), the numerical precision of values is not as important. The discounted cash flow and decision tree models are readily available in popular spreadsheet software.

Figure 4.1 shows five regions for management action with respect to the firm's opportunity options associated with potential opportunities. Management action may vary from one firm to another for the same opportunity since the managerial perception of the uncertainty associated with the opportunity and the managerial estimates of the opportunity value may vary. In addition, a firm may have different set of real options associated with the same opportunity as each firm has a different resource bundle. An opportunity option may move from one region to another as the opportunity is monitored and more information is gathered. The estimates of the opportunity's value-to-investment ratio and the risk of loss with the opportunity are continually monitored as more information is gathered over time through experimentation and learning. As noted earlier, the direction of the change in the management estimates and the use of the same valuation models consistently are more important than the precise numerical values of opportunities.

Furthermore, entrepreneurial organizations actively exploit the uncertainty associated with an opportunity. A manager empowered with entrepreneurial incentives is not necessarily to take action to reduce the uncertainty but to proactively exploit the uncertainty in the firm's favor. When an opportunity option is exercised, an initial investment is made by the firm. However, the investment in the opportunity is made in several stages. Moreover, the staging of the investment in an opportunity limits the firm's risk of loss in case some outcomes turn out to be unfavorable. By staging the investment in an opportunity underlying an opportunity option, the management actively learns, develops new organizational capabilities, enriches the firm's core resources, creates additional opportunity options, and proactively exploits the uncertainty with the opportunity to resolve in the firm's favor.

The investment in an opportunity is made in several stages; each stage is a real option on the next stage. Thus, each stage investment is a compound investment option. These resultant investment options can be monitored in the opportunity space as well. For example, a second investment in an opportunity may be deferred until the outcome of current investment turns out to be favorable, or management may choose to abandon the opportunity altogether. Active learning occurs with staged investments in the firm's opportunities, which further enhances the firm's core resources. Further, stage learning helps the management refine their estimates of the opportunity value and risk of loss. Learning benefits are always captured by the organization by enhancing their core resources. Even though a firm may choose to finally abandon an opportunity, the learning effects enhance the firm's core resources that further enhance the firm's portfolio of opportunity options.

Exercising Opportunity Options

Now returning to Fig. 4.1, consider region 1. In this region, the opportunity delta exceeds one; that is, the opportunity value-to-investment is higher than the critical positive value warranted by the risk of loss associated with the underlying opportunity. A value opportunity to be seized must have the opportunity delta that exceeds one.

When the opportunity delta exceeds one and the opportunity is in region 1, the opportunity option may be exercised and the value opportunity may be seized. When an opportunity moves to region 1, the opportunity option may be exercised and thereby the value opportunity is seized. The exercise of the opportunity option requires an investment in firm resources. The investment may be made in stages and thus a series of real options are created. Therefore, there need not be a full commitment to an opportunity when the opportunity is seized.

Now consider region 4, where the value-to-investment ratio of the opportunity is less than one, and most of the uncertainty with the opportunity is resolved or the window of opportunity is about to close. It may be too late to take advantage of the opportunity, in which case the opportunity option will be likely abandoned. This might happen when the time has run out with the opportunity, competitors have preempted the opportunity resulting a crowded competitive space, or a technology is leapfrogged. In the tomato garden metaphor, region 1 contains ripe tomatoes, and region 4 contains either late blossoms or the ones stolen by squirrels.

Consider region 2 in Fig. 4.1. The opportunity's value-to-investment ratio exceeds one but the opportunity delta is less than one (i.e., the region lies to the left of the opportunity delta curve). The net present value of the opportunity is positive; however, the present value does not exceed the positive critical value appropriate for the risk of loss associated with the opportunity. The possibility, however, exists that the opportunity option may move to region 1. In this region, the opportunity option may still be exercised if there are early mover advantages. Wernerfelt and Karnani (1987) propose that it is optimal to seize an opportunity early before the uncertainty is completely resolved if there are early mover advantages and the management has the ability to influence the way the uncertainty can be resolved. The firm may have access to some strategic resources that gives the firm an advantage to resolve the uncertainty associated with the opportunity to resolve in the firm's favor. Moreover, early mover advantages are greater in some industries, especially in technology industries or in high-growth industries with high customer switching costs, intellectual property protection, network externalities, or learning effects.

Furthermore, entrepreneurial organizations may have the ability to actively influence the way the uncertainty with an opportunity is resolved. In industries with early mover advantages or in firms with specialized assets to influence the direction of uncertainty resolution, the opportunity options in region 2 may be exercised even though the opportunity delta is less than one. When a firm has a strategic resource to influence the opportunity uncertainty to resolve effectively in the firm's favor, it is optimal to exercise the opportunity options in region 2. Otherwise it is optimal to defer the exercise of region 2 opportunity options. Thus, the firm's strategic resources are valuable when they enhance the value of the firm's opportunity options.

In region 2, opportunity options are in the money (i.e., the intrinsic value of the option is positive or the value-to-investment ratio exceeds one) but the opportunity is not ripe enough to be seized since the opportunity delta is less than one. The exercise of opportunity options may be deferred in region 2. However, as stated above, early mover advantages and the presence of specialized and co-specialized resources warrant the exercise of these opportunity options. Using the tomato garden metaphor, in region 2, the tomatoes are picked early even if they are imperfectly ripe but they are edible (that is, if we predict that squirrels will get them otherwise). Otherwise the exercise of opportunity options in region 2 is deferred. The change in the environmental variables changes the value-to-investment ratio and the risk of loss estimates with these opportunities as the firm continues to monitor them.

Consider region 3 in Fig. 4.1. In this region, the value-to-investment ratio is less than one and the risk of loss with the opportunity is high. These opportunities are probably too early to act upon. Management will actively monitor and cultivate these opportunities; and when the payoff from the opportunity is such that the opportunity delta exceeds one and the opportunity moves to region 1 or region 2 (with early mover advantages or specialized resources), the opportunity option may be exercised, possibly before the window of opportunity closes. With high uncertainty, the time value of the opportunity option is high. To decide which of these opportunities the firm should monitor, the management may use some heuristics to rank order the available opportunities (e.g., using payback period, the internal rate of return, or another investment rule) and monitor the ones that are more acceptable to the firm.

In region 4 in Fig. 4.1, the value-to-investment ratio is less than one but most of the uncertainty is resolved. It may be too late to exercise these opportunity options. In tomato garden metaphor, region 4 contains late blossoms. The firm's opportunity options in region 4 are less promising. However, region 3 opportunity options are more valuable than those in region 4. Using the tomato garden metaphor, region 3 contains promising green tomatoes and region 4, late blossoms. In region 4, tomatoes are unlikely to ripen before the season ends, or the value opportunities expire or likely to get preempted by competitors. In region 4, the management may perceive that the window of opportunity is about to close. It may be too late to exploit these opportunities profitably (e.g., a technology that is about to change or a customer preference that has changed). In region 4, the uncertainty is low and thus the time value of the opportunity option is low. These options are less valuable. In contrast, the uncertainty is high in region 3 and these opportunity options are more valuable and they are more likely to move into regions 1 or 2. Thus, the opportunity options in region 3 are more valuable than those in region 4 for the same level of the value-to-investment ratio.

Region 3 opportunity options should be nurtured through experimentation and learning even though these options are out-of-the-money at present. An opportunity option in region 3 may move to region 2. Region 4 opportunities are late blossoms and the opportunity options in this region may never be exercised. Region 5 contains rotten opportunities and should be quickly discarded. There is no positive probability that the opportunity might succeed in that the risk of loss in region 5 is greater than 100 percent. An opportunity option may fall in one region for one firm and in another region for another firm since the managers perceive the risk of loss with the opportunity differently and their estimates of the opportunity value-to-investment ratio may vary. The management logics influence the manager's estimates of an opportunity's value-to-investment ratio and the risk of loss and thus influences the decision to exercise the opportunity options. Further, entrepreneurial organizations proactively exploit the type of uncertainty associated with an opportunity, and thus they can maneuver an opportunity option to move from a less desirable region to a more desirable region.

When an opportunity option is exercised and the opportunity is seized, it triggers a series of real options. A real option gives management the right to invest in a real asset or a capability, and thus enables the firm's dynamic capabilities. Exercising a real option by investing in a resource or capability may create additional real options. Real options further include flexibility options, growth options, switching options, deferral options, and abandonment options, among others. Entrepreneurial organizations proactively manage the firm's real options associated with an opportunity to exploit the uncertainty to resolve in the firm's favor. The real options enhance the firm's dynamic capabilities that support the risk management capacity. The real options enable the firm to enhance their capabilities, or investments are made to develop or acquire new capabilities. Initially when an investment is made in an opportunity, the net present value of the underlying opportunity may be negative, but as long as there is a positive probability that the return to the firm with the opportunity will exceed the investment cost of the opportunity (see Fig. 4.1), the value of the opportunity option is positive.

Entrepreneurial organizations explore multiple opportunities when their resources and knowledge assets permit. However, Wernerfelt and Karnani (1987) propose that managers may concentrate their resources on one opportunity as opposed to developing or pursuing multiple opportunities simultaneously, when the opportunity has high-scale economies and the management can actively influence the way the uncertainty with the opportunity is resolved. Wernerfelt and Karnani further propose that the greater the number of competitors in an industry is, the greater are the incentives for the management to act early and commit to the opportunity. Large firms without a resource constraint may bet on several value opportunities even when one of the opportunities has large economies of scale and early mover advantages. In contrast, a firm with resource constraint has no choice but to bet its available resources on one value opportunity so its limited resources are not spread too thin across multiple opportunities. Further, within our entrepreneurial logic, a firm when it chooses to focus on one opportunity does so where the management can actively influence the resolution of the opportunity uncertainty in the firm's favor or improve the opportunity value-to-investment ratio. Further, a firm with a competitive disadvantage will bet on a more risky opportunity with a smaller chance to win a large payoff than a large chance to win a smaller payoff.

Opportunity options are embodied in the firm's knowledge capital which is embedded in the core resources. As the firm actively learns, it acquires new knowledge and thus its opportunity options multiply. However, management is not always cognizant of all opportunity options available to a firm. Management logics enhance the management's situation awareness that further enhances the management ability to recognize the opportunity options available to the firm including the trigger signals indicating when to exercise the opportunity options. Further, experimentation and active learning in organizations enhance management logics and hence the firm's situation awareness. Entrepreneurial incentives that enhance active learning in the organization further enhance the recognition and timely exercise of the firm's opportunity options. Failure to identify opportunity options or not exercise them in a timely manner is often due to stagnant management logics or poor attentional resources of the organization. Entrepreneurial incentives enhance the management logics and management's situation awareness that enable the managers to sense and seize cognitively distant value opportunities in a timely manner to build and sustain the firm's competitive advantage.

Exploiting Uncertainty

To proactively exploit the uncertainty associated with the firm's opportunity options, managers must develop and cultivate a broad range of opportunity options and maintain an active opportunity option portfolio. The portfolio of opportunity options is regularly updated and monitored, so that management does not fail to recognize and act on an opportunity in a timely manner. The organization thus exploits the uncertainty in their favor by exercising in-the-money opportunity options in a timely manner. The uncertainty is a friend of an opportunity focused entrepreneurial manager powered by entrepreneurial incentives, not their enemy. The opportunity options enable entrepreneurial organizations to take advantage of change in the environmental conditions that is most likely in the firm's favor. Entrepreneurial organizations are quick to recognize the firm's opportunity options.

To act in a timely manner does not mean to act first or even early. Early mover advantages are not always present. A first mover may not always gain competitive advantage over others. An opportunity focused manager is always quick to act when the opportunity option is in the money. Not all opportunity options in the firm's portfolio will pay off, and some will be discarded or left unexpired. Some opportunities will expire when their windows are shut or preempted by competitors. Some opportunities have a shorter window. An unexpired opportunity option is always valuable when there is a positive probability that its opportunity delta might exceed one, but it does not mean that the option is currently in the money; that the net present value of the underlying opportunities can be currently negative. By proactively exploiting the uncertainty associated with the opportunity, the management nurtures the opportunity option to favor the firm and enhance their business model advantage.

Strategies to proactively exploit the opportunity in the firm's favor depend on the nature of the uncertainty. The uncertainty associated with the firm's opportunities may be defined at five levels. At level 1 uncertainty, the firm's environment is stable and the future is predictable. At this level, forecasting the future is helpful. The environmental elements are relatively stable and predictable. Level 2 uncertainty can be described as a future that consists of few discrete scenarios (Courtney et al. 1997). It is difficult to predict the outcome but it is possible to attach probabilities to the alternate scenarios. At level 2, the environmental variables are not randomly distributed; rather, they are clustered or hang together in certain ways such that it is possible to divide the future into discrete scenarios (Emery and Trist 1963).

Moderate to high-velocity environments, however, demand more strategic flexibility. In a more uncertain environment, it is difficult to predict discrete scenarios. It is not helpful to use standard financial valuation tools. Level 3 uncertainty contains a range of future scenarios on a continuum (Courtney et al. 1997). Thus the future cannot be described by discrete scenarios. The potential outcomes are defined by a limited set of key environmental variables. The opportunity outcome can lie anywhere on a continuum bounded by a predictable range. The span covering the range of potential outcomes is however fairly predictable under level 3 uncertainty. Level 3 uncertainties often associate with opportunities in emerging industries and emerging markets. Moreover, level 3 uncertainties often arise from the interaction of competing organizations in an industry. Firms have a sense of the general direction in which the market is evolving but it is difficult to predict discrete scenarios. Each firm's actions to enhance their competitive position are persistent.

Level 4 environments are hypercompetitive. Emery and Trist (1963) compare level 4 environment to "that of a company of soldiers marching in step over a bridge" [26]. As the firm's environment changes rapidly and firms actively seek to compete, the industry soon changes from a level 3 to a level 4. D'Aveni (1994) claims that "there are few industries in the United States and other parts of the world that have escaped hypercompetition" [155]. Even traditional, stable industries, such as aerospace, steel, and automotive, among others, now are hypercompetitive. Hypercompetition is "a condition of rapidly escalating competition based on price-quality positioning, competition to create new know-how and establish first-mover advantage, competition to protect or invade established products or geographic markets, and competition based on deep pockets and the creation of even deeper pocketed alliances" (D Aveni 1994: 1).

In a hypercompetitive environment, actions of incumbent organizations create a continual disequilibrium in the market. The organizations respond to the opportunities created by the continual disequilibrium, and their response escalates the level of competition and the level of uncertainty in the market. The environment thus escalates toward a higher level of dynamism and the competitive forces in the industry shift continually. Competitive advantages of firms in level 4 environments rapidly become obsolete. Thus competitive advantage is regenerated and sustained when the firm's business model configuration continuously morph in a hypercompetitive environment. The business model configuration constitutes the management logics, value opportunities, core resources, and value activities (see Chapter 5). In level 4 environments, a firm thus must continually create a series of new advantages to sustain superior performance even though the firm currently may be enjoying competitive advantage. Thus, firms in an industry continually attempting to create competitive advantage escalate the level of competition in the industry leading to a hypercompetitive environment.

Level 5 environments are hyperturbulent or ambiguous, such that multiple variables interact to create an environment that is virtually unpredictable. In level 5 environments, turbulence is further intensified as environmental changes exceed the collective adaptive capacities of organizations sharing the environment. Further, it might be impossible to identify, much less predict, all the relevant variables that will define the future. Level 5 uncertainties are rare but they could exist in an industry, albeit temporarily. However, over time hyperturbulent situations mitigate as the industry transitions to level 3 or 4 conditions.

Strategies for Exploiting Uncertainty

Courtney et al. (1997) describe three moves for managers to proactively exploit an uncertainty in the firm's favor, namely, big bets, options, and no-regrets. Big bets are major capital investments or acquisitions that might result in large payoffs in some scenarios but large losses in others. For example, shaping opportunities might make big bets. Second, options strategies are designed to secure large payoffs in some scenarios while minimizing the losses in other scenarios. Most options involve making modest investments to reserve-the-right-to-play in the future. Finally, no-regret moves are actions that will pay off no matter what.

It is possible to be an industry shaper in a level 1 environment but that is risky (Courtney et al. 1997). Shaping opportunities attempt to alter long standing industry logics. The best level 1 proactive adapters enhance the firm value through product or business model innovations, without fundamentally changing industry rules. Level 1 adapters may make some big bets but in that case they will hedge their positions using options strategies. Best proactive adapters in level 2 situations closely monitor trigger signals in the market. Trigger signals are often simple to identify in a level 2 environment. Since it is relatively easy to monitor the trigger variables, it can be easy to proactively adapt in level 2 environments. Level 2 adapters may use the reserve-the-right-to-play strategy by making small upfront investments in opportunity options that give the firm privileged access to value opportunities in the future as the future unfolds in a discrete predictable manner.

In level 3 situations in which the future scenarios are not discrete but lie on a continuum in a predictable bounded range, industry shapers try to move the market in a general direction towards a desired outcome. However, in level 3 situations, since it is not possible to predict the discrete futures, the firm cannot predict a discrete outcome. Thus, the firm will try to move the market in a general direction towards a desired discrete outcome. Shaping opportunities may involve big bets hedged with options to give the firm flexibility to adjust the course.

Adapters in level 3 situations primarily make investments in resources that increase the firm's flexibility and keep their opportunity options open. An investment in flexibility is sensible in level 3 situations for proactive adapters. A common strategy for a firm in level 3 situations is the reserve-the-right-to-play by making small investments in opportunity options. Opportunity options provide the firms strategic flexibility in reserving the right to make investments later if the outcomes of their earlier investments turn out to be favorable.

In level 4 situations, no player knows the best strategy, so the role of shapers is crucial in bringing a sense of direction to the industry (Courtney et al. 1997). Even though the uncertainty is high in level 4 situations, the payoffs are higher for shapers than in level 2 or 3 situations. The market demand is uncertain and potential products are continually redefined in level 4 situations, with the players still figuring out the rules of competition. Shapers by coordinating the strategies of other players in the industry provide a vision for the industry and bring order to the product market with possibly a more favorable outcome and higher payoff for themselves. However, the shapers must have high credibility in their industry or own dominant resources to have the acceptance of other players.

In a high-velocity environment, shaping opportunities create order by reducing the level of industry uncertainty. A shaping opportunity increases the likelihood that a favorable scenario will emerge in the firm's favor. Shapers may make big bets to build new capacity in the industry before there is an upturn in market demand to preempt competition, or they may consolidate the industry through mergers and acquisitions. However, best shapers in level 4 environments must be prepared to proactively adapt their course when necessary, so they may use opportunity options to build flexibility in their strategy. Best shapers hedge their bets with opportunity options so that if required they can change their course quickly.

Reserving the right to play using opportunity options is common in level 4 situations but given that the rules in the industry are still evolving, the investment in resource flexibility may not pay off (Courtney et al.

1997). The difficulty in managing opportunity options in level 4 situations drives the firm towards an adapter strategy in which firms adapt to the vision and standards set by the industry's dominant players. With the adaptation strategy firms make investments in resources in areas led by dominant players. Dominant players create platform standards for other players to coalesce around and as a result the industry logics evolve.

Level 5 situations are transitional in nature often occurring after a major technological or legislative shock. Most strategies for level 4 situations apply to level 5 environments but the risk of loss is high and the payoff is low. Shapers try to provide a vision for the industry but it is too risky for the shapers. Investments in flexibility and opportunity options may not be as effective since the rules of competition are truly ambiguous. Customer demand and preferences are highly uncertain. New opportunities abound but no one knows who will win or lose and when industry transitions occur. Incumbent firms may be overtaken by upstart new entrants. Dominant players take time to emerge since it is not credible that large firms with deep pockets can provide a vision. However, level 5 situations are rare; and when they occur, they are of short duration.

Adverse Investment Incentives

In this section we consider adverse managerial incentives associated with opportunities, namely, escalation of management commitment to a failing opportunity, overinvestment in negative net present value opportunities, underinvestment in positive net present value opportunities, and management overconfidence. Management overcommitment arises when mangers believe that further investment of time and effort can turn around a failing investment. The overinvestment problem may arise with excess financial slack in a firm that has few growth opportunities. Further, management overconfidence may lead to an overinvestment problem when the firm has financial slack. The underinvestment problem may arise when adverse selection exists with high growth opportunities.

Managerial Overcommitment

Managerial overcommitment is a tendency of management to "throw good money after bad" in support of their prior investments in opportunities where the outcomes are uncertain. Most managers tend to be optimistic and overconfident about the prospects of a new opportunity.

Further, staged investments in an opportunity that should minimize the risk of investment loss often create an escalation of management commitment to the opportunity. Management may find it difficult to abandon an opportunity when they are vested in it. Overcommitment may occur for several reasons including management's self-justification (Brockner 1992), the firm's reward system, management's loss aversion (Kahneman and Tversky 1979), and the firm's capital budgeting system, among others. It is important for management to know when to change the course and abandon the pursuit of an opportunity.

Overcommitment applies to "situations in which losses have resulted from an original course of action, but where there is the possibility of turning the situation around by investing further time, money, or effort" (Staw and Ross 1989: 216). Scholars assume that the means of overcoming overcommitment are by management engaging in more effortful and analytical decision processes. However, merely pursuing analytical decision-making processes may actually escalate management commitment (Hodgkinson and Healy 2011). Thus, managers with rational styles may feel the pressure to vindicate their prior choices more intensely. Rational decision making may escalate management commitment because management may attend to the underlying causes of unfavorable situations once these are made salient or clear to them (Staw and Ross 1989).

Obvious determinants of possible overcommitment to a failing opportunity are whether an unfavorable outcome is judged to be a temporary setback, whether further investment can correct the problem, and how large is the payoff resulting from continuing the investment. Further, management's previous experience with similar projects can escalate their commitment to a current initiative. Some investments, such as a new product or process development, have a long delay between the investment and payoffs; in such cases losses are expected to occur in the beginning, thus increasing the possibility of escalation of management's commitment. In some situations, the costs of shutting down a project are substantial, thus leading to the continuation of the project in spite of large losses. In other situations, managers already may have incurred large investments in the projects and thus they are trapped into continuing the projects so that they may escape public embarrassment for their failure.

Psychological variables may influence the escalation of management commitment. Sunk costs may be economically irrelevant in deciding to continue an investment but they are certainly psychologically important to management. Prospect theory (Kahneman and Tversky 1979) suggests that managers may be more risk seeking when they view a situation as a losing situation since they believe continuing investments hold the promise of turning around a bad situation. Self-justification and self-inference biases are other psychological causes of commitment escalation by continuing failed investments. Self-justification is when managers try to justify their prior choices. As a result managers try to save the ongoing projects by committing additional resources. Self-inference conditions (Kisler 1971) resulting in an overcommitment to ongoing projects occur when the manager's actions are explicit or unambiguous, when their behavior is irrevocable and not easily undone, when the manager has initiated the action, when the project is important to the manager, when the project is highly visible, and when similar projects were undertaken in the past (Staw and Ross 1989).

Self-regulation is suggested as an important means of overcoming overcommitment. Self-regulation involves individuals controlling internal ego-protective goals. Most overcommitment situations are driven by personal ego. Further, when considering whether to continue a failing investment, stimulating negative emotions in individuals such as a prevention focus rather than a promotion focus may alleviate escalation of management commitment. However, as prospect theory suggests, due to their loss aversion, managers may become more risk seeking and further escalate their commitment hoping that additional investments may turn around the firm's failing opportunities. Moreover, staged investments in an opportunity based on performance milestones can theoretically de-escalate management overcommitment, but in practice many managers do not use milestones since it is often difficult to determine the milestones in advance.

Capital Market Adverse Incentives

Unless the firm has sufficient cash to fund their current operations and new opportunities, the firm will need external capital. The firm raises external capital by issuing equity, debt, or both in the capital market. The implication of capital market financing is that management may have to forego some positive net present value opportunities in certain situations to act in the best interests of the shareholders. In these instances the firm has an underinvestment problem. The underinvestment problem, however, does not arise because of agency costs from a lack of incentive alignment between shareholders and managers. The underinvestment problem arises because of the adverse selection in the capital market due to information asymmetry between managers and external investors. Managers always have more real time information than do capital market investors. It is difficult for external investors to perfectly assess the true value of a firm, or its resources and opportunities, in spite of detailed disclosures required by regulatory agencies. Managers often present the most favorable information about their firm and attempt to suppress unfavorable information in their regular communication to external capital providers. Moreover, certain company information is proprietary and competitively sensitive, and thus management will try not to provide such information to external parties for fear that it may be used by competitors.

Myers and Majluf (1984) show that the financial slack in a firm may alleviate the underinvestment problem when growth opportunities are present. Financial slack is the cash on hand, unused debt capacity, and marketable securities of the firm. It is the liquid assets that are immediately available to the firm to invest in current operations or new opportunities. Further, the greater the financial slack, the less is the firm's reliance on external finance. However, the greater and more uncertain a firm's growth opportunities, the worse is the adverse selection in the capital market and the worse is the firm's underinvestment problem. In this situation, the greater is the need for the firm to carry sufficient financial slack. Financial slack relaxes the firm's reliance on external capital and thus alleviates the underinvestment problem. However, when growth opportunities are absent, excess financial slack results in an overinvestment problem; that is, managers may invest the excess cash in the pet projects that have negative net present value.

Firms normally carry sufficient cash and marketable securities to finance their working capital associated with current operations. Myers and Majluf (1984), however, recommend the firm build up additional financial slack, especially when sufficient growth opportunities are present. A firm may build up financial slack by raising capital in regular intervals even when the firm may not need capital. The presence of sufficient financial slack ensures that the firm does not have to forego a value creating opportunity. Moreover, raising capital is a costly and time-consuming process. Further, investors penalize firms raising equity since investors believe that managers want to use the equity to fund their less valuable opportunities because the equity is cheaper for the firm when it is overvalued. Thus a new equity issue will depress the stock price of the firm. However, when the firm's capital raising program is regular and more predictable, equity investors may not penalize the stock price of the firm.

Furthermore, since raising capital is a time-consuming process, thus by the time external capital is obtained by the firm, a competitor may have preempted the opportunity, or the window of opportunity may have closed for the firm. Additionally, there is always uncertainty whether the firm will be able to raise the needed capital in favorable terms to justify an investment in the new opportunity. It is thus advisable for the firm to build up financial slack in excess of what is needed to sustain the current operations when growth opportunities are present. Further, it is also consistent with Penrose's (1959) theory of the growth of the firm, in that resource slack supports the firm's growth.

Myers and Majluf (1984) show that a firm may actually lose value by undertaking positive net present value opportunities in some situations when the external finance is used to fund the growth opportunities, in that these situations arise because capital market investors have incomplete information about the firm. This occurs even when agency costs are absent in that the management is acting in the best interests of the shareholders. Furthermore, there is no capital rationing by the capital market either, in that the firm is able to raise capital at a risk-adjusted cost when the firm needs it. Myers and Majluf show that management will refuse to issue new equity or debt to fund the new opportunities in some situations. However, if the firm is forced to raise capital in these situations, the firm will prefer debt financing to equity financing. The most preferred alternative for the firm is to use financial slack or internal cash flow. Thus there is a pecking order for financing new investments; namely, the firm's internal cash flow is preferred to the debt financing, and the debt financing to the equity financing.

Financial slack thus carries positive signaling value because without sufficient financial slack the firm would rather pass up a good opportunity. Thus, unless the firm has been pursuing a successful growth strategy in the past and raising capital regularly, investors would consider a new stock issue as a signal that the management considers the firm's stock is overvalued. Thus the new stock issue will depress the stock price. The value of an opportunity includes both a cash flow value and a growth option value. Investors may be able to estimate imperfectly the cash flow value with the information provided by the firm's management but it is difficult to estimate the firm's growth option value. However, the management has more information about the value of the growth option with the opportunity. The growth opportunity options create an information asymmetry between the firm and the external capital providers even when the management may disclose sufficient cash flow information at the time of issuing new stock. The main implication of capital market financing is that unless the firm has sufficient financial slack, management may not invest in all value opportunities.

Further, Myers (1977) shows that the presence of excess debt on the firm's balance sheet exacerbates the firm's underinvestment problem, known as the debt overhang effect (or agency costs of debt), and as a result, the firm will forego some positive net present value opportunities. The value of growth opportunities of the firm is inversely related to the level of existing debt of the firm. The firm's growth opportunities (e.g., opportunity options) are embedded in the firm's knowledge assets, as explained earlier in the chapter. The value of the firm's knowledge assets is thus reduced when the firm has excess debt.

The agency costs of debt or the loss of value in the firm's growth opportunities can be significant in high-growth firms such as technology firms. In high-growth firms, a significant proportion of value lies in the firm's growth opportunities, not in their current operations. It is the opposite in the case of low growth firms. The greater the firm's growth opportunities, the greater are the agency costs of debt and thus less debt financing is preferred in high-growth firms. Debt is typically issued to capture tax shields (i.e., interest on debt is tax deductible), but tax advantages have to be balanced with the disadvantage of the agency costs of debt.

Because issuing debt reduces the value of growth opportunities (thus the value of the firm's knowledge assets), debt financing is less preferred to the use of internal cash to fund the firm's growth. Firms may borrow against their existing assets to support their current operations. Firms could issue equity to fund growth opportunities but earlier we showed that equity is not desirable to fund growth opportunities because of the adverse selection in the capital market. Therefore, financial slack is most desirable to fund the opportunities in high-growth firms when the agency costs of equity are already minimized by aligning the interests of management with those of shareholders through powerful entrepreneurial incentives.

Firms with greater financial slack, unless management incentives are aligned with those of shareholders, incur agency costs of equity and thus these firms may become attractive takeover targets (Jensen 1986). Jensen proposes the free cash flow theory of takeovers, which postulates that a firm with excess free cash flow or financial slack incurs high agency costs; and the market for corporate control disciplines the management in that the incumbent management is replaced by the acquiring firm. The free cash flow is the excess cash available after the firm has invested in positive net present value opportunities. The greater the free cash flow, the greater is the financial slack of the firm. We have argued that financial slack is beneficial for a high-growth firm when the entrepreneurial incentives are present.

Jensen (1986) considers the market for corporate control as the managerial labor market. Jensen shows that a firm with high free cash flow is an attractive takeover target in the market for corporate control, and the target firm's management is replaced by the acquiring firm. Excess financial slack thus can be a liability and poses a takeover threat when the firm does not have sufficient growth opportunities, or when the capital market cannot determine whether the firm has sufficient growth opportunities (e.g., the firm has not been growing in the recent past).

Jensen proposes that debt financing can discipline firms with excess free cash flow as the free cash flow will be used to service the firm's debt. However, because the debt will increase the agency costs of debt, debt financing can reduce the value of the firm's growth opportunities and thus the value of their knowledge assets. With debt financing, the management may forego some positive net present value opportunities. Thus debt financing may not be optimal for high-growth firms to discipline an incompetent management; and therefore the market for corporate control could be more effective. In low growth firms, however, debt financing may discipline an incompetent management and reduce the agency costs associated with excess financial slack.

In Fig. 4.2, the firm's financial slack is on the horizontal axis and the firm's growth opportunities on the vertical axis. When the financial slack is high but the growth opportunities are low (bottom-right quadrant in Fig. 4.2), the agency problem postulated by the free cash flow theory arises and the management might overinvest (i.e., invest in negative net present value opportunities). The market for corporate control may discipline these managers, and the acquiring firm with high growth opportunities can use the excess financial slack of the acquired firm.

The firm's underinvestment problem is shown in the top-left quadrant in Fig. 4.2, where the growth opportunities are high but the financial slack is low. Some growth opportunities will be passed up because the management will be unwilling to raise external capital since there is not enough financial slack to fund the growth opportunities. Raising equity

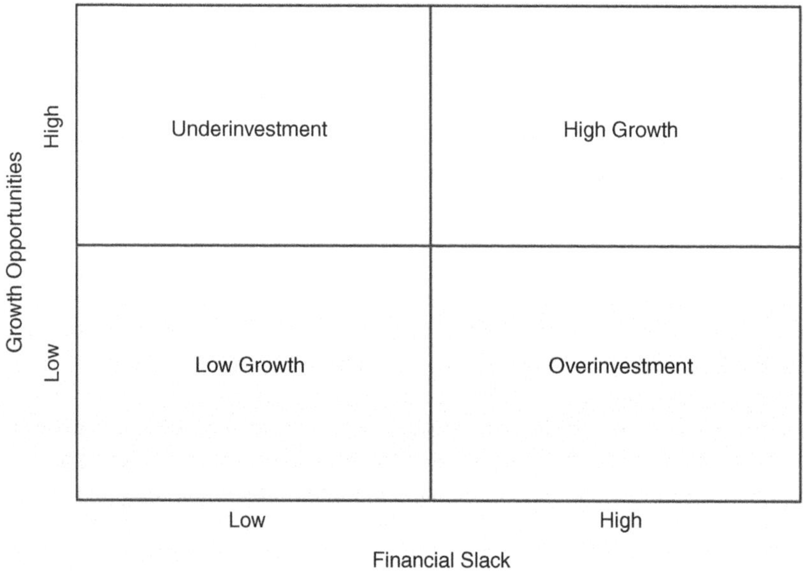

Fig. 4.2 Investment incentives

capital to fund growth opportunities will actually depress the value of the firm's stock. Firms in the top-left quadrant are also attractive takeover targets since acquiring firms with sufficient financial slack can exploit the acquired firms' growth opportunities. Further, high growth results when the firm has high growth opportunities and sufficient financial slack to fund these opportunities (top-right quadrant in Fig. 4.2). These firms use a regular capital raising program to replenish their financial slack.

The firms that are underinvesting in growth opportunities (top-left quadrant in Fig. 4.2) are potential takeover targets. These acquired firms would benefit from excess financial slack in the acquiring firms. Firms with a growth-resource mismatch (i.e., firms in top-left and bottom-right quadrants in Fig. 4.2) are candidates for takeover targets. Thus, low growth is optimal (in bottom-left quadrant in Fig. 4.2) for firms with low growth opportunities and low financial slack. Firms in the bottom-right quadrant in Fig. 4.2 could be also candidates for buyouts by private equity firms. Private equity firms acquire firms by financing the buyout price with high leverage and then using the excess financial slack to pay off the debt. Private equity investors restructure the acquired firms by cutting their spending on growth since not many profitable growth opportunities are available to the acquired firms.

High growth is expected from firms in the top-right quadrant in Fig. 4.2, when the firms carry sufficient financial slack and have high growth opportunities. However, if these firms fail to invest in their growth opportunities in a timely manner or when the financial slack is wasted by investing in management's pet projects, these firms could be potentially acquired by more entrepreneurial firms. The firms in the top-right quadrant in Fig. 4.2 need entrepreneurial incentives to achieve high growth, which provides the management an entrepreneurial surplus. However, in the absence of growth opportunities, firms should not build up excess financial slack; otherwise the firms will attract the attention of potential bidders and be acquired in the market for corporate control.

Management Overconfidence

Entrepreneurial incentives enhance the manager's promotion focus (disposed to believe in positive outcomes). They are more optimistic about the prospects of the firm and generally overconfident in their capacity to control the future of the firm. Managerial overconfidence arises from the "better-than-average" effect; that is, when managers are asked to evaluate their skills relative to their peers, they tend to overstate their abilities and evaluate themselves as better than average. These individuals believe they will succeed even when the likelihood of success is slim and their peers have failed in the past.

Overconfident managers have an internal locus of control; that is, they attribute their success to their actions and their failure to bad luck (Miller and Ross 1975). Overconfidence problems also arise from a manager's high promotion focus, a high belief in positive outcomes and a low belief in negative outcomes. Furthermore, overconfidence can arise when there is an illusion of control in that overconfident individuals believe they can largely control the future outcome. Overconfident managers use an abstract performance reference, which makes it difficult to compare their performance with their peers (Weinstein 1980). Further, overconfident managers are likely to overestimate the probability of a good outcome and underestimate the probability of a bad outcome. As well, overconfident managers overestimate the value of an opportunity and underestimate the risks.

Overconfident managers may overinvest when the firm has excess financial slack but not sufficient growth opportunities. The overinvestment problem thus occurs when the management invests in negative net present value opportunities. At the same time overconfident managers feel that the capital market undervalues their firm's stock and thus they are reluctant to issue new stock, thus creating an underinvestment by passing up positive net present value opportunities. Thus, overconfident managers may overinvest when the firm has excess financial slack, and may underinvest in the absence of sufficient financial slack. Therefore, the firm may have an overinvestment or underinvest problem with managerial overconfidence, even though the manager acts in the best interest of shareholders and there are no agency costs of free cash flow, or there is low adverse selection in the capital market. In addition, adverse selection problems with high growth opportunities and agency issues with free cash flow are exacerbated by the adverse incentives of managerial overconfidence.

Heaton (2002) explains the relationship between managerial overconfidence and strategic investments. In Heaton's model, there are no agency costs of free cash flow or adverse selection in the capital market. Managers act in the best interests of shareholders. The stock prices reflect the future value of the firms. Managerial overconfidence occurs when managers overestimate the probability of a good outcome or underestimate the probability of a bad outcome. The firm has no capital rationing; that is, the firm has unconstrained access to capital at a risk-adjusted cost.

Several implications are suggested by the managerial overconfidence model. First, a pecking order of financing preference arises, in which managers prefer internal cash to debt financing to equity financing when funding a firm's growth opportunities. Second, overconfident managers may fall short of meeting their cash flow forecasts since their cash flow projections are systematically upward biased. Third, managers perceive their stock is undervalued in the capital market and they are likely to repurchase their stock. Thus, overconfident managers are likely to repurchase their firm's stock when the growth opportunities are low but the financial slack is high. Further, managerial perception of the high cost of capital results in an underinvestment problem in the firm when the growth opportunities are high.

Fourth, overconfident managers overestimate the value of an opportunity and therefore they may overinvest in negative net present value opportunities. The value of opportunities is upward biased because the manager's cash flow projections are upward biased and the discount rate is downward biased because the risk factors are underestimated. Finally, overconfident managers are also more likely to resist takeover offers for their firm since they believe that bidders are not paying enough for their firm's stock. Their takeover resistance is not because of an agency problem since overconfident managers truly believe that in the best interests of the shareholders they must reject takeover offers unless bidders are willing to pay a sufficiently high price. In these instances the manager's resistance to takeovers arises from overconfidence in the firm's future prospects.

Summary

Entrepreneurial incentives empower managers to seek cognitively distant value opportunities to build and sustain competitive advantage. Value opportunities drive the value creation mechanism in a firm. A value opportunity is an opportunity that has the potential to enhance the firm value and the value added must commensurate with the opportunity risk and investment. Further, the opportunity options are unrealized value potential embodied in the firm's knowledge assets. The firm monitors and regularly evaluates its opportunity options. The timing of when to exercise an opportunity option and seize a value opportunity depends on the opportunity delta in that the net present value of a value opportunity must exceed a critical positive value. The opportunity delta is a function of the firm's risk of loss associated with the opportunity. The value opportunities enhance the firm's value creation and appropriation mechanism and enable the firm to renew or build competitive advantage. Value opportunities provide the firm the fuel to run the value creation engine.

To spot cognitively distant value opportunities may require that managers recognize complex stimuli in the environment. Superior opportunities are cognitively distant for managers. Opportunity recognition by managers is enhanced with the entrepreneurial incentives. Managers with entrepreneurial incentives overcome traditional behavioral rationality bounds and may spot cognitively distant value opportunities in a timely manner. Superior value opportunities lie in the environment in several sources including incongruities in industry best practices, misalignment in industry structure, demographic changes, underserved and overserved markets, changes in consumer perception and preferences, and regulatory and technology changes, among others.

Value opportunities differ in their uncertainty, difficulty, and complexity. Superior value opportunities are innovative and innovatively imitative opportunities that are cognitively distant and not visible to all firms. Entrepreneurial incentives enhance the firm's value opportunities. In Miles and Snow's (2003) typology, prospectors who pursue innovative opportunities and analyzers who pursue innovatively imitative opportunities are both entrepreneurial. Prospectors and analyzers both have high entrepreneurial orientation. Further, entrepreneurial organizations proactively manage a portfolio of opportunity options to exploit the uncertainty to resolve in the firm's favor. The greater the uncertainty, the more time left for the opportunity to expire, the greater the present value of the opportunity, or the lower the investment required to exploit the opportunity, the more valuable is the opportunity option. The more valuable are the opportunity options, the more valuable are the firm's core resources.

Value opportunities are classified under four categories: architectural opportunities, niche opportunities, regular opportunities, and revolutionary opportunities. Architectural opportunities create new firm competencies and new markets; niche opportunities enhance the firm's existing competencies while creating new markets; regular opportunities incrementally and continually enhance the firm's existing competencies and market linkages; and revolutionary opportunities strengthen the firm's existing markets while creating new competencies.

Some managers are more successful than others in identifying, shaping, and exploiting cognitively distant value opportunities. Entrepreneurial incentives enhance the managerial ability to recognize and exploit superior value opportunities. Managers with entrepreneurial incentives are alert, agile, and cognitively adaptive; they continually examine and enhance the management logics. Further, entrepreneurial organizations pursue value opportunities while attending to the needs of their existing operations; that is, they are ambidextrous. Entrepreneurial executives are more likely to overcome traditional behavioral rationality bounds and perceive complex patterns of stimuli in an environment. Entrepreneurial decision makers have a habitual promotion focus with mildly tempered prevention focus. With predominant promotion focus, executives with entrepreneurial incentives are more likely to recognize cognitively distant opportunities that traditional managers may miss because of their greater prevention focus and resource orientation.

The firm may be viewed as a collection of entrepreneurial business units. Each business unit may be viewed as a series of entrepreneurial startups which seek value opportunities and over time each startup creates competitive advantage that is only of a short duration. Thus the firm's long-term strategy should regularly identify a portfolio of value opportunities that each business unit can exploit in a series over time. Further, the strategy for each business unit should include a plan to transition from one opportunity to another. Such a long-term strategy for a firm needs entrepreneurial incentives that enable the managers to exploit a series of opportunities over time using a business model mechanism that continually adapts to changing market conditions.

Organizations enhance the business model mechanism when they exercise opportunity options and exploit the value opportunities. Opportunity options are unrealized value potential for an organization. Value opportunities are seized when the firm exercises opportunity options. Exercising opportunity options result in series of real options that enable the firm to reconfigure its resources and activities. The exercise of opportunity options enhances the firm's resource orchestration. However, it is difficult for managers to recognize triggering stimuli indicating the time to exercise the firm's opportunity options. Further, the firm's management logics and managerial incentives influence when managers recognize and exercise opportunity options.

Executives with entrepreneurial incentives are adept at recognizing the firm's opportunity options and exercising them in a timely manner. Entrepreneurial organizations actively cultivate opportunity options through active learning and making small investments in experimentation, and they proactively exploit the environmental uncertainty to resolve in the firm's favor. The entrepreneurial incentives increase the likelihood that the opportunity options will be in the money before the opportunities expire or are preempted by competitors. Opportunity options enable a firm to exploit environmental uncertainty and provide flexibility in a moderately to high-velocity environment.

Entrepreneurial organizations continually create and nurture opportunity options, and evaluate their opportunity space. The opportunities are thus identified and nurtured by the firm. The opportunity space predicts whether and when the firm's value opportunities are seized or the opportunity options exercised. Further, the opportunity space is defined by two key dimensions, namely, the opportunity's value-to-investment ratio and the opportunity uncertainty. When the opportunities lie above the opportunity delta curve in the opportunity space, they are ripe to be seized immediately by the firm. Other promising opportunities in the opportunities space are cultivated further. Some opportunities that are being cultivated may be discarded because they will never be seized by the firm. Managers with entrepreneurial incentives are successful risk managers who actively exploit the uncertainty and cultivate the firm's opportunity options such that the uncertainty associated with the opportunities resolves in the firm's favor (Mishra 2015).

Adverse managerial incentives associated with a firm's opportunity exploitation include management overcommitment to failing opportunities, overinvestment in negative net present value opportunities, underinvestment in positive net present value opportunities, and managerial overconfidence. Financial slack alleviates the firm's underinvestment problem associated with the adverse selection in the capital market, and thus financial slack enables a firm to invest in growth opportunities. However, in the absence of sufficient growth opportunities, financial slack increases a firm's agency costs and encourages managers to overinvest in negative net present value opportunities. Debt financing constrains the firm's value opportunities and reduces the value of the firm's core resources. Furthermore, managerial overconfidence can engender an overinvestment problem when the firm has excess financial slack.

CHAPTER 5

Business Model Mechanism

Introduction

The business model mechanism drives value creation and appropriation in the firm. The business model mechanism underlies the firm's competitive advantage. The business model mechanism is the powertrain that drives and sustains the firm value. The entrepreneurial incentives enhance the value creation and appropriation mechanism wherein the competitive advantage lies. The entrepreneurial incentive is the uncertain performance-based compensation in the executive pay, in that the performance is set by an external arbiter such as the capital market. Superior business models are scalable, sustainable, and adaptable. Further, the buyer value is created, delivered, sustained, monetized, and appropriated using the firm's business model (Mishra 2015).

The greater the buyer value added and the more of the buyer value appropriated by the firm relative to the competitors, the greater is the firm's business model advantage. The business model mechanism drives the firm's value creating activities and enables the revenue models and signaling activities to appropriate the value created. Value activities are the firm's activities that enhance the buyer value. The buyer value is created when the buyer cost is lowered or the buyer performance is raised, or both. The greater the buyer value added by the firm, the greater is the buyer's willingness to pay for the firm's product or service. The buyer value drivers are at the heart of the firm's business model design.

C.S. Mishra, *Creating and Sustaining Competitive Advantage*,
DOI 10.1007/978-3-319-54540-0_5

The entrepreneurial incentives to proactively exploit the market uncertainty in the firm's favor and act on the cognitively distant value opportunities in a timely manner are a source of competitive advantage. To seize and exploit value opportunities in a timely manner, the firm must regularly test and revise the management logics. Management must be alert to and focus their attention on the critical aspects of the environment to recognize cognitively distant value opportunities. Further, with high-powered entrepreneurial incentives, managers will seize and exploit cognitively distant value opportunities in a timely manner, enhancing the firm's value creation and appropriation mechanism that provides the firm competitive advantage. Thus, the competitive advantage lies in the firm's value creation and appropriation mechanism. Further, the entrepreneurial incentives enable a firm to create and sustain competitive advantage.

The business model mechanism implements and executes the firm's strategy, where the strategy determines where and how the firm competes to achieve a desirable strategic position. The business model implementation requires the firm to determine which buyer segments and buyer needs the firm will serve, how the firm will acquire and retain buyers, how the firm will create and deliver the buyer value, which revenue models and drivers the firm will employ, and what cost structure and drivers will support the value activities (Mishra 2015). The buyer value design is central to the business model mechanism. The business model mechanism acquires and retains customers, creates and delivers the buyer value, enhances the buyer's willingness to pay, optimizes the firm's value activities and cost structure, and thus enables the firm to extract and appropriate the value created. Thus, the business model mechanism constitutes the firm's value creation and appropriation drivers. The value creation is driven by the firm's value opportunities, core resources, and value activities. The value appropriation is enhanced by the firm's signaling activities and revenue drivers. The revenue drivers enhance the buyer's willingness to pay. The cost drivers must be optimized to achieve the business model efficiency. The cost drivers lower the activity costs.

The firm's business model advantage is greater when it is more efficient, sustainable, and adaptable. Entrepreneurial incentives enhance the business model efficiency, sustainability, and adaptability. The business model advantage is enhanced when the business model is scalable, sustainable, and adaptable. The business model advantage enhances the value appropriability. The efficiency provides the firm scale economies; the sustainability sustains the firm's cash flow growth; and the adaptability provides the firm flexibility in changing competitive conditions. The business model efficiency must be balanced with the business model adaptability. Further, the business model with balanced efficiency and adaptability is sustainable. The entrepreneurial incentives enhance the firm's dynamic capabilities that further enhance the business model advantage. Business model designs to sustain competitive advantage must adapt to changing competitive conditions.

In the literature, several definitions of the business model are available. Some definitions consider the business model as the management's hypothesis or mental model, etc. One useful definition found in Johnson et al. (2008) is that a business model constitutes four components, namely, buyer value proposition, a profit formula, key resources, and key processes. Another definition is that the business model creates, delivers, sustains, monetizes, and appropriates the buyer value (Mishra 2015). The buyer value design constitutes the choice of buyer segments the firm will serve, the buyer needs they will fulfill, and the product or service features the firm may offer, the price point the buyer will be more likely willing to pay, and the firm's marginal cost to serve a buyer (Mishra 2015).

The buyer criteria determine the buyer value design. The buyer value is central to the business model design. Buyer value propositions define what the firm provides its customers, at what price point, and at what cost (Mishra 2015). The firm's resources and capabilities enable the value activities (or the value chain). The firm's value activities generate the buyer value, and the revenue drivers and signaling activities enhance the buyer's willingness to pay and enable the firm's value appropriation. The value creation and appropriation mechanism that implements the firm's strategy and exploits the value opportunities underlies the competitive advantage.

The business model may use several revenue models targeting different customer groups and channels. Further, each revenue model may contain several revenue streams. Furthermore, each revenue stream may use more than one price point for different product configurations. The revenue model and its drivers are designed to enhance the buyer's willingness to pay, and the revenue model design must be consistent with the buyer value design. For example, a freemium model is a revenue model (not a business model as mistakenly used in practice). With freemium revenue model, the firm provides certain product features at no cost or low cost, and the other product features at a premium price.

Similarly, another example of revenue model is the razor-blade model in that a product is available at low cost to the customer but the accessories for the product are offered at a premium price.

Several revenue model choices are available to a firm. The revenue model design is tricky, however. For example, in a freemium model, the firm must determine which features should be offered at no cost and which features should be priced at a premium. The revenue models identify the revenue streams, pricing strategy, and revenue drivers underlying the firm's value appropriation mechanism (Mishra 2015). Revenue models are used interchangeably with business models. However, the business model mechanism that constitutes the firm's value creation and appropriation drivers include the core resources, revenue drivers, cost drivers, and value opportunities. The business model mechanism thus constitutes the value drivers enabling the firm's value creation and appropriation mechanism. Entrepreneurial incentives that enhance the management logics enhance the firm's value creation and appropriation mechanism. Further, the firm's combinative capabilities enhance the activity drivers that further enhance the business model mechanism.

Teece (2007) admits that a firm's success is contingent upon how astutely the business model is crafted. The business model design reflects what the buyers want, how the firm can best meet the buyer needs, and how the firm can get paid. Further, the business model design centers on the buyer value creation and a mechanism to appropriate the value created to sustain the value activities and pay the resource providers, including an adequate return to the shareholders who provide investment capital and to the employees who provide human capital, social capital, and knowledge capital. A firm may have a superior strategy, strategic resources, or superior value opportunities relative to the competitors, but without a superior business model implementation and adequate incentives for the management the firm is unlikely to achieve competitive advantage.

Our theory of entrepreneurial rent argues that the firm's competitive advantage lies in the value creation and appropriation mechanism powered by superior entrepreneurial incentives for the executives. The firm's superior strategy or strategic resources when executed with a poor or flawed business model is unlikely to achieve competitive advantage. Further, the extant strategic logics such as resource-based and positioning views assume that the implementation mechanism always creates and appropriates firm value when a strategic resource is present or an attractive strategic position is found. However, the source of a firm's competitive advantage lies in the superior execution of the business model powered by the entrepreneurial incentives even in the absence of superior resources.

The average variance in firm profits across firms in an industry is about four times larger than the average variance of profits across industries. Resource-based theories claim that the dispersion of firm profits across firms in an industry is due to the unique resources the firms possess. Porter (1996), however, proposes that it is not the firm's resource bundles but the activity systems that explain the profit dispersion in an industry. Porter asserts that the firm's activity drivers that enhance the value activities are the real sources of competitive advantage. The business model mechanism constitutes the firm's management logics, core resources, value opportunities, and value activities that are linked to the buyer value drivers.

Further, the buyer value drivers are enhanced by the firm's value opportunities, activity drivers, and core resources. Thus, the heterogeneity in the firm's choice of activity drivers, value opportunities, and core resources, and their linkages with the buyer value drivers may explain the profit dispersion across firms in an industry, according to our theory of entrepreneurial rent. The configuration of value opportunities, value activities, revenue models, and firm capabilities may vary across firms in an industry. Business model configuration differences thus may explain the profit dispersion across firms in an industry. The buyer value is enhanced when the business model configuration is efficient, sustainable, and adaptable.

The business model efficiency is enhanced by optimizing the value activities and activity drivers. The business model sustainability is enhanced when customer and supplier lock-in, business model novelty and specificity, and business model tacitness, complexity, and activity complementaries are high. Customer lock-in and supplier lock-in are high when the customer and supplier switching costs are high. Business model novelty and specificity is achieved when the firm's value activities can be configured in innovative ways to create and deliver the buyer value. Furthermore, the revenue models and revenue drivers can be configured in innovative ways to extract the buyer value created.

The business model novelty and specificity are enhanced when the value activities and revenue models are linked innovatively. Because of the tacitness and complexity of the business model configuration, business models are causally ambiguous and sustainable. Competitors may copy a high-performing firm's superior strategy, strategic resources, value opportunities, or value activities, but it is difficult for the competitors to copy and implement the firm's complex, tacit, and causally ambiguous business model configuration. The firm's business model configuration is a complex adaptive system. Business model configurations thus have an emergent order as the business model drivers adapt to changing competitive conditions. Furthermore, the organizations with high-powered entrepreneurial incentives revise their management logics continually and are likely to have more efficient, sustainable, and adaptable business models. Business models are more adaptable in entrepreneurial organizations in that the management has the incentives to proactively adapt the business model to changing competitive conditions. Thus, organizations that proactively adapt their business model configuration to changing competitive conditions are likely to be entrepreneurial. Entrepreneurial organizations are alert, agile, absorptive, proactive, adaptive, and opportunity driven (see Chapter 3).

Entrepreneurial organizations regardless of their resource position continually seek value opportunities and execute their business models with superior incentives, thereby enhancing the value creation and appropriation that further enhances the competitive advantage. The theory of entrepreneurial rent argues that the greater the entrepreneurial incentives in a firm or the more entrepreneurial a firm, the greater is the likelihood of the firm achieving competitive advantage. The entrepreneurial incentives enhance the business model advantage, namely, business model scalability, sustainability, and adaptability. Further, the entrepreneurial incentives enhance the firm's entrepreneurial orientation.

The business model mechanism constitutes the firm's management logics, core resources, value activities, and value opportunities. The entrepreneurial incentives enhance the business model mechanism, which sustains the firm's value creation and appropriation. The business model mechanism is enhanced by the firm's active learning, which is further enhanced by the entrepreneurial incentives in the firm. The buyer value drivers underlie the buyer value chain. The core resources link the firm's value chain to the buyer's value chain. Further, the business model enhances the buyer value added and hence the buyer's willingness to pay. The buyer value created is appropriated using the firm's revenue models.

The business model value drivers underlie the firm's value chain and revenue models. The business model value drivers are the firm's activity drivers, value opportunities, and core resources. The business model value drivers underlie the firm's value creation and appropriation mechanism that underlie the firm's competitive advantage. The entrepreneurial incentives in the firm enhance the business model value drivers. The activity drivers constitute the revenue drivers and cost drivers. The value activities and revenue models are linked to the buyer value chain and thus to the buyer value drivers. The activity drivers underlie the firm's value activities and are enhanced by the core resources and value opportunities. The revenue drivers underlying the firm's revenue models are linked to the buyer value drivers that enhance the buyer value and their willingness to pay. The buyer value is created by raising the buyer performance or lowering the buyer cost, or both. The revenue models enable the firm to appropriate the buyer created, which generates and sustains the firm's cash flow growth and hence enhances the firm value.

The primary value drivers underlying the value creation and appropriation mechanism are revenue drivers and cost drivers, which are enhanced by the firm's value opportunities and core resources. Further, the revenue drivers are linked to the buyer value drivers, which enhance the buyer's willingness to pay. The cost drivers are linked to the buyer value drivers, which lower the activity costs. The core resources and value opportunities enhance and sustain the firm value creation and appropriation. The activity drivers that enhance and sustain the buyer value enhance the activity differentiation. The activity drivers, value opportunities, and core resources enhance the value chain effectiveness and revenue model effectiveness. The business model value drivers must be consistent with the buyer value drivers. Furthermore, the business model configuration is a complex adaptive system and therefore the business model value drivers are emergent and self-organizing.

Figure 5.1 illustrates the firm's value creation and appropriation mechanism. The high-powered entrepreneurial incentives enhance the firm's management logics, value opportunities, core resources, and value activities. The greater the entrepreneurial incentives in a firm relative to the competitors, the more enhanced are the firm's active learning, combinative capabilities, dynamic capabilities, and management cognition, which further enhance the core resources, value opportunities, and value activities. The entrepreneurial incentives enhance the business model mechanism.

The core resources strengthen the linkages between the firm's value activities and the buyer value drivers. Entrepreneurial incentives enhance the management logics that further enhance the management cognition, which further enhance the value opportunities that are exploited by the business model mechanism to create the buyer value. Active learning and

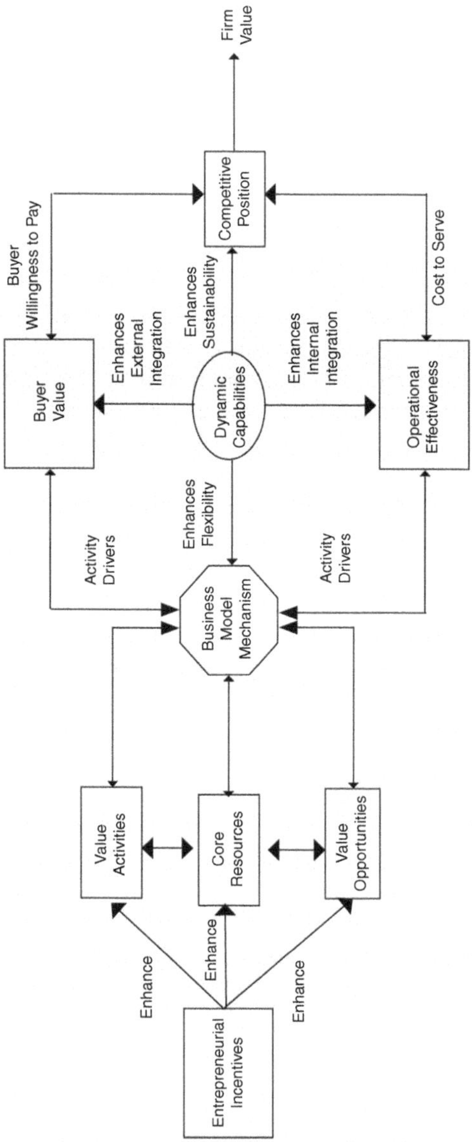

Fig. 5.1 Value creation and appropriation

combinative capabilities enhance the organizational capabilities and value activities. Further, entrepreneurial incentives empower the management team to earn an entrepreneurial surplus.

The business model mechanism implements the firm's strategy in that the business model configures the firm's value activities, organizational capabilities, and value opportunities that are consistent with the firm's strategic position. The entrepreneurial incentives that enhance the management logics further enhance the firm's strategic position, organizational capabilities, value opportunities, and value activities. The management logics enhance the linkages between the firm's activity drivers and the buyer value drivers, enhancing the firm value appropriation. The firm's management logics, core resources, value opportunities, and value activities are enhanced with the entrepreneurial incentives. The value opportunities enable the firm's value chain to sustain value creation. The entrepreneurial incentives enhance the proactive adaptation that further enhances the activity drivers, namely, the revenue drivers and cost drivers, underlying the value activities. The activity drivers are configured to maximize the firm's ability to create and appropriate the buyer value. Entrepreneurial incentives that enhance the firm's learning and management logics further enhance the value creation and appropriation mechanism.

The firm's strategy is the choices the firm makes regarding where to compete and how to compete. The business model mechanism implements the firm's strategy. The decision of where to compete is the choice of which buyer groups as well as what buyer needs to serve, and further, with which strategic groups to compete. The decision of how to compete and appropriate value will depend on the firm's choice of strategic position, namely, low cost position, or product or service differentiation. The firm's strategic position is further enhanced with the entrepreneurial incentives. Further, the value opportunities and value activities determine the firm's resource needs.

Entrepreneurial organizations with high-powered entrepreneurial incentives and enhanced management logics seize and exploit cognitively distant value opportunities in a timely manner. The active learning enhances the core resources underlying the activity drivers. Furthermore, the business model mechanism exploits the value opportunities to sustain buyer value creation and appropriation. The business model mechanism is self-realigning when the firm is proactive and entrepreneurial, in that the business model value drivers, namely, the firm's management logics, core resources, value opportunities, and value activities adapt in changing competitive conditions to sustain buyer value creation and appropriation. Further, the value creation and appropriation mechanism is enhanced by the management logics that are enhanced by active learning and entrepreneurial incentives. The firm's business model mechanism is the powertrain that sustains the value creation and appropriation and hence the firm's competitive advantage, powered by the entrepreneurial incentives.

The revenue drivers link the firm's value chain to the buyer's value chain. The buyer value chain creates the buyer value; that is, it enhances the buyer performance or lowers the buyer cost, or both. The buyer's willingness to pay depends on the buyer's perceived value of the firm's product or service. The buyer's willingness to pay further depends on the firm's signaling activities such as advertising, promotion, etc. The buyer value drivers are linked to the firm's revenue drivers that enhance the buyer's willingness to pay. The revenue drivers and signaling activities maximize the buyer value appropriated by the firm. The buyer value drivers underlie the buyer value chain, and the revenue drivers and signaling activities are linked to the buyer value drivers. The firm's revenue model effectiveness is measured by the ratio of the price the buyer is willing to pay to the buyer value added. The revenue drivers enhance the revenue model effectiveness and thereby the business model advantage.

The activity drivers, namely, the revenue drivers and cost drivers, underlie the firm's value activities. The activity drivers enhance the firm's value activities; that is, they enhance the activity performance or lower the activity cost, or both. The activity drivers enhance the value chain effectiveness and the business model advantage. The value chain effectiveness is the ratio of the buyer value added to the firm's marginal cost to serve. Furthermore, the revenue model effectiveness is the ratio of the price the buyer is willing to pay to the buyer value added. The business model advantage is the product of the value chain effectiveness and the revenue model effectiveness. The business model advantage is thus defined as the ratio of the price the buyer is willing to pay to the firm's marginal cost to serve. Entrepreneurial incentives enhance the firm's business model advantage.

A firm has competitive advantage when its business model advantage is greater than that of its competitors. The business model advantage enhances the firm's competitive position. The business model advantage and hence the competitive position of a firm change over time. The business model advantage is high when the revenue model effectiveness and the value chain effectiveness are high. Further, the revenue drivers determine the effectiveness of the revenue models employed by the firm; and the activity drivers determine the effectiveness of the value chain employed. The revenue drivers thus link the revenue models and value activities. The firm's management logics, revenue drivers, cost drivers, value activities, buyer value drivers, value opportunities, and core resources underlie the business model advantage. Entrepreneurial incentives enhance the business model value drivers that further enhance the business model advantage and the competitive position.

Dynamic capabilities and active adaptation enhances the firm's products and services, and the processes and value activities. Active adaptation further enhances the management logics and strategic position. Entrepreneurial organizations are proactively adaptive. Active learning enhances the firm's proactive adaptation in a dynamic environment or its dynamic capabilities. The entrepreneurial incentives that enhance active learning enhance the firm's agility, alertness, adaptability, and absorptivity. Further, active adaptation or dynamic capabilities enhances the firm's business model efficiency, sustainability, and adaptability, and hence the business model advantage.

Thus, the firm's dynamic capabilities and active adaptation enhance the value creation and appropriation and therefore the business model advantage. The greater the entrepreneurial incentives and the more enhanced the firm's active learning and adaptation, the more efficient, sustainable, and adaptable is the business model. Active learning in the organization enhances the firm's value potential and thus their ability to proactively adapt to changing competitive conditions. Further, the entrepreneurial incentives are greater when the firm's value potential is enhanced, and the executives may expect to earn an entrepreneurial surplus (see Chapter 3). The entrepreneurial surplus is enhanced with the firm's dynamic capabilities.

The more entrepreneurial the firm, that is, the greater the entrepreneurial incentives, the greater are the business model efficiency, sustainability, and adaptability, and the greater is the potential for the firm to achieve and sustain competitive advantage. Thus, the greater the business model advantage, the greater is the likelihood of the firm's achieving competitive advantage. The business model advantage enhances the firm's competitive position. Further, the business model advantage is the product of the value chain effectiveness and revenue model effectiveness. Thus, the business model advantage is the ratio of the price the buyer is willing to pay to the firm's marginal cost to serve. The business model advantage of firms in an industry can be compared to determine a firm's relative competitive position. The business model advantage enhances the firm value and shareholder return.

Buyer Value Drivers

The buyer value added is the increase in the buyer benefits or decrease in the buyer cost, or both. Buyer value links the buyer need to the firm's value offering at a price point the buyer is willing to pay (Mishra 2015). The price the buyer is willing to pay cannot exceed the buyer value added. Mishra provides a formula to estimate the maximum price a firm can receive from the buyer in a competitive market. The competitive price of a product or service is not necessarily the lowest price in the product category, nor is the competitive price always above the firm's marginal cost to serve. The firm's marginal cost to serve includes product development costs, production costs, distribution costs, and sales and marketing costs, among others. In the long run, the unit price of the product or service must exceed the unit marginal cost to serve for the firm to be profitable.

Buyer value is at the heart of the business model design. The business model mechanism creates, delivers, sustains, monetizes, and appropriates buyer value (Mishra 2015). The business model design fails when the buyer value offering is flawed; that is, when the buyer value offered does not enhance the buyer performance or lower the buyer costs. The business model design based on a flawed buyer value offering is not sustainable. The buyer value offering is configured by identifying the customer segments to be served, determining the customer needs to be met, developing product (or service) solutions and value propositions that enhance the buyer value added, and deciding a price point for the product offering which the buyer will be willing to pay. Flaws in any of the above choices will certainly fail the buyer value offering. The buyer value offering is an integral part of the firm's product market strategy. The buyer value design can be differentiated vis-à-vis the competitors in any of the above dimensions, namely, buyer criteria, product features, buyer benefits, price point, and unit cost.

To design the buyer value offering requires the effective segmentation of the market. The market can be segmented using demographics, sociographics, psychographics, geographies, and other creative segmentation strategies. A market segment is a homogeneous group of customers who share similar characteristics and preferences. A product or service may be viewed as getting the customer's job done or their problem solved. The more creative the market segmentation, the more effective is the buyer value design. Identifying unserved, underserved, and overserved customer segments and packaging a differentiated product offering to satisfy the buyer value criteria are central to the buyer value design. An effective buyer value design is at the heart of the business model design. Further, Mishra (2015) offers a framework to identify customer pain points and design a differentiated buyer value offering that enhances the buyer value.

The key drivers of the buyer value offering include the buyer criteria including the buyer pain points addressed, buyer benefits, buyer willingness to pay, product or service features, and the firm's marginal cost to serve (Mishra 2015). Further, the buyer value design is central to the business model design that creates, delivers, monetizes, sustains, and appropriates the buyer value. The business model drivers include determining the value opportunities, core resources, and activity drivers. The activity drivers support the value activities that create and deliver the buyer value. The activity drivers constitute the revenue drivers and cost drivers. The cost drivers lower the cost of value activities. The revenue drivers and signaling activities enable the firm to appropriate the value created. Furthermore, the value appropriated by the firm cannot exceed the buyer value added.

The buyer value is central to competitive advantage creation. The firm when designing a buyer offering chooses which buyer segments to target, which buyer needs or pain points to address, which buyer benefits must be offered, how the buyer benefits are differentiated, which product or service features are to be included, what price point the benefit bundle can fetch, and how much it will cost the firm to create and deliver the benefit bundle. The revenue drivers that extract and appropriate the buyer value underlie the revenue models that are linked to the buyer value chain.

The buyer criteria determine the buyer value offering. To determine the buyer criteria, consider the buyer's value chain in that the buyer is hiring the firm's product or service to get their job done or problem solved. Examine the buyer value chain that gets the buyer's job done and then identify the buyer hurdles or buyer pain points. The firm's product or service offering must help the buyer to overcome the hurdles in getting their job done or problem solved. Mishra (2015) provides a framework to identify the buyer pain points, and prioritize the pain points that can be addressed through the firm's product offering. The firm must decide which buyer hurdles or pain points their product offering will address and which benefits they will offer to meet the buyer criteria and enhance the buyer value.

Porter (1985) describes how the buyer value chain can be linked to the firm's value chain. A firm's product or service offering is a purchased input to the buyer value chain. It is important to understand the job the buyer wants to get done in order to understand the buyer value chain and determine the buyer value drivers. The firm's product or service offering should enhance the buyer performance or lower the buyer hurdles. The firm may focus on one or a few critical value activities in the buyer value chain. The product or service solutions link the firm's value chain to the buyer value chain. The greater the number of linkages between the firm's value chain and the buyer value chain, the greater is the potential to enhance the buyer's willingness to pay. The core resources enhance the linkages between the firm's value chain and the buyer value chain.

Buyer benefits offered by the firm must be chosen to address the buyer hurdles or pain points in getting the buyer's job done or problem solved. The buyer benefits offered enhance the buyer value by lowering the buyer cost or raising the buyer performance. The greater the buyer value added, the greater is the price premium the buyer is willing to pay. The buyer value added is the value of the buyer benefits minus the costs of getting the buyer's job done (or the cost of the buyer activities). The buyer may need complementary products or services in getting their job done, the costs of which should be included in the buyer costs. The buyer costs include not only their financial costs but the opportunity costs of their time and inconvenience as well. The financial costs of the buyer may be direct or indirect costs. The buyer value is also enhanced by raising the buyer performance, and the buyer performance can be enhanced by raising the buyer satisfaction or lowering the buyer risk of the product usage. It is easier to estimate the savings in the buyer costs with a new product offering than estimate the increase in the buyer satisfaction or reduction in the buyer risk of product usage.

The buyer benefits offered must enhance the buyer performance or lower the buyer costs, or both. Analyze the buyer's cost structure and identify opportunities that can significantly lower the buyer costs. The firm has several opportunities to lower the buyer costs, including lowering the buyer's installation and financing costs, direct and indirect costs of using the product, and expected costs of product failure, among others (Porter 1985). The firm may also enhance the linkages between its value chain and the buyer value chain by providing presale consultations and after-sale service support. In essence, the firm is a strategic partner to the buyer such that the buyer benefits offered enhance the buyer value. In seeking and prioritizing opportunities to lower the buyer costs, the firm must understand how their product will move through the buyer value chain or consumption chain. The firm must also understand the complementary products and services the buyer may need in addition to the firm's product or service in getting the buyer's job done or problem solved.

To raise the buyer performance a firm must understand the buyer expectations and the criteria they use to compare the firm's products with those of the competitors. The firm must understand the expectations not only of the end users but also those of payers, influencers, and purchasers. These different buyer groups have different motivations and criteria when judging the product performance relative to what is available on the market. The firm must also meet the minimum desirable performance criteria for its product to be seriously considered by the buyer. The buyer's expectations and criteria are important determinants in seeking opportunities to raise the buyer performance. For corporate buyers, the firm must also understand the buyer's buyers and the downstream value chains. It is important to meet and exceed the buyer's economic and noneconomic criteria and expectations. Noneconomic criteria include the buyer's reputation, status, tastes, and preferences.

With new products, there is an adverse selection problem because sellers often overvalue their products whereas the buyers are skeptical of product performance and sellers' claims. When introducing a new product, the product performance must be sufficiently superior to overcome buyer skepticism. It is difficult for buyers to assess the performance of a new category product. Not only it is difficult for buyers to assess the product performance, but also it is more difficult to assess how well the seller can provide customer support for a new product. Often buyers judge a product based on its price and fail to assess the hidden costs associated with the product usage.

Furthermore, buyers are often unaware of their value chain and the buyer value drivers underlying the performance of their value chain. Therefore, the firm must signal the value of the product and how it enhances the buyer performance and meets the buyer's latent criteria. The firm's signaling activities include customer education, advertising, endorsements, samples, promotion, etc. The buyer's willingness to pay for a product depends on the perceived value of the product. It is the perceived value of the buyer which is more important than the true value offered to the buyer. A firm that delivers modest buyer value but signals the buyer value more effectively can command a price premium compared to a firm that offers higher buyer value but signals weakly. In the long run, however, it is the actual buyer value created that determines the buyer's willingness to pay (Porter 1985).

The buyer's willingness to pay for a product depends on the sources of buyer value and the measurability of the buyer value added. The sources of buyer value include the factors that influence the buyer costs or buyer performance. The buyer's willingness to pay is often higher when the buyer costs are lowered and the cost savings are readily measurable. However, when the buyer value added is more difficult to measure, the buyer's willingness to pay will be lower. Moreover, the cost of the firm's signaling activities (e.g., marketing and advertising costs) will be higher when the buyer value is more difficult to measure. Thus, the firm's marginal cost to serve will be greater when the buyer value added is more difficult to measure. Further, it is more difficult to quantify the buyer value added when the sources of buyer value are the factors raising the buyer performance; therefore, in these situations the buyer's willingness to pay will be lower and the firm's cost of signaling activities will be higher.

Selection of product features is important in determining the buyer value configuration. Several combinations of product features can be envisaged to deliver the same buyer benefits. However, each buyer segment may rank their preferences for product features differently; thus, to enhance the buyer value added for a specific buyer segment, the product or service features must be carefully selected. Product features also drive the buyer's willingness to pay and their perceived value of the product. Further, the product features also determine the firm's marginal cost to serve. Moreover, the product or service features offered are constrained by the firm's resources and capabilities. In any case, the product features offered must meet the buyer criteria and enhance the buyer value added for the buyer segments served. Further, it is difficult to determine features of novel products especially when the new products require a change in the buyer's usage behavior. When a change in buyer usage behavior is expected, the firm's cost of signaling activities will be higher.

When designing the buyer value configuration and in identifying the buyer value drivers, the firm makes several determinations, namely, which buyer segments to serve and what the buyer criteria are, which buyer needs to address, which benefits to be offered, what determines the buyer's willingness to pay, what revenue model to use, what the firm's marginal cost to serve is, and what product and service features must be included with the product offering. The firm's goal is to enhance the perceived value of the buyer and increase their willingness to pay, while controlling the firm's marginal cost to serve. Not only must the firm enhance the buyer value, the firm must also capture the value created with an appropriate revenue model.

Activity Drivers

The activity drivers underlie the firm's value creation and appropriation mechanism. The activity drivers enhance the activity leverage and the value chain effectiveness. The activity leverage is measured by the ratio of an activity's contribution to the buyer value to the cost of the activity. Thus, activity leverage is enhanced when the activity enhances the buyer value, or the activity cost is reduced, or both. The activity leverage enhances the value chain effectiveness. The value chain effectiveness is the ratio of the buyer value added to the firm's marginal cost to serve. The activity leverage is a measure of an activity's effectiveness. When the firm's value activities are optimized, the activity leverage of individual activities and their complementaries are enhanced. Activity complementaries enhance the business model efficiency. Further, the activities that do not contribute to the buyer value are eliminated.

In the positioning logic, the source of competitive advantage centers on the firm's activity drivers (Porter 1996). A firm is a collection of discrete activities. The firm's strategy defines the value activities and how they interrelate. According to Porter, the firm's competitive advantage results when the value activities are performed at a lower cost or differently in that they enhance the buyer value. When the buyer value is enhanced, the firm may command a price premium. When the firm's activities are performed at a lower cost relative to its competitors, the firm has cost advantage. Similarly, when the firm's activities enhance the buyer value greater than the rivals can, the firm has differentiation advantage. The value chain effectiveness of the firm is greater relative to the competitors' with cost advantage or differentiation advantage. However, the activity drivers underlying cost advantage in an industry can be different from the activity drivers underlying differentiation advantage. Thus, few firms can achieve cost advantage and differentiation advantage at the same time since the underlying activity drivers may be at odds. Further, the corporate cultures in these firms employing cost or differentiation advantage are very different.

The core of competitive advantage, be it a cost or differentiation advantage, lies in the firm's activity system. The firm's activity system or value chain is the core of the value creation mechanism. The firm's value chain is linked to the value chains of the upstream suppliers and downstream buyers. The value chains of buyers include those of the distributors, retailers, and end users. The firm's business model determines how its value chain is configured such that it creates and delivers the buyer value differently or at a lower cost relative to the competitors'.

The firm's value chain comprises primary and support value activities (Porter 1985). The primary activities create and deliver the products and services that enhance the buyer value. The primary activities include product development, production, marketing, sales, service, logistics, etc. The support activities enhance the primary activities. The support activities include human resource, technology management, procurement, infrastructure, etc. The value activities of a firm are interdependent. The cost or performance of one activity may depend on one or several other value activities. The value activities are not only linked within the firm, they are also linked to the value activities of suppliers, distributors, and complementors.

The effectiveness of the value chain is dependent not only on the performance of value activities but also on the linkages between the activities both within and outside the firm. It is difficult to imitate a firm's activity system because of the complex linkages between activities. Many of the activity linkages are tacit and thus the value chain is causally ambiguous. Further, to perform value activities requires resources that may be tangible or intangible. The resources may exist inside or outside the firm. Tangible resources include physical assets, financial assets, and management systems. Intangible resources include the firm's human capital, social capital, and technology assets. The resources may be owned by the firm or available through partnerships, alliances, outsourcing, and other contractual relationships. Resource-based theory emphasizes that strategic resources underlie the firm's competitive advantage. However, strategic resources can become a liability and constrain the firm's value activities, thus resulting in a loss of firm performance.

When the strategic resources enhance the value chain effectiveness, they may provide the firm competitive advantage when the value created can be appropriated. However, when the firm resources, regardless of how rare they are, constrain the value activities, they do not provide the firm a competitive advantage. Further, according to our theory of entrepreneurial rent, when the firm's strategic resources enhance the linkages between the value chain and the buyer value, they are likely to provide the firm a competitive advantage. However, strategic resources, which are rare, hard to accumulate, immobile, and imperfectly imitable, when they weaken the linkages between the firm's value chain and the buyer value chain, do not provide the firm a competitive advantage.

Strategic resources are valuable when they enhance the value activities. However, the firm's activities that are inconsistent with the buyer's needs are not value activities; rather, they may create liabilities for the firm. Further, it is not that a rare and imperfectly imitable resource in and of itself can provide the firm a competitive advantage. When the firm's strategic resource enhances the linkages between the value activities, the strategic resource may sustain the firm's competitive advantage. To be sources of competitive advantage, resources must be considered within the context of the firm's value activities.

Furthermore, a firm's value activities exploit its value opportunities. The firm's strategy defines the value opportunities and the value activities, resources, and capabilities necessary to exploit the value opportunities. The business model mechanism implements the firm's strategy, and thus exploits the value opportunities to create, deliver, and monetize the buyer value through the value activities supported by the firm's resources. The greater the entrepreneurial incentives or the entrepreneurial orientation, the greater is the value chain effectiveness, and the greater is the likelihood that the firm may achieve competitive advantage. The value opportunities enhance the activity drivers; thus, the superior value opportunities are sources of superior performance. The entrepreneurial incentives enhance the value opportunities and value activities. Further, the core resources enhance the linkage between the value opportunities, value activities, and activity drivers. The activity drivers constitute revenue divers and cost drivers.

The activity drivers enhance the activity performance or lower the activity costs. Why do some firms perform the activities at a lower cost or in ways that enhance the buyer's willingness to pay? The entrepreneurial incentives enhance the firm's active learning that further enhances the activity drivers and the value chain effectiveness. The activity drivers that lower the activity costs are the cost drivers; and the activity drivers that enhance the buyer's willingness to pay are the revenue drivers. The cost drivers and revenue drivers underlie the firm's value activities and therefore enhance the value chain effectiveness. The activity drivers raise the buyer performance or lower the firm's marginal cost to serve, or both. The activity drivers are the sources of cost or differentiation advantage for a firm. The buyer value drivers underlying the buyer's value chain are linked to the activity drivers. The core resources link the activity drivers and the buyer value drivers.

The linkage between the activity drivers and the buyer value drivers enhance the value chain effectiveness. The core resources and value opportunities enhance the linkages between the firm's activity drivers and the buyer value. The importance and mix of activity drivers employed vary by business model design, firm, and industry. The value opportunities enhance the activity drivers. Thus, by identifying the activity drivers, it is easier to recognize the value opportunities. Why are some firms more successful even though they are investing in the same activity drivers that their competitors utilize? The answer lies in the entrepreneurial incentives that enhances the management logics and provides powerful incentives that further enhance the value creation and appropriation mechanism where the firm's source of competitive advantage lies. It is the firm's superior execution of value activities powered by entrepreneurial incentives, which provides the firm competitive advantage.

A firm identifies a valuable strategic position and the strategic position determines a set of value activities and the resources to achieve the strategic position (Porter 1996). The strategic positions available to a firm are a low cost position or a product differentiation position. Within each broad strategic position, the firm may focus on specific customer segments, customer needs, or customer access channels (Porter 1996). The value activities of the firm may differ for these strategic positions. The customer need focus is appropriate when a firm has a relative advantage in creating and delivering specific products and services that enhance the buyer value. Second, the customer segment focus is appropriate when the firm can serve specific customer segments better than its competitors. Third, the customer access focus is appropriate when the firm has an advantage within a location or particular channel. It may be possible for a firm to focus on all three positions, that is, to focus on specific needs of specific customer segments through specific channels. The choice of the firm's value activities and thus the business model employed will be tailored to the firm's strategic position.

The choice of a strategic position requires management to make tradeoffs in choosing the value activities. The value activities are complementary and interdependent, and consistent with the choice of the firm's strategic position. Thus, it may be easy for a competitor to copy a firm's strategic position but it is difficult to copy the firm's interlocking activities. Therefore, a firm's competitive advantage when supported by the firm's activity system is sustainable. Each firm has to make tradeoffs among their value activities even when the competing firms choose the same strategic position. Further, firms make tradeoffs in their resources even when they choose the same activity systems. The business model mechanism, a complex adaptive system, configures the firm's organizational capabilities and value activities, consistent with their strategic position.

Three factors drive the tradeoffs between the value activities, namely, the firm's signaling needs, the differences in strategic positions, and the consistency of the activities with the firm's values and norms (Porter 1996). The choice of value activities must be consistent with the firm's image, or the activities will create confusion in the market. Second, different strategic positions require different activity configurations. Finally, the activities chosen must be consistent with the firm's values and norms; otherwise the activities will create internal confusion. Further, a firm's strategic position requires a different set of activities that are consistent with the firm's priorities and reward system. Firms must make tradeoffs when choosing the value activities, making it difficult for competitors to copy a firm's business model. Otherwise, a strategy of a firm can be easily imitated.

The activity leverage is enhanced when the activity is tailored to enhance the buyer value and optimized to enhance the value chain effectiveness. The activity drivers enhance the activity leverage and value chain effectiveness. The greater the value chain effectiveness, the greater is the firm's business model advantage and the higher is its competitive position. The activity drivers enhance the firm's value chain differentiation or lower the marginal cost to serve. The activity drivers thus enhance the firm's competitive position. Because of the complexity and tacitness of the linkages between the value activities and the underlying activity drivers, it is difficult for competitors to copy the firm's business model even when the competitors share the same strategic position.

Business Model Construct

The business model mechanism sustains the value creation and value appropriation. The business model construct comprises three dimensions, namely, scalability, adaptability, and sustainability. The business model design is scalable when it is efficient and the firm's value chain is optimally configured and the activity complementaries are high. The business model has high sustainability when the customer and supplier lock-in, and the business model novelty and specificity are high. Furthermore, the business model sustainability is high when the activity configuration is tacit, complex, and causally ambiguous. The business model sustainability is high when the product market complementaries are high. The business model is adaptable when it adapts to changing competitive conditions. The greater the business model advantage, the greater is the likelihood that the firm achieves competitive advantage. The entrepreneurial incentives further enhance the business model advantage and provide the firm an entrepreneurial rent. The more entrepreneurial a firm relative to its competitors or the greater the entrepreneurial incentives, the greater is the likelihood of a higher business model advantage.

The firm's business model is superior when it has high scalability, sustainability, and adaptability relative to the competitors. When a business model has high efficiency, adaptability, and sustainability, the business model provides increasing returns to scale (Mishra 2015). With increasing returns to scale, the firm's operating margin increases at an increasing rate with the sales volume. The firm's competitive position is enhanced when the business model design is more scalable, sustainable, and adaptable. Entrepreneurial incentives are likely to enhance the business model scalability, sustainability, and adaptability.

The business model construct constitutes the firm's efficiency, cash flow sustainability, and business model adaptability. Further, the business model sustainability is enhanced by the firm's isolating mechanisms and imitation barriers. Furthermore, the firm's value creation and appropriation is sustainable when the business model is efficient and adaptable. The business model efficiency must be balanced with the business model adaptability. A sustainable business model provides sustainable cash flow growth. Furthermore, the business model advantage enhances the firm value. The business model advantage is the ratio of the price the buyer is willing to pay to the firm's marginal cost to serve the buyer.

A business model is efficient when the activity system is optimized, the activity costs are minimized, the activities that incur costs but do not enhance the buyer value are eliminated, and the cost drivers are optimized to achieve a desirable cost position. To achieve the business model efficiency, managers should examine the activity cost drivers and compare them with those of the competitors. Business model efficiency is a key performance indicator for firms pursuing a low cost position. An efficient business model is scalable. Efficient business models use firm resources efficiently. Information technology and process technologies enhance business model efficiency. To enhance business model efficiency, the activity cost drivers must be identified and the activity system optimized.

Activity complementaries enhance the business model efficiency. Value activities are complementary when the value created by one activity is not nullified by the other activities, and the activities reinforce each other. Activity complementaries enhance the activity linkages. The core resources enhance the activity complementaries, which further enhance the business model advantage. Activity complementaries also enhance the business model's causal ambiguity and imitation barriers. With greater activity complementaries, it is difficult for competitors to imitate a firm's business model.

The firm's value activities are complementary in that the advantage with one activity is not cancelled out by another activity. Three levels of activity complementaries are identified by Porter (1996). The first-order complementarity requires that the value activities are consistent with the firm's strategic position. The second-order complementarity requires that the activities reinforce each other; that is, the value of the activity system is greater than the sum of the values of individual activities. The third-order complementarity requires that the unnecessary activities are eliminated and the activities are optimized such that the costly activities are replaced by less costly activities. When an activity system has achieved third-order complementarity, the firm's value activities are optimized and the activity configuration is unique relative to its competitors. The activity leverage and value chain effectiveness increase with the activity complementarity.

The business model efficiency is measured by the firm's operating margin, that is, the operating income divided by the net sales. The business model efficiency enhances the value chain effectiveness and thus the firm's business model advantage. The business model efficiency lowers the firm's marginal cost to serve and thus enhance the business model advantage. Moreover, business model efficiency and business model novelty are complements rather than substitutes. The business model novelty enhances the business model sustainability. The business model efficiency and sustainability are complements. However, the business model efficiency must be balanced with the business model adaptability.

The business model sustainability is enhanced by enhancing the business model lock-in, that is, by enhancing the customer and supplier lock-in, and by enhancing the business model novelty and specificity. Business model novelty and specificity increase the causal ambiguity, making it difficult for competitors to copy the firm's business model. Business model novelty is enhanced when the value chain and revenue model configurations are novel and creative. Value chain innovation enhances the value chain effectiveness and revenue model innovation enhances the revenue model effectiveness. The business model advantage is further enhanced when the value chain effectiveness and revenue model effectiveness are enhanced. The linkages between the firm's value chain and the buyer value chain further enhance the business model novelty and specificity. Thus, the core resources that strengthen the linkages between the firm's value chain and the buyer value chain enhance the business model novelty and specificity.

Customer lock-in enhances the business model sustainability and the business model advantage. Enhancing the buyer value drivers, raising the buyer performance or lowering the buyer costs, enhances the customer lock-in. Furthermore, customer lock-in enhances customer switching costs. A firm can invest in information technologies and signaling activities to enhance the customer lock-in. High switching costs make it difficult for customers to switch to the firm's competitors. Further, supplier lock-in enhances the business model sustainability. A firm may require customers, suppliers, and strategic partners to make early investments in their time, learning, and resources to enhance the business model lock-in. The firm must understand the buyer value chains and supplier chains well enough to increase buyer and supplier switching costs to enhance their lock-in. The customer lock-in increases customer loyalty and sustains revenue growth. Supplier lock-in enhances the supplier reliability and reduces cost uncertainty.

The activity system complexity, tacitness, and causal ambiguity enhance the business model sustainability. The activity system complexity and product market complementaries enhance the barriers to imitation and hence the business model sustainability. The complexity, tacitness, and causal ambiguity of the activity linkages further enhance the business model sustainability. Furthermore, active learning in organizations enhances the core resources that enhance the activity and product market complementaries, which further enhance the business model novelty and specificity. Entrepreneurial organizations have a greater capacity for active learning and thus they are likely to have more novel business models.

Product market complementaries are high when the business model supports existing and new products in the firm's existing and adjacent markets. The greater the number of products offered, the greater the number of markets served, or the greater the number of channels used, the more sustainable is the business model, and the greater is the cash flow growth. The product market complementaries create positive feedback and thus provide increasing returns to scale. Product market complementaries enhance the buyer value added, and hence increase the buyer's willingness to pay and customer lock-in. Furthermore, network externalities are enhanced when the business model complementaries are high. Success with one customer group or in one market feeds back positively to other customer groups and markets. Product market complementaries thus provide increasing returns to scale. The product market complementaries are likely to be high in entrepreneurial organizations in that active learning enhances the activity linkages and complementaries, enhancing the business model advantage. Further, activity complementaries enhance the product market complementaries. The business model efficiency and sustainability are thus complements.

Finally, the business model adaptability must be balanced against the business model efficiency. Adaptability may come at the expense of the business model efficiency. Further, adaptability without the business model sustainability is chaos. However, instability can result with excess flexibility in the business model. Adaptability is the middle course between business model rigidity and overreaction. A lack of business model adaptability creates organizational inertia and core rigidity. However, excess business model flexibility makes the firm overreact to minor changes in an environment.

The business model construct thus constitutes three dimensions, namely, scalability, sustainability, and adaptability. The business model scalability is enhanced by optimizing value activities and activity complementaries. The business model sustainability is enhanced by the product market complementaries, customer and supplier switching costs, and business model novelty and specificity. The business model sustainability is enhanced with the activity causal ambiguity, tacitness, and complexity. Furthermore, the business model adaptability is enhanced with activity multiplexity, redundancy, and loose–tight coupling (discussed later in the chapter).

The firm's business model construct can be compared with the competitors along three dimensions, namely, scalability, sustainability, and adaptability. Furthermore, an efficient and adaptable business model is sustainable.

A tradeoff is required between the business model efficiency and adaptability. The greater the environmental uncertainty or the more dynamic the market conditions, the greater is the need for the business model adaptability. The more stable and predictable is the environment, the greater can be the business model efficiency.

The more entrepreneurial the organization, the greater is the business model advantage. Thus, the business model efficiency, sustainability, and adaptability are key dimensions of the business model construct that underlies the firm's superior performance. Organizations need to balance the business model design that is efficient and adaptable. In addition, the business model advantage requires high managerial incentives. Entrepreneurial incentives provide the managers an entrepreneurial surplus (see Chapter 3). Entrepreneurial organizations continually learn and adapt the management logics that further enhance the business model advantage. Thus, the more enhanced the management logics, the greater is the firm's business model advantage. Further, the entrepreneurial incentives enhance effective implementation and execution of the business model mechanism. Entrepreneurial organizations are alert, agile, proactively adaptive, absorptive, and opportunity driven. The business model advantage of entrepreneurial organizations is likely to be greater relative to their competitors. The business model advantage further enhances the firm's competitive position.

The business model construct can be alternatively viewed by the four perspectives of the balanced scorecard. The strategy map links a firm's financial perspective, buyer perspective, internal process perspective, and learning and growth perspective (Kaplan and Norton 1992). Building a strategy map for an organization clarifies the business model logic of how the value is created and appropriated (see Fig. 5.2). The financial perspective provides the tangible performance measures such as the profit margin, sales growth, return on assets, or return on equity, among others. The buyer perspective defines the buyer value propositions that provide the context for the firm's resources and activities to create the buyer value. For example, if the buyers value the product quality and reliability, then the value activities that contribute to the product quality and timely delivery are valuable to the firm. The buyer perspective determines whether a resource or an activity of the firm enhances the buyer value and thus if the firm's resource or activity is valuable to the organization.

The internal process perspective identifies the value activities that create and deliver the buyer value. The value activities enhance the buyer value and thus the financial performance. Firms may choose different value

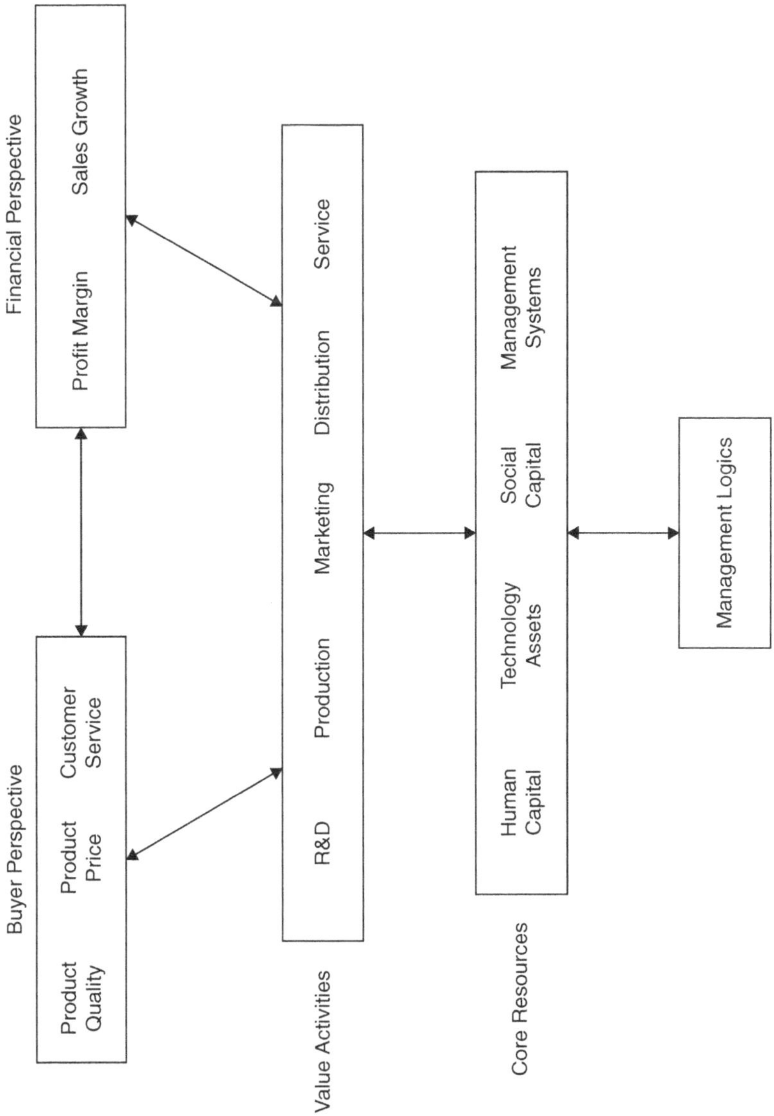

Fig. 5.2 Strategy map

activities to deliver the buyer value. Further, the learning and growth perspective identifies the firm's core resources, namely, the human capital, social capital, technology assets, and management systems that sustain the value activities. The learning and growth perspective further determines which human resources, which technology systems, which management systems, and what kind of social climate the organization may need to support the value activities. The business model effectiveness requires that the four perspectives are closely aligned. The business model construct can be viewed by the four perspectives of the balanced scorecard. The strategy map thus can uncover the inconsistencies between the firm's financial performance, buyer value drivers, value activities, and core resources.

The strategy map is based on the balanced scorecard (Kaplan and Norton 1992). The balanced scorecard includes the firm's financial and nonfinancial performance measures. The financial performance measures reflect the value appropriated by a firm, while the nonfinancial performance measures reflect the firm's value creation potential. The nonfinancial performance measures include buyer satisfaction, process effectiveness, and the firm's ability to learn and grow. Further, buyer satisfaction is captured in the buyer perspective, process effectiveness in the internal process perspective, and the firm's ability to learn and grow in the learning and growth perspective.

Competitive Position

The firm's value activities enhance the buyer value added. However, the firm performance and competitive position depend upon the cash flow generated or the value appropriated by the firm. The firm's revenue model design captures the buyer value created. The revenue drivers link the revenue models and value activities. The revenue model consists of the revenue streams and the mechanism for the buyer to pay for the firm's products and services. To achieve competitive advantage, the firm not only needs a superior value chain to create and deliver the buyer value, it must also monetize and appropriate the buyer value. The value creation and value appropriation mechanisms are central to the firm's ability to achieve and sustain competitive advantage. The business model comprises the value creation and appropriation mechanisms. The business model mechanism employs the value chain and revenue models that are linked to the buyer value chain.

We have defined the value chain effectiveness as the ratio of the buyer value added to the firm's marginal cost to serve. Thus, the greater the value chain effectiveness, the greater is the buyer value added or the lower the activity costs, or both. We have defined the revenue model effectiveness as the ratio of the price the buyer is willing to pay to the buyer value created by the firm. The greater the revenue model effectiveness, the greater is the buyer value appropriated by the firm.

The buyer value added is the buyer benefits minus the buyer costs associated with the product usage. The greater the buyer value added by the value chain and the more effective the revenue model design, the greater is the likelihood that the buyer will be willing to pay more. Further, the firm's signaling activities determine how much the buyer will be willing to pay for the firm's product or service. We have defined the business model advantage as the product of the value chain effectiveness and the revenue model effectiveness. The value chain effectiveness and revenue model effectiveness determine the firm's competitive position. The firm's business model advantage and thus their competitive position may change over time as the business model drivers adapt to changing competitive conditions. Thus:

$$\begin{aligned} \textit{Business Model Advantage} &= \textit{Value Chain Effectiveness} \\ &\quad \times \textit{Revenue Model Effectiveness} \end{aligned}$$

The firm's business model advantage is thus the product of the value chain effectiveness and the revenue model effectiveness. Simplifying the above equation, we get a measure for the business model advantage:

$$\textit{Business Model Advantage} = \frac{\textit{Price Buyer Willing to Pay}}{\textit{Marginal Cost to Serve}}$$

The firm's business model advantage, or the ratio of the price the buyer is willing to pay to the firm's marginal cost to serve, enhances the firm's share of the added value. Brandenburger and Stuart (1996) define the added value as the total value created in the firm's supply chain. The supply chain includes the value chains of the firm's suppliers, buyers, partners, distributors, and complementors, among others. The total value created in the firm's supply chain is distributed among the participants. The added value of a firm is thus the total value created in the supply chain minus the value that would have been created without the firm in the chain. The added value is the maximum value the firm may capture or appropriate. In a competitive market, the firm will capture less than the added value. Further, the value appropriated by the firm is less than the added value. It is not the added value but the appropriated value that determines the firm's competitive position. The value appropriated by a firm is less than or equal to the added value.

Thus, the firm's share of added value is high when the firm's business model advantage is high; that is, when the value chain effectiveness and revenue model effectiveness are high. The firm's business model advantage is high when the signaling value activities and revenue models enhance the buyer's willingness to pay or when the value activities cost less, or both. The value activities cost less when the resource suppliers provide the resources at a lower cost. The buyer value added is high when the buyer benefits are high or the buyer costs are low. The knowledge of the buyer value chains and supplier value chains enables the firm to identify opportunities to enhance the added value and the business model advantage. The greater the added value, the greater is the value created in the supply chain and the greater is the value available for the firm to appropriate. Furthermore, the value appropriated by the firm depends on their business model design in that the business model advantage determines the firm's bargaining power relative to the other participants in the supply chain. The firm's competitive advantage is enhanced by the business model advantage.

The greater the buyer value added or the greater the difference between the buyer benefits and buyer costs, the greater is the buyer's willingness to pay. The opportunity costs of suppliers of the resources influence the firm's marginal cost to serve. The opportunity costs of suppliers depend on the next best alternatives for which their resources can be employed. For example, an employee's opportunity cost is the highest compensation the employee may receive in an alternative employment. Thus, it is not the actual compensation paid by the firm to the employee but the employee's opportunity cost that determines the added value in the firm's supply chain. The added value created in the supply chain is the difference between the buyer value added and the suppliers' opportunity costs. The firm's share of the added value is less than the added value. Further, the amount the buyer is willing to pay is less than the buyer value created by the firm.

The value appropriated by the firm or the firm's share of the added value is the firm's revenues minus the costs to serve. The supplier's share of the added value is the payment received from the firm for the resources supplied minus the supplier's opportunity costs. The buyer's share of the added value is the buyer value added minus the amount the buyer is willing to pay. The buyer value added by the firm is greater than or equal to the amount the buyer may be willing to pay, wherein the buyer value added is the difference between the buyer benefits and buyer costs. The value appropriated by each party in the supply chain depends on their relative bargaining power, which further depends on their business model design.

The firm's business model advantage is enhanced when the buyer is willing to pay more for the product or service, the suppliers' opportunity costs are lowered, or both. Through product or service differentiation, the buyer's willingness to pay can be enhanced. Further, by increasing the suppliers' switching costs, the firm's marginal cost to serve can be lower. Thus, lower cost, product differentiation, or effective supply chains further enhance the business model advantage. The strategic positions such as cost leadership and product differentiation enhance the firm's business model advantage and hence the business model advantage. The low cost and product differentiation strategies enhance the firm's business model advantage and the competitive position.

Bradenburger and Stuart (1996) offer four strategies to enhance the firm's share of the added value and hence their business model advantage. First, the firm can enhance the buyer's willingness to pay for the product or service, or lower the buyer's willingness to pay for the competitors' products or services. For example, product differentiation can enhance the buyer's willingness to pay for the firm's products and services. Further, negative advertising about the competitors may lower the buyer's willingness to pay for the competitors' products. Finally, the firm can enhance the supplier lock-in by helping its suppliers lower their costs of doing business with the firm or increase the costs of doing business with the firm's competitors. The firm may share technology or management know-how to lock in the suppliers and strategic partners and help them lower their costs. Further, by increasing the switching costs of suppliers and partners, the firm can raise the suppliers' opportunity costs of doing business with the firm's competitors.

The firm's business model advantage or the ratio of the amount the buyer is willing to pay to the firm's marginal cost to serve, can be approximated by the business model leverage (Mishra 2015). The business model leverage is the firm's net sales divided by the operating costs. Mishra defines the firm's return on equity (ROE) or the ratio of the operating income to the market value of equity as:

$$ROE = Operating\ Margin \times Business\ Model\ Leverage \times Capital\ Leverage$$

The operating margin is the operating income divided by the net sales; the business model leverage is the net sales divided by the operating costs; and the capital leverage is the operating costs divided by the market value of equity. The firm's business model leverage approximates the business model advantage. That is, the greater the firm's business model leverage, the greater is their business model advantage. Thus, the greater the value chain effectiveness and revenue model effectiveness, the greater is the business model advantage and the greater will be the firm's business model leverage. Further, the business model advantage enhances the firm's competitive position. The operating margin is determined by the industry conditions, and the capital leverage is determined by the capital market conditions. However, the firm's business model leverage is a business model measure that is determined by the firm's business model design.

Furthermore, the capital leverage, the ratio of the operating costs to the market value of equity, can be further stated as:

$$Capital\ Leverage = Supply\ Chain\ Leverage \times Financial\ Leverage$$

The supply chain leverage is the ratio of the operating costs to the firm's total assets; and the financial leverage is the ratio of the total assets to the market value of equity. Note that the firm's total assets equal the total capital (or the sum of the debt and equity). The financial leverage ratio is well known in finance literature. The financial leverage captures the effects of debt financing, which measures the firm's debt capacity. However, the debt financing may constrain the firm's growth; further, excess debt increases the likelihood of the firm's bankruptcy (see Chapter 4).

The supply chain leverage is enhanced when the firm owns fewer assets and outsources more value activities. Strategic networks enhance the firm's supply chain leverage. The supply chain leverage measures the effectiveness of the firm's supply chain and enhances the firm's share of the added value. Further, in industries with low operating margins, a

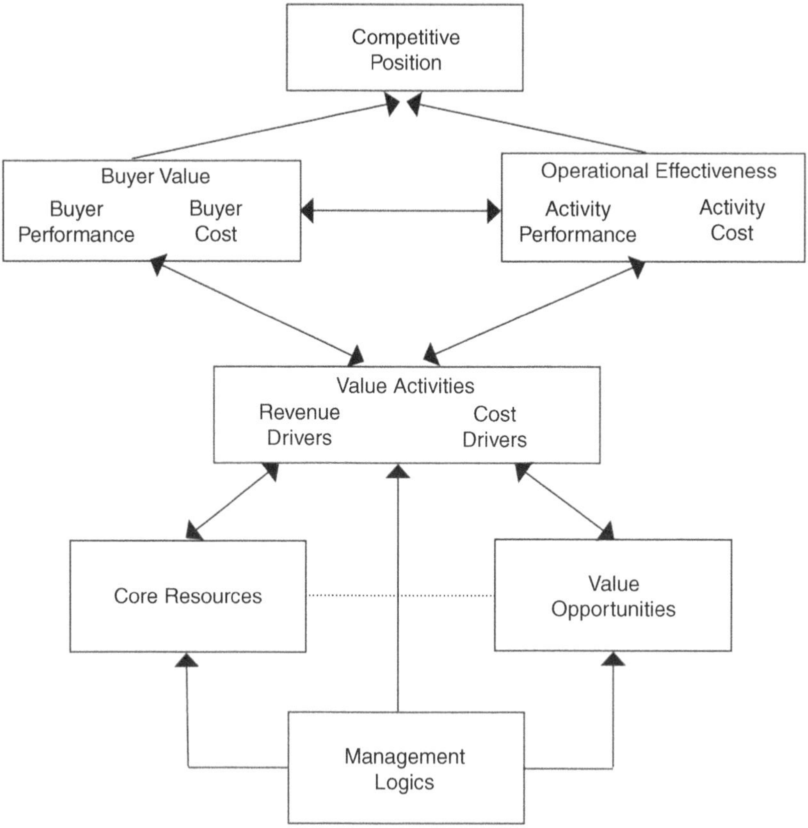

Fig. 5.3 Business model value drivers

firm's return on equity can be enhanced by reducing the firm's asset ownership (enhancing the supply chain leverage), enhancing the business model design (enhancing the business model leverage), and restructuring the firm's capital structure (enhancing the financial leverage). Thus, the business model leverage measures the business model effectiveness, the supply chain leverage the supply chain effectiveness, and the financial leverage the firm's debt capacity.

Figure 5.3 illustrates the relations between the key business model value drivers, namely, management logics, core resources, value opportunities, and activity drivers. The business model drivers are enhanced by the entrepreneurial incentives. Further, the business model value drivers enhance the buyer value and operational effectiveness and hence the firm's competitive position. The core resources underlie the organizational capabilities. The core resources include the human capital, technology assets, social capital, and management systems. The activity drivers include the revenue drivers and cost drivers. The revenue drivers enhance the buyer performance or lower the buyer cost, or both. The cost drivers enhance the activity performance or lower the activity cost, or both, and thereby enhance the activity leverage. The activity performance enhances the buyer value and thus the buyer's willingness to pay. The cost drivers determine the firm's cost structure. Enhancing the revenue and cost drivers increases the wedge between the buyer value added and the firm's marginal cost to serve, thus enhancing the value creation and appropriation and the business model advantage. Furthermore, the revenue and cost drivers are enhanced by the core resources and value opportunities. Entrepreneurial incentives enhance the organization's active learning and thereby the management logics, which further enhance the core resources, value opportunities, and the activity drivers.

The revenue drivers are linked to the buyer value drivers and thus to the buyer value chain. Further, the firm's signaling activities enhance the perceived value of the firm's products and services and enhance the buyer's willingness to pay. The buyer value drivers raise the buyer performance and lower the buyer costs. The revenue drivers enhance the buyer's willingness to pay and the revenue model provides a mechanism for the buyer to pay for the firm's product and service. The revenue drivers are linked to the firm's signaling value activities.

The cost drivers determine the firm's cost structure and operational effectiveness. The business model value drivers, namely, core resources, value opportunities, revenue drivers, and cost drivers, enhance the business model leverage and hence the firm performance such as the return on assets or the return on equity. The return on assets is the product of the firm's operating margin, business model leverage, and supply chain leverage. The firm's operating margin is the operating income divided by the net sales; the business model leverage is the net sales divided by the operating costs; and the supply chain leverage is the operating costs divided by the total assets. The firm's return on equity is the return on assets times the financial leverage.

The firm's operating margin and financial leverage are largely industry determined. The business model leverage measures the business model effectiveness, determined by the firm's business model design. The supply chain leverage is determined by the supply chain design. The business model effectiveness is raised by the business model value drivers. Active adaptation or dynamic capabilities enhance the business model value drivers and the value potential of the firm. Entrepreneurial incentives enhance the business model value drivers and hence enhance the business model advantage, and thus the firm's competitive position. Further, active learning and the management logics enhance the business model value drivers and hence the business model advantage. Furthermore, the business model value drivers illustrated in Fig. 5.3 show how these value drivers are interrelated.

Business Model Adaptability

Effective business model designs must adapt to changing environmental conditions. The more entrepreneurial the firm, or the more alert, agile, proactive, adaptive, and absorptive the firm, the greater is their business model adaptability. Firms must quickly and proactively adapt the parts of their business model configuration that are vulnerable to changing competitive conditions. The firm's dynamic capabilities enable the business model adaptability. Firms must quickly shift their resources and configure the activities to adapt their business models to respond to changing conditions in the environment.

"[A] company's real core capability – perhaps its only sustainable one – is its ability to design and redesign its value chain in order to continually find sources of maximum, albeit temporary advantage" (Fine et al. 2002: 70). Teece (2007) defines the organization's ability to adapt as its dynamic capabilities. Teece proposes that "the capacity an enterprise has to create, adjust, hone, and if necessary, replace business model is foundational to dynamic capabilities" [1330].

Business model adaptability requires the adaptability of the firm's management logics, core resources, value activities, and value opportunities. Sanchez (1995) defines strategic flexibility to emphasize the inherent flexibility of the firm's resources and in the deployment of its resources. Rindova and Kotha (2001) found that technological and human capital resources, namely, the firm's core resources, afforded the firms' different degrees of strategic flexibility when pursuing their strategies in changing industry conditions. Further, active learning enhances the core resources including technological and human capital resources and thus enhances the business model adaptability. The firm's core resources provide the knowledge assets that enable the dynamic capabilities adapt the business model to changing environmental conditions. The core resources thus enhance the business model adaptability.

Business model adaptability enables continuous morphing when the firm's competitive conditions shift. Continuous morphing involves active adaptation in the firm's product offerings, resources, activities, and governance (Rindova and Kotha 2001). Continuous morphing enables a firm to sustain competitive advantage when the competitive conditions shift. Entrepreneurial incentives enhance the firm's continuous morphing ability. Entrepreneurial organizations have the ability to continuously morph because of their high business model adaptability. The business model is enhanced when the firm morphs continuously. Thus, continuous morphing enhances the business model advantage and competitive position.

Entrepreneurial incentives empower the organizations to proactively adapt their value opportunities, organizational capabilities, and value activities. The firm's value opportunities, organizational capabilities, and value activities are reconfigured and realigned with the product market strategy and the buyer value drivers. The buyer value drivers underlie the buyer value chain that gets the buyer's job done or problem solved. The buyer value is enhanced when the buyer performance is raised or the buyer cost is lowered, or both.

A firm may pursue a generic product market strategy such as a low cost producer or product differentiation. Within a generic product market strategy, the firm may focus on a customer segment, a customer need, or a channel. A firm may identify a new product market opportunity, which will then require adjustments in the firm's value activities and capabilities. Further, the firm may modify its value activities, which would require a different resource and capability configuration, giving rise to new product opportunities. Furthermore, the firm may acquire and develop a new resource which will create new product market opportunities and require a change in the value activities. Continuous morphing thus reconfigures the firm's value activities, value opportunities, and organizational capabilities when competitive conditions shift. The business model is changed when the value activities, organizational capabilities, or value opportunities have changed.

Continuous morphing of firms may accelerate competition in the industry and may lead to hypercompetitive conditions. Thus, when firms proactively respond to changing competitive conditions and morph continuously, it results in a hypercompetitive environment. Further, in a hypercompetitive industry, business model adaptability is crucial to the firm's survival. Business model adaptability requires entrepreneurial response to changing competitive conditions in that these organizations are more alert, agile, proactive, adaptive, absorptive, and opportunity driven. Active learning enhances the firm's proactive adaptation in a hypercompetitive environment. The more entrepreneurial the firm, the greater is the business model adaptability. Further, the greater the market dynamism, the greater is the need for the business model adaptability.

A system can enhance its adaptive capacity through multiplexity, redundancy, and loose–tight coupling (Staber and Sydow 2002). Business model adaptive capacity can be enhanced by enhancing activity multiplexity, task and resource redundancy, and loose–tight coupling of value activities. Active learning enhances the firm's knowledge assets or core resources that enhance the business model adaptive capacity. When active learning takes place at a rate faster than the rate of change in conditions that require the dismantling old activities and creating new ones, the business model adaptive capacity is higher. Organizations who search for solutions using their existing competencies have limited adaptive capacity in that these organizations develop core rigidity and are stuck in competency traps.

Multiplexity refers to the number and diversity of linkages between value activities. The greater the multiplexity of the linkages, the greater is the business model adaptive capacity. The greater the number of linkages between the firm's cross-functional activities, the greater is the knowledge sharing and the faster is the knowledge integration within the organization; and the greater is the firm's combinative capabilities, and the greater is the business model adaptive capacity. Thus, the knowledge integration in the firm enhances the dynamic capabilities and resource orchestration. However, having a greater number of and diverse linkages between activities is not enough. The activity linkages have to be coordinated effectively that requires entrepreneurial incentives. The firm's reward system and incentive structure must be effective in leveraging cross-functional activity linkages. Further, the managerial attention is crucial in managing the cross-functional activity linkages for enhancing the adaptive capacity of the business model. The design of the firm's operating and governance channels that situate and distribute the management attention is thus crucial to the business model adaptability and the dynamic capabilities.

Redundancy enhances the business model adaptive capacity, namely, through resource redundancy, task redundancy, and activity linkage redundancy. Resource redundancy is the resource slack or excess resource the firm has relative to that which their activities require. Resource slack is considered waste and inefficient by agency theorists and transaction cost theorists. However, behavioral theorists (e.g., Cyert and March 1963) consider resource slack as necessary to enhance the organization's ability to cope with unforeseen challenges as well as reward experimentation.

According to our theory of entrepreneurial rent, absence of resource slack in a high growth firm may cause an underinvestment problem in that the firm may pass up some positive net present value growth opportunities (see Chapter 4). Further, Penrose (1959) in her theory of the growth of the firm emphasizes the role of resource slack as essential for the firm's growth. Growth firms thus need resource slack. In the absence of growth opportunities, however, a firm's resource slack may be considered as waste and inefficient.

Among all organizational resources, redundancy in the information resource is especially crucial to enhance the business model adaptive capacity. Information redundancy enhances the reliability of the firm's operating and governance channels, which enhances the management attention. With information redundancy, it is easier to detect errors in value activities and thus the errors can be quickly corrected. Further, enhanced management attention also increases the firm's agility and hence the entrepreneurial orientation. With resource redundancy, the firm's efficiency is compromised in the short term but the business model adaptability is improved. Resource redundancy permits experimentation, innovation, and risk taking, enhancing the business model novelty and sustainability.

Task redundancy in a business model refers to redundancy in value activities such that not all activities are pursued at all times. Because not all activities are required at all times, the failure of one activity to adapt to a changing competitive condition can be replaced while another activity is responding to the changed condition. Task redundancy requires that a value activity can accomplish more than one task, or alternative value activities perform the same task. In startups, for example, employees work on several activities simultaneously and the boundary between job descriptions and activities is open and flexible. Resources are quickly shifted to prioritized activities in order to respond to a changed competitive condition, thus enhancing the firm's dynamic capabilities.

Finally, redundancy in linkages between the value activities means that a linkage that fails can be replaced easily if duplicating linkages can sustain the relations in the meantime. Furthermore, redundancy of linkages in a firm's supply chain enhances the business model reliability and adaptability. With resource redundancy, task redundancy, and linkage redundancy are available, the business model is more adaptable and error-friendly. Further, with redundancy, an organization is more conducive to experimentation, improvisation, and innovation, thereby enhancing the firm's absorptive capacity and active learning and thus their entrepreneurial orientation.

Another dimension of the business model adaptability is the strength of the linkages between value activities. Loose coupling of the activity linkages enhances the business model adaptability while tight coupling enhances the business model efficiency. Thus, a loose–tight coupling of the linkages between the activities balances the business model efficiency and adaptability. Loose coupling of the value activities raises the business model adaptability to changing competitive conditions. A system is loosely coupled when its elements share a few variables in common or when the common variables shared by the elements are weak relative to the other variables driving the performance of the elements (Glassman 1973). Loose coupling of the elements means that the system's elements are relatively independent and can adjust quickly to changing conditions.

Loose coupling is enhanced with outsourcing of the firm's value activities. A firm's decision to insource or outsource a value activity depends on how critical the activity is to the buyer, how rapidly the underlying technology is changing, how important the activity is to the firm's competitive position, how capable and reliable the supplier base is, and how integral the activity is to the business model (Fine et al. 2002). The firm's value activities that are of high importance to the buyers, that are critical to the firm's competitive position, that do not have a capable and reliable supplier base, or that are integral to the functioning of the business model mechanism should not be outsourced.

Loose coupling of value activities is especially advantageous in a dynamic and uncertain environment. Loose coupling reduces the likelihood of repeating mistakes and the possibility of commitment escalation (see Chapter 4). Further, loose coupling is beneficial when the knowledge acquired by a firm is unclear and its application requires experimentation. Loose coupling and resource redundancy enhance the firm's learning capacity, namely, the capacity to experiment, create, and assimilate knowledge.

The business model adaptive capacity and efficiency increase when the activity linkages employ loose–tight coupling. The business model efficiency requires a tight coupling while the business model adaptability requires a loose coupling. Thus, an effective business model design uses loose–tight coupling. The business model adaptability must be higher when business models operate in more dynamic environments. In a more stable environment, the business model efficiency is more desirable.

Robust Business Models

Business model configuration is a complex adaptive system. Complex adaptive systems are self-organizing and emergent. Further, complex adaptive systems are robust to changing conditions. Robust business models are thus emergent and self-organizing. The business model elements, namely, the management logics, value opportunities, core resources, revenue drivers, cost drivers, organizational capabilities, and value activities, are self-realigning in a dynamic environment when the entrepreneurial incentives are present in the organization. Further, business models are emergent in entrepreneurial organizations as these organizations actively learn and proactively adapt to the changing environmental conditions.

A complex adaptive system is an open system with interacting elements. An open system dissipates energy that must be replenished to sustain the system. Open systems interact with their environment from where they draw energy. Complex systems exchange information with their environment. Unlike equilibrium systems which are closed systems, complex adaptive systems are open systems and exhibit dynamic disequilibrium. Complex adaptive systems have emergent properties in that the system elements and linkages coevolve as they interact, and as they adapt to changing environmental conditions. Thus, complex adaptive systems exhibit emergent order, bounded instability, and path dependency. Complex adaptive systems are robust and emergent.

Many biological systems are complex adaptive systems. For example, ant colonies are self-organizing, complex adaptive systems. Similarly, many economic systems such as business organizations are complex adaptive systems. Business model configurations in entrepreneurial organizations are complex adaptive. The business models in entrepreneurial organizations, that is, the value opportunities, value activities, revenue drivers, cost drivers, and organizational capabilities, coevolve and self-organize as the business model adapts to changing environmental conditions.

Similarly, an industry is a higher order complex adaptive system. The complex adaptive systems exist at multiple levels. A system of a group of complex adaptive systems is a complex adaptive system. For example, the constituents of an industry-level complex adaptive system include interacting organizations, buyers, suppliers, and complementors. Similarly, a market economy constituting several interacting industries is a higher order complex adaptive system. These complex adaptive systems are self-organizing and emergent.

The rules of interaction between system elements within a complex adaptive system also evolve as the system learns and adapts to its changing environmental conditions. Furthermore, a complex adaptive system exchanges energy with its environment (e.g., opportunities, in the case of business organizations). Complex adaptive systems follow the second law of thermodynamics in that the system dissipates energy over time and can wind down unless it is replenished with more energy (or new value opportunities). Business organizations must continually seek new value opportunities to survive and thrive. Entrepreneurial organizations are constantly seeking value opportunities to build competitive advantage. Thus, the value opportunities replenish the organization's dissipated energy and prevent them from winding down.

Beinhocker (1997) describes four key aspects of complex adaptive systems. A complex adaptive system when it has relatively few elements and linkages will be less adaptable because the number of states the system can be in will be fewer in comparison to the number of situations it might encounter. Earlier we explained how the multiplexity of an activity system can enhance the business model adaptability. The system multiplexity refers to the number and diversity of the linkages between system elements. As the system becomes more complex, the number of states the system can operate in and therefore the number of possible responses to changing environmental conditions grows exponentially. The greater the activity multiplexity, the greater is the business model adaptability and the more enhanced are the firm's dynamic capabilities. In a hypercompetitive industry, the business models must be complex adaptive. Further, the greater the complexity of the business model, the greater is the causal ambiguity of the business model mechanism and the more difficult it is for competitors to imitate the business model; thus, the business model advantage is sustained. The business model adaptability and hence the dynamic capabilities thus sustain the firm's competitive advantage.

However, beyond a certain level of complexity, the system will cease to be adaptable, causing complexity catastrophes. Complexity catastrophes occur when the complex system exhibits inertia or chaos. That is, complexity catastrophe occurs when there is too little or too much complexity. For example, when the system has too little complexity, the system cannot be in enough states to have sufficient response to changing environmental conditions and thus the system will exhibit inertia. However, when the system has too much complexity, the system will exhibit chaos. The properties of complex adaptive systems are achieved when the complexity is between the edge of order and the edge of chaos. Complexity catastrophes thus occur when the system complexity falls below the edge of order or rises above the edge of chaos.

Further, when a complex system with positive feedback builds up too much complexity, the system will exhibit chaos; similarly, in a system with too little complexity, a positive change in one element has too little changes elsewhere, resulting in the system's failure to adapt. At a certain level of complexity, a complex adaptive system has optimal adaptive capacity; that is, at the optimal level of complexity, a system is said to be "at the edge of chaos" (Kauffman 1991). A business model configuration that has optimal complexity such that it operates at the edge of chaos will have high business model advantage and provide the firm increasing returns to scale.

Second, complex adaptive systems exhibit the Red Queen effect (Kauffman 1995). The Red Queen effect occurs when a predator learns to run faster, then the prey responds creatively. With the Red Queen effect in a competitive industry, a single competitive advantage of a firm is not sustainable over a long period since competitors will catch up sooner or later. A superior business model configuration thus can only offer a temporary advantage. Rather the firm's business model must continually seek value opportunities and thus replenish its business model with energy to build a series of competitive advantages. Studies have found that competitive advantages in an industry do not last more than five years at a time (Beinhocker 1997).

Third, a complex adaptive system achieves superior performance when the system operates at the edge of chaos. Furthermore, at the edge of chaos, the system is simultaneously conservative and radical. A system is conservative when it is making incremental changes; and the system is radical when the changes are significant and innovative. At the edge of chaos, the system is making both incremental and radical changes. When the business model operates at the edge of chaos, the management makes incremental, continuous improvements of their resources and activities, but at the same time they make bold experiments and pursue radical opportunities to build the firm's next competitive advantage.

At the edge of chaos, the management pursues efficiency, sustainability, and adaptability at the same time. The firm's current operations are sustained while new competitive advantages are built; that is, the organization is ambidextrous. The organization is thus ambidextrous when their business model operates at the edge of chaos. The organization actively learns and their core resources are continually enhanced. Active learning enhances the organizational knowledge and improves the organization's products, processes, systems, and social values such that the business model value drivers are enhanced. Thus, the business model efficiency, sustainability, and adaptability are enhanced, thereby enhancing the business model advantage or fitness. Entrepreneurial incentives that enhance active learning in the organization further enhance the business model to operate at the edge of chaos. Entrepreneurial organizations are ambidextrous. They continually improve their current processes and products, but at the same time pursue bold experimentation with new value opportunities to build new competencies.

Fourth, for an organization with its business model to create a series of competitive advantages to sustain superior performance such that it stays ahead in the Red Queen race, it must balance the business model efficiency with business model flexibility. Standardization enhances the business model efficiency and provides scale economies. Flexibility enables an organization to respond to changing competitive conditions. Few organizations can strike a balance between the business model efficiency and flexibility. Entrepreneurial organizations have the ambidexterity to balance efficiency and adaptability, as well as standardization with variation. To build flexibility, the organization must seize and exercise opportunity options to experiment with new opportunities, and proactively create and manage real options to exploit the environmental uncertainty to resolve in the firm's favor (see Chapter 4). However, developing flexibility is costly but may be beneficial to a firm in an uncertain environment with rapidly changing competitive conditions. An effective business model must balance efficiency with flexibility for the firm to be competitive and stay ahead of the Red Queen race.

Furthermore, the firm's business model must be simultaneously focused and robust. A focused business model is necessary in the short term but is not sufficient in the long run. A business model is robust when it can perform in changing competitive conditions. Complex adaptive systems are robust to changing environmental conditions. Entrepreneurial organizations proactively adapt to changing environmental conditions; thus, the entrepreneurial incentives enhance the business model robustness. For example, an organization may pursue shaping bets, hedges, or no-regret moves at the same time. Shaping bets are value opportunities that will shape the rules of competition in an industry; hedges are opportunities that limit the firm's risk of loss; and no-regret moves are opportunities that yield positive outcomes regardless of the future state of the environment. Thus, a robust business model calls for the firm to pursue multiple value opportunities simultaneously.

Entrepreneurial organizations employ robust business models. They constantly seek value opportunities to sustain and enhance competitive advantage. The firm's value opportunities are at different stages of development. The value opportunities are identified and carefully managed to sustain the firm's competitive advantage (see Chapter 4). New opportunities replenish energy in a dissipating business model system. In the absence of new value opportunities, an organization as a complex adaptive system will wind down and fail. Thus, business model configurations when continually replenished with new opportunities survive and thrive in the long run.

Entrepreneurial organizations actively cultivate a portfolio of value opportunities, and exploit them in a timely manner (see Chapter 4). A robust business model provides flexibility to exploit the value opportunities and enhances the business model advantage. Entrepreneurial organizations employ robust business models, and actively learn and adapt to new opportunities. Business models of entrepreneurial organizations thus have self-organizing, emergent properties.

When a complex system displays the responsiveness of the whole without displaying the distinctiveness of its parts, the system is tightly coupled (Orton and Weick 1990). Similarly, when the complex system displays the distinctiveness of the parts without the responsiveness of the whole, the system is decoupled. Only when the system displays both the responsiveness of the whole and the distinctiveness of the parts, the system is loosely coupled. The business model configurations of entrepreneurial organizations are loosely coupled, coordinated, and enhanced by the management logics. Furthermore, when a system is neither responsive nor distinctive, the system is not really a complex system.

Loosely coupled systems are distinctive and responsive at the same time. The empirical evidence supports that high-performing organizations are frequently loosely coupled systems that demonstrate their responsiveness as entities while displaying the distinctiveness of their parts. The business model activity drivers of entrepreneurial organizations are loosely coupled.

Top management plays a key role in managing a loosely coupled activity system in an organization. Entrepreneurial incentives that enhance the management logics are crucial when managing a loosely coupled organization. Spender and Grinyer (1995) assert that the role of top management and their incentives are crucial in managing loosely coupled organizations. Spender and Grinyer examined firms undergoing strategic reorganization and found that firms rearranged and reconfigured their activities and resources led by top management that believed their firm was loosely coupled and a reconfiguration was always possible. Management logics are central to the robustness of the business model mechanism. Management logics play a key role when reconfiguring the business model configuration.

Orton and Weick (1990) further assert that the effective management of loosely coupled organizations calls for greater entrepreneurial orientation. Weick (1982) argues that university administrators should give more attention to the "glue" that holds loosely coupled educational institutions. The management logics are the "glue" that hold a firm's loosely coupled value activities together. Entrepreneurial incentives enhance the firm's management logics that enhance the effectiveness of loosely coupled activity systems. Entrepreneurial organizations continually learn and adapt the management logics in order to enhance their ability to manage loosely coupled activity systems and enhance the value creation and appropriation mechanism.

Competitive Landscape

Business model configurations may be viewed in terms of fitness landscapes (Kauffman 1993). Fitness landscapes have many peaks and valleys, where the height of a peak represents the fitness of the landscape (e.g., the business model advantage). The greater the height of a peak, the greater is the fitness level. Fitness landscapes have certain regular properties that can be employed to understand business model adaptation. For example, fitness landscapes can take various shapes. A random fitness landscape has lots of peaks and valleys that are not correlated to each other. In contrast, competitive landscapes have peaks that are correlated. The greater the complexity of competitive landscape, the greater is the correlation between peaks. A competitive landscape has peaks that are correlated such that fitness levels of nearby business model peaks differ incrementally.

Consider a competitive landscape where each business model peak represents a possible business model driver configuration. The business model driver configuration or peak constitutes the firm's value opportunities, core resources, value activities, revenue drivers, and cost drivers. The height of a business model peak is the business model advantage. The higher the business model peak, the greater is the business model fitness or the greater is the business model advantage. In a competitive landscape, the firm is continually searching for higher peaks. The properties of fitness landscapes can help a manager enhance the firm's competitive position by proactively adapting the business model configuration to enhance the business model advantage in changing competitive conditions.

A competitive landscape has peaks that are not fixed; the peaks are a mountain range that is constantly bucking and heaving as the firm's competitive conditions change. Thus, the height of a peak on the competitive landscape is changing continually as the environmental conditions change. A business model configuration that is superior today may not survive in the future. The firm's strategy is to find a profitable business model configuration or a higher peak on its competitive landscape. For the firm to create and sustain competitive advantage, the firm's adaptation strategy involves an evolutionary search for higher peaks on its competitive landscape. A firm's competitive landscape can be viewed in an industry environment with alternative business model configurations (or peaks) possible for the given firm.

A manager is thus a hiker on the competitive landscape. Beinhocker (1999) describes a hiker's journey in the search for higher peaks on a fitness landscape. A hiker can find food only on higher peaks. The hiker can carry only a limited amount of food on the journey. If the hiker gets stuck in a valley too long, the hiker might die of starvation. Second, the hiker has no map of the region and must rely on sight. Moreover, it is very foggy and the hiker can only see a few feet ahead. Most importantly, the landscape experiences earthquakes, which changes the landscape periodically. What would be the hiker's strategy for survival?

A proactive adaptation strategy for a manger to find higher business model peaks on the competitive landscape is to keep moving, deploy platoons of hikers, and mix short and long jumps (Beinhocker 1999). Organizational inertia is death. If a firm is not constantly seeking value opportunities, they will not find higher business model peaks and starve to death. Even though a firm is presently on a high peak and successful, their competitive position will soon change as the competitive landscape changes. Further, organizations must constantly learn, explore, and seek new value opportunities to find higher business model peaks on the competitive landscape, or starve to death. Entrepreneurial organizations never settle for the current peaks they stand on; they always aspire for higher business model peaks. They are proactively adaptive and aspire for higher potential performance, thereby increasing the gap between their potential performance and their actual performance. Entrepreneurial organizations keep moving, actively learning, experimenting, and exploring new value opportunities. They are constantly striving for improvement even when their performance is superior relative to their competitors'.

Second, to improve the odds of finding higher peaks, management must deploy platoons of hikers or explore multiple opportunities at the same time. The greater the number of value opportunities explored, the greater are the odds of finding a higher peak and the greater are the odds of achieving competitive advantage. Thus, the management's exploration strategy is to use a parallel search rather than a sequential search. Parallel exploration of value opportunities has three benefits. Parallel exploration increases the odds of finding a higher business model peak and hedges the firm when some of the opportunities do not work out. Further, a parallel search diversifies the firm's risk as opposed to the firm concentrating all its resources on a single value opportunity. Small investments made in several opportunity options allow the firm to experiment and pilot test before it commits to a superior value opportunity.

In addition to keep moving and deploying a platoon of hikers to explore multiple business model peaks, the manager should use a mix of short and long jumps to reach nearby and farther peaks in the competitive landscape. Short jumps are incremental improvement opportunities, whereas long jumps are more innovative or innovatively imitative opportunities. The hikers have limited visibility and can see only a few feet ahead at a time. The surrounding area is barely discernible. Further, the fog may lift for a short while or could thicken at times.

A short jump or an incremental improvement is an "adaptive walk." Adaptive walks are efficient local searches for higher peaks. The drawback with adaptive walks is that the hiker may choose a local high peak and stop exploring the region further to find the global high peak. The local high peak is a local maximum; that is, the highest peak in the immediate vicinity of the hiker. A long jump helps the hiker to explore farther areas in the region. Long jumps are to find more innovative opportunities. The hiker can use a pogo stick to jump to peaks far away from their immediate vicinity (Beinhocker 1999). The use of the pogo stick improves the odds of reaching higher peaks in a farther region. The disadvantage of a pogo jump is that the hiker does not know where they will land. The hiker may land in a low valley instead. The pogo jumps are innovative or innovatively imitative value opportunities and carry high risk and high reward.

The best active adaptation strategy for the manager is to use a mix of short and long jumps, or combine adaptive walks with medium to long pogo jumps. The adaptive walks help the firm to keep moving toward a higher fitness level or business model advantage, while medium to long pogo jumps help the firm not to get stuck on a local high peak and enhance the possibilities for significant improvements. A firm may pursue a mix of short-term, medium-term, and long-term value opportunities. Short-term opportunities include continuous improvements that are geared to defend and incrementally increase firm performance. Medium-term opportunities include value opportunities that leverage existing business model configuration, whereas long-term opportunities are the value opportunities that plant the seeds for building new business models. In an uncertain environment, a firm should cultivate and nurture a portfolio of value opportunities that improves the firm's near-term performance, plants the seeds for building future advantages, and hedges against key uncertainties. Managers may view the firm's portfolio of opportunities in terms of whether the payoffs are near-term to long-term, whether the risks are low to high, and whether the opportunities are incrementally extending the current advantage to laying out foundations for new advantages.

Summary

The business model mechanism drives the firm's value creation and appropriation activities. Further, the business model implements and executes the firm's strategy. The firm's strategy determines where and how the firm competes to achieve a desirable strategic position. The buyer value is at the heart of the business model design. The buyer value drivers underlying the buyer value chain are central to the effectiveness of the business model design. The business model creates, delivers, sustains, monetizes, and appropriates the buyer value. Further, the competitive advantage is achieved when the firm's business model mechanism can create and appropriate greater added value than the competitors can. The firm's entrepreneurial capacity to proactively exploit the market uncertainty in their favor and act on the value opportunities in a timely manner is a source of competitive advantage.

To seize and exploit value opportunities in a timely manner, the firm must maintain sufficient situation awareness by regularly testing and revising the management logics. The management attention must focus on the critical aspects of the environment. With learning and enhanced management logics, managers with entrepreneurial incentives achieve coarse foresight that enables them to recognize cognitively distant value opportunities. Further, entrepreneurial organizations create and manage opportunity options and exploit the uncertainty associated with the value opportunities to resolve in the firm's favor. With the entrepreneurial incentives and enhanced management logics, entrepreneurial organizations seize and exploit value opportunities in a timely manner which enhances the firm's value creation and appropriation mechanism and the competitive advantage. Thus, the entrepreneurial incentives in the organization empower the management to create and sustain competitive advantage, and thereby the management earns an entrepreneurial surplus.

The buyer value is enhanced when the buyer performance or satisfaction is raised, or the buyer costs or risks are lowered, or both. The buyer value added enhances the business model advantage and hence the firm's competitive position. The greater the buyer value added by the firm, the more the buyer is willing to pay for the product or service. The value appropriated by the firm is higher when the buyer is willing to pay more or the value activities cost less. The revenue drivers underlie the buyer's willingness to pay and the cost drivers underlie the activity costs. Activity drivers constitute the revenue drivers and cost drivers. Activity drivers enhance the activity leverage and hence the value chain effectiveness. The buyer value drivers underlie the buyer value chain and are linked to the firm's value chain. The core resources strengthen the linkages between the firm's value chain and the buyer value chain.

The business model mechanism links the business model value drivers, namely, revenue drivers, cost drivers, core resources, and value opportunities, to the buyer value drivers and buyer value chain. Activity drivers enhance the value chain effectiveness. Revenue drivers enhance the buyer's willingness to pay and the revenue model effectiveness. Revenue drivers and cost drivers vary with the business model design. Further, value opportunities provide to the firm the fuel that the value creation engine requires to sustain the business model; that is, to create, deliver, and sustain the buyer value. The management logics bind and enhance the value activities. Further, the value activities enable the value creation by exploiting the value opportunities with the firm resources. The business model design determines the value activities, value opportunities, cost drivers, and revenue drivers necessary to achieve a desirable strategic position. The firm's strategic position may be a low cost or a differentiation position, within which the firm may choose to focus on selected customer segments, customer needs, and channel access.

The entrepreneurial incentives enhance the business model value drivers, namely, value opportunities, management logics, core resources, and activity drivers. The value opportunities provide the fuel. The management logics bind the value activities by strengthening the activity linkages. The core resources strengthen the linkages between the firm's value chain and the buyer value chain. Further, activity drivers enhance the buyer's willingness to pay and lower the firm's cost to serve. The activity drivers constitute the firm's cost drivers and revenue drivers. The entrepreneurial incentives enhance the firm's business model advantage. The business model construct constitutes three dimensions, namely, the business model scalability, adaptability, and sustainability. Continuous morphing of the business model enhances the firm's value activities, products, processes, resources, and strategic position. Further, active learning and adaptation in the organization enhances the business model efficiency, sustainability, and adaptability. Moreover, the greater the firm's value potential, the greater is the potential for the entrepreneurial surplus and thus the greater will be the entrepreneurial incentives. The dynamic capabilities enhance the firm's value potential and hence the available entrepreneurial surplus.

Business model advantage is the product of the value chain effectiveness and the revenue model effectiveness. Further, business model advantage is the ratio of the buyer's willingness to pay to the firm's marginal cost to serve. The firm's share of the added value is enhanced with the business model advantage. Business model advantage enhances the firm's competitive position. The business model advantage thus is a measure of the degree of competitive advantage. Further, the greater the business model advantage of the firm relative to its competitors the higher is its competitive position or the greater is its degree of competitive advantage. The business model advantage can be approximated by the firm's business model leverage, that is, the ratio of the net sales to the operating costs. The higher the net sales or lower the activity costs, the greater is its business model leverage relative to its competitors and hence the greater is the firm's business model advantage. The business model advantage enhances the shareholder return. Furthermore, strategic resources are valuable when they enhance the firm's business model advantage, not when they can become liabilities by constraining the business model mechanism.

The firm's revenue drivers are linked to the buyer value drivers that underlie the buyer value chain. The buyer value chain gets the buyer's job done or their problem solved. The buyer value chain is central to the buyer value creation and thus to the firm's value creation. The buyer value drivers enhance the buyer value. Further, the firm's revenue drivers and signaling activities enhance the buyer's willingness to pay. The firm may achieve competitive advantage when it can enhance greater buyer value and appropriate a greater share of the buyer value it creates than the competitors can. The entrepreneurial incentives enhance the value creation and appropriation mechanism that underlie the firm's competitive advantage, according to our theory of entrepreneurial rent.

Entrepreneurial incentives enhance the business model advantage. Entrepreneurial firms are alert, agile, proactive, adaptive, absorptive, and opportunity driven. The more entrepreneurial the firm or the greater the entrepreneurial incentives in the firm, the greater is the likelihood of the firm achieving competitive advantage. The competitive advantage creation may be viewed in a two-stage framework; in that in the first stage, entrepreneurial incentives stimulate the firm's entrepreneurial behavior, enhancing the firm's active learning, management logics, management cognition, combinative capabilities, and dynamic capabilities. In the second stage, the firm's entrepreneurial advantage provides superior execution of the firm's business model mechanism, which further enhances the business model advantage and the firm's competitive position.

PART III

Summing Up: Entrepreneurial Advantage to Competitive Advantage

CHAPTER 6

The Theory of Entrepreneurial Rent

Introduction

Competitive advantage is the rationale underlying a firm's superior performance relative to its competitors. How does a firm create and sustain competitive advantage? The resource-based view advocates that strategic resources underlie a firm's competitive advantage. However, the resource-based view assumes that the firm's value creation and appropriation mechanism always delivers superior performance when a strategic resource is present. The positioning view advocates that it is not the resources but the firm's value activities, consistent with their strategic position, that provide the firm competitive advantage. The positioning view assumes that managers will always recognize and seize superior strategic positions; and, furthermore, when an attractive strategic position is chosen, the managers will always select superior value activities to provide the firm competitive advantage. However, managers often fail to recognize and seize superior opportunities in a timely manner.

Why do some firms pick superior resources, opportunities, or activities? The answer is found by entrepreneurial logic in that the firm's competitive advantage lies in the value creation and appropriation mechanism powered by the entrepreneurial incentives. Further, the entrepreneurial incentive is the uncertain performance-based compensation in the executive pay, where the firm performance is determined by an external arbiter, such as the capital market. The entrepreneurial incentives enhance management

C.S. Mishra, *Creating and Sustaining Competitive Advantage*,
DOI 10.1007/978-3-319-54540-0_6

logics that further enhance the management cognition, enabling the executives to overcome traditional behavioral bounds, in that the executives pick superior opportunities and reconfigure the resources and value activities. The entrepreneurial behavior sustained by the entrepreneurial incentives, namely, the firm's enhanced alertness, agility, absorptive capacity, proactive adaptation, and opportunity focus, is a source of competitive advantage that generates an entrepreneurial rent for the firm and provides the firm executives an entrepreneurial surplus.

The entrepreneurial incentives induce the entrepreneurial behavior in the organization in that the organization is alert, agile, absorptive, adaptable, proactive, and opportunity driven. The managers with entrepreneurial incentives recognize and seize cognitively distant superior value opportunities in a timely manner to build competitive advantage. Managers are motivated by the potential to earn an entrepreneurial surplus, that is, an excess compensation relative to that of their peers', based on the firm's superior performance. Managers earn an entrepreneurial surplus for bearing the excess firm-specific risk. Further, shareholders are compensated for investment capital at a return commensurate with the firm's systematic risk, whereas the managers are compensated for human capital at a return commensurate with the firm's total risk, that is, the sum of the firm's systematic risk and unsystematic risk. Shareholders invest in diversified portfolios of securities such as mutual funds, in that the firm-specific risk is mostly diversified away for a shareholder. However, the firm's managers assume and actively manage the firm-specific risk in addition to the systematic risk, and thus managerial human capital must earn an excess return commensurate with the firm's total risk. The total risk is the sum of the firm's systematic risk and firm-specific unsystematic risk.

Entrepreneurial incentives empower executives to constantly seek value opportunities to build and sustain competitive advantage. The firm's competitive advantage lies in the value creation and appropriation engine, which is fueled by cognitively distant superior opportunities that are barely visible to all managers. Cognitively proximate opportunities more easily found by a local search may not provide superior performance. Further, the entrepreneurial incentives enhance the management capacity to seek value opportunities while simultaneously attending to the firm's current operations, that is, their ambidexterity. Enhanced management attention sustained by the entrepreneurial incentives enhances the organizational ambidexterity. Further, enhanced management capacity enables a firm to actively exploit the environmental uncertainty to resolve in their favor, which provides the firm with superior value opportunities that sustain the firm's competitive advantage. Entrepreneurial incentives are thus central to the firm's competitive advantage.

The entrepreneurial incentives enhance the management logics, which enhance the management cognition, enabling the executives to recognize and seize cognitively distant value opportunities. Thus, the entrepreneurial incentives empower the decision makers to overcome traditional behavioral bounds assumed in conventional behavioral theory. Thus, entrepreneurial organizations are more successful at identifying superior value opportunities. Managers with entrepreneurial incentives have a promotional focus mildly tempered with prevention focus that enables them to evaluate a greater number of opportunities. Thus, these managers are more likely to recognize superior value opportunities. Entrepreneurial incentives provide the managers a greater ability to recognize complex stimuli associated with superior opportunities. Powerful entrepreneurial incentives enhance the management learning and managerial cognitive adaptability that further enhance the management cognition to overcome traditional behavioral bounds.

Entrepreneurial incentives in a firm empower the executives with the opportunity to earn an entrepreneurial surplus, analogous to a startup's entrepreneurs earning an entrepreneurial reward (Mishra and Zachary 2014, 2015). Entrepreneurial surplus is the executive's excess compensation for bearing the excess firm-specific risk associated with the likelihood of the firm achieving superior performance. Entrepreneurial surplus is accrued to the executives in firms that are more entrepreneurial. Entrepreneurial corporations are more alert, agile, proactive, adaptive, absorptive, and opportunity driven. These organizations continually learn and proactively exploit the environmental uncertainty and complexity, and constantly pursue superior opportunities while not constrained by their current resource limitations. Entrepreneurial firms therefore assume and actively manage a greater firm-specific risk relative to their peers. The firm-specific risk can be measured by the firm's stock option volatility the variance of abnormal returns or market model residuals, or earnings volatility.

Managers with entrepreneurial incentives have the potential to earn an entrepreneurial surplus or an excess compensation when compared to their counterparts in firms with the same level of systematic risk. The firm's systematic risk is measured by the firm's stock beta. Thus, within a group of competitors, where the stock betas of the firms are in close proximity, managers of a firm with a higher firm-specific risk must have the potential to earn an excess compensation or entrepreneurial surplus in order for managers to be adequately incentivized for the firm to achieve superior performance, according to our theory of entrepreneurial rent. In strategy literature, we often ask what constitutes a firm's competitors. In an industry, firms with the stock betas in close proximity may be considered as a group of competitors. Furthermore, the entrepreneurial rent is the excess profit from the firm's superior performance relative to its competitors, which accrues to the firm from the superior execution of the firm's value creation and appropriation mechanism. The entrepreneurial rent for a firm accrues from the firm's business model execution advantage powered by superior entrepreneurial incentives. The entrepreneurial surplus is therefore the excess executive compensation appropriated by the management when the firm creates and appropriates the entrepreneurial rent. Entrepreneurially oriented firms earn entrepreneurial rent and provide their executives an entrepreneurial surplus through equity-linked compensation vehicles.

Our theory of competitive advantage, namely, the theory of entrepreneurial rent, is premised on the entrepreneurial behavior of a firm sustained by powerful executive incentives in enhancing the firm's value creation and appropriation mechanism wherein the competitive advantage lies. The entrepreneurial incentives are at the heart of the entrepreneurial logic that underlies the theory of entrepreneurial rent. Further, the firm's value creation and appropriation mechanism constituting the value opportunities, core resources, activity drivers, and value activities enhances the firm's competitive position. The business model thus constitutes the firm's value creation and appropriation mechanism. The business model construct constitutes the business model scalability, adaptability, and sustainability. The efficient and adaptable business models are sustainable. However, the business model efficiency must be balanced with the business model adaptability. The greater a firm's business model advantage, the higher is the firm's competitive position. The firm's business model advantage is the unit price the buyer is willing to pay divided by the firm's marginal cost to serve.

Entrepreneurial incentives enhance the business model advantage. Entrepreneurial firms are alert, agile, proactive, adaptive, absorptive, and opportunity driven. The more entrepreneurial the firm or the greater the entrepreneurial incentives in the firm, the greater is their likelihood of achieving competitive advantage. The competitive advantage creation may be viewed in a two-stage framework; in the first stage, the entrepreneurial incentives enhance the firm's entrepreneurial orientation (behavior), or the firm's alertness, agility, absorptivity, and proactive adaptiveness, which further enhances the firm's entrepreneurial competence, namely, enhanced management logics, combinative capabilities, management cognition, and dynamic capabilities. In the second stage, the entrepreneurial competence enhances the execution of the firm's value creation and appropriation mechanism, which further enhances the business model advantage and the firm's competitive position.

Extant strategic logics assume the firm's value creation and appropriation mechanism always provides the firm with competitive advantage when a strategic resource is present or an attractive market position is found. Since the firm's competitive advantage lies in the execution of the value creation and appropriation mechanism, unless the firm's business model mechanism is identified, it is difficult to identify and test a firm's sources of competitive advantage. The two most-studied strategic logics of competitive advantage are the positioning logic and the resource-based logic.

The resource-based logic claims that a firm's strategic resource is a source of competitive advantage. In the resource-based logic, strategic resources are a priori valuable, rare, inimitable, and nonsubstitutable (Barney 1991). The resource-based logic assumes that the firm's business model mechanism always delivers competitive advantage whenever the firm controls a strategic resource. However, the value creation and appropriation mechanism is a "black box" in the resource-based logic. The resource-based logic thus does not provide the interior processes of value creation and appropriation underlying the competitive advantage creation when the firm controls a strategic resource.

In our entrepreneurial logic, the firm's strategic resources are valuable a priori when the strategic resources controlled by the firm embody valuable opportunity options for the firm. The greater the uncertainty associated with the opportunity underlying the opportunity option, the more time left for the opportunity to expire, the greater the present value of the opportunity, or the lower the investment required to exploit the opportunity, the more valuable is the opportunity option. For a strategic asset to be valuable for the firm, the strategic asset must reduce the risk of loss for the firm in pursuing the opportunity underlying the opportunity option embodied in the strategic asset, extend the opportunity's time to expiration, enhance the present value of cash flows from the opportunity, or reduce the investment required to exploit the opportunity.

To assess that a strategic resource is valuable a priori for the firm, the firm's opportunity options embodied in the strategic resource must be explicitly identified and it must be shown that these opportunity options have not expired or been already preempted by competitors. The associated opportunity options must be valuable for the strategic resource to be valuable a priori. However, it is difficult to spot the firm's opportunity options so it is difficult to know whether the strategic asset is valuable a priori. Thus, a strategic resource provides superior performance or competitive advantage only if the focal firm had exploited the underlying opportunities with the strategic resource better than its competitors exploited similar opportunities without the identified strategic resource. Thus, the interior processes of firm value creation and appropriation mechanism must be explicitly controlled when empirically testing the resource-based theory in that whether a firm's strategic resource identified by the criteria prescribed by the resource-based theory is a source of competitive advantage for the firm.

Further, the definition of resource is vague in the resource-based logic. Anything and everything associated with a firm is a resource. For example, the firm's inputs, processes, and attributes are all considered to be resources. It then follows that the firm's competitive advantage is also a resource. A clear definition of a resource is thus necessary to identify strategic resources in a firm. We define the factor inputs as the firm's resources. In our strategic framework, the firm's core strategic resources constitute the human capital, social capital, technology assets, and management systems. The entrepreneurial incentives are necessary for the firm's core resources to provide superior performance.

The resource-based logic further suggests that firms can accumulate or acquire strategic resources employed by the competitors to achieve superior firm performance. However, the competitor's value creation and appropriation mechanism that employs a strategic resource is causally ambiguous. It is difficult for the firm to learn how the competitor deploys the strategic resource that the firm wants to deploy in its business model mechanism. Firms may have different business model implementations. Thus, a high-performing competitor may have a different business model implementation and its strategic resource may not enhance the imitating firm's business model advantage, and hence may not provide the imitator superior performance. Further, it is not always incentive compatible for a firm to imitate the strategic resources of high-performing competitors in that the strategic resources may not be incentive compatible for the managerial capability of an imitating firm, since an average-ability manager will not choose the same strategic resource that a high-ability manager chooses. The strategic resource of a high-ability competitor may impose a greater risk on an imitating firm's executive pay and the managers may not choose the same strategic resource. The firm's choice of a strategic resource is thus an incentive signal of the managerial ability.

Peteraf (1993) provides the conditions of competitive advantage under which a firm may earn excess profits. A source of competitive advantage is scarce, imperfectly imitable, and imperfectly mobile. Peteraf included a fourth condition, namely, limited competition. However, we have argued that limited competition may inhibit the firm's value appropriation mechanism. A source of competitive advantage provides Ricardian and firm-specific quasi-rents. In our theory of entrepreneurial rent, the entrepreneurial behavior of a firm is a source of competitive advantage in that the firm has the potential to generate an entrepreneurial rent (excess profit) and the managers an entrepreneurial surplus. Further, the entrepreneurial behavior is scarce, imperfectly imitable, and imperfectly mobile. The entrepreneurial behavior of a firm can sustain the firm's competitive advantage.

The firm's core resources, namely, the human capital, social capital, technology assets, and management systems, are strategic resources that are imperfectly imitable and imperfectly mobile. In our framework, the firm's core resources embody the firm's opportunity options that strengthen the linkages between the firm's value activities and the buyer value chain, thereby enhancing the firm's value creation and appropriation. Further, the entrepreneurial incentives enhance the deployment of the firm's core resources and the exploitation of opportunity options in the business model mechanism through the firm's absorptive capacity and dynamic capabilities. The entrepreneurial incentives enhance the firm's active learning, absorptive capacity and dynamic capabilities.

The dynamic capabilities adapt the firm's resources to changing competitive conditions. However, it is not clear what constitutes the dynamic capabilities. In Teece's (2007) definition, the dynamic capabilities are firm-specific strategic capabilities situated with the management. However, in Eisenhardt and Martin's (2000) definition, industry-best practices and operational capabilities are included in the dynamic capabilities. We define the dynamic capabilities as the firm's ability to proactively adapt to changing competitive conditions. In proactive adaptation, the stimulus to widen the gap between the firm's potential performance and actual performance comes from within the firm. In contrast, in preactive adaptation, stimulus comes from an external source. Thus, industry best practices are included in preactive adaptation, in that by adopting industry best practices the firm is trying to catch up with its competitors. Industry best practices are thus not included in the firm's proactive dynamic capabilities in our framework.

By defining the dynamic capabilities as the firm's ability to proactively adapt, it will be easier to identify the dynamic capabilities and test its impact on firm performance. Indeed, the greater the firm's entrepreneurial orientation, the greater are the firm's dynamic capabilities. The dynamic capabilities may be proxied by the firm's entrepreneurial orientation construct, which constitutes the firm's alertness, agility, proactiveness, adaptiveness, absorptivity, and opportunity focus (see Chapter 3). When the entrepreneurial incentives are high, the firm's entrepreneurial orientation is enhanced and thus their dynamic capabilities will be greater. The entrepreneurial incentives therefore enhance the firm's dynamic capabilities. The dynamic capabilities help the firm exploit the environmental uncertainty and sustain firm growth.

Another strategic logic explaining the firm's competitive advantage is the positioning view (Porter 1996). The positioning view attributes the rationale underlying a firm's competitive advantage to the firm's choice of an attractive strategic position and an optimal activity system consistent with the strategic position. Porter argues that it is the value activities that a firm does differently that create and sustain the firm's competitive advantage. Firms may choose a different set of value activities even though they may have similar resource bundles. Thus, it is not the firm resource heterogeneity, but the activity differentiation that provides them competitive advantage in the positioning logic.

The activity drivers differentiate an activity system from another. According to Porter (1996), the firm's activity drivers are the source of competitive advantage. The activity drivers enhance the buyer value or lower the activity cost, or both. Further, the firm's activity system is causally ambiguous. It is difficult for a competitor to copy the firm's activity system. The competitive advantage associated with an activity system is thus sustainable. Competitive advantage results from a firm's ability to perform the value activities at a lower cost or perform some activities in unique ways. However, the positioning view assumes that the firm's managers will always choose an attractive strategic position and an optimal activity system, and the firm's activity system will be continually adapted to the changing competitive conditions. Porter admits that the choice of strategic position and activity system is dependent on the management. Thus, the management incentives are critical for the choice of superior strategic position and value activities. Further, the management logics, namely, the management mental models and theories, influence the choice of the firm's strategic position and value activities.

To perform the activities at a lower cost or in unique ways may require firm-specific resources. Within the firm's business model implementation, the strategic resources embody value opportunities that enable the firm to lower the activity costs or enhance the buyer value. Under certain conditions, a firm's strategic resources may enhance the buyer value or lower the activity costs. The entrepreneurial incentives and management logics play an important role in determining when the strategic resources may or may not be valuable. Thus, the business model conditions under which a firm's strategic resources enhance the value activities are not explored in the resource-based logic. The entrepreneurial logic fills that void. Under the entrepreneurial logic, the business model configuration provides the conditions when a firm's strategic resources may enhance the value activities. Within the resource-based logic, the value-maximizing business model implementation with the firm's strategic resources is always presumed. In the positioning logic, the managerial choice of attractive strategic position and complementary value activities is presumed. The entrepreneurial incentives that enhance the management choice and their ability to execute the value creation and appropriation mechanism better than the competitors can are thus central to the competitive advantage creation.

The firm's competitive advantage is created and sustained in their business model implementation that constitutes the management logics, value opportunities, core resources, and value activities. Thus, the firm's managerial ability to execute its business model mechanism is crucial to the competitive advantage creation. In our theory of entrepreneurial rent, the business model or the value creation and appropriation mechanism is where the firm's competitive advantage lies. Further, the execution of the business model is enhanced by powerful entrepreneurial incentives. The entrepreneurial incentives provide the management an opportunity to earn entrepreneurial surplus and provide the firm an entrepreneurial rent. The entrepreneurial surplus is an excess compensation for bearing excess firm-specific risk. The entrepreneurial rent is the excess profits accrued from the firm's superior execution of the value creation and appropriation mechanism.

Organizations with entrepreneurial incentives are more likely to find attractive strategic positions and value opportunities, or deploy the resources more effectively in enhancing the value activities. Our entrepreneurial logic thus enhances resource-based and positioning logics. The entrepreneurial logic argues that it is the superior execution of the firm's business model mechanism where the competitive advantage is created and sustained. Furthermore, the business model mechanism constitutes the management logics, value opportunities, core resources, and value activities, which are enhanced by the entrepreneurial incentives (see Chapter 5). Thus, the entrepreneurial incentives that enhance the business model value drivers further enhance the firm's competitive position. Therefore, the entrepreneurial incentive is the uncertain performance-based compensation in the executive pay, such that the firm performance is set and evaluated by an external arbiter.

Thus, the theory of entrepreneurial rent argues that the source of competitive advantage lies in the firm's value creation and appropriation mechanism enhanced by the entrepreneurial behavior that is sustained by the entrepreneurial incentives. Our entrepreneurial logic is consistent with the emerging behavioral logic in that it is the entrepreneurial behavior, induced by the entrepreneurial incentives, which overcomes traditional behavioral bounds of decision makers. Conventional behavioral theory emphasizes problemistic local search and proximate opportunities, whereas our entrepreneurial logic emphasizes the firm's proactive exploitation of environmental uncertainty, recognition of complex stimuli, organizational agility, opportunity focus, and distant searches for superior opportunities. To enable distant searches, and enhance organizational agility and promotional focus of decision makers, the entrepreneurial incentives are needed in the organization. The entrepreneurial logic emphasizes the execution of the firm's value creation and appropriation mechanism wherein the firm's competitive advantage is created.

Entrepreneurial logic is different from strategic leadership logic. Strategic leadership logic, an extension of the upper-echelons theory, emphasizes the leadership traits of top management, whereas entrepreneurial logic emphasizes the entrepreneurial behavior of the organization, not the managerial traits. It is the firm's entrepreneurial behavior, namely, their alertness, agility, absorptive capacity, proactive adaptability, and opportunity focus, sustained by the entrepreneurial incentives, that underlies the competitive advantage creation according to the theory of entrepreneurial rent. Further, it is the management's desire to earn an entrepreneurial surplus that primarily drives the firm's superior performance. Entrepreneurial incentives in an organization induce an entrepreneurial culture, and the entrepreneurial culture enhances an opportunity focus in the organization.

Entrepreneurial incentives are thus key to the firm's achieving superior performance. In an interview with the *Harvard Business Review*,

Hatsopoulos (1995), Chairman and CEO of Thermo Electron Corporation, asserts: "When executives from other companies ask me what they need to do to increase new business activity, the first advice I give them is to change their organizations' basic incentive structures." In addition, Holt (1995), Vice President for Research and Technology at Xerox Corporation, states: "If innovation is the ability to recognize opportunity, then the essence of being an entrepreneur is being able to mobilize talent and resources quickly to seize that opportunity and turn it into a business." It is the entrepreneurial execution of the firm's business model mechanism wherein the competitive advantage is created. The buyer value design and the firm's business model mechanism that creates, delivers, sustains, monetizes, and appropriates the buyer value are central to the competitive advantage creation. The business model advantage enhances the firm's competitive position.

More distant value opportunities are Schumpeterian (Schumpeter 1934). Schumpeterian opportunities disrupt the market equilibrium, alter industry structure, and crush market entry barriers. In contrast, proximate opportunities are Kirzerian (Kirzner 1997), which are proximate and incremental in nature, and can be identified by a problemistic, local search in the environment. Proximate opportunities are visible to most firms in the industry. Even with the proximate opportunities, not all managers will act on them in a timely manner, and therefore the entrepreneurial incentives are still important to the exploitation of proximate opportunities in a timely manner. Kirzerian opportunities arise when product and factor markets are in temporary disequilibrium, and exploiting Kirzerian opportunities restores the market equilibrium. In contrast, exploiting Schumpeterian opportunities disrupts the market equilibrium and industry structure. Schumpeterian opportunities that include innovative and innovatively imitative opportunities are the source of competitive advantage for a firm competing in a dynamic environment.

The more entrepreneurial the firm, the less is the organizational inertia. Further, the more entrepreneurial the firm, the greater is the likelihood that the firm will seize and exploit distant value opportunities. Organizations with entrepreneurial incentives display superior dynamic capabilities that quickly reconfigure the resources and value activities to exploit the distant value opportunities in a timely manner. Active learning enhanced by the entrepreneurial incentives enhances the firm's dynamic capabilities. Thus, managers with entrepreneurial incentives have the ability to lead and shape the firm's social values such that multiple parties can be persuaded easily, and the firm resources can be mobilized quickly to reconfigure the value activities to exploit the firm's value opportunities in a timely manner. Entrepreneurial incentives enhance the firm's value creation and appropriation mechanism wherein the competitive advantage lies. It is the superior execution of the business model that exploits the firm's value opportunities in a timely manner sustained by the entrepreneurial incentives, which creates and sustains the firm's competitive advantage.

The Theory of Entrepreneurial Rent

The theory of entrepreneurial rent argues that the source of competitive advantage lies in the execution of the firm's value creation and appropriation mechanism that is enhanced by the firm's entrepreneurial behavior and sustained by the entrepreneurial incentives. It is the superior execution of the business model mechanism that provides the firm competitive advantage. The interior processes underlying the competitive advantage creation may be viewed in two stages. In the first stage, the entrepreneurial incentives enhance the entrepreneurial orientation of the firm, namely, the firm's agility, alertness, adaptability, proactiveness, and absorptive capacity, which further enhances the firm's active learning, management cognition, and dynamic capabilities.

In the second stage, the superior execution of the business model mechanism enhances the business model advantage that further enhances the firm's competitive position. The business model mechanism constitutes the management logics, core resources, value opportunities, and value activities, which are enhanced by the firm's active learning, management cognition, and dynamic capabilities. The business model value drivers enhance the value activities and revenue models that enhance the firm's value creation and appropriation. The firm's dynamic capabilities enable the firm to proactively adapt the business model to changing competitive conditions. The management logics enhance the management cognition that enables the firm's executives to sense and seize cognitively distant value opportunities. Further, the firm's active learning and absorptive capacity enhance the management logics and dynamic capabilities. The theory of entrepreneurial rent is illustrated in Fig. 6.1.

Entrepreneurial Incentives

The entrepreneurial incentives enhance the firm's entrepreneurial orientation, namely, the firm's agility, absorptivity, alertness, proactiveness, adaptiveness, and opportunity focus, which further enhance the business

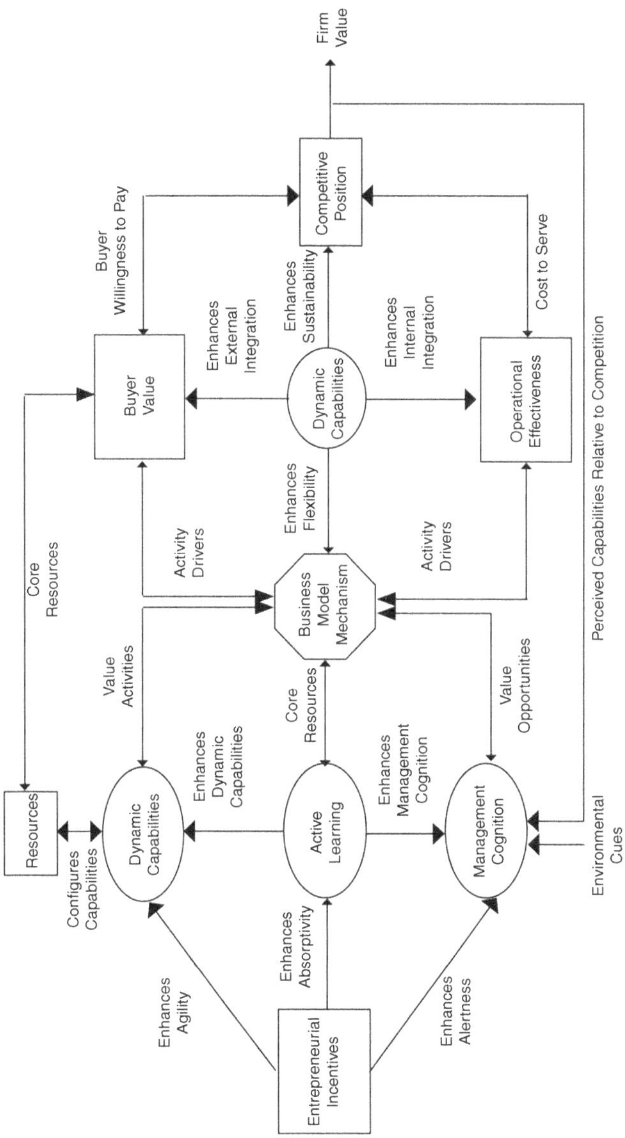

Fig. 6.1 The theory of entrepreneurial rent

model mechanism wherein the firm's competitive advantage is created and sustained. The entrepreneurial incentives provide the management the potential to earn an entrepreneurial surplus (above-industry-average compensation). The entrepreneurial surplus is the excess executive compensation when the firm has achieved superior performance relative to their peers in the industry. The entrepreneurial surplus is thus the excess compensation for the management when the firm's total risk is higher than the industry average. The firm's total risk is the sum of the systematic risk (measured by the stock beta) and the firm-specific risk (measured by the market model residual uncertainty or stock option volatility).

The entrepreneurial incentive is the uncertain compensation in the executive pay, where the firm performance is set by an external arbiter such as the capital market. The proportion of the equity-linked compensation in the executive pay measures the executive's entrepreneurial incentives. The entrepreneurial incentives are higher when the firm's management pay-performance sensitivity is higher relative to the competitors. The greater the entrepreneurial incentives in a firm, the greater will be the firm's entrepreneurial orientation or the greater will be the firm's alertness, agility, absorptivity, proactiveness, adaptiveness, and opportunity focus. The management pay-performance sensitivity or alternatively the percentage of equity-based management compensation thus measures the level of the entrepreneurial incentives in a firm. The greater the management pay-performance sensitivity, the greater is the potential for the management to earn an entrepreneurial surplus.

Proposition 1: The greater the entrepreneurial incentives or the greater the management pay-performance sensitivity, the greater is the firm's entrepreneurial orientation and the greater are the firm's agility, alertness, absorptive capacity, proactive adaptability, and opportunity focus.
Proposition 2: The greater the firm's entrepreneurial orientation, the greater is the firm-specific risk.
Proposition 3: The greater the firm's entrepreneurial orientation, the greater is the likelihood of earning entrepreneurial surplus.
Proposition 4: The greater the firm's entrepreneurial orientation or the greater the entrepreneurial incentives, the more likely the firm is to achieve superior performance (above industry average).
Proposition 5: The higher the firm performance above the industry average, the greater is the entrepreneurial surplus for the management.

The firm's pay-performance sensitivity is an incentive signal of the management ability. High-ability managers will accept greater pay-performance sensitivity, or a greater proportion of their pay may be based on an uncertain firm performance measure such as the market value of the firm's equity. Firm performance on which the entrepreneurial incentives are based must be truly uncertain so that the firm performance is not readily predictable. Thus, the accounting performance measures on which many executive performance plans are based are not truly uncertain; therefore, accounting-based performance plans may not be counted toward the firm's entrepreneurial incentives. The more uncertain component of the executive pay is equity-linked and includes stock options and restricted stock. In the entrepreneurial incentives, the firm performance is evaluated by an external arbiter such as the capital market. Some high-performing firms have their management pay constitute 80 to 90 percent in the firm's restricted stock and stock options. Further, it is not always incentive compatible for a firm to imitate the strategic resources of high-performing competitors in that the strategic resources may not be incentive compatible for the managers of the imitating firm, since an average-ability manager will not choose the same strategic resource that a high-ability manager chooses. The firm's choice of a strategic resource is thus an incentive signal of the managerial ability. And the strategic resource choice of a firm must be incentive compatible to the level of management pay-performance sensitivity.

> *Proposition 6: The greater the proportion of the stock options and restricted stock in the management pay, the greater are the firm's entrepreneurial orientation and the level of entrepreneurial surplus.*
> *Proposition 7: The firm's choice of a strategic resource must be consistent with the level of managerial pay-performance sensitivity and is an incentive signal of the management ability.*

Low-ability managers will not accept a high proportion of their pay in uncertain, equity-linked compensation. Low-ability managers prefer their pay tied to predictable accounting firm performance measures such as the return on assets or the return on equity (accounting-based). Entrepreneurial firms thus have high management pay-performance sensitivity relative to their peers. The pay-performance sensitivity increases with the management ability. Furthermore, the level of pay-performance sensitivity increases with the market dynamism. When the environment is more dynamic, the firm-specific risk is higher and thus the return to managerial human capital must be higher; therefore, the manager's entrepreneurial surplus is greater in a dynamic environment. The need for entrepreneurial incentives is more critical in a more dynamic or hypercompetitive environment.

The greater the entrepreneurial incentives or the greater the pay-performance sensitivity, the greater is the likelihood of an entrepreneurial surplus. However, low-ability managers may not choose higher pay-performance sensitivity since a high pay-performance sensitivity imposes a greater risk on their pay in a more dynamic environment. Managers who choose a lower pay-performance sensitivity are less likely to achieve superior performance in a dynamic environment. Further, in a dynamic environment, equity-linked pay, because of their option-like characteristics, is more valuable to high-ability managers; thus, the entrepreneurial surplus will be greater in a more dynamic environment.

Proposition 8: The greater the management ability, the greater is the management pay-performance sensitivity and the greater is the entrepreneurial surplus.
Proposition 9: The more dynamic the firm's environment, the greater is the pay-performance sensitivity and the greater is the manager's entrepreneurial surplus.

The firm's managerial human capital must earn a higher rate of return than the shareholder's financial capital for the management to be adequately incentivized. Shareholders are rewarded for the firm's systematic risk since shareholders diversify away the firm-specific risk (or the firm's unsystematic risk) by holding a diversified portfolio of stocks or by investing in a diversified stock mutual fund. Thus, the firm's shareholders may not be compensated for the firm-specific risk. However, the management bears and actively manages the firm-specific risk and so the managerial human capital must earn a higher rate of return than the shareholder financial capital. Beck and Zorn (1982) show that shares awarded to the management must be priced at a discount, or the management must earn entrepreneurial surplus through the price discount in the shares they are awarded. Shareholders earn a return on their investment capital commensurate with the firm's systematic risk, whereas managers earn a return on their human capital commensurate with the firm's total risk, the sum of the systematic risk and firm-specific risk. The greater the firm-specific risk, the greater is the potential for the management's entrepreneurial surplus.

Proposition 10a: The management earns an entrepreneurial surplus or a relative performance bonus relative to their competitors when their performance is higher than the competitors.
Proposition 10b: The greater the firm's entrepreneurial orientation, the greater is the relative performance bonus awarded to the management.

Proposition 10c: The greater the firm-specific risk, the greater is the relative performance bonus awarded to the management.

The greater the firm-specific risk, the greater must be the manager's entrepreneurial surplus. Entrepreneurial organizations exploiting cognitively distant value opportunities have a higher firm-specific risk; therefore, the entrepreneurial surplus must be greater in organizations with entrepreneurial incentives. Further, innovative or innovatively imitative opportunities are cognitively distant. The entrepreneurial surplus should be greater when firms pursue innovative or innovatively imitative opportunities. In Miles and Snow's (2003) typology, prospectors pursue innovative opportunities and analyzers pursue innovatively imitative opportunities. Thus, both prospectors and analyzers have a higher entrepreneurial orientation in that they are alert, agile, proactive, adaptive, absorptive, and opportunity driven. We expect the entrepreneurial incentives and entrepreneurial surplus are higher in prospectors and analyzers.

Proposition 11: Prospectors and analyzers have a greater entrepreneurial orientation.
Proposition 12a: Prospectors and analyzers have higher management pay-performance sensitivity relative to their industry peers.
Proposition 12b: The management of prospectors and analyzers earn an entrepreneurial surplus or relative performance bonus.
Proposition 12c: Prospectors and analyzers are more likely to choose cognitively distant value opportunities.

In entrepreneurial organizations, management teams require greater team collaboration and more interdependence; thus, executive tournament incentives can break down and as a result the firm's performance may suffer in entrepreneurial organizations. Tournament incentives are provided through large pay dispersions among the executives of an organization. Since team collaboration and interdependence is crucial to the success of entrepreneurial-oriented organizations, executive tournament incentives can have detrimental effects on the firm performance in entrepreneurial organizations. With tournament incentives, the firm managers may put forth great effort, but the team performance may suffer as sabotage often occurs between the executives.

Entrepreneurial organizations face a task environment that is more dynamic and complex; there is a need for greater team interdependence and team collaboration, and therefore the executive tournament incentives are more detrimental to firm performance. Further, the more dynamic and complex the task environment, the greater are the detrimental effects of tournament incentives in entrepreneurial organizations. Thus, the larger the pay dispersion among top executives in an entrepreneurial organization, the lower will be the firm's relative performance. Moreover, product market competition may be considered as an intra-industry tournament. Therefore, we may observe large pay dispersions across firms in an industry.

Proposition 13: The greater the firm's entrepreneurial orientation, the lower the likelihood of employing executive tournament incentives.
Proposition 14: The more dynamic the environment, the lower the firm performance with tournament incentives. The detrimental effect on the firm's performance increases with the firm's entrepreneurial orientation.
Proposition 15: The greater the market dynamism, the greater is the CEO pay dispersion among firms in an industry. Thus, the CEO pay dispersion is greater in hypercompetitive industries.
Proposition 16: The greater the market share of a firm in a hypercompetitive industry, the greater is the management's entrepreneurial surplus or relative performance bonus.

Dynamic Capabilities

The firm's dynamic capabilities enable the firm to proactively adapt to changing competitive conditions. The greater the firm's entrepreneurial orientation or the greater the firm's alertness, agility, proactiveness, adaptiveness, and absorptive capacity, the greater are the firm's dynamic capabilities. Entrepreneurial organizations are proactively adaptive and dynamic. Further, active adaptation occurs when the firm's potential performance increases, resulting in an increased gap between the firm's potential performance and their actual performance. Proactive adaptation occurs when the stimulus to increase the firm's potential performance comes from within the firm, not from an external stimulus such as the industry or competitor benchmarking. When the stimulus comes from an external source such as industry-best practices, preactive adaptation occurs. Thus, active adaption may be proactive or preactive. In our framework, the firm's dynamic capabilities enable the firm to proactively adapt. In preactive adaptation, the firm is trying to catch up with the competitors. The greater the firm's entrepreneurial orientation, the greater is the firm's proactive adaptation.

Proposition 17: The greater the firm's entrepreneurial orientation, the more enhanced are the firm's dynamic capabilities.
Proposition 18: The greater the management pay-performance sensitivity in an industry, the more enhanced are the firm's dynamic capabilities.
Proposition 19: The more enhanced the firm's dynamic capabilities, the greater is the management's entrepreneurial surplus.
Proposition 20: The more enhanced the firm's dynamic capabilities, the greater is the likelihood of the management exploiting cognitively distant value opportunities.

Teece's (2007) view of dynamic capabilities is consistent with the firm's proactive adaptation, whereas Eisenhardt and Martin's (2000) view of dynamic capabilities is consistent with the firm's preactive adaptation in that the stimulus to enhance the firm's potential performance comes from outside the firm, such as through competitive benchmarking and industry best practices. Proactive adaptation is driven by firms constantly seeking value opportunities to enhance their business model mechanism and entrepreneurial rent, whereas preactive adaptation is driven by firms constantly enhancing their resource position and catching up with their competitors. The greater the firm's entrepreneurial incentives, the more likely the firm is to be proactively adaptive and thus opportunity driven.

Proposition 21: The greater the firm's proactive dynamic capabilities and the more dynamic the environment, the greater is the likelihood of the firm pursuing cognitively distant value opportunities.
Proposition 22: The more dynamic the environment and the greater the entrepreneurial incentives, the greater is the firm's entrepreneurial orientation and more proactive are the firm's dynamic capabilities.

The dynamic capabilities enhance the firm's business model mechanism. The business model mechanism constitutes the management logics, core resources, value opportunities, and value activities. The dynamic capabilities enhance the firm's value creation and appropriation. As illustrated in Fig. 6.1, the proactive dynamic capabilities enhance the buyer value, business model flexibility, self-cannibalization and business model sustainability, and operational effectiveness. The buyer value is enhanced through the firm's products and services. The firm's operational effectiveness is enhanced by reconfiguring the resources and value activities. Thus, the more enhanced the firm's dynamic capabilities, the greater is the value chain effectiveness. The value chain effectiveness is the ratio of the buyer value added to the firm's marginal cost to serve. The firm's proactive dynamic capabilities are enhanced when the entrepreneurial incentives are high.

Proposition 23: The more enhanced the firm's dynamic capabilities, the greater is the value chain effectiveness.
Proposition 24: The more enhanced the firm's dynamic capabilities, the greater is the business model adaptability and the more robust is the business model.

Teece (2007) describes the dynamic capabilities as the firm's ability to sense and seize value opportunities, and reconfigure the firm resources to adapt to changing competitive conditions. The dynamic capabilities include the firm's capabilities for external integration, internal integration, operational flexibility, and self-cannibalization. External integration capabilities enhance the buyer value; internal integration capabilities enhance the operational effectiveness; operational flexibility enhances the business model adaptability and robustness; and self-cannibalization capabilities sustain the firm's competitive position. The dynamic capabilities are enhanced with the entrepreneurial incentives.

External integration capabilities enable a firm to integrate the customer knowledge and market intelligence within the firm to enhance the product and service quality. Thus, external integration enhances the consumer acceptance of the firm's products and services, which further enhance the buyer value. External integration capabilities include market probe and learn, market research, competitive intelligence, and other capabilities that enhance the firm's market linkages and customer relationships. External integration also includes the internal learning routines that assimilate the external information into the product and customer service outcomes.

Internal integration capabilities enable a firm to be more efficient and effective. Internal integration is achieved when the firm's functional areas are tightly connected and the value activities are optimally configured. Internal integration enhances the activity linkages, thereby enhancing the speed and efficiency of the organizational processes. Internal integration enhances the firm's operational efficiency that lowers the firm's marginal cost to serve. The firm's value chain effectiveness is enhanced with a lower marginal cost to serve.

Product flexibility affords a quick change in the firm's product mix on short notice, while process flexibility allows for rapid and easy changeovers in production setups. Modular product design enhances the product flexibility and variety. However, the product and process flexibility must be balanced with the operational efficiency. Flexibility is costly, so the benefits of flexibility must be weighed against the costs. In addition, the external and internal integration capabilities enhance the business model flexibility. Active learning enhances the product, process, and business model flexibility. And active learning is enhanced by the entrepreneurial incentives in a firm. The business model configuration must be flexible enough to adapt to the firm's changing competitive conditions but at the same time it must be efficient enough to achieve sufficient scale economies.

Self-cannibalization sustains the firm's competitiveness and prevents competitors from entering the firm's market space. A firm self-cannibalizes when it replaces its existing products or processes with new products or processes. However, most companies are reluctant to self-cannibalize because that would reduce the firm's current profits. The greater the entrepreneurial orientation of the firm or the greater the entrepreneurial incentives, the greater is the likelihood of the firm to self-cannibalize. Further, the greater the organizational ambidexterity, the greater is the likelihood of self-cannibalization.

Proposition 25: The more enhanced the firm's dynamic capabilities, the greater is the firm's self-cannibalization and the more sustainable is the firm's competitive position.

Proposition 26: The more enhanced the firm's dynamic capabilities, the greater is the buyer value added through superior products and services.

Proposition 27: The more enhanced the firm's dynamic capabilities, the greater is the firm's operational effectiveness through optimal reconfiguration of the value activities.

Proposition 28: The greater the firm's entrepreneurial orientation or the greater the entrepreneurial incentives, the greater is the likelihood of the firm self-cannibalizing its products or processes.

The organizational ambidexterity is the firm's ability to implement and exploit the value opportunities while phasing out their existing products and processes. Self-cannibalization thus requires organizational ambidexterity. Self-cannibalization includes two capabilities, namely, the ability to seize value opportunities in a timely manner and the ability of ambidexterity. With organizational ambidexterity, the firm pursues new value opportunities while it simultaneously manages and supports its current product lines and processes. Organizational ambidexterity is crucial for the firm's proactive adaptation. The entrepreneurial incentives further enhance the organizational ambidexterity and self-cannibalization capabilities. Self-cannibalization is akin to Schumpeter's concept of "creative destruction." The firms who fail to self-cannibalize in a timely manner will lose market share and competitiveness.

Proposition 29: The greater the firm's ambidexterity, the greater is the likelihood of the firm's self-cannibalizing its products or processes.
Proposition 30: The more enhanced the firm's dynamic capabilities, the greater is their ambidexterity.
Proposition 31: The greater the entrepreneurial incentives or the greater the firm's entrepreneurial orientation, the greater is the firm's ambidexterity.
Proposition 32: The greater the firm's ambidexterity, the more sustainable is the firm's market share and competitive position.

Absorptive Capacity

The absorptive capacity enhances the dynamic capabilities and proactive adaptation. The firm's absorptive capacity constitutes two capabilities, namely, active learning (knowledge generation) and combinative capabilities (knowledge integration). Entrepreneurial organizations are learning organizations. Entrepreneurial incentives enhance the firm's absorptive capacity in that their active learning and combinative capabilities. Entrepreneurial organizations continually learn and build resources to exploit superior opportunities. Active learning further enhances the firm's core resources, namely, the human capital, social capital, technology assets, and management systems. Active learning enhances tacit and explicit knowledge of individuals and the organization. The firm's knowledge capital resides in their core resources, namely, in their human capital, social capital, technology assets, and management systems.

Combinative capabilities integrate the knowledge generated or acquired within the firm and enable the firm's dynamic capabilities and resource orchestration. Combinative capabilities thus enhance the firm's resource combination and coordination capabilities that enable the firm to exploit their value opportunities. The firm's capability configuration occurs in two steps occurring simultaneously (see Fig. 6.1). Active learning enhances the management cognition that enables the firm to seek cognitively distant value opportunities. Furthermore, active learning enhances the dynamic capabilities that reconfigure the organizational capabilities to enable the firm to exploit those value opportunities. When the value opportunities are seized by the firm, a sequence of real options is created, which drive the firm's dynamic capabilities and resource reconfiguration. The entrepreneurial incentives enhance the firm's active learning and combinative capabilities.

Proposition 33: The greater the entrepreneurial incentives or the greater the firm's entrepreneurial orientation, the greater is the firm's absorptive capacity and the greater are the firm's active learning and combinative capabilities.
Proposition 34: The greater the firm's absorptive capacity, the greater are the dynamic capabilities and management cognition.
Proposition 35: The greater the firm's absorptive capacity, the greater are the core resources or the more enhanced are the firm's human capital, social capital, technology assets, and management systems.
Proposition 36: The greater the firm's absorptive capacity, the more enhanced are the management logics and the superior are the firm's value opportunities.

The dynamic capabilities facilitated by the firm's core resources and enhanced by the absorptive capacity reconfigure the firm's organizational capabilities. The firm's absorptive capacity enhances the core resources. The core resources are the shared knowledge of the individuals, embedded in the firm's human capital, social capital, technology assets, and management systems. The firm's dynamic capabilities enhance the resource orchestration processes, namely, resource substitution, evolution, and transformation, enabled by the sequence of the real options that result when the firm seizes the value opportunities. The firm's value opportunities and organizational capabilities are configured simultaneously. Active learning that enhances the management logics and management cognitive adaptability further enhance the management cognition and situation awareness. Active learning powered by the entrepreneurial incentives thus enables the firm to sense and seize cognitively superior opportunities. Entrepreneurial incentives enhance active learning in an organization.

Active learning enhances the firm's proactive dynamic capabilities and management cognition that further enhance the firm's value opportunities and the resource and activity orchestration. The entrepreneurial incentives that enhance firm's active learning, core resources, management logics, management cognition, and dynamic capabilities may explain the capability heterogeneity across firms in an industry. Thus, the greater the entrepreneurial incentives or the greater the firm's entrepreneurial orientation, the superior are the firm's management logics, core resources, value opportunities and organizational capabilities.

Proposition 37: The greater the firm's active learning and dynamic capabilities, the more aligned are the core resources with the value opportunities and the more enhanced are the organizational capabilities and value activities.
Proposition 38: The greater the firm's entrepreneurial orientation and active learning, the more enhanced are the management logics, the more enhanced is

> *the management cognition and the more cognitively distant are the seized value opportunities. Innovative or innovatively imitative opportunities are cognitively distant.*
> *Proposition 39: The greater the management pay-performance sensitivity, the less likely the firm is to have organizational inertia or core rigidity.*

Active learning enables the firm's combinative capabilities or knowledge integration, which enhances the management logics and resource orchestration. Active learning is defined as knowledge generation by an individual, a group, or an organization. Organizational and team learning are enhanced through the firm's combinative capabilities, namely, knowledge externalization, internalization, combination, and socialization. Organizational learning enhances the firm's core sources, namely, the human capital, social capital, technology assets, and management systems. Furthermore, the organizational knowledge is absorbed by the individuals and groups through internalization, enhancing the human capital. The organizational knowledge enhanced by entrepreneurial incentives and active learning thus enhances the value creation and appropriation mechanism wherein the firm's competitive advantage lies. Thus, the organizational knowledge enhances the business model advantage. The organizational knowledge enhances the management logics and hence the business model adaptability and sustainability.

> *Proposition 40a: The greater the firm's absorptive capacity, the greater is the business model advantage.*
> *Proposition 40b: The greater the firm's absorptive capacity, the greater are the business model scalability, sustainability, and flexibility.*
> *Proposition 40c: The greater the firm's absorptive capacity, the greater are the management logics, core resources, management cognition, and dynamic capabilities.*

Organizational knowledge includes tacit knowledge and explicit (codified) knowledge. Active learning enhances the organizational tacit and explicit knowledge. Active learning is a continuous process of individual and organizational knowledge creation and integration that occurs at the interfaces between the organization and its environment. Furthermore, efficient knowledge creation and integration in the organization requires the organizational transactive memory such that the organizational members know who knows what information, and no member will be overloaded with more information than necessary for their functional needs. Active learning enhances the organization's ability to acquire, create, integrate, exploit, and accumulate knowledge continuously through interactive processes between the teams and individuals, between the organization and teams, and between the organization and external stakeholders.

> *Proposition 41a: The more enhanced the firm's transactive memory, the more enhanced are the firm's absorptive capacity, management logics, dynamic capabilities, core resources, and management cognition.*
> *Proposition 41b: The greater the entrepreneurial incentives or the greater the firm's entrepreneurial orientation, the more enhanced is the organization's transactive memory.*
> *Proposition 41c: The more enhanced the firm's transactive memory, the more enhanced are the firm's business model scalability, adaptability, and sustainability, and the greater is the business model advantage.*

Value activities further enhance the individual and organizational learning. An individual's learning cycle includes four parts, namely, assess, design, implement, and action (see Chapter 3). Individual knowledge enhances the organizational knowledge through knowledge externalization and socialization, while the organizational knowledge further enhances the individual knowledge through knowledge internalization and integration. The combinative capabilities thus include the knowledge externalization, socialization, internalization, and integration processes. Further, the combinative capabilities enhance the firm's management logics and core resources that enable the firm's dynamic capabilities and proactive adaptation. The value activities thus further enhance the firm's active learning. The more enhanced the value activities, the greater is the value chain effectiveness. The value chain effectiveness is the ratio of the buyer value added to the firm's marginal cost to serve.

> *Proposition 42: The more enhanced the firm's combinative capabilities, the more enhanced are the firm's management logics, core resources, and dynamic capabilities.*
> *Proposition 43: The more enhanced the firm's combinative capabilities, the superior are the firm's value activities and value opportunities.*

The management logics, core resources, and dynamic capabilities are continually enhanced by the firm's active learning cycle. The organizational knowledge generated by active learning is assessed using the organization's justification standards, and if the knowledge is considered as worthwhile to the organization, it is retained and further enhanced through the active learning cycle. The organizational knowledge enhances the management logics that further enhance the management cognition and value opportunities. The greater a firm's active learning and thus the more enhanced the management logics, the narrower will be the gap between the organizational activities and the espoused theory.

> *Proposition 44: The greater the firm's absorptive capacity, the more enhanced are the management logics and the narrower is the gap between the firm's value activities and the management's espoused theory of how the value creation and appropriation takes place in the organization.*

The combinative capabilities enable effective integration and utilization of generated or acquired knowledge by the organization. The combinative capabilities enhanced by the entrepreneurial incentives enhance the dynamic capabilities that reconfigure the firm's product and process capabilities. The organizational knowledge embeds the firm's opportunity options (see Chapter 4). Thus, the firm's knowledge assets enhanced by the combinative capabilities serve as platform investments embodying the firm's opportunity options. Furthermore, the exercise of the firm's opportunity options triggers a series of real options, the exercise of which enables the firm's dynamic capabilities and resource orchestration. Thus, the knowledge assets enhance the dynamic capabilities that further enhance the firm's organizational capabilities and value activities.

The management knowledge base thus enhances the firm's dynamic capabilities when pursuing the value opportunities. The active learning enhances the management logics that further enhance the value opportunities. The management logics, value opportunities, and core resources enhance the firm's value creation and appropriation mechanism, where the firm's competitive advantage lies. Thus, active learning enhances the value creation and appropriation mechanism, enhancing the firm's competitive advantage. Further, the entrepreneurial incentives enhance active learning and management logics in the organization so that the business model execution advantage is enhanced and the firm may achieve superior performance.

Management Cognition

Entrepreneurial incentives enhance the firm's alertness and agility that enable the management to sense and seize cognitively distant opportunities in a timely manner, overcoming traditional behavioral bounds assumed in conventional behavioral theory of the firm. Entrepreneurial organizations are sufficiently alert to spot faint market signals when the signals are just a glimmer and before the signals are readily apparent to everyone. Entrepreneurial incentives also enhance the management's cognitive adaptability that further enhances the management cognition. Additionally, active learning powered by entrepreneurial incentives enhances the management logics that further enhance the management cognition.

The management logics constitute management's mental models and management's espoused theories of how their business works. The management logics or management mental models are enhanced by the firm's absorptive capacity, which is further enhanced by the entrepreneurial incentives. The management logics provide the basis the management employs when sensing the value opportunities, reconfiguring the firm resources, selecting strategic market positions, and reconfiguring and coordinating the value activities. Built on their past experience, active learning, and accumulated over time, the management logics are the management's knowledge, theories, and beliefs of how their business works and how the value is created and appropriated in their business. The management logics when are stagnant inhibit the management cognition and situation awareness in a dynamic environment, increasing organizational inertia and core rigidity. However, with greater entrepreneurial incentives and an entrepreneurial orientation that stimulate management learning and cognitive adaptability, the management logics are regularly tested and updated. The management logics when updated continually in a dynamic environment through active learning and management cognitive adaptability enhance the management cognition and the firm's portfolio of value opportunities.

In a dynamic environment, management must continually test and enhance their mental models and theories. Senge (1992) argues that many of the best ideas in an industry are known to a firm's managers, yet these ideas are never put into practice. The lack of implementation or insufficient execution is not the result of poor management skills, but rather the new ideas are at odds with the extant management logics. Often the management logics remain unexamined and unchanged in most organizations. The entrepreneurial incentives in an organization enhance the management learning and their cognitive adaptability, which further enhances the management knowledge and thus the management logics. Enhanced management logics boost the firm's value creation and appropriation mechanism.

Proposition 45a: The greater the entrepreneurial incentives or the greater the firm's entrepreneurial orientation, the greater is the management cognitive adaptability.
Proposition 45b: The greater the entrepreneurial incentives or the greater the firm's entrepreneurial orientation, the more enhanced are the management cognition and situation awareness.
Proposition 45c: The greater the entrepreneurial incentives or the greater the firm's entrepreneurial orientation, the greater are the management cognitive adaptability and the management learning.
Proposition 45d: The greater the entrepreneurial incentives or the greater the firm's entrepreneurial orientation, the richer the abstractness, complexity, and organization of the management logics.
Proposition 45e: The greater the entrepreneurial incentives or the greater the firm's entrepreneurial orientation, the greater is the firm's peripheral vision and the greater is the management's ability to spot weak signals before they are apparent to other firms.
Proposition 45f: The greater the entrepreneurial incentives or the greater the firm's entrepreneurial orientation, the greater is the management's ability to recognize novel stimuli and complex patterns in the environment and to seize more innovative or innovatively imitative value opportunities.

The entrepreneurial incentives enhance the management goals that can reduce the load on the management attention, enhancing management cognition and situation awareness. Management attention is generally a primary bottleneck to a firm achieving sufficient situation awareness required to spot superior value opportunities. Management attention is recognized as a scarce resource in an organization. The second primary bottleneck for a firm to achieving sufficient situation awareness is the executive working memory. The entrepreneurial incentives enhance active learning, which further enhances the transactive memory which reduces the load on the executive working memory and management attention. The executive working memory, a managerial capability enhanced by the organizational transactive memory, is another primary bottleneck to the management cognitive adaptability and the management achieving sufficient cognition and situation awareness. The firm's procedural and communication channels, or the organizational attentional resources, situate and distribute the management attention and enhance the executive working memory capacity.

The management attention and executive working memory are the primary bottlenecks to the management cognition and situation awareness. The management attention is the management capacity to focus on specific information in the environment, while the executive working memory is the management capacity to hold the transient information active for further processing. The transactive memory reduces the load on the management attention and executive working memory requirements. The entrepreneurial incentives that enhance the management goals reduce the workload on the management attention and executive working memory, enhancing the management cognition. The management learning that enhances the management logics further reduces the load on the management attention and executive working memory.

Management attentional resources are critical for the management to achieve sufficient situation awareness. Further, the management attention is situated and distributed by the firm's operating and governance channels. The firm's operating and governance channels thus focus, situate, and distribute the management attention (Ocasio and Joseph 2005). The attention-based view of the firm posits that the firm behavior is influenced by the firm's attentional resources. The three principles underlying the attention-based view of the firm are the principle of selective attention, the principle of situated attention, and the principle of distributed attention. The principle of selective attention states that executives will be selective with respect to the specific issues and initiatives to which they will attend. The management goals driven by the entrepreneurial incentives largely determine the selection of the issues and initiatives the executives will attend to at a given time.

The principle of situational attention states that the focus of executive attention depends on the situational context and thus the executive's attention focus will vary with the decision context. Further, the principle of distribution of attention states that the manager's attentional focus depends on the organizational procedural and communication channels that regulate and distribute the issues and initiatives (Ocasio 1997). The greater the entrepreneurial incentives or the more entrepreneurial the firm, the more agile the firm is and the quicker the management responds to a changing environment and the available value opportunities. The managerial attentional capacity and the distribution of the management attention in an organization determine the availability and exploitation of the value opportunities.

The firm's operating and governance channels situate and distribute the management attention. The entrepreneurial incentives enhance the management goals and organizational transactive memory and thus enhance the distribution of the management attention. The greater the entrepreneurial incentives, the greater are the firm's alertness, agility, absorptivity, adaptiveness, proactiveness, and opportunity focus, and the greater are the management learning and cognitive adaptability. In a more dynamic environment, the management powered by the entrepreneurial incentives may allocate more attention to seeking and exploiting the value opportunities.

Proposition 46a: Management goals reduce the load on the management attention and executive working memory, thus enhancing the management learning, their cognitive adaptability, and management cognition and situation awareness.
Proposition 46b: Automatic scanning reduces the load on the management attention and executive working memory resources.
Proposition 46c: Management goals direct the selection of the management mental model and management's espoused theory, thus enhancing the management learning, cognitive adaptability, and management cognition and situation awareness.
Proposition 47: The management learning and management's situation awareness is limited by the management attentional resources and executive working memory capacity.
Proposition 48a: The greater the entrepreneurial incentives, the more enhanced the organization's transactive memory, and the greater is the management cognition and situation awareness.
Proposition 48b: The more enhanced the organization's transactive memory, the greater is the executive memory capacity in the organization and the greater are the management learning and their cognitive adaptability.
Proposition 49: With enhanced transactive memory, situation awareness is distributed within an organization, requiring a greater coordination by the top management through effective design and implementation of the firm's operating and governance channels. Thus the enhanced transactive memory increases the load on the organizational attentional resources and management information systems.
Proposition 50: The more enhanced the organization's transactive memory, the greater are the firm's absorptive capacity and dynamic capabilities. Thus the enhanced transactive memory facilitates active learning and proactive adaptation in the organization.
Proposition 51: The entrepreneurial incentives enhance the speed and effectiveness of the firm's procedural and communication channels and thus enhance the management attention.

The management cognition constitutes the management's perception of the available information in the environment, their comprehension and interpretation of the information, and the projection of the key environmental variables and their impact on the firm performance in the near future.

Management cognition results in the management's situation awareness of their environment or their awareness of what is going on in their environment. Situation awareness is a shared state of knowledge of the environment in an organization. Managers differ in their cognitive abilities and thus their situation awareness varies across firms in an industry. Managers differ in their ability to recognize and evaluate potential value opportunities, to adapt to changing competitive conditions, and take timely actions on improving current operations and exploiting opportunities.

Management perception is how the available information is encoded and organized. The perception of the environmental information involves the managerial ability to recognize patterns and prototypes, and categorize available information. The management logics enhanced by the management goals influence the speed and accuracy of the management perception. The management logics when enhanced by management learning increase the speed and accuracy of the management perception. The entrepreneurial incentives enhance the management perception, enabling the management to recognize novel and complex stimuli in the environment. The entrepreneurial incentives enable the management to sense weak and cognitively distant signals. Signals may be categorized as opportunities or threats depending on whether there is a potential gain or loss, whether their impact on the firm performance is positive or negative, and whether the firm has more or less control over the situation.

Proposition 52: The management logics when enhanced through active learning increase the speed and accuracy of the management perception.
Proposition 53: The entrepreneurial incentives enhance the management's perception of the weak signals and cognitively distant cues.
Proposition 54: Small competitive threats enhance the management attention and situation awareness. However, more enhanced threats negatively affect the management attention and situation awareness.
Proposition 55: The entrepreneurial incentives (or the firm's entrepreneurial orientation) influence the speed and accuracy of the management perception.
Proposition 56: Automatic scanning improves the speed of management perception but not the accuracy of information.
Proposition 57: The more enhanced the entrepreneurial incentives, the more likely an event is to be categorized as an opportunity rather than a threat.
Proposition 58: Management goals reduce the workload on the management attention and enhance the management perception.

Management comprehension is the management' synthesis of the disparate information received in light of the management goals and incentives. The management logics and management attention enhance the management comprehension, and the management comprehension further enhances the management logics. Management thus constructs cause-and-effect relations between the information elements or the environmental state variables. The five principles that govern the management comprehension are the augmentation principle, the discounting principle, illusory correlation, illusory causation, and automaticity. These five principles guide the management in determining what and how available information is incorporated in constructing a holistic picture of the state of the firm's environment.

The entrepreneurial incentives and the entrepreneurial orientation of the firm enhance the management goals and thus the management logics, further enhancing the management comprehension. Automaticity reduces the load on the management attention and improves the speed of management comprehension. However, if the management is not actively conscious of the cognitive processes leading to an outcome, the accuracy of the management comprehension may suffer, especially in a novel task environment or when the management goals have changed. Furthermore, the management comprehension is enhanced when top-down (goal-driven) and bottom-up (data-driven) information processing activities are employed simultaneously.

Proposition 59: Management cognition is enhanced when a combination of top-down (goal-directed) and bottom-up (data-directed) information processing is employed in an organization.

Proposition 60: Situation awareness may be lower with the firm's automatic scanning in a dynamic environment.

Management projection is the management's ability to extrapolate the current trends and project their impact on the near-term firm performance. Projection is not forecasting of environmental variables. Rather, the management projection is the management's ability to forge a coherent relationship between the firm's present and future. Thus the management projects when they comprehend and extrapolate the current trends that have an ongoing impact in the industry. The management projection is enhanced with the management logics, and the management logics are further revised and enhanced by the situation awareness. The management goals enhance and are enhanced by the management logics and situation awareness. Further, the entrepreneurial incentives and the firm's entrepreneurial orientation enhance the management projection in light of the enhanced management goals. It is critical to recognize the current trends in the environment that have an ongoing impact, the full potential of which is not yet realized.

Proposition 61: The more entrepreneurial the firm or the greater the entrepreneurial incentives, the more enhanced is the management projection and situation awareness.
Proposition 62: The more foresightful the manager or the more enhanced the manager's projection ability, the more enhanced are the management logics and the more aligned are the firm's core resources with their value opportunities.
Proposition 63: The more foresightful the manager or the more enhanced the manager's projection ability, the greater the likelihood that the manager will choose a higher pay-performance sensitivity and entrepreneurial incentives.

Management learning enhances the management logics and therefore the management cognition and situation awareness. Management learning enhances the management's cognitive adaptability, enabling the managers overcome traditional behavioral bounds and better recognize complex and novel stimuli in the firm's task environment. Further, the entrepreneurial incentives and the firm's entrepreneurial orientation enhance the management learning and their cognitive adaptability. Management learning enhances the management logics, further enhancing the management cognition. Management learning includes the skills of reflection, inquiry, and advocacy skills that test and enhance the management logics, in that the management mental models and theories are surfaced, tested, and updated. Management learning enhances the abstractness, complexity, and organization of the management logics, enabling the management to recognize complex and novel stimuli.

Proposition 64: Management learning enhances the management cognition, enabling the management to sense cognitively distant opportunities.
Proposition 65: Management learning focuses and situates the management attention on the key variables in the environment.
Proposition 66: The management logics of more experienced managers have greater abstractness, complexity, and organization.

In a more dynamic environment, the management cognition is enhanced by enhancing management mental model complexity, implementing rapid decision making, and through active learning and taking experimental actions. The managers in entrepreneurial organizations have greater cognitive adaptability and thus more enhanced management cognition. Decision making is rapid and experimental actions are more prevalent in proactive entrepreneurial organizations that encourage an entrepreneurial culture and have a greater tolerance for failure. The entrepreneurial incentives enhance creative problem solving, rapid decision making, and experimental actions in organizations, which enhance management cognitive adaptability and the dynamic capabilities.

Proposition 67: Rapid decision making, enhanced managerial cognitive complexity, and experimental actions enhance the management logics and the firm's value opportunities.
Proposition 68: Rapid decision making, enhanced managerial cognitive complexity, and experimental actions are enhanced with the entrepreneurial incentives.

Management metacognition is the management's knowledge-generating behavior that can be intentionally manipulated, for example, by means of the entrepreneurial incentives and active learning. Metacognitive processes regulate and enhance the cognitive abilities of managers and enhance the management logics. Metacognitive processes thus improve the effectiveness of the manager's perception and comprehension of complex and novel stimuli in the environment. With greater metacognition, the management can effectively and quickly adapt the management logics or their mental models and espoused theories to novel stimuli in a changing environment. Management metacognition generates alternate and coherent stories that are further tested and retained to fill the gaps in the management logics, thus improving the management logics and enhancing the management cognition and situation awareness. Furthermore, the management goals are also revised and enhanced by management metacognition processes.

Proposition 69: Management learning and metacognition enhance the management logics and the firm's opportunity options.
Proposition 70: Management metacognition enhances the management goals, thus enhancing the management cognition and situation awareness.
Proposition 71: The more abstract and complex the management logics, the more enhanced the management learning and metacognition. The more enhanced the management metacognition, the more enhanced are the management cognition and situation awareness, and the more superior are the firm's available value opportunities.

Value Opportunities

Entrepreneurial organizations are constantly seeking value opportunities to build competitive advantage. The entrepreneurial incentives that enhance the management logics further enhance the management cognition, enabling the managers to recognize cognitively distant opportunity options. Entrepreneurial organizations are opportunity driven, and they are quick to seize an opportunity and exploit it in a timely manner. Exercising the firm's opportunity options and real options in a timely fashion enhances the business model advantage and the firm's competitive position. Opportunity options are unrealized value potential within the firm's knowledge resources. Further, the management logics enhance the firm's opportunity options that enhance the value opportunities and the real options that reconfigure the organizational capabilities. The entrepreneurial incentives provide the management the potential to earn an entrepreneurial surplus, which enhances the management goals and management logics that enable the managers to seize cognitively distant opportunities and exploit the opportunities by quickly reconfiguring the firm's resources.

The value opportunities provide the firm's value creation engine fuel to enhance and sustain the firm performance. Value opportunities must meet three conditions: (1) the opportunity has the potential to enhance the firm value, (2) the value added is commensurate with the risk and effort undertaken, and (3) the potential value created is appropriable by the firm. The net present value of a value opportunity must exceed a critical positive value determined by the level of uncertainty associated with the value opportunity. Value opportunities available to a firm differ in their risk, difficulty, novelty, and complexity.

Cognitively distant opportunities are less contested than proximate value opportunities. Further, cognitively distant opportunities are Schumpeterian. Schumpeterian opportunities disrupt market equilibrium, whereas proximate Kirzerian opportunities restore market equilibrium. Kirzerian opportunities are incremental in nature. Schumpeterian opportunities may require powerful entrepreneurial incentives that enhance the management logics and cognitive adaptability. Further, firms sense the opportunity characteristics differently, may act on them too early or late, or not at all. The theory of entrepreneurial rent predicts that organizations with entrepreneurial incentives are more likely to sense cognitively distant value opportunities, seize them in a timely manner, and exploit them successfully such that the firm's business model advantage and competitive position are enhanced.

> *Proposition 72a: The more entrepreneurial the firm or the greater the entrepreneurial incentives, the greater is the likelihood that the firm will sense and seize cognitively distant opportunities.*
> *Proposition 72b: The more enhanced the management logics, the greater is the likelihood that the firm will pursue cognitively distant opportunities.*
> *Proposition 73a: The more cognitively distant a value opportunity, the more risky is the opportunity.*
> *Proposition 73b: Innovative and innovatively imitative opportunities are more likely to be cognitively distant.*
> *Proposition 73c: Schumpeterian opportunities are likely to be cognitively distant.*
> *Proposition 73d: Cognitively proximate opportunities are Kirzerian or equilibrium-restoring, and are generally incremental in nature.*
> *Proposition 74: The more cognitively distant the firm's value opportunities, the greater the likelihood of the management earning an entrepreneurial surplus.*

Why are some executives more successful at identifying and exploiting superior value opportunities? The answer lies in the executive's ability to recognize complex and novel stimuli in the environment and employing a greater promotion focus enhanced by the entrepreneurial incentives. The entrepreneurial incentives enhance the executive's opportunity focus, away from a resource focus. Entrepreneurial organizations build resources, whereas traditional organizations build on resources. Traditional managers complain that their resource constraint does not permit them to pursue a certain opportunity, but managers empowered by the entrepreneurial incentives are not constrained by the existing resources. Entrepreneurial managers have a greater internal locus of control, cognitive complexity, and field independence (see Chapter 2 for the traits of entrepreneurial managers). Traditional organizations thus miss an opportunity unless they have sufficient resources, whereas entrepreneurial organizations seek opportunities regardless of their current resource position.

Managers who adopt a greater promotion focus rather than a prevention focus are more likely to examine more opportunity options and recognize more complex and novel patterns of cues in the environment. Entrepreneurial incentives enhance the manager's promotion focus. Thus, with entrepreneurial incentives, managers are more likely to sense and seize distant value opportunities in a timely manner. In comparison, resource-focused managers who have a greater prevention focus evaluate fewer opportunity options permitted by their resource position; thus, these managers are less likely to spot cognitively distant value opportunities. Entrepreneurially driven managers employ a greater promotion focus mildly tempered with prevention focus, and they are more likely to spot superior opportunities and make correct rejections. Promotion focus of an executive enhances the firm's odds of seizing a valuable opportunity in a timely manner.

Proposition 75a: Managers with a greater promotion focus are more likely to recognize a value opportunity when it is truly present.
Proposition 75b: Managers with a greater prevention focus are more likely to recognize the absence of opportunities when they are truly absent.
Proposition 75c: Managers with a greater promotion focus are more likely to explore a greater number of potential value opportunities.
Proposition 75d: Managers with a greater promotion focus are more likely to use less stringent criteria when evaluating prospective opportunities.
Proposition 75e: Managers with a greater prevention focus are more likely to use more stringent criteria to qualify a value opportunity.
Proposition 75f: Managers with a greater prevention focus are more likely to miss more opportunities or seize them too late.
Proposition 75g: Managers with a greater promotion focus are more likely to recognize cognitively distant opportunities.
Proposition 76: The greater the entrepreneurial incentives, the more likely the managers are to have a promotion focus.
Proposition 77: The greater the manager's promotion focus, the more enhanced are the manager's attentional engagement and situation awareness.

Value opportunities for a firm may arise from several sources such as incongruities in industry-best practices, structural changes in the industry, changes in consumer perception and preferences, changes in technologies and regulations, and unexpected occurrences in the organization. The greater the complexity and more dynamic the firm's environment, the greater is the number of value opportunities available to the firm. Further, the entrepreneurial incentives enhance the executive's ability to actively exploit the environmental uncertainty and seek opportunity options that steer the environmental uncertainty to resolve in the firm's favor. To proactively exploit the environmental uncertainty the firm develops and nurtures a portfolio of opportunity options.

Active exploitation of environmental uncertainty includes strategies such as big bets, opportunity options, and no-regrets. Big bets are major investments that might result in large payoffs in some scenarios but large losses in others. Big bets are often industry-shaping value opportunities that are of high risk but have potential to provide high reward. Opportunity options are designed by a firm to secure large payoffs in some scenarios while minimizing the losses in other scenarios. Firms thus make small investments upfront in developing opportunity options and reserve their right to invest further in the future. The greater the level of uncertainty, the more valuable and abundant are the firm's opportunity options. The management logics enhance the recognition and exercise of the firm's opportunity options in a timely manner. Finally, no-regret opportunities are hedged investments that pay off to the firm no matter what.

> *Proposition 78a: In a low to moderate velocity environment with predictable discrete scenarios, firms are more likely to invest in opportunity options.*
> *Proposition 78b: In a high-velocity environment, firms are more likely to make big bets that have large payoffs for the firm, combined with a hedge to minimize possible losses.*

The knowledge capital embodied in the firm's human capital, social capital, technology assets, and management systems embeds the firm's opportunity options. An opportunity option gives the firm a preferential access to a future value opportunity. The firm's knowledge resources are valuable when the embedded opportunity options are valuable, in that the underlying value opportunities have not expired or not been preempted by competitors. The greater the uncertainty of the underlying opportunity, the more time is left for the opportunity to expire before it is preempted by competitors, the more cognitively distant the opportunity, the greater the net present value of the opportunity, or the lower the investment outlay required for exploiting the opportunity, the more valuable is the opportunity option and the more valuable is the knowledge resource that embeds the opportunity option. The firm's knowledge resources are valuable a priori, when their embedded opportunity options are valuable. However, it is difficult for most firms to spot the opportunity options associated with the knowledge assets and evaluate them in practice. Thus, to assess whether a knowledge resource is valuable a priori, the management must be able to identify and value the opportunity options associated with the knowledge resource.

The firm's opportunity options are often difficult to spot and evaluate. Moreover, many organizations recognize their opportunity options too late or not at all, and fail to act upon them in a timely manner. The entrepreneurial incentives enhance the manager's promotion focus that further enhances the likelihood of recognizing the firm's value opportunities. Exercising an opportunity option results in a series of real options, enabling the firm's resource and activity reconfiguration. The exercise of opportunity options thus enable the firm's resource reconfiguration. In addition, active learning and combinative capabilities that enhances the knowledge resources further enhances the firm's opportunity options. Enhanced management logics also increase the likelihood of identifying the firm's opportunity options in a timely manner. The firm's knowledge resources and value opportunities are enhanced with the firm's active learning. The dynamic capabilities further enhance the firm's value opportunities and resource reconfiguration.

Proposition 79: The greater the firm's absorptive capacity, the greater are the firm's opportunity options.
Proposition 80a: The more valuable the opportunity options, the more valuable are the firm's knowledge resources.
Proposition 80b: The greater the uncertainty of the underlying opportunity, the more time left for the opportunity to expire, the lower the invest cost to exploit the opportunity, the more distant the opportunity, or the more valuable the opportunity, the more valuable is the opportunity option and the more valuable is the associated knowledge resource.

Management attention is critical for seizing and exploiting the firm's value opportunities in a timely manner. Management attention is defined as the manager's intentional, conscious, sustained allocation of cognitive resources to guide the managerial activities. Insufficient management attention resulting from poorly designed procedural and communication channels can inhibit the management cognition and the exercise of the opportunity options in a timely manner. Further, managers when preoccupied with the firm's current operations may fail to spot or exercise the opportunity options in a timely manner. Moreover, the relative importance between the firm's current operations and new value opportunities depends on the sustainability with the current operations. Management attention is a scarce resource. It is difficult for managers who are preoccupied with current operations to give sufficient attention to finding and exercising valuable opportunity options. Ambidextrous organizations can effectively identify the value opportunities, and distribute and optimize the management attention between current operations and the new opportunities. Entrepreneurial incentives enhance the organizational ambidexterity. Entrepreneurial organizations are ambidexterous.

Proposition 81: The more enhanced the firm's attentional resources, the more likely the firm is to exercise the opportunity options in a timely manner.

Proposition 82: The greater the entrepreneurial incentives, the more likely the firm is to exercise the opportunity options in a timely manner.
Proposition 83a: The firm is more likely to be ambidextrous when the opportunity options are more valuable.
Proposition 83b: The firm is more likely to be ambidextrous when the firm's absorptive capacity is high.
Proposition 83c: The firm is more likely to be ambidextrous when the firm has high financial slack and growth opportunities.
Proposition 84: The greater the sustainability of the firm's current operations, the less likely the firm is to pursue new opportunities in the absence of entrepreneurial incentives.

Real option theory does not consider the managerial motives that can prevent managers from exercising the firm's real options. Thus, the entrepreneurial incentives that enhance the management goals further ensure that the management is more likely to exercise the opportunity options in a timely manner and exercise the real options that enable the firm to reconfigure the resources to exploit the value opportunities. In the absence of powerful incentives, the opportunity options and the associated real options may not be exercised or exercised too late.

As illustrated in Fig. 6.1, the entrepreneurial incentives that enhances active learning enhance the management cognition and situation awareness, which enables the management to sense and seize the value opportunities in a timely manner. The entrepreneurial orientation of the firm thus enhances the management logics that further enhance the management cognition and situation awareness. The entrepreneurial incentives also enhance the management goals as the managers can earn an entrepreneurial surplus when the firm achieves superior performance. The management logics, core resources, value opportunities, and value activities are enhanced by the entrepreneurial incentives, which enhance the value creation and appropriation mechanism. The business model mechanism that adapts to a dynamic environment enhances the firm's competitive position.

Proposition 85: Entrepreneurial organizations are quick to spot the firm's opportunity options and exercise the opportunity options in a timely manner.
Proposition 86: The greater the management cognitive adaptability, the more likely the managers are to spot and exercise the firm's opportunity options in a timely manner.

Proposition 87: Entrepreneurial organizations are quick to align the core resources with the firm's value opportunities.
Proposition 88: The more enhanced the management logics, the more quickly the firm will reconfigure their capabilities to exploit the value opportunities in a timely manner.

Adverse managerial incentives associated with a firm's opportunity identification and exploitation include managerial overcommitment to failing opportunities, overinvestment in negative net present value opportunities, underinvestment in positive net present value opportunities, and managerial overconfidence. Financial slack alleviates the firm's underinvestment problem associated with the adverse selection when the growth opportunities are present. In the absence of growth opportunities, however, financial slack increases the agency costs of free cash flow and encourages managers to overinvest in negative net present value opportunities. Debt financing can constrain the firm's value opportunities and firm growth. Moreover, managerial overconfidence can engender an overinvestment problem in a firm with high financial slack.

Proposition 89: Debt above industry average constrains the firm from pursuing cognitively distant opportunities.
Proposition 90: Financial slack alleviates the firm's underinvestment problem when the firm has high-growth opportunities.
Proposition 91: Managerial overconfidence increases overinvestment when the firm has financial slack.
Proposition 92: Staged investment in an opportunity in the absence of entrepreneurial incentives can enhance managerial overcommitment to the opportunity.
Proposition 93: The level of managerial commitment to exploiting an opportunity varies with the firm's reward system, capital budgeting system, and prior experience of the management.
Proposition 94: Analytical decision making processes, as opposed to heuristics, when employed in management decisions escalate managerial overcommitment to the firm's failing opportunities.
Proposition 95a: Managerial overcommitment to a failing opportunity escalates when the costs to abandon the project are substantial.
Proposition 95b: Managerial commitment to an opportunity escalates when there is a lengthy delay between the investment in the opportunity and the payoff.
Proposition 95c: Managerial commitment to an opportunity increases with the amount of the investment in the opportunity.

Proposition 96a: A greater promotion focus escalates the managerial overcommitment to a failing opportunity.
Proposition 96b: A greater prevention focus alleviates the managerial overcommitment to a failing opportunity.
Proposition 96c: Managerial overconfidence escalates managerial overcommitment to a failing opportunity.
Proposition 97: Managerial overconfidence increases the likelihood of the firm to invest in negative net present value projects in the absence of growth opportunities.
Proposition 98a: Financial slack enhances the managerial overcommitment when the firm has fewer high-growth opportunities.
Proposition 98b: In the absence of growth opportunities, firms with high financial slack are attractive takeover targets.
Proposition 99: The value of the firm's knowledge assets is reduced when the firm has excess debt (above-industry average).
Proposition 100a: The entrepreneurial incentives enhance the positive relation between the financial slack and the firm performance when the firm has high-growth opportunities.
Proposition 100b: The entrepreneurial incentives alleviate the negative relation between the financial slack and the firm performance when the firm has low-growth opportunities.
Proposition 101: The number of acquisitions is greater in high-growth industries than in low-growth industries. The market for corporate control is more active in high-growth industries.
Proposition 102: Debt financing is more prevalent in low-growth industries than in high-growth industries.
Proposition 103: The likelihood of underinvestment is high when the firm's growth opportunities are high but the financial slack is low.
Proposition 104: Firms with high-growth opportunities but low financial slack are attractive takeover targets.
Proposition 105a: Firms with high-growth opportunities and high financial slack will sustain high firm growth when the entrepreneurial incentives are high.
Proposition 105b: Firms with high-growth opportunities and high financial slack are likely to be takeover targets in the absence of entrepreneurial incentives.
Proposition 106: Overconfident managers overestimate the value of opportunities and underestimate the potential risks.
Proposition 107a: Overconfident managers are reluctant to issue new equity to finance growth opportunities.
Proposition 107b: Overconfident managers are more likely to repurchase the firm's stock when the growth opportunities are low and the financial slack is high.
Proposition 108: Overconfident managers are more likely to resist takeover bids.

Business Model Mechanism

The business model mechanism is the value creation and appropriation mechanism wherein the firm's competitive advantage is created and sustained. The entrepreneurial incentives enhance the business model advantage. The business model construct constitutes scalability, adaptability, and sustainability. The business model advantage is enhanced when the buyer's willingness to pay is enhanced or the firm's cost to serve is lowered, or both. The business model advantage enhances the firm's competitive position. The business model mechanism constitutes the management logics, value opportunities, core resources, and value activities. The core resources are valuable when they enhance the linkage between the firm's value chain and the buyer value drivers. Further, a robust business model adapts continually to changing competitive conditions. Moreover, the business model efficiency must be balanced with the business model adaptability.

Proposition 109: The higher the business model advantage, the higher is the firm's competitive position.
Proposition 110: The more enhanced the linkages between the firm's value chain and the buyer value drivers, the more valuable are the firm's core resources.
Proposition 111: The greater the firm's business model advantage, the higher is the management's entrepreneurial surplus.
Proposition 112a: Entrepreneurial organizations are likely to have more novel business models.
Proposition 112b: Entrepreneurial organizations are likely to have more robust business models.
Proposition 113: The firm's balanced scorecard is enhanced with the business model advantage.

The value opportunities provide the necessary fuel to run the firm's value creation engine. The firm's core resources and value opportunities enable the value activities. The activity drivers enhance the firm value creation and appropriation. The revenue drivers enhance the buyer's willingness to pay and the cost drivers enhance the suppliers' opportunity costs. Further, the value opportunities and core resources support the activity drivers that enhance the buyer's willingness to pay or lower activity costs, or both. The business model is enhanced with the firm's active learning and combinative capabilities, and the value activities further enhance the firm's active learning. The activity drivers are linked to the revenue model and the operations model, and the revenue and cost drivers are configured to maximize the firm's ability to create and appropriate the buyer value. The revenue drivers enhance the revenue model effectiveness, and the cost drivers enhance the operations model effectiveness.

Proposition 114a: Active learning enhances the firm's business model advantage, namely, the business model scalability, adaptability, and sustainability.
Proposition 114b: The management logics enhance the activity drivers and the value activity linkages.
Proposition 115: The activity drivers enhance the firm's revenue model effectiveness and value chain effectiveness.
Proposition 116: The core resources and value opportunities enhance the firm's activity drivers that underlie the value activities.

The firm's value chain is linked to the buyer value chain. The buyer value drivers underlie the buyer value chain. The business model creates, delivers, sustains, and monetizes the buyer value (Mishra 2015). The core resources strengthen the linkages between the firm's value chain and the buyer value chain; thus, the core resources that enhance the buyer value or lower the activity costs enhance the business model advantage and competitive position. The greater the buyer value added and the greater the firm's share of the added value relative to its competitors, the greater is the business model advantage. The buyer value is created when the buyer cost is lowered or the buyer performance is raised, or both. The greater the buyer value added, the greater is the buyer's willingness to pay for the firm's product and the greater is the business model advantage.

The business model mechanism implements and executes the firm's strategy. The business model thus employs the firm's resources to exploit the firm's value opportunities. The management logics thus align the firm's resources with the value opportunities undertaken by the firm. The business model mechanism that creates and appropriates the buyer value constitutes the management logics, core resources, value opportunities, and value activities, all linked to the buyer value drivers. The firm's strategy determines where and how the firm will compete to achieve a desired strategic position that enhances the buyer value. Further, the firm's strategic position may be to become a low cost producer or a product differentiator, or both. The business model design requires the firm to determine which buyer segments and buyer needs the firm will serve; how the buyers will be acquired and retained; how the firm will create, deliver, sustain, and monetize the buyer value; what revenue models and revenue drivers the firm will employ; and what cost structure and cost drivers will support the firm's value activities that employs the firm's resources to exploit the value opportunities driven by the management logics and sustained by the management incentives. (Mishra 2015).

The business model design creates and delivers the buyer value (operations model); enhances the buyer's willingness to pay (revenue model); optimizes the firm's value activities, resources, and cost structure; acquires and retains customers (marketing model); and enhances the buyer value appropriability that enhances the firm's share of the added value. The business model mechanism constitutes the firm's value creation and appropriation drivers. The business model advantage is higher when the firm's business model is more efficient, robust, and sustainable relative to the business models of competitors. The business model advantage is measured by the ratio of the price the buyer is willing to pay to the firm's marginal cost to serve. The higher the business model advantage, the higher is the firm's competitive position. The entrepreneurial incentives enhance the business model advantage and competitive position. The greater the business model scalability, adaptability, and sustainability relative to the competitors, the greater is the business model advantage and the greater is the potential for entrepreneurial rent.

The entrepreneurial incentives enhance the firm's absorptive capacity and dynamic capabilities that enhance the business model efficiency, adaptability, and sustainability. The firm's absorptive capacity constitutes active learning and combinative capabilities enhancing the buyer value and lowering the activity costs. The dynamic capabilities enable the firm's external integration and thus enhance the buyer value; enable the internal integration and enhance the firm's efficiency and agility; enhance the firm's operational and strategic flexibility; and enable the firm's self-cannibalization and sustain the competitive advantage. The firm's external integration capability enhances the firm's market linkages through enhancing the products and services. The external integration capability supports the buyer value drivers through the revenue model design and the revenue drivers. The internal integration capability enhances the firm's resource linkages through optimizing the processes and value activities. Further, the internal integration optimizes the firm's cost structure and cost drivers. The firm's absorptive capacity enhances the dynamic capabilities. The entrepreneurial incentives enhance the firm's absorptive capacity and dynamic capabilities.

Self-cannibalization is a dynamic capability observed among entrepreneurial firms. However, self-cannibalization is time inconsistent in that a firm that enjoys superior performance must self-cannibalize its current competencies and build new competencies to sustain superior performance. The entrepreneurial incentives enhance the firm's ability to self-cannibalize in that the firm will more likely seek value opportunities to replace or strengthen the current competencies. Thus, the firm's ability to self-cannibalize their competencies enhances the business model advantage. The business model advantage is high when the business model efficiency, adaptability, and sustainability are high.

The business model efficiency is enhanced by optimizing the firm's value activities and activity linkages. The management logics guide the activity configuration. The business model efficiency enhances the value chain effectiveness. The value chain effectiveness is the buyer value added divided by the firm's cost to serve. Further, the revenue models can be configured in innovative ways to enhance the buyer's willingness to pay and thus enhance the business model advantage. The revenue model effectiveness is the ratio of the price the buyer is willing to pay to the buyer value added. The business model advantage is the product of the value chain effectiveness and the revenue model effectiveness.

The business model sustainability is enhanced when the customer and supplier lock-in are high, and when the business model novelty and specificity are high. Furthermore, the business model sustainability and efficiency enhance the buyer value appropriability and the firm's share of the added value. The added value is the buyer value added minus the suppliers' opportunity costs. The firm's share of added value is thus enhanced when the business model advantage is enhanced. For example, when the customer and supplier lock-in are enhanced, the customer and supplier switching costs increase, thereby enhancing the firm's relative bargaining power along the supply chain to extract a greater proportion of the added value. The firm's share of the added value is the total added value minus the added value appropriated by the buyers, suppliers, and complementors.

Proposition 117: The greater the firm's business model advantage relative to the complementors, the greater is the firm's bargaining power in the supply chain and the greater is the firm's share of the added value.
Proposition 118a: The firm's external integration capabilities enhance the product market linkages and thus enhance the business model advantage.
Proposition 118b: The firm's internal integration capabilities enhance the resource and activity linkages and thus enhance the business model advantage.
Proposition 118c: The firm's self-cannibalization capabilities enhance the core resources and thus enhance the business model advantage.

Proposition 118d: The firm's operational and strategic flexibility enhance the business model adaptability and thus enhance the business model advantage.

The business model sustainability is enhanced when the business model tacitness, complexity, and product market complementaries are high. With tacitness and activity complexity, the business model is causally ambiguous; thus, imitators find it difficult to copy the firm's business model. Further, the greater the number of products or services offered, the greater the number of market segments served, or the greater the number of channels employed, the greater are the product market complementaries and the more sustainable is the firm's business model. The product market complementaries create positive feedback and can provide increasing returns. The product market complementaries enhance the buyer's willingness to pay and hence enhance the revenue model effectiveness and the firm value appropriability. The product market complementaries also enhance the customer lock-in.

Proposition 119: Product market complementaries increase the buyer's willingness to pay and customer lock-in.
Proposition 120: The business model advantage is sustained with the customer lock-in and supplier lock-in, business model novelty and specificity, and business model tacitness and complexity.
Proposition 121a: The business model advantage is enhanced and sustained when the value activities and revenue models are linked innovatively to the buyer value drivers.
Proposition 122b: The business model advantage is enhanced and sustained when the firm's value chain and the buyer value chain are linked innovatively.

Effective business models are adaptable and thus are robust to changing competitive conditions. Organizations must continually examine the parts of their business model that are vulnerable to changing competitive conditions. The firm's dynamic capabilities enhance the business model adaptability. Organizations must quickly shift their resources and reconfigure the activities to adapt the business model to respond to changing competitive conditions. The business model adaptability requires a realignment of the firm's management logics, value opportunities, core resources, and value activities. A robust business model is thus self-realigning and emergent. Further, active learning enhances the business model adaptability. Active learning in the firm enhances the management logics to further enhance the value opportunities selection, enhances the firm's core resources to further enhance the linkages between the firm's value chain and the buyer value drivers, and enhances the dynamic capabilities that reconfigure the firm's resources and activities. Active learning and combinative capabilities constitute the firm's absorptive capacity. The firm's absorptive capacity is the capacity for organizational knowledge generation and integration.

Proposition 123: The management logics realign the firm's core resources, value opportunities, and value activities when the competitive conditions shift.
Proposition 124: When the firm's active learning takes place faster than the rate of change in competitive conditions, the business model mechanism is enhanced, and the business model advantage is sustained.

The business model adaptability enables continuous morphing in that the firm's product offerings, resources, and activities shift with the changing competitive conditions. Continuous morphing sustains a firm's competitive advantage. Entrepreneurial organizations continuously morph. When firms continuously morph, the business model mechanism self-realigns. The linkages between the business model configuration and the buyer value chain are further enhanced. The buyer value drivers underlie the buyer value chain that gets the buyer's job done or problem solved. The buyer value is enhanced when the buyer performance is raised or the buyer cost is lowered, or both. In hypercompetitive industries, firms that are entrepreneurial, namely, being agile, alert, absorptive, proactive, opportunity driven continuously morph their business model configuration to sustain competitive advantage. Powerful entrepreneurial incentives enable the firm to morph continuously.

Proposition 125: Continuous morphing enhances the business model advantage and the firm's competitive position in a dynamic environment.
Proposition 126a: Entrepreneurial incentives enhance the firm's absorptive capacity and management logics and thereby enhance the firm's ability to morph continuously.
Proposition 126b: Entrepreneurial surplus for management is sustained when the firm morphs continuously. Entrepreneurial rent is sustained when the firm's business model morphs in changing competitive conditions.
Proposition 126c: Active learning and combinative capabilities enhance the firm's continuous morphing.
Proposition 126d: The more enhanced the entrepreneurial incentives and management logics, the greater is the likelihood that the firm will morph continuously.

The business model adaptability is enhanced through activity multiplexity, task and resource redundancies, and loose–tight coupling of activities. Activity multiplexity refers to the number and diversity of the linkages between the value activities. The greater the number of activity linkages, the greater is the activity multiplexity and the greater is the knowledge sharing in the firm, thus enhancing the firm's active learning and combinative capabilities, which further enhances the dynamic capabilities and business model adaptability. The entrepreneurial incentives enhance the management logics that further enhance the activity coordination through the activity reconfiguration. Thus, the firm's reward system and incentive structure must be effective in leveraging cross-functional activity linkages. The firm's operating and governance channels that distribute the management attention are critical for enhancing the activity linkages. Therefore, the organizational attentional resources can become a bottleneck to the business model adaptability.

Proposition 127: The more enhanced the firm's operating and governance channels, the greater is the business model adaptability.
Proposition 128: The more enhanced the absorptive capacity and management logics, the greater is the business model adaptability.
Proposition 129: The more enhanced the firm's reward system, the greater is the business model adaptability.
Proposition 130: The more entrepreneurial the firm or the greater the entrepreneurial incentives, the greater is the business model adaptability.
Proposition 131: The greater the activity multiplexity, the greater is the business model adaptability.

Resource and task redundancies enhance the business model adaptability and the firm's dynamic capabilities. Resource slack is considered waste and inefficient by economists; however, behavioral theorists consider resource slack essential to enhance the firm's ability to adapt and cope with unforeseen challenges. In the absence of financial slack, a high-growth firm may have an underinvestment problem in that the firm must pass up positive net present value opportunities. Penrose (1959) in the theory of the growth of the firm emphasizes the role of resource slack as essential to support the firm growth. In the absence of growth opportunities, however, a firm's resource slack may be considered as waste and inefficient. Further, resource redundancy allows experimentation and learning, innovation, and risk taking in the organization when the entrepreneurial incentives are present.

Task redundancy requires that a value activity can accomplish more than one task, and alternative activities can perform the same task. Because not all activities are required at all times, the failure of one value activity to adapt to a changed condition can be replaced while another value activity is responding to the change. Redundancy in activity and resource linkages ensures that if one activity linkage fails, it can be replaced easily if alternative linkages can sustain the activity relations in the meantime. The redundancy in activity linkages thus enhances the business model reliability. With resource, task, activity linkage redundancies, the business model is more reliable and robust. The more robust the business model, the greater is the firm's absorptive capacity and the more disposed is the organization to experimentation and innovation.

Proposition 132a: Task and resource redundancies enhance the effectiveness of the firm's dynamic capabilities.
Proposition 132b: Task and resource redundancies enhance continuous morphing and the business model configuration reliability.
Proposition 132c: The greater the business model absorptive capacity, the more enhanced are the firm's dynamic capabilities.
Proposition 132d: The greater the number of linkages between the firm's cross-functional activities, the more robust is the business model.

Furthermore, loose coupling of the activities enhances the business model adaptability, while tight coupling enhances the business model efficiency. Loose-tight coupling of value activities supports continuous morphing and sustains the business model advantage. Thus, loose–tight coupling of the value activities balances business model efficiency with business model adaptability. A system is loosely coupled when its elements share a few variables in common. Loose coupling of system elements means that the elements are relatively independent but can adjust quickly to changing conditions, thus enhancing the system's robustness. Further, linkage multiplexity and task redundancies enhance the business model robustness. Outsourcing some of the activities enhances loose coupling in the firm's value chain and further enhances the business model flexibility.

Proposition 133: The less critical the value activity to the buyer, the more rapidly a technology underlying the activity is changing, the less important the activity to the firm's competitive position, the more reliable the supplier base,

or the less integral the activity to the firm's business model, the more likely the value activity will be outsourced.
Proposition 134: The greater the entrepreneurial incentives, the more balanced is the loose-tight coupling of the value activities, and the more robust is the business model.
Proposition 135: The more enhanced the management logics, the more balanced is the loose–tight coupling of activities and the greater is the business model sustainability.

The business model is a complex adaptive system; it is self-realigning in changing competitive conditions when the organization is proactive and entrepreneurial. The business model is more robust when the entrepreneurial incentives are high and the firm has high absorptive capacity. The business model mechanism constitutes the management logics, value opportunities, core resources, and value activities that coevolve and self-organize when the firm is entrepreneurial or the entrepreneurial incentives are high. Further, robust business models can sustain the firm's value creation and appropriation mechanism wherein the competitive advantage lies. Robust business models enable a firm to stay ahead of the Red Queen race, such that the firm's competitive advantage is sustained. The Red Queen effect occurs when a predator learns to run faster, but the prey responds creatively to stay ahead. Thus, a firm must constantly seek superior value opportunities to stay ahead of the Red Queen race. At the edge of chaos (optimal business model complexity), the business model advantage is sustained. Further, entrepreneurial organizations constantly seek higher business model peaks.

Proposition 136a: At the optimal business model configuration complexity, the business model advantage is maximized.
Proposition 136b: At the optimal business model configuration, business model efficiency is balanced with business model adaptability and the firm's competitive position is sustained.
Proposition 137: Firms with robust business models exploit multiple value opportunities simultaneously.
Proposition 138: Firms with robust business models hold a portfolio of short-term, medium-term, and long-term opportunity options with varying degrees of risks, payoffs, and complexity.
Proposition 139: The more complex, abstract, and organized the management logics, the more robust is the business model.
Proposition 140: The more innovative or innovatively imitative the value opportunities, the more complex is the business model.

Summary

Entrepreneurial incentives stimulate entrepreneurial behavior in the organization and empower executives to overcome traditional behavioral bounds. Entrepreneurial incentives provide the management the potential to earn an entrepreneurial surplus. Entrepreneurial incentives enhance the management cognitive adaptability, which further enhances the management cognition and enables them to sense cognitively distant value opportunities. Further, entrepreneurial incentives enhance the firm's active learning and combinative capabilities to further enhance the management logics, cognitive adaptability, and business model advantage. The firm's absorptive capacity enhances the business model mechanism. The management logics enhance the firm's value creation and appropriation mechanism wherein the competitive advantage lies. Entrepreneurial incentives enhance the firm's absorptive capacity.

The theory of entrepreneurial rent argues that the source of competitive advantage lies in the firm's value creation and appropriation mechanism enhanced by the entrepreneurial behavior and sustained by the entrepreneurial incentives (Fig. 6.1). The entrepreneurial incentive is provided through the uncertain performance-based compensation in the executive pay, where the firm performance is set and evaluated by an external arbiter such as the capital market or product market. The entrepreneurial incentives thus enhance the entrepreneurial orientation of the firm, namely, the firm's agility, alertness, proactive adaptiveness, absorptive capacity, and opportunity focus. The entrepreneurial incentives provide the firm an entrepreneurial leverage that enhances the firm's value creation and appropriation mechanism. Further, the business model constitutes the firm's value creation and appropriation mechanism wherein the firm's competitive advantage is created and sustained. The greater the uncertain compensation in the management pay or the greater is the management pay-performance sensitivity, the greater is the potential for the management to earn an entrepreneurial surplus, the greater are the entrepreneurial incentives and the more entrepreneurial will be the organization.

The entrepreneurial incentives enhance the firm's alertness, agility, absorptive capacity, proactive adaptability, and opportunity focus. The firm's entrepreneurial behavior is a source of competitive advantage that provides the firm an entrepreneurial rent and the management an entrepreneurial surplus. The firm's entrepreneurial behavior is scarce, imperfectly imitable, and imperfectly mobile; thus, the firm's entrepreneurial behavior meets the conditions of the source of competitive advantage. The more entrepreneurial the firm or the greater the entrepreneurial incentives, the more likely the firm is to achieve competitive advantage. Competitive advantage is the rationale underlying a firm's superior performance. Further, in our theory of the entrepreneurial rent, the competitive advantage lies in the firm's superior execution of the value creation and appropriation mechanism sustained by the entrepreneurial incentives.

The entrepreneurial incentives empower the managers to overcome traditional behavioral bounds. The entrepreneurial incentives thus enable the managers to sense and seize cognitively distant value opportunities in a timely manner. Entrepreneurial organizations constantly seek value opportunities to build competitive advantage. Entrepreneurial organizations when pursuing value opportunities are not constrained by their current resource positions. Entrepreneurial incentives are at the heart of entrepreneurial organizations. Entrepreneurial organizations build resources, whereas traditional organizations build on resources. The theory of entrepreneurial rent asserts that a firm can build and sustain competitive advantage without the need for strategic resources. The more entrepreneurial the firm, the greater the likelihood of achieving competitive advantage in spite of a lack of strategic resources. It is the business model execution advantage that provides the firm competitive advantage.

The firm's absorptive capacity constitutes the firm's active learning (knowledge generation) and combinative capabilities (knowledge integration). Entrepreneurial organizations are absorptive in that they actively learn and generate knowledge that reconfigures the firm's capabilities. Further, active learning enhances the firm's core resources, management logics, management cognition, value opportunities, and dynamic capabilities (see Fig. 6.1). The management logics are enhanced to support the management cognition and dynamic capabilities. Enhanced management cognition and situation awareness further enhances the value opportunities, and the dynamic capabilities enhance the organizational capabilities. Thus, the firm's value opportunities and organizational capabilities are developed simultaneously, enhanced by the management logics and sustained by the entrepreneurial incentives. Prior resources and capabilities do not constrain a firm's value opportunities when executives are empowered with entrepreneurial incentives.

Entrepreneurial organizations continually learn, test, and revise their management logics. The management logics are the management mental models and espoused theories of how their business works and how the firm value is created and appropriated. The management logics enhance the execution of the firm's value creation and appropriation mechanism. Further, the management logics when continually updated enhance the management cognition, which enables the management to sense and seize cognitively distant value opportunities. Furthermore, the entrepreneurial incentives enhance the management goals that reduce the load on the management attention and executive working memory that are the primary bottlenecks to achieving superior management cognition and sufficient situation awareness. The management attention, a scarce firm resource, is further enhanced by the firm's design of its operating and governance channels that situate and distribute the management attention. Management attentional capacity constrains the business model cashflow advantage and firm growth (Penrose 1959). The entrepreneurial incentives enhance the organizational attentional resources and enrich the management goals.

Active learning enhances the firm's core resources, namely, their human capital, social capital, technology assets, and management systems. Active learning enables the combinative capabilities that further enable the firm's knowledge integration and capability reconfiguration to exploit the firm's value opportunities. The core resources strengthen the linkages between the firm's value chain and the buyer value drivers. The buyer value chain gets the buyer's job done or problem solved. The core resources thus enhance the buyer's willingness to pay in that the core resources enhance the buyer value by raising the buyer performance or lowering the buyer cost, or both. The firm's knowledge capital within the core resources embodies the firm's opportunity options. When the firm's opportunity options are valuable in that the underlying value opportunities have not expired or not been preempted by competitors, the firm's knowledge resources are valuable. Active learning enhances the value of the core resources and the portfolio of opportunity options.

Active learning enhances the management's cognitive adaptability, which further enhances the management's cognition and situation awareness. Situation awareness is the firm's knowledge of what is going on in their environment. The firm's situation awareness is a shared awareness of the senior executives in the organization. The greater the situation awareness, the greater is the firm's agility, adaptability, and proactiveness. The greater the situation awareness, the more proactively adaptive is the firm and the greater are their dynamic capabilities. The transactive memory that constitutes who knows what information in the organization, enhances the situation awareness and hence the firm's dynamic capabilities.

The entrepreneurial incentives enhance the promotion focus of the executives. With the promotion focus, the executives examine a greater number of potential opportunities and thus they are less likely to miss a superior opportunity. With the promotion focus, the executives can sense weak signals in the environment before the signals are readily apparent to everyone. The promotion focus enhances the executive's peripheral vision. The promotion focus that is mildly tempered with prevention focus enables the executives to sense cognitively distant value opportunities.

Management attention is a scarce resource in an organization. Management attention is the manager's intentional, conscious, sustained allocation of cognitive resources to guide the managerial activities. The entrepreneurial incentives enhance the management alertness and attentional engagement. Insufficient management attention resulting from poorly designed operating and governance channels of the firm can inhibit the management's recognition and exercise of the value opportunities in a timely manner. Managers when preoccupied with current operations may fail to recognize or exercise the firm's opportunity options in a timely manner. The allocation of the management attention between the firm's current operations and new opportunities depends on the firm's business model sustainability with current operations. It is difficult for managers who are preoccupied with the firm's current operations to give sufficient attention to identifying and exercising valuable opportunity options. Ambidextrous organizations effectively distribute the management attention between the firm's current operations and new opportunities. The entrepreneurial incentives enhance the organizational ambidexterity.

Insufficient management attention constrains the management cognition and the firm's dynamic capabilities, thus limiting the firm's value opportunities and capability reconfiguration and thereby limiting the firm's potential to earn entreprenurial rent. Insufficient management attention is a bottleneck to the firm's achieving superior performance. Further, management attentional engagement enhances the firm's value creation and appropriation. The entrepreneurial incentives enhance the management's attentional engagement. The business model value creation and appropriation drivers, namely, the management logics, value opportunities, core resources, and value activities, are enhanced with the management's sustained attentional engagement. The dynamic capabilities that enhance the business model adaptability and sustainability are further enhanced with the management's sustained attentional engagement. The management goals supported by powerful entrepreneurial incentives sustain the management's attentional engagement.

The business model constitutes the firm's value creation and appropriation mechanism. The business model construct constitutes the business model scalability, adaptability, and sustainability. The firm's activity system enhances the business model scalability. The dynamic capabilities enhance the business model efficiency, adaptability, and sustainability. The active learning and combinative capabilities enhance the dynamic capabilities that further enhance the firm's self-cannibalization and business model sustainability. The dynamic capabilities constitute the firm's capabilities for external integration, internal integration, operating flexibility, and self-cannibalization. Further, the entrepreneurial incentives enhance the dynamic capabilities. The management logics enhance the firm's dynamic capabilities, management cognition, and business model. In addition, the exercise of opportunity options results in a series of real options, which, when exercised, enables the dynamic capabilities and reconfigures the firm's resources and value activities. Seizing value opportunities in a timely manner thus deploys the dynamic capabilities and enhances the firm's resource reconfiguration.

The business model drivers constitute the management logics, value opportunities, core resources, and value activities that support the firm's value creation and appropriation. The value activities and the activity drivers therein enhance the buyer value and lower the firm's cost to serve. The activity drivers include the revenue drivers and cost drivers. The revenue drivers enhance the buyer's willingness to pay, and the cost drivers lower the activity costs. The core resources and value opportunities enhance the activity drivers. The activity drivers enhance the value activities and revenue models. The value activities enhance the value chain effectiveness or the ratio of the buyer value added to the firm's cost to serve. The revenue models enhance the revenue model effectiveness or the ratio of the price the buyer is willing to pay to the buyer value added. The revenue models and signaling activities enhance the firm value appropriability. The business model advantage is the product of the value chain effectiveness and revenue model effectiveness. The business model advantage is thus the ratio of the price the buyer is willing to pay for the firm's product or service to the firm's marginal cost to serve the buyer. The entrepreneurial incentives enhance the business model execution advantage which sustains the firm's competitive position.

The business model construct constitutes the business model scalability, adaptability, and sustainability. Further, the greater the business model scalability, adaptability, or sustainability, the greater is the business model advantage and the higher is the firm's competitive position. The greater the business model efficiency and adaptability, the greater is the cash flow sustainability. The business model efficiency must be balanced with the business model adaptability. Robust business models are sustainable. The entrepreneurial incentives enhance the business model efficiency, adaptability, and sustainability, further enhancing the business model advantage and the firm's competitive position. In a low-velocity environment, the business model efficiency is more desirable, whereas in a moderate- to high-velocity environment, the greater business model adaptability is desirable. The firm's dynamic capabilities balance the business model efficiency and adaptability, thus enhancing the business model sustainability.

The business model adaptability and the firm's dynamic capabilities are enhanced with greater activity multiplexity, task and resource redundancies, and loose–tight coupling of the value activities. The multiplexity increases the number and diversity of activity linkages. The loose–tight coupling of activities balances the business model efficiency and adaptability. Task and resource redundancies enhance the business model reliability. Furthermore, robust business models enable the firms to stay ahead of the Red Queen race and sustain the firm's competitive position. With entrepreneurial incentives, the firm's core resources, organizational capabilities, management logics, value opportunities, activity drivers, and value activities coevolve and self-organize when the competitive conditions change in a dynamic environment. The firm's business model mechanism enhanced by powerful entrepreneurial incentives sustains the buyer value added and the firm's competitive advantage.

CHAPTER 7

The Theory of Franchising

Introduction

Why do some firms franchise and others not? Why is the franchising business model found to persist; that is, why do mature franchisors without capital constraints continue franchising? Why do department stores and supermarket chains with geographically dispersed outlets not choose to franchise? Why are the units in some regions, although closer to their regional headquarters, franchised rather than company-owned? The theory of franchising provides explanations to these and other questions related to why and when retail firms choose the franchising model for expansion.

The theory of franchising provides firm-specific and location-specific conditions when a firm may choose the franchising business model, how the franchise payment should be structured, how the franchising strategy evolves over the franchisor's life cycle, and whether a specific outlet should be franchised or company-owned. The theory of franchising provides specific guidance to the empirical research in franchising. Without an adequate theory of franchising, the empirical franchising literature suffers from misdirected empirical designs, confounding findings, and potential misinterpretations. The theory of franchising fills an important gap in franchising literature.

Entrepreneurial value creation is the key to the franchising strategy. Franchising business models leverage the entrepreneurial mechanism to reduce the cash flow uncertainty and sustain competitive position.

C.S. Mishra, *Creating and Sustaining Competitive Advantage*,
DOI 10.1007/978-3-319-54540-0_7

The franchising model is employed when the value appropriability is uncertain. The franchising structure enhances value appropriability. The franchise business model provides leveraged growth and entrepreneurial flexibility when the cash flow uncertainty is high.

The theory of franchising postulates that the franchising strategy relaxes an underinvestment condition associated with adverse selection when the firm growth potential is high; enhances the business model sustainability; reduces firm value appropriation uncertainty; enhances the brand value and competitive position; provides entrepreneurial flexibility; and minimizes the firm's monitoring, coordination, and customer acquisition costs. The theory of franchising draws on business model conditions to explain why and when some firms may franchise and others do not. The magnitude and uncertainty of the appropriable rent determine the firm's choice of whether to franchise and the sustainable rate of franchising.

Geographic dispersion leading to franchising is predicted by agency theory. However, firms do not necessarily choose to franchise because of the geographic dispersion of their outlets. Several department stores and supermarket chains, although their outlets are geographically dispersed, choose not to franchise their outlets. Several restaurants and hair salons also choose not to franchise but rather wholly own their retail units. The agency theory suggests that the franchising model provides superior incentives and lowers employee monitoring costs, because employee monitoring is costly when the retail units are geographically dispersed; and as franchisees are residual claimants, therefore their interests are more aligned with the franchisor's objectives in maximizing firm profitability. However, some firms choose not to franchise but rather wholly own their retail units. The agency theory alone cannot explain the firm's decision not to franchise at all.

Similarly, the resource scarcity theory predicts that retail firms franchise when they are capital constrained. However, many franchisors offer financial assistance to their franchisees; thus, these firms choose to franchise their units even when they are not capital constrained. Further, among mature franchisors (who are not necessarily capital constrained), the average percentage of outlets franchised is about 80 percent, and only about 20 percent of the outlets are corporate-owned. If franchising is to occur under capital constraint as postulated by the resource scarcity theory, then as franchisors mature and their capital constraint is removed, the franchisors should invest in only company-owned outlets. However, empirical evidence does not support this conclusion. Mature franchisors continue to franchise and maintain a stable ratio of franchised units to company-owned units. Franchising is therefore a sustainable business model even after the firm's capital constraints, if any, are removed. Thus, the resource scarcity theory cannot explain the franchising phenomena.

Franchising is a business model decision. Further, franchising employs the entrepreneurial mechanism. The theory of franchising identifies firm-specific conditions such as value appropriability, cash flow uncertainty, and growth opportunities to explain the firm's choice to franchise. In particular, when the firm's growth potential is high but its business model design is such that the value appropriability may be more uncertain, the firm may choose to franchise to enhance and sustain its competitive position. The entrepreneurial firm is opportunity driven, not resource driven. Thus, firms who choose to franchise have a competitive focus on opportunities, not on resources. Entrepreneurial firms invest in new opportunities regardless of their current resource position. Further, when a firm has low asset specificity, less complex organizational routines, and low tacit knowledge, then the value appropriability is more uncertain; and these firms may choose to franchise their outlets to secure and enhance their competitive position.

The theory of franchising also explains location-specific conditions for an outlet to be franchised or company-owned, given that the firm has chosen to franchise some of its outlets. To explain the location-specific conditions, the theory of franchising draws on the agency theory, search cost theory, and transaction costs theory. For example, if the outlets are geographically dispersed in a region or they are distant from the regional monitoring headquarters, franchising is preferred to company ownership. Even when the outlets are geographically concentrated, if the demand variability is high in a region such that the customer acquisition costs are high, the outlets would preferably be franchised. Entrepreneurial franchisees are highly motivated to acquire and retain customers at a lower cost.

Further, when a firm's outlets are geographically concentrated and the regional demand variability is low such that the customer acquisition costs are low and the customer retention rate is high, franchising still may be preferred when the demand externality is low or when the region's customer mix includes fewer nonrepeat customers. However, when the firm's outlets are geographically concentrated, the regional demand externality is high (i.e., when there is a greater number of nonrepeat customers in the region), and the regional demand variability is low, then the franchisor may choose to own the outlets in the region. In these cases, there is a potential for franchisee free-riding; that is, the franchisee may underinvest in local advertising and customer development since the demand is more certain and the customer retention is better assured in that region.

In the theory of franchising, a potential franchisor in the early stage must demonstrate their franchise competence to potential franchisees and if necessary to venture capital investors through investment in prototype company-owned units. The units must achieve sustained profit prior to commencing franchising. The franchisor must also demonstrate that the concept has growth potential and unit profitability can be sustained with sales growth. The franchisor thus signals their franchise competence by investing in company-owned units. The franchisor may not face a capital constraint when it has access to venture capital financing although venture capital is expensive. However, franchisee capital is also expensive.

Young franchisors do not have access to public capital markets such as stock and bond markets. The only alternative to franchisee capital is venture capital, which is very expensive. However, when the franchisor can credibly signal their unit profit potential and growth potential to potential franchisees, the capital constraint can be relaxed through franchising. Franchising thus can relax a high-growth franchisor's underinvestment condition associated with a potential adverse selection. An adverse selection occurs when information asymmetry exists between a franchisor and their potential franchisees. Less competent franchisors, however, will fail to credibly signal their entrepreneurial competence with an investment in company-owned prototype units since they will fail to achieve sustained profitability and sales growth with their investments in prototype units. Less competent franchisors thus will not attract franchisee capital or venture capital.

In the early stages of franchising, a franchisor's cost of capital is high since the alternative capital sources to a young competent franchisor are either franchisee capital or venture capital. As the franchise matures, its cost of capital is lower as the franchisor obtains access to public and private equity markets. Thus, Rubin's (1978) argument against resource scarcity theory, in that franchising does not occur with capital constraint binding because the franchisor's cost of capital is always lower than the franchisee's, may be valid for mature franchisors. For young franchisors, however, the alternative source of capital is venture capital if available and that is not cheaper than franchisee capital.

However, even in the early stages of franchising, when the franchisor's cost of capital is high and thus the capital constraint may be binding, the franchisor may not be able to convince prospective franchisees to invest unless it can credibly signal franchise competence through investments in company-owned prototype units demonstrating the concept's high growth potential and unit profitability. Less competent franchisors may succeed initially to attract a few franchisees but they will fail to attract more when the company-owned units fail to demonstrate profitability and growth.

The franchising business model should provide sustained advantage for the franchisor. The franchisee is the value lever that enhances the value creation in the franchising business model. Franchising can sustain a chain's competitive advantage when the franchisor's growth potential is high but the value appropriability is more uncertain. A firm that finds the franchising business model attractive would prefer to franchise its outlets unless there is a high potential for franchisee free-riding in a region. Franchisee free-riding occurs when the franchisee chisels at the product or service quality, or underinvests in the local advertising and customer development.

The potential for franchisee free-riding exists when the customer retention rate is high and the franchisor's brand value is high. Franchisee free-riding increases the franchisor's monitoring and coordination costs. The theory of franchising predicts the conditions under which franchisee free-riding may occur in a region, and the theory explains the conditions when the franchisor may own some of the outlets in a region. By owning some of the outlets in the region the franchisor can ratchet up local franchisees' performance and thus lower the monitoring and coordination costs (Bradach 1997).

In the next section, the theory of franchising is developed. The theory delineates firm-specific conditions, location-specific conditions, franchise payment design, and franchise life cycle conditions to explain why and when some firms choose to franchise and others do not; and when a firm chooses to franchise, why it then chooses which units it will franchise and which it will own. Next, several testable propositions are derived from the theory of franchising. The theory of franchising predicts the rate of franchising under firm and locational conditions including unit profitability, firm growth potential, value appropriability, cost of capital, barriers-to-imitation, asset specificity, geographic dispersion, demand variability, and demand externality. The final section summarizes these findings.

The Theory of Franchising

The two theories that are particularly tested and accepted in franchising literature are agency theory and resource scarcity theory. Three other related theories are transaction costs theory, search cost theory, and signaling theory. These theories are tested as competing theories to explain the rate of franchising, but they are complementary and explain different facets of a firm's franchising strategy. Below we briefly explain these theories.

Resource scarcity theory postulates that firms franchise because they are capital resource constrained (Oxenfeldt and Kelly 1969; Caves and Murphy 1976). Resources here are primarily capital resource. Other resources that are less emphasized are intangible core resources such as a firm's managerial, information, and knowledge resources. However, some empirical evidence is available that indicates franchising relaxes the managerial capacity constraint to growth (also known as the Penrose constraint). Nevertheless, the franchisor's capital constraint is the principal resource that is emphasized by the resource scarcity theory. In the early stage of franchising, many franchisors lack enough capital to grow rapidly to secure market share and achieve efficient scale. These firms adopt the franchising strategy, in that franchisees provide the capital needed for growth. The underlying premise is that these firms prefer owning the outlets to franchising, but the capital constraint forces these firms to franchise.

The resource scarcity theory implies that when franchisors mature and their capital constraint is relaxed, then they will discontinue franchising and invest in company-owned units only. In practice, however, mature franchisors continue to franchise. Indeed, several franchisors provide financial assistance to their franchisees. On average, among mature franchisors, 80 percent of their outlets are franchised and about 20 percent are company-owned. Thus, there is a stable ratio of franchised outlets to company-owned outlets for mature franchisors. Franchising seems to be a sustainable business model with or without capital constraint. Capital constraint cannot explain mature firms' need to franchise. Further, the resource scarcity theory does not explain the conditions under which franchisors can franchise in the initial stage. The theory of franchising explains the initial conditions under which a franchisor who is initially capital constrained can franchise.

However, Rubin (1978) posits that capital constraint cannot explain franchising because the franchisor's cost of capital is cheaper when franchisors can raise capital more cheaply from public capital markets than from their franchisees. Franchisees have a higher cost of capital since they have limited capital that is invested in one or a small number of units, whereas a franchisor owns several units and thus is more diversified.

Therefore, the cost of capital is cheaper for the franchisor than for the franchisee. Accordingly, the franchisor is better off not raising the capital from the franchisees. However, Rubin assumes that franchisors have access to capital from public capital markets in the early stage of franchising. It is more likely that franchisors may have access to private capital markets, in which case the franchisor's cost of capital may not be cheaper than the franchisee's.

Rubin (1978) suggests that franchising occurs due to the geographic dispersion of the franchisor's outlets, as the geographic dispersion increases the franchisor's costs of monitoring the outlet managers. Rubin thus employs the agency theory to explain a firm's rate of franchising. Franchising lowers the employee monitoring costs by providing a superior incentive alignment between the store operators and the franchisor. Lower monitoring costs maximize the value creation in the franchise system. Store operators by owning the stores become residual claimants to the store's cash flows and are less likely to shirk responsibilities or underperform. Franchisees will work harder than company-owned store managers and in so doing maximize the outlet performance.

The costs of monitoring the franchised outlets by the franchisor are lower and thus the operating performance of the franchise system improves. The agency theory suggests franchising occurs since the franchising model offers a superior incentive alignment mechanism compared to bonus-based compensation paid to company-owned store managers. In these cases, a franchisor should then franchise all its outlets and eliminate the need to monitor the store managers completely. However, in practice, most franchisors prefer to own some outlets, not to franchise all their outlets.

Most franchise systems have both company-owned stores and franchised stores. Thus, the presence of both company-owned and franchised outlets is further explained by the possibility of franchisee free-riding and opportunism. A franchisee may underinvest in maintaining the quality of the product or service, or underinvest in local customer development and advertising costs. Thus, a franchisee may attempt to free-ride on the franchisor's brand name and reputation, or shirk responsibilities when the customer retention rate is high. Franchisee free-riding can harm the franchisor's brand value and reputation. To prevent franchisee free-riding and opportunism, the franchisor should own some outlets, especially where there is a greater likelihood of franchisee free-riding. Furthermore, where the frequency of nonrepeat customers is high (or the demand externality is high), franchisee opportunism can be high and the likelihood of franchisee free-riding will be high.

The transaction costs theory stating that a firm may rather own the asset that is provided by a partner when the cost of partner opportunism and the likelihood of the partner hold-up are high explains why some outlets should be owned by the franchisor rather than the franchisees. In practice, however, there is not much empirical support for increasing company ownership with franchisee opportunism and free-riding. Indeed, most franchisee contracts require mandatory standards for franchisees to invest in local advertising and product development. Also, credible threats of potential termination of franchise contracts when franchisees are caught cheating can deter such cheating by franchisees, as these franchisees would then lose their initial investments when their contracts are terminated. Furthermore, several franchisors require their franchisees to purchase their supplies from the franchisor or franchisor-approved suppliers to maintain product quality and consistency. Such contractual measures certainly minimize franchisee opportunism.

Two other theories of franchising are related to the agency theory, in that these theories are also premised on asymmetric information, namely, the signaling theory (Gallini and Lutz 1992) and the search cost theory (Minkler 1992). The signaling theory postulates that a franchisor may use the franchise payments, such as royalty rate and franchise fee, and the proportion of company-owned outlets to signal the franchisor type (entrepreneurial competence) to potential franchisees. These signals are incentive signals, in that only high-ability franchisors can sustain these signals in the long run, whereas low-ability franchisors, if they imitate the high-ability franchisors, will fail. However, current empirical evidence does not support the signaling theory. Royalty rates and franchise fees do not change over time for a franchisor, nor are royalty rates and franchise fees inversely related, as postulated by the signaling theory. The postulations of the signaling theory of franchising are not supported empirically at present.

Another related theory is the search cost theory (Minkler 1992), which postulates that firms franchise because they lack local market knowledge, as presumably franchisees possess superior local market knowledge. Further, as the franchisor learns more about the local market conditions from its franchisees, there would be less need for franchising; the franchisor would then establish company-owned stores in the area. Franchising would then not be needed after the franchisor has gathered local market knowledge. However, that is not the case in practice. Franchisors continue to franchise in a region where they have established franchisees. Further, prospective franchisees may not have superior knowledge of local market conditions. Indeed most franchisors provide their franchisees with information about local market conditions and marketing expertise. Furthermore, there is very little empirical evidence to support the search cost theory.

Our theory of franchising draws on the theory of entrepreneurship (Mishra and Zachary 2014), namely, the entrepreneurial value creation theory, that explains how entrepreneurs sustain value creation and appropriation. Mishra and Zachary propose a two-stage value creation theory that explains the entrepreneurial process of value creation and appropriation. In the first stage, an entrepreneurial opportunity is recognized and developed by an entrepreneur, modulated by the entrepreneurial intention, effectuating the entrepreneurial competence in that the entrepreneur proves the market and growth potential of the venture. The entrepreneurial competence then provides a temporary advantage to the entrepreneur. The entrepreneurial competence resulting in stage one may not be rare, nor is it initially profitable, inimitable or nonsubstitutable; thus, the entrepreneurial competence does not obey the conditions prescribed by the resource-based theory (Barney 1991). Entrepreneurial behavior underlies the entrepreneurial advantage of the firm.

In the second stage of value creation, the entrepreneurial competence formulated in stage one is further leveraged by acquiring and developing complementary capabilities, which drives a business model mechanism that generates sustainable value and appropriates the entrepreneurial reward. The second stage of value creation and appropriation is explained by the business model theory and business model mechanism, whereas the first stage of value creation is explained by the theory of entrepreneurial competence and effectuation mechanism.

In each stage of value creation, the firm value is enhanced and amplified, as the initial entrepreneurial opportunity is reconfigured and the entrepreneurial resources and complementary capabilities are leveraged to generate and appropriate an entrepreneurial reward. In the case of franchising, the franchisees and the entrepreneurial mechanism inherent in the franchising business model provide the firm with complementary capabilities to generate, sustain, and appropriate entrepreneurial reward. The franchising business model thus leverages the franchisor competence and the franchisee complementary capabilities to create, sustain, and appropriate entrepreneurial reward.

In the case of franchising, the entrepreneurial competence formulated in the first stage of value creation is the franchise competence. In the early stage of franchising, the franchisor has the incentive to signal their entrepreneurial ability and the quality of the franchise concept to prospective franchisees through a predetermined royalty rate and franchisee fee. The franchisor further signals their franchise competence by investing in prototype company-owned units such that they can credibly demonstrate the sustained profit and sales growth in these prototype units. The franchisor also needs to demonstrate their franchise competence in managing geographical growth; thus, they should invest in company-owned units in more than one region.

The franchisor, when the franchise concept has high growth potential, may raise venture capital, if necessary, to invest in more company-owned prototype units. However, venture capital is expensive and scarce; the growth rate that can then be achieved with venture capital is limited. Further, a venture capital investor would invest in a young franchisor if the investor believes that there is a strong likelihood of franchisee participation in the future. Furthermore, when the appropriable rent is sufficiently high and sustainable, the venture capital investor may not require franchisee participation and would instead support the geographic expansion through a wholly owned chain.

Figure 7.1 illustrates the theory of franchising. The figure is divided into two parts: the first part provides firm-specific conditions explaining why a firm would franchise and the second part explains location-specific conditions of when to franchise or company-own an outlet given that the firm has chosen the franchising business model. The first part of the theory of franchising is driven by the firm's business model conditions that determine the extent of potential sustainable and appropriable rent. The first part consists of the two stages of value creation and appropriation explained in the theory of entrepreneurship (Mishra and Zachary 2014), namely, the effectuation mechanism and the business model mechanism.

The second part of the theory of franchising develops location-specific conditions that minimize the franchisor's monitoring, coordination, and customer acquisition costs. Thus, in the second part, the conditions are developed on whether the franchisor chooses to franchise an outlet or company-own it. In our framework, when the chain prefers to use a franchising business model, it has a preference to franchise its outlets unless the location-specific conditions require the chain to own some of the outlets.

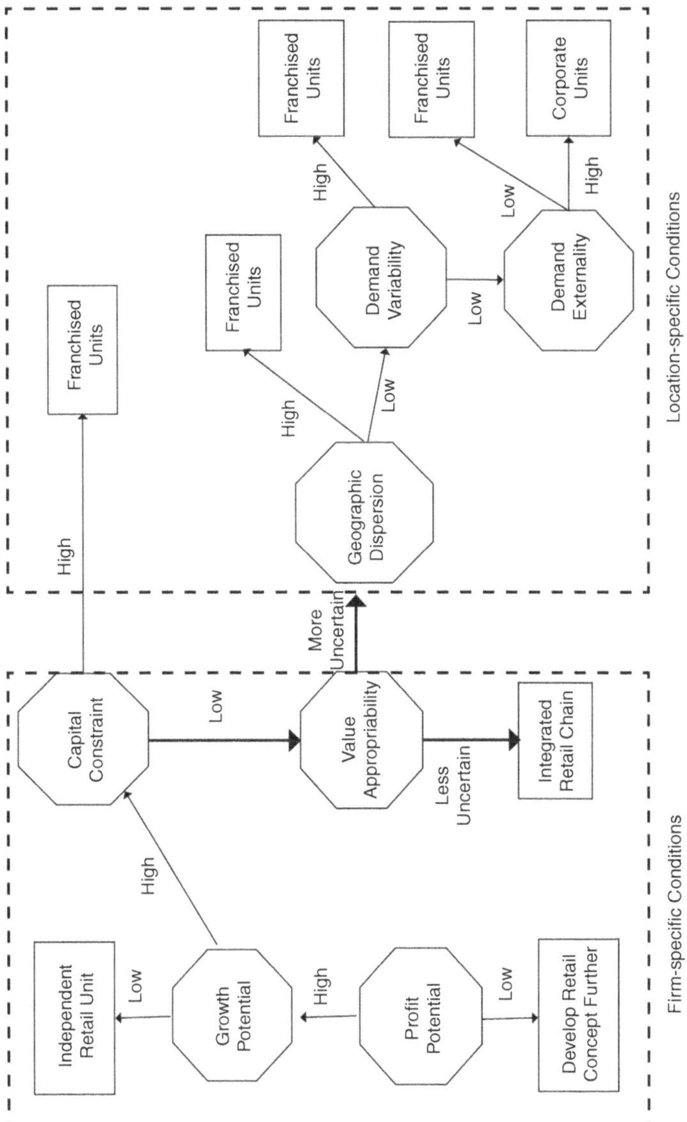

Fig. 7.1 The theory of franchising

Firm-Specific Conditions

The first part of Fig. 7.1 has two columns. The first column describes the formulation of the franchise concept, similar to the first stage of entrepreneurial value creation consisting of the effectuation mechanism. The second column refers to the second stage of the value creation using a business model mechanism. The franchise competence is signaled by a franchisor by demonstrating sustained profit and sales growth at company-owned prototype units. Thus, the franchisor first develops and tests the franchise concept with an investment in company-owned units. The franchisor must wait until sufficient franchise competence is developed. Franchising early might cause the franchise system to fail. Or the franchisor may fail to attract prospective franchisees.

The franchise competence requires that the potential franchisor can demonstrate the concept's profit potential by achieving sustained profit with one or a few company-owned units. The potential franchisor may further invest in geographically dispersed corporate units to demonstrate the concept's high growth potential with sustained profitability under various market conditions, and further that the franchisor has the ability to manage geographically dispersed and distant units. If the unit profitability is low, then the potential franchisor must develop the franchise concept further. Further, if the growth potential is limited then growth through franchising is not possible. The entrepreneur will then operate only one or a small number of local units.

The process of developing franchise competence can take a few years. Many potential franchisors may fail at this stage. If the potential franchisor can demonstrate that unit profit can be sustained under various market conditions through an investment in more company-owned units, then the chain may grow to become a regional or national chain, either through a franchising strategy or company ownership as determined by the chain's business model conditions.

At this stage, after the franchise competence is demonstrated and signaled, the potential franchisor moves to the second column of the firm-specific conditions as shown in the first part of Fig. 7.1. The firm at this stage may or may not face a capital constraint. If the firm has venture capital backing, it may not initially face a capital constraint, although the cost of venture capital is very high. However, when the capital constraint is binding but the firm's growth potential has been demonstrated as being high, then the firm will suffer from an underinvestment condition since the firm would not have enough capital to finance its growth opportunities. The underinvestment condition can be relaxed by financing the growth through franchising.

However, as the franchisor is new and their franchise competence may not be proven, prospective franchisees will be skeptical of the young franchisor's ability to support growth and provide operational assistance. If the franchisor has venture capital backing, although the capital constraint is still binding as the venture capital provided to the franchisor is limited and costly, then the franchisor has stronger credibility due to its affiliation with the venture capital investor. In this case, the venture capital affiliation provides potential franchisees a screening mechanism to sort franchisor ability and the quality of the franchise concept.

In any case, with or without the venture capital backing in the early stages, the franchisor has an incentive to signal their ability and the quality of the franchise concept by investing early in a few prototype company-owned units. However, the number of early units is not as important as the sustainability of unit profit under various market conditions. The greater the profit and sales growth in the prototype units, the greater will be the franchisor's royalty rate and franchise fee. The franchisor may limit its geographic expansion initially and should open outlets in more familiar markets.

As the retail firm continues to demonstrate profitability and growth in the prefranchising period, it refines the franchise concept further and develops sufficient franchise competence. The firm may then begin franchising and gradually increase the rate of franchising, or the firm may choose not to franchise and thus wholly own the units. When the capital constraint is not binding and the appropriable rent is high and less uncertain, in that the barriers-to-imitation are high and the value appropriability and sustainability are more certain, the firm may choose not to franchise but to own all the units. In this case, the potential appropriable rent is high and the firm would therefore prefer to retain control over the rent creation and appropriation.

The appropriable rent is high when the ratio of the price the buyer is willing to pay for the firm's product or service to the firm's marginal cost to serve the buyer is high. Further, when the business model has less uncertain appropriability and sustainability, the firm's profit margin increases at an increasing rate with its sales volume; that is, the firm can achieve increasing returns to scale. In this case, control of the chain is necessary to maximize the rent appropriation and to minimize the likelihood of a partner hold-up problem; the firm then will choose to wholly own the units. The average outlet size is also larger and the unit efficiency is high. Therefore, there are significant economies of scale, as a small increase in the operating expenses will yield a larger volume of sales (i.e., the firm has a higher business model sustainability). Further, high barriers-to-imitation protect and sustain the appropriable rent from dissipation to competitors.

Capital Constraint

For a young franchisor that does not have access to public capital markets, the alternative to franchisee capital is venture capital. Since venture capital is expensive and scarce, the cost of capital for a young franchisor is very high. Many young franchisors with sustained profitability and high growth potential may receive limited venture capital because of the adverse selection problem associated with venture capital financing. Adverse selection occurs when the investors have incomplete information about the entrepreneurs and their ventures. In these situations, the capital constraint is binding and the underinvestment condition exists in that franchisors may pass up positive net present value opportunities.

The alternative for a young franchisor is to seek franchisee capital, which is also very expensive but is less stringent and less scarce than venture capital. Further, a franchisee owns a 100 percent equity in the outlet whereas a venture capital investor owns less; thus, the cost of franchisee capital is lower than the cost of venture capital due to a franchisee control premium. The right comparison for an alternative source of capital for a young franchisor is then not the public capital markets consisting of diversified stock and bond investors, but the availability of scarce and costly venture capital.

A venture capital investor may require an investment return 10 times the investment amount and would like to exit in five years or so. Further, the investors may not invest in a franchising business model when their capital may be stuck in the business for several years before they can achieve investment liquidity. Furthermore, venture capital comes with stringent investment conditions and a loss of operational flexibility for the franchisor. Thus, franchisee capital when available is cheaper, and provides more flexibility and control to a young franchisor.

Franchising thus relaxes the underinvestment condition associated with a venture capital market adverse selection when the franchisor has high growth potential and the capital constraint is binding. With an underinvestment in growth, the firm will fail to achieve a competitive cost structure and may fail to appropriate sufficient rent, and thus may fail entirely. When the capital constraint is relaxed through franchising, the early period of rapid growth may last several years. A franchisor may fail in this period if they cannot achieve sufficient growth; or the firm's growth may be limited to local and regional expansion as long the units are profitable. Thus, the theory of franchising predicts that when the capital constraint is binding and more importantly, when the growth potential is high, the underinvestment condition that constrains firm growth can be relaxed efficiently through franchising. However, capital constraint alone in the absence of the franchisor's growth potential would not increase the rate of franchising.

Furthermore, if the franchise concept's growth potential is limited and not proven but the franchisor franchises, the franchisor may fail due to an overinvestment condition as the new units franchised would not be profitable. The likelihood of the overinvestment condition thus separates the high-ability franchisors from the low-ability franchisors. Low-ability franchisors when trying to imitate high-ability franchisors will suffer from an overinvestment condition and are likely to fail. High-ability franchisors thus have an incentive to develop franchise competence sufficiently before commencing franchising and signal their high franchise competence with an investment in more than one company-owned unit.

Capital constraint thus works as a screening mechanism to separate the high-ability franchisors from low-ability franchisors. Capital constraint incentivizes and necessitates the franchisors to signal their ability truthfully to prospective franchisees and requires the franchisor to develop their franchise competence sufficiently prior to commencing franchising. Franchise competence is developed by investing in prototype company-owned units and demonstrating sustainable profit and sales growth. Low-ability franchisors will commence franchising too early. Further, there is a greater likelihood of franchisor failure if they commence franchising too early.

Value Appropriability

When the capital constraint is not binding and the growth potential is high, the firm's value appropriability conditions determine the rate of franchising. The business model is the firm's value creation and appropriation mechanism. The value appropriability is the firm's potential for value appropriation. The value appropriability can be approximated by the firm's net sales divided by the operating expenses.

Further, the higher the barriers-to-imitation or the more complex the activity system, the greater is the business model sustainability and the less uncertain are the cash flows generated by the business model. The less uncertain the cash flow growth or the greater the business model sustainability, the less uncertain is the value appropriability. The higher the business model sustainability and appropriability, the greater is the likelihood of increasing returns to scale, such that the firm's profit margin, the gap between the unit product price and the unit cost, increases at an increasing rate with the sales volume. The less sustainable or more uncertain the value appropriability, the greater is the rate of franchising. Further, the less uncertain the cash flow appropriability, the greater is the likelihood of the firm wholly owning the units or the lower is the likelihood of the firm to franchise. Further, when the company owns its outlets, the outlet size is larger.

With less uncertain value appropriability, the rate of franchising is lower, the average outlet size is larger, the labor intensity is lower, and the inventory turnover is higher. The theory of franchising predicts that the firms with higher inventory turnover and lower labor intensity would franchise fewer outlets, as their value appropriability is less uncertain. The value appropriability conditions determine the firm's choice whether to franchise or wholly own the outlets. When the value appropriability is more uncertain, the firm will choose to franchise. In this case, the outlets are also smaller. When the value appropriability is more uncertain, the entrepreneurial incentives associated with franchising enhances value appropriation and sustains cash flow growth.

The value appropriability conditions depend on the business model design. The value appropriability thus can be enhanced by improving the business model design (Mishra 2015). Business models vary from one firm to another even in the same industry; thus, intraindustry franchising rates may vary. Furthermore, the value appropriability can be enhanced by greater customer lock-in, supplier lock-in, and operating efficiency. The customer lock-in is high when the customer switching costs are high or the customer retention rate is high. Thus, when the value appropriability is less uncertain, the customer lock-in is high, and a franchisee has the potential to free-ride since it is less likely to lose customers. Therefore, when the value appropriability is less uncertain, the firm may want to own more outlets. Further, when the barriers-to-imitation are sufficiently high such that the firm can sustain appropriation and cash flow growth, the value appropriability is less uncertain and the firm may want to wholly own the units to maximize the rent appropriation.

Further, the greater the business model efficiency, the lower is the firm's marginal cost to serve and the less uncertain is the value appropriability assuming that the price a buyer is willing to pay does not decrease by a rate higher than the rate of decrease in the marginal cost. For example, the operating efficiency is high when the inventory turnover (i.e., net sales divided by inventory costs) is high or the labor intensity (i.e., labor costs to sales) is low. With higher operating efficiency, the value appropriability is less uncertain and thus the firm may choose to own more units and the rate of franchising will be lower. Further, when the value appropriability is less uncertain, there is a risk of franchisee hold-up and thus the risk of losing competitive advantage unless the firm can respond quickly to competitive threats. With less uncertain value appropriability, the rent appropriation is more certain, but the appropriable rent may not be sustainable unless the firm has high barriers-to-imitation.

When the business model barriers-to-imitation are high so that the appropriable rent is less uncertain, the firm will choose to wholly own the units. The business model barriers-to-imitation are high when the firm possesses greater knowledge assets, tacit knowledge, greater asset specificity, or complex organizational routines. The firm's barriers-to-imitation sustains appropriation of the rent created by its business model. The firm's business model is its value creation and appropriation mechanism. However, over time the firm's barriers-to-imitation may weaken. In these cases, some mature wholly owned chains may begin franchising to sustain their competitive position.

The barriers-to-imitation, given the business model design, will determine how sustainable the firm's appropriable rent is. The business model's causal ambiguity, such as tacit knowledge, interdependent organizational routines, and asset specificity, raise the barriers-to-imitation as the competitors cannot fully comprehend the firm's business model advantage. Tacit knowledge is an implicit, noncodifiable accumulation of skills that result from learning by doing (Polanyi 1967). Tacit knowledge is thus knowledge accumulated through experience and refined by practice (Reed and DeFillippi 1990).

With the business model tacitness, the causal relationship between some of the firm's activities and the firm performance remains unclear, such that a skilled manager is unable to codify the decision rules and protocols that underlie the firm performance. A competitor thus cannot fully comprehend the causal relationships underlying the firm's business model. Tacit knowledge is deeply rooted in the individual's involvement within a specific context. Explicit knowledge, in contrast, can be codified and transmitted in a formal document such as a franchisor's operating manual. Furthermore, production knowledge can be explicit and easier to codify, whereas marketing knowledge is more tacit and difficult to transfer between individuals. Thus, the greater the franchisor's specific know-how or the less codifiable the franchisor's knowledge, the more tacit is the knowledge and the greater is the barrier-to-imitation, and the more sustainable is the business model and the less likely is the firm to franchise or the lower will be the rate of franchising.

Asset specificity also increases the height of barriers-to-imitation and lowers the cash flow uncertainty. Asset specificity is high when there are specialized assets and capabilities. Williamson (1985) identifies four types of asset specificity, namely, site specificity, physical asset specificity, dedicated assets, and human capital. Another type of asset specificity arises from brand name or reputational capital. Asset specificity is high when the assets cannot be redeployed easily without the loss of productive value. Specialized human capital, dedicated assets, and intangible assets including brand assets have high asset specificity. Asset specificity further increases causal ambiguity, which increases the height of barriers-to-imitation and lowers the uncertainty associated with the value appropriability. A firm may internalize the asset when the asset specificity is high to prevent franchisee hold-up and lower the uncertainty of value appropriation. The higher the franchisor's asset specificity, the greater the control the firm will want over the outlets, and the less likely it is that the firm will franchise.

The complexity of organizational routines or activity linkages raises the business model barriers-to-imitation. The more complex the organizational routines and the greater the number of activity linkages, the more difficult it is to grasp the factors underlying the firm's business model advantage and how these factors impact the firm performance. This prevents potential expropriation by the employees when they leave the firm to join competitors. Interdependent routines and activities give rise to the business model causal ambiguity; thus, it is difficult for competitors to imitate the firm's activities through observation. Furthermore, tacit knowledge, asset specificity, and organizational routine complexity reinforce one another to enhance causal ambiguity and raise the barriers-to-imitation further. The greater the business model complexity and causal ambiguity or the higher the business model barriers-to-imitation, the more sustainable is the rent and the less uncertain is the value appropriability (see Fig. 7.1). In this case, the firm would prefer to own their units to maximize value appropriation and minimize franchisee hold-up.

When the business model barriers-to-imitation are low or there is greater uncertainty with the value appropriability, the economic rent is subject to competitive dissipation and the cash flow growth is not sustainable. In this case, franchising enhances the firm's competitive position. Franchising is a strategic network that benefits from partner lock-in, which enhances the value appropriability when the barriers-to-imitation are low. Franchising further provides a superior incentive mechanism for franchisees and positive network externalities that provide increasing returns to scale (Mishra and Zachary 2014). Increasing returns to scale are achieved when the operating margin increases at an increasing rate with an increase in the sales volume. Superior incentives and greater strategic partner lock-in create positive feedback such that the success of one franchisee enhances the success of the entire franchise network. When the appropriable rent is not sustainable due to low barriers-to-imitation, or there is greater appropriability uncertainty, a franchise network can protect the rent from competitive dissipation. Furthermore, the franchising mechanism provides entrepreneurial incentives that enhances the firm's value appropriability.

Location-Specific Conditions

The second part of Fig. 7.1 describes the location-specific conditions for a unit to be franchised or company-owned, given that the firm has decided to franchise. In these situations, franchising is a sustainable strategy, and the firm's preference is to franchise its units unless the locational conditions require it to own some of these units. Geographic dispersion of the outlets, locational demand variability, and demand externality (i.e., customer mix consisting of repeat and nonrepeat customers) primarily determine if the units in a region should be franchised or company-owned (see Fig. 7.1). When the units are geographically concentrated, the locational demand variability is low, and the demand externality is high, the franchisor may own the outlets in the region. In this case, the potential for franchisee free-riding is high. In other cases, the firm will franchise its units.

The firm minimizes the monitoring, coordination, and customer acquisition costs when it chooses a location to be franchised or company-owned. The agency theory suggests that an outlet distant from the monitoring headquarters should be franchised. Company-owned stores need more frequent monitoring; thus, the more distant the unit, the greater are the monitoring costs if the unit is company-owned. Thus, the more geographically dispersed the units, or the more distant the units are from the regional headquarters, the greater is the likelihood for the units to be franchised as doing so minimizes the franchisor's monitoring costs. A company-owned unit may require monitoring three times more often than a franchised unit. In the case of franchised units, the franchisor may monitor the output (i.e., the sales and product quality). However, in company-owned units, the franchisor needs to monitor and supervise the effort and performance of the store managers. Franchising the units provides superior incentives, as the franchisee owns the unit and works hard for the unit to be successful. The franchising model provides entrepreneurial leverage and high-powered entrepreneurial incentives in that the franchisee works hard to earn an entrepreneurial reward (Mishra and Zachary 2015). Franchising thus provides an entrepreneurial rent.

Further, when the units are not geographically dispersed, this does not suggest that the units should be owned by the franchisor. If the demand at a location is more variable, the units should be franchised. It is not that the units are more risky and that the franchisor wants to shed the risk to the franchisees. If that is the case, a franchisee would be reluctant to acquire such a unit and the franchisor would be unable to recruit franchisees for that region. When the demand is more variable at a location, the unit needs greater entrepreneurial skills and flexibility to acquire and retain customers. Entrepreneurial competence involves greater alertness, agility, and flexibility.

The entrepreneurial ability of the franchisee is thus more valuable when the locational demand is more variable, as the customer acquisition costs are high and the customer retention rate is low. A franchisee with more entrepreneurial abilities can better manage the unit and develop the customer base at such a location than can a company-operated store manager. Franchisees are entrepreneurs and thus they are more entrepreneurial than are the store employees. When the external uncertainty is high and the unit performance is more uncertain, franchising the unit can provide superior incentive alignment and improve the unit performance

(Prendergast 2002). An alternative explanation is that the demand variability increases the franchisor's monitoring costs as it is difficult to attribute the poor performance of the outlet to the store manager's effort. Thus, the employee monitoring costs and the customer acquisition costs are reduced, and the customer retention rate is enhanced, when the outlet is franchised at a location where the demand is more variable. Furthermore, franchisors prefer to franchise to entrepreneurial owner-operators and not to passive investors because of the entrepreneurial skills of the franchisees.

Furthermore, when the units are geographically concentrated and the demand variability is low in the region, it still does not suggest that the units should be company-owned (see Fig. 7.1). Franchisors still prefer franchising to company-ownership of units since franchising provides entrepreneurial incentives to sustain the firm's competitive position, according to the theory of franchising. The advantage with franchising is that the franchisee is an entrepreneur, unlike a store manager who is a company employee. Thus, there is an entrepreneurial advantage with franchising.

However, in a location where the demand variability is low but the demand externality is high (i.e., the customer mix includes a greater proportion of nonrepeat customers or out-of-town travelers), there is a strong potential for franchisee free-riding; in these cases, the franchisor may want to own the units. In such cases, the customer acquisition cost is low so the franchisees may underinvest in local advertising and market development. The franchisee at such a location may chisel at the product or service quality to save money to maximize their profits as the customer retention is assured, especially when the franchisor's brand value is high and the value appropriability is more certain. The franchisor by owning these units in the region protects the brand value and prevents franchisee opportunism and free-riding.

Franchisee free-riding can arise when the units are geographically concentrated and the demand variability in the region is low; thus, the customer acquisition costs are low and the customer retention rate is high. In these cases, since the uncertainty with the appropriability is less, the franchisor prefers to own the units; thus, the rate of franchising will be lower. The rate of company ownership in a region increases with the value appropriability, such as an increase in the franchisor's asset specificity, complexity and interdependence of routines, tacitness of the routines, and other factors giving rise to the causal ambiguity and sustainability of the franchisor's business model.

Furthermore, in the case of highway outlets, the demand can be more variable. Thus, it makes more sense to franchise highway outlets as the entrepreneurial skills of franchisees are especially important to lower the customer acquisition costs and compete more effectively with nearby businesses. When the demand is more variable and the customer retention is not assured as in the case of highway outlets, the franchisees are less likely to underinvest in local advertising or free-ride, especially when the nearby competition is high. However, when the nearby competition is low and the demand is more certain at a busy highway, and the units are geographically concentrated, a high degree of demand externality can increase the franchisor's monitoring and coordination costs to maintain the system integrity and brand value, in which case the franchisor would rather own the highway units to prevent the likelihood of franchisee hold-up and opportunism.

Franchise Payment Structure

The franchise payment structure depends on the size of appropriable rent and the value appropriability conditions. Empirical support indicates that royalty rates increase with the brand value (asset specificity), decrease with the rate of franchising, decrease with outlet size, and decrease with the franchise risk. Royalty rates and franchise fees do not vary much over time for a franchisor. Franchisors may use their payment structure and investment in corporate units to signal their franchising ability and the franchise's growth potential to prospective franchisees.

The franchisor's royalty rate (i.e., the royalties divided by the outlet sales) can be written as follows:

$$\frac{Royalties}{Sales} = \frac{Royalties}{PAT} \times \frac{PAT}{Sales}$$

In the above equation, PAT = Franchisee's profit after taxes. By denoting the operating margin as the profit after taxes divided by the franchisee sales, and by denoting Franchisor Share as the royalties divided by the profit after taxes, the above equation can be rewritten as:

$$Royalty\ Rate = FranchisorShare \times Operating\ Margin$$

Furthermore, the franchisor's share of the operating margin depends on the franchisor's competitive position and value appropriability. When the franchisor share is 100 percent, the outlet is company-owned as 100 percent of the profit margin is received by the franchisor. In other cases, when the units are franchised, the franchisor's share is less than 100 percent. In the above equation, holding the franchise share constant, the higher the operating margin, the higher is the royalty rate. However, the royalty rate follows market or industry norms and cannot be arbitrarily high. When in a region where the franchisor's unit profit potential is very high due to a higher appropriable rent and the royalty rate is constrained by the market norms, the units would be owned by the franchisor. Since the royalty rates do not change over time, an increase in the unit profitability in a region will further increase company ownership.

Thus, the more profitable units of a franchisor would be owned by the franchisor since the royalty rate is constrained by the market norms. The theory of franchising thus predicts that the franchisor should set a higher royalty rate when the franchise's operating margin potential is high. However, since the royalty rates are constrained by the industry norms, the franchisor will own the outlets when the operating margin is high and less uncertain. Further, the franchisor's royalty rate does not vary much from one location to another. The theory of franchising is thus consistent with a fixed royalty rate but with a higher percentage of corporate units and a lower rate of franchising when the franchise's operating margin potential is high and less uncertain.

The greater the franchisor's brand value and thus the less uncertain is the value appropriability, the greater is the franchisor share in the above equation and the greater is the royalty rate. However, since the royalty rate is constrained by the market norms, the theory of franchising predicts a higher percentage of corporate units and a lower rate of franchising when the franchisor's brand value is high. Furthermore, the less uncertain the franchisor's value appropriability, the higher is the royalty rate; but as the royalty rate is constrained by the market norms, the greater will be the percentage of corporate units. Furthermore, the greater the franchisor's dependence on the franchisees or the greater the value-added by franchisees, the lower will be the franchisor share and the lower will be the royalty rate; in which case the greater will be the rate of franchising.

Consider the case of a franchisor that is indifferent between whether to enter a new market through a company-owned unit or through a franchised unit. It can be shown that (the proof is straightforward):

$$\textit{Franchise Fee} - \textit{Franchisee Development Cost} = \textit{Franchisee Profit} - \textit{Capital Cost per Outlet}$$

In the above equation, the franchisee profit is the operating income net of royalties and taxes; and the capital cost per outlet is the franchisor's cost of capital times the initial capital investment required per outlet. Further, the franchisee development cost declines over time, but the franchise fee does not vary much over time. Thus, the left-hand side of the above equation increases over time, and the difference between the franchisee profit and the capital cost per outlet increases over time. The increase in the franchisee profit over the franchisor's capital cost is the entrepreneurial reward for the franchisee. Further, when the franchise fee equals the long-run average franchisee development cost, an average franchisee earns a profit after royalties that equals the franchisor's capital cost plus an entrepreneurial reward for the franchisee. Thus, the theory of franchising predicts that an average franchisee's return on investment equals the franchisor's cost of capital plus an entrepreneurial surplus for the franchisee.

Rubin (1978) argues that the franchisor's franchise fee extracts the franchisee's profit after royalties over the life of the franchise contract. However, in that case, the franchise mechanism will fail to provide an entrepreneurial reward to the franchisees. Rearranging the franchisor's indifference equation, when franchising is preferred, the franchise fee net of the franchisee development cost is less than the present value of the difference between the franchisee profit net of royalties and the franchisor's capital cost per outlet amortized over the life of the franchise contract.

The franchise fee is typically the franchisor's long-run average franchisee development cost. When the franchisor's cost of capital is high, or if the initial investment per outlet is high, holding the franchisee profit constant, the franchise fee would be lower, which is contrary to the prediction of the resource scarcity theory, which predicts that a higher franchise fee is associated with a greater cost of capital for the franchisor. Furthermore, the greater the long-run average franchisee development cost, the greater is the franchise fee; but the franchise fee is constrained by the market norms. Thus, the rate of franchising decreases and the rate of corporate ownership increases with the rise in franchisee development cost.

Franchise fees and royalty rates are initially set by the franchisor and do not vary much over time. However, across franchisors, there can be some variation in these fees subject to the market norms. The franchisor's value appropriability conditions determine the royalty rate and franchise fee, according to our theory of franchising. Further, the greater the operating margin or the franchisor's competitive position, the greater is the royalty rate subject to an upper limit set by the market norms.

Franchise Life Cycle

There is a general consensus that the rate of franchising first increases and then decreases as the franchisors mature. Figure 7.2 predicts the rate of franchising over the life cycle of a franchisor. In the early stages of franchising, a young franchisor has limited capital available and thus will commit to low geographic expansion in the familiar and nearby markets. The franchisor needs to prove the franchise competence by demonstrating sustained profit in the prototype company-owned units.

The rate of franchising is low at the early stage since franchise competence is yet to be proven. The young franchisor further needs to signal the concept's growth potential and their franchise competence through managing additional units in diverse and high-volume markets. The early stage can last from five to seven years. During this period, some franchisors, especially the low-growth types, may fail either by overinvesting in company-owned units or by failing to attract prospective franchisees.

If a young franchisor is successful in the franchise competence development stage, the franchisor then enters a rapid growth stage with high geographic expansion (see Fig. 7.2). The franchisor's competitive position may be still low but the franchisor has successfully proved franchise competence by demonstrating sustained unit profitability and high growth potential through company-owned prototype units and possibly with a few franchised units. The capital constraint may or may not be binding. It is the franchisor's sustained unit profitability and high growth potential that propels rapid growth in the franchising rate. Capital constraint, however, creates a need for the franchisor to signal its high franchise competence to potential franchisees. At this stage, franchising relaxes an

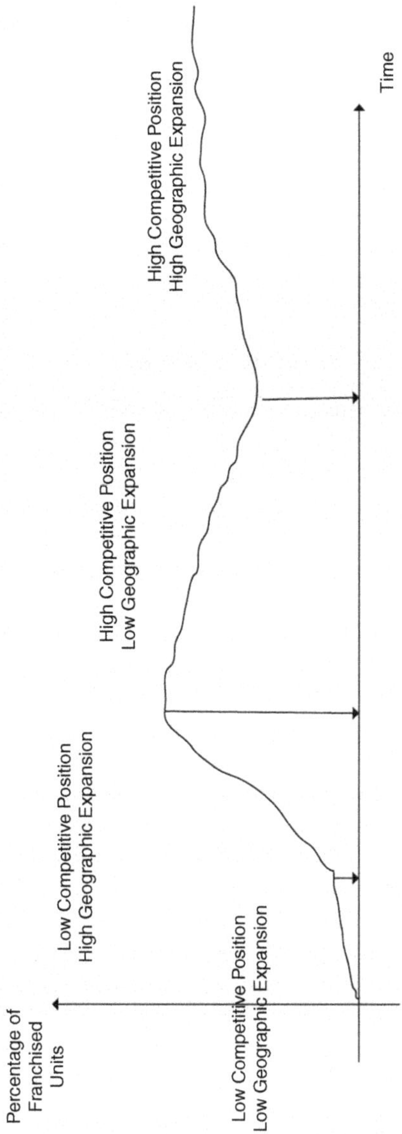

Fig. 7.2 Franchise life cycle

underinvestment condition associated with the franchisor's high growth potential and the adverse selection in capital markets, as postulated by the theory of franchising. Franchising provides leveraged growth to relax the underinvestment condition when the franchisor's growth potential is high.

After the rapid growth, the franchisor may have achieved a high competitive position. At this stage, when the franchisor has achieved a moderate competitive position and the cash flow uncertainty is reduced, the franchising rate may slow and the franchisor may choose to grow by opening more corporate units to protect the brand value from franchisee opportunism and hold-up and enhance the value appropriability. The franchisor would ratchet up franchisee performance further by opening some corporate units in the same region where the franchised units are located. The corporate units ratchet up the performance of the franchised units (Bradach 1997). The franchisor does this to enhance the value appropriability and sustain its competitive position. The rate of franchising remains low for a few years as the franchisor opens more corporate units in geographic locations where the existing franchisees are located.

When the average franchisee performance is stabilized, then the franchisor picks up the rate of growth again through franchising as it begins greater geographic expansion, including foreign markets and unfamiliar markets. At this major expansion stage, the franchisor has high competitive position and its brand value is high. This franchising growth rate is lower, however, than the rapid growth rate that a young franchisor has undertaken. The rate of franchising is then maintained preferably at a stable rate to sustain the franchisor's value appropriability and an efficient cost structure. The stable rate of franchising is determined by the franchisor's business model conditions, namely, its value appropriability and sustainability.

The rate of franchising may differ significantly over the life cycle of a franchisor, across firms within an industry, and across industries. The likelihood of franchisee hold-up and the rent uncertainty determine a sustainable rate of franchising for a mature franchisor. As the theory of franchising suggests, once a firm has chosen to leverage its growth potential through franchising, it has a preference to franchise its units unless there is a concern for franchisee free-riding and hold-up. Franchise free-riding occurs when the local demand variability is low and the demand externality is high (see Fig. 7.1). Thus, a mature franchisor maintains a stable rate of franchising and the brand value is sustained. The stable rate of franchising on average in an industry is about 80 percent franchised stores and 20 percent company-owned stores as suggested by the empirical literature. The long-run rate of franchising is, however, determined by the franchisor's value appropriability conditions.

Empirical Implications

In this section, we discuss the empirical implications of the theory of franchising and derive several research propositions. Additional propositions can be developed when the theory is applied to specific franchising conditions and sectors.

Franchisor Profitability and Growth Potential

The theory of franchising predicts that a franchising strategy relaxes an underinvestment condition when the firm's growth potential is high. Thus, to acquire franchisee capital, a franchisor in the early stages needs to demonstrate sustained profitability and growth potential through company-owned prototype units. Further, the franchisor needs to demonstrate high franchise competence by managing multiple units under various market conditions. In addition, as argued earlier, the franchisor should set a higher royalty rate when the unit profit potential is high, but royalty rates are constrained by market norms; thus, the rate of franchising first increases with the unit profit potential but then decreases at higher unit profitability. Therefore,

> *Proposition 1. The rate of franchising first increases and then decreases in the unit profit margin.*
> *Proposition 2. The rate of franchising increases with the franchisor's growth potential and franchise competence.*

Thus, an inverted U-shaped relation is expected between the rate of franchising and the unit profitability. The franchise competence requires that the franchisor can demonstrate the unit profitability and the concept's growth potential. Furthermore, the franchising rate increases with the franchisor growth rate. The growth rate first increases rapidly and then at a slower rate when the franchisor's competitive position improves.

Shane (1996) showed that the rate of franchising is positively associated with the franchisor's growth rate. Shane examined whether franchisors can overcome managerial limits to growth (or the Penrose (1959) constraint) using franchising as an alternative organization form. Penrose's theory of the growth of the firm is premised on the supposition that a firm's growth is constrained by their managerial capacity.

The franchising model that provides entrepreneurial incentives can relax the managerial capacity constraint to growth. Thus, Shane tested the hypothesis that the rate of franchising is higher the faster the firm grows. Further, franchising enables a young firm facing rapid growth to achieve minimum efficient scale quickly to survive the competition and enhance the competitive position. The survival of a young franchisor thus depends on their ability to grow the number of outlets quickly to achieve an efficient scale and a competitive cost structure.

Shane (1996) found that the rate of franchising was positively related to firm growth rate. Firm growth was measured by the growth in the number of outlets. The rate of franchising was measured by the ratio of the number of new franchised outlets to the number of new company-owned outlets for the period prior to the year under study. Shane's result is consistent with the notion that franchising allows a firm to grow faster than if the firm were to grow through the establishment of company-owned units. The franchising model thus overcomes an underinvestment condition associated with the firm's growth opportunities. However, Shane interpreted his result as evidence that franchising removes managerial limits to firm growth and survival.

Additional tests are needed to confirm whether franchising can remove the managerial capacity constraint of the franchisor since franchisees may not have superior managerial skills compared to company store managers. However, franchisees have high-powered entrepreneurial incentives that enhance their managerial capacity. Additional tests are also needed to evaluate the relation between the rate of franchising and the franchisee's entrepreneurial capacity in a region where the demand growth rate is high. The franchisee's entrepreneurial capacity can be measured, for example, in the reduction of the customer acquisition costs between a company-owned store and a franchised store in a given region.

It might be productive to assess the relation between the franchisor survival rate and the rate of franchising under high-growth and low-growth conditions to test the underinvestment hypothesis and the related incentive signaling hypothesis. Furthermore, the capital constraint by itself would not lead to a greater rate of franchising unless the franchisor's growth potential is high. A low-ability franchisor under capital constraint may seek franchisee capital but such a firm will fail unless its growth potential is high because of an overinvestment in the number of outlets. Thus,

> *Proposition 3a. The greater the rate of franchising in the early stage, the lower is the likelihood of franchisor survival when their growth potential is low.*
> *Proposition 3b. The longer the franchisor's pre-franchising period, the greater is the franchise competence and the greater is the likelihood of the franchisor's survival.*

Shane (1996) found that the use of franchising enhanced the survival rate of new firms. However, he did not examine the firm survival likelihood under high-growth and low-growth conditions. An examination of the relation between the franchisor growth rate and their survival rate would test the incentive signaling theory. In our framework, low-ability franchisors will fail since their growth potential is limited. Low-ability franchisors overinvest in the number of outlets and they will fail as their growth potential is actually low. High-ability franchisors, those with high growth potential, signal high growth by investing in and managing more outlets. The franchisor survival rate, particularly in the early stages, can therefore test the incentive signaling hypothesis in our framework. Further, the relation between the franchisor profitability and the rate of franchising in the early stages of franchising can be examined. The greater the franchisor profitability, the greater is the rate of franchising for young franchisors when their growth potential is high.

A young franchisor signals their ability and type by demonstrating the profitability and growth in their prototype units. The relation between a mature franchisor and their profitability will be different as the signaling needs of a mature franchisor under low capital constraint are likely different from those of a young franchisor under high capital constraint. Thus, the signaling hypotheses should be tested for mature and young franchisors separately, and the same for high-growth and low-growth conditions. For example, under low-growth conditions even with young franchisors, we may not see an incentive signaling effect. The franchisor's capital constraint, their growth potential, and their need for incentive signaling are thus related.

Franchise Risk and Cost of Capital

The opportunity cost of capital of a young franchisor, as an alternative to franchisee capital, is venture capital and private equity, not public capital markets. A young franchisor may not have access to public capital markets. Since both venture capital and franchisee capital are expensive, the cost of capital for a young franchisor is very high. As a franchisor matures, however, their cost of capital decreases, and may be lower than the cost of franchisee capital. Thus, for mature franchisors, our framework is consistent with Rubin's (1978) argument that the capital constraint does not explain or determine the rate of franchising.

However, a young franchisor's alternative to franchisee capital is expensive venture capital and private equity. Further, the greater the cost of capital for the franchisor and the higher their growth potential, the more binding is the capital constraint, and the greater will be the need for franchisee capital and the greater will be the rate of franchising. Further, the greater the franchisor risk, the higher is the franchisor's cost of capital and the greater will be the rate of franchising. However, with the greater franchise risk, there is a greater dependence on the franchisees and thus the royalty rate will be lower.

> *Proposition 4a. The greater the franchisor's cost of capital, the greater is the rate of franchising, and the relation is stronger when the franchisor's growth potential is high.*
> *Proposition 4b. The lower the franchisee development cost, the greater is the rate of franchising, and the relation is stronger when the franchisor's growth potential is high.*
> *Proposition 5. The rate of franchising increases with the franchise risk, and the relation is stronger when the franchisor's growth potential is high.*

Combs and Ketchen (1999) examined several variables to assess the effects of capital constraint on the rate of franchising. Capital constraint was measured by variables such as the franchisor's price-to-earnings ratio, debt-to-equity ratio, liquid capital, and return on assets. Further, these financial variables are associated with the firm's cost of capital. The lower the firm's price-to-earnings ratio, the higher the debt-to-equity ratio, the lower the liquid capital, or the lower the return on assets, the higher is the firm's cost of capital and the more binding is the capital constraint.

Combs and Ketchen found that the more binding the capital constraint, or, as implied, when the franchisor's cost of capital is higher, the higher is the rate of franchising. In their study, the relation between the debt-to-equity ratio and the rate of franchising was insignificant. But if they had adjusted the debt-to-equity ratio for the industry average, they might have found a significant effect on the rate of franchising. The relation between the firm's cost of capital and the debt-to-equity ratio is nonlinear, as the cost of capital first decreases with the debt-to-equity ratio (i.e., debt is cheaper than equity because of the tax benefits of debt interest payments), but the firm's cost of capital increases when the firm's debt-to-equity ratio exceeds the industry average (because of the agency costs of debt and potential costs of bankruptcy).

The firm's cost of capital is also higher when the firm risk is higher. Several authors have tested the relation between the franchise risk and the rate of franchising. Martin (1988) found a positive relation between the franchise risk and the rate of franchising. The franchise risk was measured by the unexplained variance in the firm's sales. Further, the greater the franchise risk, the greater is the franchisor's cost of capital; thus, the capital constraint will be more binding when the franchise risk is high, especially when the franchisor's growth potential is high.

The positive relation between the rate of franchising and the franchise risk is interpreted as a case of greater monitoring costs associated with greater franchise risk. Martin thus suggests that the monitoring costs are reduced when risky locations are franchised. Thus, the franchisor will try to shed the risky locations to franchisees. However, in practice the risky locations will be unattractive to potential franchisees. Thus, it is not the franchisor shedding risk to franchisees, but rather the franchise risk increasing the franchisor's cost of capital, especially when their growth potential is high, that causes the franchising rate to be high with greater franchise risk. Indeed, one may see that when the franchise risk is high, the rate of franchising will be greater in regions where the growth potential is high.

Martin's study is an example of how the two theories, namely, resource scarcity theory and agency theory, are complementary and reinforcing, not competing, as both theories predict a similar result. Agency problems are exacerbated under capital constraints, especially when the firm's growth opportunities are high. The agency theory predicts greater unit monitoring costs with increased franchise risk. The resource scarcity theory predicts the rate of franchising is higher with an increase in the franchisor's cost of capital. Both theories predict a positive relation between the franchise risk and the rate of franchising, and the relation is stronger when the franchisor's growth potential is high.

Lafontaine (1992) also found a positive relation between the franchise risk (measured by the average discontinuation rate of outlets in a given sector) and the rate of franchising in the sector. Lafontaine argues that the rate of discontinuation of outlets in a given sector reflects the probability of bankruptcy and is a better measure of the exogenous risk than the one using the franchisor's sales variability. Lafontaine interprets her result as supporting the notion that the greater the exogenous risk, the greater is the need for franchising incentives and the greater will be the rate of franchising, an interpretation consistent with the agency theory. However, the greater the exogenous risk, the greater also is the franchisor's cost of capital; thus, a greater cost of capital may also justify a greater rate of franchising, consistent with the resource scarcity theory.

The resource scarcity theory predicts that the rate of franchising is higher when the capital constraint is binding. However, as stated earlier, the theory of franchising predicts a higher rate of franchising with capital constraint only when the franchisor's growth potential is high. Thus, the franchisor must be able to credibly signal their high-growth type when the capital constraint is binding. Further, the lower the cash flow sustainability or the more uncertain the value appropriability, the greater is the need for the franchising mechanism to sustain a competitive cost structure. Entrepreneurial incentives associated with the franchising mechanism therefore provide a sustainable advantage to the franchisor when the value appropriability is less uncertain.

Value Appropriability

The theory of franchising predicts that the more uncertain the value appropriability is of the franchisor, the greater is the rate of franchising (see Fig. 7.1). Further, the appropriable rent can be measured by the net sales divided by the operating expenses including the working capital. Further, the smaller the size of the appropriable rent, the smaller will be average outlet size. Moreover, the higher the labor intensity and the lower the inventory turnover, the more uncertain is the appropriable rent. Further, the greater the customer lock-in or brand value, the less uncertain is the value appropriability and therefore the lower will be the rate of franchising.

Proposition 6a. The lower the inventory turnover, the greater is the rate of franchising.

Proposition 6b. The higher the labor intensity, the greater is the rate of franchising.
Proposition 6c. The smaller the average outlet size, the greater is the rate of franchising.

Labor intensity was examined by Norton (1988) and Michael (1996). Norton based his hypothesis on the idea that it is humans who shirk responsibilities, not machines; thus, the greater the labor intensity, the greater are the franchisor's monitoring costs and the greater will be the rate of franchising to lower monitoring costs (i.e., consistent with agency theory predictions). Norton found support for the hypothesis that the likelihood of franchising is greater when the labor intensity is higher.

Michael (1996), however, did not find a significant relationship between labor intensity and the rate of franchising in an industry. The labor intensity is the ratio of the average number of employees to the average sales in an industry or the number of employees per outlet in an industry; or alternately, it is measured by the restriction in the franchise contract that the franchisor requires the franchisee to be an owner-operator, not a passive investor. Michael's premise was that the more important the labor is to production (i.e., a firm with greater labor intensity), the more important the supervision of labor is; thus, for the supervision to be more effective, the supervisor should be granted greater incentives by making the supervisor a franchisee (consistent with agency theory predictions).

The theory of franchising posits that higher labor intensity is associated with a greater uncertainty in the cash flow appropriability and thus the franchising model may be employed to achieve a sustained cost structure, even when the outlet monitoring costs are low. In terms of average outlet size, Martin (1988) found that the average sales of company-owned outlets are three times larger than the average sales of franchised outlets in most industries in his data. This result is inconsistent with the agency theory since the store monitoring costs are higher for company-owned stores; thus, larger company stores would further increase the monitoring costs. However, the result that company-owned outlets are larger is consistent with our theory of franchising, in that there is a positive relation between company ownership and the cash flow appropriability, in which case the size of the company-owned outlets will be larger.

However, Martin interpreted his results as supporting the notion that franchisors retain more profitable units and franchise out the less profitable ones. Our theory of franchising argues that the average franchised outlets are smaller because the franchising model is used when the cash flow appropriability is more uncertain. Furthermore, when the cash flow appropriability is less uncertain, the proportion of company-owned outlets is high because of a greater potential of franchisee hold-up (see Fig. 7.1). Lafontaine (1992) further found that the smaller the outlet size, the greater is the rate of franchising, consistent with our theory of franchising.

The theory of franchising predicts that when the business model barriers-to-imitation are lower, or the value appropriability is more uncertain, which occurs when the firm's tacit knowledge, asset specificity, site specificity, brand specificity, etc., are lower, the greater will be the rate of franchising. Barriers-to-imitation and isolating mechanisms help to sustain the economic rent accrued with the business model mechanism. With higher barriers-to-imitation and thus with less uncertain appropriability, the firm would prefer to retain control of their outlets to maximize the rent appropriation and minimize the potential for franchisee hold-up; in which case, the rate of franchising would be lower since the firms will maintain control of the outlets. Further, when the appropriable rent is high warranting a higher royalty rate and since the royalty rate cannot be arbitrarily increased, the rate of franchising will decrease. The rate of franchising increases when the appropriability is more uncertain or when the size of rent decreases.

Proposition 7a. The lower the franchisor's specific know-how, the greater is the rate of franchising.
Proposition 7b. The lower the franchisor's isolating mechanisms, the greater is the rate of franchising.
Proposition 7c. The lower the franchisor's location specificity, the greater is the rate of franchising.
Proposition 7d. The lower the franchisor's human capital specificity, the greater is the rate of franchising.
Proposition 7e. The lower the franchisor's brand value and customer lock-in, the greater is the rate of franchising.

Several authors have studied the relation between asset specificity, intangible assets, brand value, etc., and the rate of franchising. Lafontaine and Shaw (2005) tested the hypothesis that franchisors with high brand value have a higher rate of company ownership of outlets, such that the franchisors can protect their brands from franchisee free-riding. Free-riding occurs when franchisees underinvest in local advertising and customer development.

Lafontaine and Shaw measured the franchisor's brand value by annual advertising expenditures. Two other brand value measures were also used, namely, the advertising fee paid by the franchisees and the number of years the franchisor spent in operation prior to when they began franchising. All three measures of brand value had strong positive effects on the percentage of company ownership of outlets, suggesting a lower rate of franchising. Further, Lafontaine and Shaw found that franchisors with higher brand value required more training for their franchisees (i.e., greater human capital specificity). The number of training days and the level of advertising expenditures correlate strongly, suggesting further that a greater company ownership of outlets is associated with a higher brand value and greater human capital specificity. Further, the franchisors with higher brand value operated larger units directly (i.e., less uncertain appropriability).

Minkler and Park (1994) measured the franchisor's brand specificity using Tobin's Q, where Tobin's Q was estimated by the difference between the firm's market value of equity and the book value of equity, normalized by dividing the revenues. Furthermore, Tobin's Q can be employed as a measure of the firm's asset specificity. Minkler and Park found a positive relation between the percentage of company ownership of outlets and the brand specificity measure. In contrast, Norton (1988) found that the greater the brand value as measured by the travel intensity in a state, the greater is the rate of franchising in one of the three industries he studied. Norton premised his hypothesis on the notion that tourists are less knowledgeable about a local seller's product quality and thus they are more likely to depend on the brand value of the product. Thus, the greater the travel intensity in a state, the greater is the need for brand value.

However, in our framework, the travel intensity in a region represents the customer mix or the demand externality condition in the region. The greater the travel intensity in a region, the greater is the demand externality. The theory of franchising predicts that with higher demand externality or travel intensity, the rate of franchising will be lower when the demand variability is low. However, when the demand variability in the region is high, the rate of franchising will be higher with the increase in the travel intensity in a region. Thus, further tests are needed to examine the relation between the travel intensity and the rate of franchising.

Combs and Ketchen (1999) tested the hypothesis that the more specific knowledge within the firm, the less the firm will rely on franchising for growth, consistent with our theory of franchising. Specific knowledge is costly or difficult to transfer between partners. It includes knowledge about how to manage day-to-day activities, improve operating effectiveness, and promote products and services. The greater the knowledge specificity, the greater is the asset specificity and hence the less uncertain is the cash flow appropriability. Furthermore, specific knowledge is tacit. The complexity and volume of knowledge is sufficient to make it specific. Combs and Ketchen measured the knowledge specificity variable by a four-item scale: (1) How long would it take to train competent store managers?; (2) How long would it take to train competent hourly employees?; (3) How difficult would it be to communicate the job requirements to unit managers?; and (4) How difficult would it be to include all job tasks in an operating manual? Specific knowledge is thus higher with greater human capital specificity. Combs and Ketchen found that the franchisor's knowledge specificity was negatively related to the rate of franchising. Thus, the greater the knowledge and human capital specificity, the less uncertain is the value appropriability and the greater is the company ownership of the outlets.

Further, Michael (1996) tested the hypothesis that the rate of franchising in an industry would be lower with a higher level of human capital specificity. He based his hypothesis on the premise that franchising does not utilize human capital completely because of the standardization inherent with franchise systems. Product design and certain marketing decisions must be made centrally, not by individual franchisees. The more important the human capital resource, the lower will be the rate of franchising. Human capital specificity was measured by the average wages paid per employee in a given industry, as wages are proportional to the level of human capital specificity.

Michael found that the greater the human capital specificity in an industry, the lower is the rate of franchising, consistent with our theory of franchising. Thus, the lower the human capital specificity, the more uncertain is the value appropriability and thus the greater will be the rate of franchising in an industry. As illustrated in Fig. 7.1, with sustainable cash flow and greater value appropriability, the rate of company ownership will be higher and the rate of franchising will be lower.

Windsperger and Dant (2006) tested the relation between noncontractible intangible assets and the rate of franchising. The authors examined the contractibility of the franchisor's system-specific assets and the rate of franchising. According to the property rights literature, intangible and noncontractible assets determine the asset ownership structure. If the franchisor's intangible assets are more important for the income generation relative to the franchisee's local market knowledge, then the more ownership rights will be transferred to the franchisor and the greater will be the percentage of company ownership of outlets.

Intangible assets include certain employee skills, knowledge, and specialized know-how that are largely stored in the mind of individuals (i.e., tacit knowledge) that cannot be easily transferred; thus, intangible assets show a low degree of contractibility and transferability. The franchisor's system-specific knowledge was measured by the number of annual training days required for the franchisees (i.e., measuring human capital specificity). Windsperger and Dant (2006) found that the percentage of company ownership of outlets is higher when the number of annual training days is greater (i.e., a proxy for the franchisor's knowledge specificity). That is, the greater the franchisor's knowledge specificity and thus the more sustainable and less uncertain the cash flow appropriability, the greater is the company ownership of outlets (see Fig. 7.1).

Thus, in general, the higher the asset specificity, human capital specificity, brand value, or tacit knowledge, the more sustainable is the business model and the less uncertain is the cash flow appropriability, and the lower is the rate of franchising. Further, the theory of franchising is consistent with the transaction costs theory, as when the firm's transaction costs are high with greater asset specificity, the firm will own or internalize the assets to minimize the transaction and coordination costs, in which case the rate of company ownership will be higher and the rate of franchising lower.

Further, the theory of franchising is consistent with the resource-based theory in that isolating mechanisms and barriers-to-imitation, because of causal ambiguity, enhance the cash flow appropriability and sustainability. Thus, when the firm's cash flow appropriability is less uncertain and the higher barriers-to-imitation protect the rent dissipation, the firm maximizes the rent appropriation if the assets are owned by the firm. Therefore, the higher the barriers-to-imitation and the greater the isolating mechanisms, the less uncertain is the appropriability and the greater is the cash flow sustainability, and therefore the higher will be the rate of company ownership and the lower the rate of franchising.

Geographic Dispersion

Next, we derive propositions based on the location-specific conditions postulated by the theory of franchising. Agency costs of monitoring are higher when the outlets are more geographically dispersed. As stated earlier, company-owned stores require more frequent monitoring. Further, the monitoring costs increase with the distance of the unit from the monitoring headquarters. Thus, the rate of franchising will be higher when the units are geographically dispersed. The theory of franchising and the agency theory predict that:

> *Proposition 8a. The greater the geographic dispersion of units, the greater is the rate of franchising.*
> *Proposition 8b. The more distant a unit is from the regional headquarters, the greater is the likelihood of the unit to be franchised.*

Several authors have tested the geographic dispersion hypothesis. Brickley and Dark (1987) found that company-owned units were located closer to their monitoring headquarters. The average distance from monitoring headquarters was 224 miles for company-owned units, whereas the average distance was 669 miles for franchised units. Furthermore, Brickley and Dark found that more company-owned units were located in more populated areas. When monitoring costs are lower, the concentration of units is higher, due to possible monitoring efficiency.

Further, Norton (1988) found that franchising is more common in rural areas (i.e., less populated areas). Lafontaine (1992) measured geographic dispersion by the number of states in which the franchisor had a presence and by the proportion of foreign outlets. She found that the rate of franchising was greater with the increase in geographic dispersion. There is a general consensus that the rate of franchising is higher with an increase in geographic dispersion of units. However, it is not clear whether the rate of franchising is lower when the units are concentrated geographically (Brickley 1999).

Demand Variability

The theory of franchising, however, in contrast to the agency theory, postulates that even when the units are geographically concentrated, the units need not be company-owned. The locational demand variability would influence whether the unit be franchised or company-owned (see Fig. 7.1).

Proposition 9a. The greater the demand uncertainty in a region, the greater is the likelihood the units in the region will be franchised.
Proposition 9b. The higher the customer search costs in a region, the greater is the percentage of units franchised.

Several authors have tested the relation between the demand variability in a region and the rate of franchising. For example, Norton (1988) found that the greater the local demand variability, the greater was the rate of franchising. The agency theory, however, posits that the greater the demand variability, the greater are the agency costs of monitoring, since a firm cannot determine whether poor outlet performance is due to the store manager's underperformance or a weak market demand. Thus, when locational demand is more variable, the outlets are franchised. The theory of franchising further predicts that when the market demand conditions are more uncertain, there is a greater need for the entrepreneurial skills of the franchisee in acquiring and retaining customers at the outlet, and thus there is a greater need to franchise the outlet.

Demand Externality

Even when the outlets are geographically concentrated and the locational demand variability is low, the theory of franchising further predicts that franchising may be preferred to company ownership of outlets unless the demand externality is high in the region (see Fig. 7.1). Demand externality is high when the customer mix at a location includes a greater number of nonrepeat customers. Thus, with high demand externality in a region, the franchisees may free-ride and underinvest in local market development or debase the product quality. In the case of highway outlets, however, the units would be franchised as the demand variability can be high at these locations. The condition of demand externality, however, applies when the locational demand variability is low and the customer retention rate is high (see Fig. 7.1).

Proposition 10. The greater the demand externality in a region, when the demand variability is low and the units are geographically concentrated, the greater is the percentage of company-owned outlets in the region.
Proposition 11. City highway outlets where the demand variability is high are more likely to be franchised. Rural highway outlets as they are geographically dispersed are more likely to be franchised.

Some studies have examined the relation between the rate of company ownership and the demand externality conditions, but no sufficient empirical evidence has yet been found to support the hypothesis that the likelihood of company ownership of the outlet is greater when the demand externality is high. Brickley and Dark (1987) found weak support for the hypothesis that the percent of franchised units is lower in industries that have a higher percentage of nonrepeat customers. These industries include travel-related businesses such as hotels, motels, fast-food restaurants, car rental agencies, and so on. The franchisee free-riding problem is more severe in such industries because of the greater number of nonrepeat customers.

However, when Brickley et al. (1991) used the unit or locational level data to test the demand externality hypothesis, they found that the effect of nonrepeat customers on the rate of franchising was positive and significant, contrary to their earlier findings using industry-level data. Brickley (1999) tested the hypothesis again that the percentage of company-owned units is greater in high-externality industries (more nonrepeat customers) but he found no significant results. Better measures of potential franchisee free-riding at the firm level could be the size and uncertainty of appropriable rent. The value appropriability can be approximated by the ratio of the net sales to the operating expenses and working capital. Furthermore, Brickley did not find a high rate of company ownership of outlets even when the units are geographically concentrated, as predicted by the agency theory. The theory of franchising predicts that the rate of company ownership may not be higher with a geographical concentration of units unless the demand variability in the region is low and the demand externality is high (see Fig. 7.1).

Michael (1996) tested the hypothesis that franchising would be chosen more frequently in industries in which customers are more mobile across local markets, as the value of the brand or trademark would be more important to these customers. According to the theory of franchising, the demand externality in a region is high with more mobile customers, but unless the demand variability is low and the units are geographically concentrated, a negative relation may not be found between the demand externality in the region and the rate of franchising. Michael found an insignificant relation between nonrepeat customer industries and the rate of franchising. Norton (1988), however, found that the greater the travel intensity in a state, the greater is the rate of franchising in one of the three industries he studied. However, when the demand variability is low and the demand externality is high with high customer mobility, the theory of franchising predicts that there should be a negative relation between the rate of franchising and nonrepeat customers.

Brickley and Dark (1987) further found that most highway outlets are franchised, and not company-owned, a result that is inconsistent with the transaction costs theory but consistent with our theory of franchising. The transaction costs theory predicts that highway customers are in the non-repeat group and thus the demand externality is high. The transaction costs theory predicts that highway units should be company-owned. In contrast to the transaction costs theory, the theory of franchising predicts that highway units are more likely to be franchised as the demand is more variable at city highway locations (see Fig. 7.1). Furthermore, in rural areas, the units are more geographically dispersed and thus the rural highway outlets will be franchised.

Franchise Payment Structure

The franchise payment structure has been examined by several authors (for example, see Sen 1993; Lafontaine 1993; Lafontaine and Shaw 1999). Carney and Gedajlovic (1991) found that franchise fees and royalty rates were the lowest for a group of unsuccessful franchisors in their sample. The franchising rate of the rapid growers group was negatively related to franchise fees and the initial investment per outlet. Sen (1993) found that franchise fees decrease with the franchisor's brand value (proxied by the total number of outlets), increase with the initial training period (human capital and knowledge specificity), increase with the geographic dispersion of outlets (outlet monitoring costs), and increase with the franchise risk (cost of capital).

Further, royalty rates increase with the brand value (asset specificity), decrease with the rate of franchising, decrease with the rate of geographic expansion, decrease with the average sales per outlet (outlet size), and decrease with the franchise risk (cost of capital). Lafontaine (1993) tested the incentive signaling theory that a high-ability franchisor signals its type through a higher royalty rate and lower franchise fee, but she found no support for the signaling theory. Lafontaine and Shaw (1999) found that royalty rates and franchise fees did not vary much over time for a franchisor, as postulated by the signaling theory. At present, there is not much study of or support for the signaling theory that franchisors use their payment structure and investment in corporate units to signal their franchising ability and concept potential to prospective franchisees.

The theory of franchising suggests that the long-run franchisee development cost, the franchisor's cost of capital, the initial investment per outlet, and the average profit margin per outlet determine the franchise fee. An average franchisee's net return on investment equals the franchisor's cost of capital plus an entrepreneurial reward. Further, the franchise fee equals the franchisor's long-run average franchisee development cost. Furthermore, when the higher unit profit margin warrants a higher royalty rate than the market norms will allow, the franchisor will own the outlets, according to the theory of franchising.

Similarly, when the high capital intensity and high franchisee development costs warrant a higher franchise fee, the franchisor will own the units. Further, to make the franchise fee more competitive, the franchisor will undertake investments in the franchisee's capital-intensive assets such as real estate and costly equipment. On average, the franchise payment is structured such that the franchisor allows an excess profit to the franchisee to the extent of their capital cost of investing in the outlet plus an entrepreneurial surplus for the franchisee.

The franchisor share is lower and the royalty rate is lower when the franchise concept is more risky since the franchisor will depend more on the franchisee. Further, as stated earlier, the franchise fee is the franchisor's long-run franchisee development cost. However, since the franchise fee is constrained by the market norms, the rate of corporate ownership increases with the franchise development cost.

Proposition 12. The royalty rate decreases with the franchise risk, and the relation is stronger when the franchisor has a greater dependence on the franchisees.

Proposition 13a. The percentage of company ownership increases when the franchise profit potential exceeds a critical value determined by the size of the appropriable rent.

Proposition 13b. The percentage of company ownership increases when the franchisee development cost exceeds a critical value determined by the capital intensity.

Proposition 14. An average franchisee's return on investment equals the franchisor's cost of capital plus an entrepreneurial surplus for the franchisee.

Franchise Life Cycle

The franchise life cycle has been examined by several authors (for example, see Martin 1988; Thompson 1994; Lafontaine and Shaw 2005; Castrogiovanni et al. 2006; Dant and Kaufman 2003). A general finding is that the rate of franchising first increases and then decreases as the franchisors mature. However, Castrogiovanni et al. (2006) found that the franchising rate may increase for more mature franchisors, whereas Lafontaine and Shaw (2005) found that the franchising rate remains stable for mature franchisors.

In the early stages of franchising, a young franchisor commits to low geographic expansion in the familiar and nearby markets. The young franchisor needs to signal the concept's growth potential and their franchise competence through managing prototype units in diverse markets. If a young franchisor is successful in the early stage, the franchisor then enters a rapid growth stage with high geographic expansion. The franchisor's competitive position may be still low and the capital constraint may or may not be binding. It is the franchisor's sustained profitability and high growth potential that propels further growth in the franchising rate.

After rapid growth, the franchisor achieves a high competitive position. At this stage, the cash flow uncertainty is reduced. The franchising rate may slow and the franchisor may choose to grow by opening corporate units to protect the brand value from franchisee hold-up. The franchisor would ratchet up franchisee performance further by opening corporate units in the region where the franchised units are located. The corporate units further ratchet up franchisee performance (Bradach 1997). Thus,

Proposition 15a. The franchising rate increases first slowly and then rapidly for young franchisors when the franchisor's growth potential is high.
Proposition 15b. The franchising rate decreases when the franchisor's competitive position changes from low to high.
Proposition 15c. The average franchisee performance increases when the rate of company ownership increases in a region.
Proposition 15d. The franchising rate increases (decreases) when the average franchisee performance increases (decreases).
Proposition 15e. The franchising rate for mature franchisors decreases with the size of the appropriable rent determined by the value appropriability.

When the average franchisee performance is sufficiently ratcheted up, then the franchisor picks up the rate of growth again through franchising as it begins greater geographic expansion. At this major expansion stage, the franchising growth rate is lower. The rate of franchising is then maintained preferably at a stable rate to sustain the firm's competitive position. A mature franchisor's long run rate of franchising is determined by their value appropriability conditions.

Summary

Why do firms franchise? Not because of the geographic dispersion of their outlets or to shed risk to franchisees as the extant theories may predict. Several department stores, supermarkets, and grocery chains have geographically dispersed outlets, but these outlets are all company-owned. Further, capital constraint does not explain the rate of franchising since many franchisors provide financial assistance to their franchisees. Why do mature franchisors without a capital constraint continue franchising? Why is the franchising business model found to persist in many industries?

Extant theories explaining franchising include the resource scarcity theory, agency theory, transaction costs theory, search cost theory, and signaling theory. The resource scarcity theory postulates that firms franchise because they are capital constrained, which further implies that when franchisors mature and their capital constraint is relaxed, they will discontinue franchising and invest in company-owned units only. In practice, however, mature franchisors with access to capital continue to franchise and maintain a stable rate of franchising. The resource scarcity theory cannot explain a mature firm's franchising decision.

The agency theory suggests that franchising lowers the franchisor's costs of monitoring the outlets. The more dispersed the outlets are or the more distant they are from the headquarters, the greater are the franchisor's monitoring costs. The agency theory implies that franchising lowers the store monitoring costs since franchisees require less frequent monitoring. However, several supermarket stores, grocery chains, and department stores have geographically dispersed outlets, but they own their outlets, and choose not to franchise them. The agency theory thus cannot explain why a chain with dispersed outlets chooses not to franchise.

Further, the transaction costs theory suggests that the franchisor should own the outlets when the franchisee opportunism and free-riding is high. Franchisees may free-ride on the franchisor's brand value and save money by underinvesting in local advertising and customer development. The franchisees may further chisel at the product or service quality when the customer retention is assured. Franchisee free-riding increases the franchisor's transaction and coordination costs. The transaction costs theory suggests that a firm should internalize an asset when it minimizes their transaction costs. That is, the franchisor should rather own and not franchise the outlets in a region when the franchisee opportunism is high. However, there is not much empirical support for an increase in company ownership when franchisee opportunism is present. Further, most franchise contracts require mandatory standards for franchisees to invest in local advertising and product development.

Two other theories, namely, the signaling theory and search cost theory, have not received much empirical support. The signaling theory postulates that a franchisor uses the franchise payment design to signal their franchise quality to potential franchisees. The signaling theory further predicts that the royalty rate and the franchise fee are inversely related and they change over time, which are not observed in practice. The search cost theory postulates that firms franchise because they lack local market knowledge, presuming that franchisees have superior knowledge of their local market. However, most franchisors offer marketing assistance to their franchisees and assistance in site selection and customer development. The search cost theory further implies that franchisors, once they have acquired the local market knowledge through their franchisees in a region, will discontinue franchising and invest in corporate units. However, this is not observed in practice. Franchisors continue to franchise in a region where their franchisees are long established.

Our theory of franchising draws on the theory of entrepreneurship (Mishra and Zachary 2014). The theory of entrepreneurship explains the entrepreneurial value creation process in two stages. In the first stage, the entrepreneur seizes an opportunity and effectuates an entrepreneurial competence, a temporary advantage for the entrepreneur. In the second stage of value creation, the entrepreneur signals their entrepreneurial competence to acquire complementary capabilities and the firm's business model mechanism leverages the entrepreneurial competence to generate sustainable rent. In the entrepreneurial value creation, entrepreneurial behavior creates the firm's competitive advantage. Entrepreneurial behavior is triggered by the entrepreneurial incentives of entrepreneurial executives who want to earn an entrepreneurial reward.

The theory of franchising develops firm-specific and location-specific conditions that explain when and why firms franchise. In the early stage of franchising, a franchisor invests in company-owned prototype units and develops a franchise competence. The franchisor waits until sufficient franchise competence is developed before commencing franchising. Franchising too early may cause the franchise system to fail. The franchise competence signals the franchisor's ability to sustain unit profitability and the concept's growth potential. The franchisor must also demonstrate that they can manage the units under diverse market conditions. It may take a few years to develop franchise competence. In this stage, many franchisors may fail, especially those who choose to franchise too early.

The franchisor in the early stage may or may not face a capital constraint. The franchisor may seek venture capital to develop franchise competence. Venture capital is expensive and does not provide flexibility. Investors impose stringent guidelines and require milestones leading to investor exit in three to five years. However, an affiliation with an established venture capitalist and their active involvement in developing franchise competence provides the young franchisor the industry expertise and the credibility to attract franchisees. The affiliation with a venture capital firm enhances the likelihood of the franchisor's survival. Franchisee capital is slightly cheaper than venture capital due to a control discount associated with franchising since the franchisee owns the outlet. Venture capital, when available, relaxes the franchisor's capital constraint. But venture capital is only a temporary source of capital and the investors require an exit in five years or sooner.

To overcome the franchisor's underinvestment problem when high growth opportunities are present, the franchisor develops and signals their franchise competence sufficiently to obtain franchisee capital. However, an overinvestment problem may result when the franchisor does not have high growth opportunities. Since venture capitalists invest in high growth opportunities, an affiliation with a venture capitalist validates the franchise concept's high growth potential and thus increases the likelihood of the franchisor's survival and success.

After the early stage, when the capital constraint is not binding, the value appropriability conditions determine the franchisor's sustainable rate of franchising. When the appropriable rent is high and less uncertain, the chain may not franchise at all and instead may own all its outlets. Further, when the franchisor's appropriable rent is less uncertain, the rate of franchising will be lower. However, when the appropriable rent is more uncertain, the rate of franchising will be higher as the chain will franchise most of its outlets. Franchising provides an entrepreneurial mechanism that enhances the value appropriation when the value appropriability is uncertain. The franchisor's business model design determines their rate of franchising; and further, the appropriability conditions determine the franchisor's long-run franchising rate and average outlet size.

Franchisors leverage franchisee incentives to enhance the firm value creation and appropriation in an uncertain environment. Franchisees possess powerful incentives to earn an entrepreneurial reward. Furthermore, the theory of franchising offers location-specific conditions to guide the franchisor whether to franchise the units in a region and their rate of franchising in the region. The location-specific conditions include the geographic dispersion of the franchisor's outlets in a region, the locational demand variability, and the demand externality in the region. The greater the dispersion is of the franchisor's outlets in the region or the more distant the outlets are from the regional headquarters, the more likely the outlets are to be franchised. Furthermore, the greater the demand variability in a region, the greater will be the rate of franchising. The greater the demand externality in a region or the greater the percentage of nonrepeat customers, when the demand variability is low, the more likely the outlets will be company-owned and the lower will be the rate of franchising.

Unless the franchisor's outlets are geographically concentrated, the locational demand variability is low, and the demand externality and thus the likelihood of franchisee free-riding is high, that is, unless all three conditions are met, the franchisor will choose not to own the outlets; and instead the outlets in the region will be franchised and the rate of franchising will be higher in the region. Thus, a franchisor in determining their outlets in a region to be franchised or company-owned minimizes the monitoring, coordination, and customer acquisition costs. In a region where the demand variability is low but the demand externality is high, there is a strong potential for franchisee free-riding, in which case the rate of company ownership increases. Further, highway outlets are franchised unless the demand variability is low. Rural highway outlets and most city highway outlets are thus franchised according to the theory of franchising.

The franchise payment design depends on the size of appropriable rent and the value appropriability conditions. The royalty rate and franchisee fee do not vary much over a franchisor's life cycle. Royalty rates and franchisee fees conform to the market norms. Across franchisors, royalty rates increase with the unit profitability, and the franchise fee increases in the franchisee development cost. When the store profit potential is high enough and less uncertain, the royalty rate will be high; however, since the royalty rate is constrained by the market norms, the franchisor will choose to own a greater percentage of the outlets. Further, an increase in store profitability in a region will trigger franchisor buyback since the franchisor cannot increase the royalty rate arbitrarily when the rate exceeds the market norms. The franchise fee increases with the franchisee development cost. However, since the franchise fee is constrained by the market norms, the rate of company ownership increases and the rate of franchising decreases when the franchisee development cost is very high.

The theory of franchising predicts that the franchisor's royalty rate will not vary much over time but the percentage of company ownership will change when the unit profit potential and brand value change. Further, the greater the franchisor's dependence on the franchisees or the greater the value-added by the franchisees, the lower will be the royalty rate and the greater will be the rate of franchising. Furthermore, an average franchisee's return on investment equals the cost of capital for the franchisor plus an entrepreneurial surplus for the franchisee.

The theory of franchising employs value appropriability conditions to explain why a chain may choose to franchise some of its outlets while another chain may wholly own their outlets. In particular, the entrepreneurial mechanism is the key to the franchising strategy of value creation and appropriation in that franchising provides entrepreneurial incentives that enhances the value appropriation when the cash flow appropriability is more uncertain. Franchising enhances the value appropriability. The franchise business model provides leveraged growth and entrepreneurial flexibility when the cash flow uncertainty is high and the barriers-to-imitations are low.

In a franchisor's early stage of development, when the capital constraint may be binding, franchising relaxes the underinvestment condition when the growth potential is high. Franchising enhances the value appropriability and reduces cash flow uncertainty; enhances the franchisor's competitive position and brand value; provides entrepreneurial flexibility in an uncertain environment; and lowers the franchisor's monitoring, coordination, and customer acquisition costs. The theory of franchising fills an important gap in the franchising and entrepreneurship literature.

References

Abernathy, W.J., and Clark, K.B. 1985. Innovation: Mapping the winds of creative destruction. *Research Policy*, 14: 3–22.

Allaire, Y., and Firsiotu, M.E. 1989. Coping with strategic uncertainty. *Sloan Management Review*, 30: 7–16.

Anthony, S.D. 2005. Can you spot the early warnings? *Strategy & Innovation*, March, Harvard Business School Publishing.

Argote, L., and Ren, Y.Q. 2012. Transactive memory systems: A microfoundation of dynamic capabilities. *Journal of Management*, 49: 1375–1382.

Baldwin, C.Y., and Clark, K.B. 1992. Capabilities and capital investment: New perspectives on capital budgeting. *Journal of Applied Corporate Finance*, 5: 67–82.

Barnett, M.L. 2008. An attention-based view of real options reasoning. *Academy of Management Review*, 33: 606–628.

Barney, J. 1991. Firm resources and sustained competitive advantage. *Journal of Management*, 17: 99–120.

Barney, J.B. 2001. Is the resource-based view a useful perspective for strategic management research? Yes. *Academy of Management Review*, 26: 41–54.

Baron, R.A. 2004. The cognitive perspective: A valuable tool for answering entrepreneurship's basic "why" questions. *Journal of Business Venturing*, 19: 221–239.

Baron, R.A., and Ensley, M.D. 2006. Opportunity recognition as the detection of meaning patterns: Evidence from comparison of novice and experienced entrepreneurs. *Management Science*, 52: 1331–1334.

Beck, P.J., and Zorn, T.S. 1982. Managerial incentives in a stock market economy. *Journal of Finance*, 37: 1151–1167.

Beinhocker, E.D. 1997. Strategy at the edge of chaos. *McKinsey Quarterly*, 24–39.

C.S. Mishra, *Creating and Sustaining Competitive Advantage*,
DOI 10.1007/978-3-319-54540-0

Beinhocker, E.D. 1999. Robust adaptive strategies. *Sloan Management Review*, Spring, 95–106.

Bhide, A. 1986. Hustle as strategy. *Harvard Business Review*, September-October, Harvard Business School Publishing.

Blyler, M., and Coff, R.W. 2003, Dynamic capabilities, social capital, and rent appropriation: Ties that split pies. *Strategic Management Journal*, 24:677–686.

Bogner, W., and Barr, P. 2000. Making sense in hypercompetitive environments: A cognitive explanation for the persistence of high velocity competition. *Organization Science*, 11: 212–226.

Bowman, E.H., and Hurry, D. 1993. Strategy through the option lens: An integrated view of resource investments and the incremental choice process. *Academy of Management Review*, 18: 760–782.

Bradach, J.L. 1997. Using the plural form in the management of restaurant chains. *Administrative Science Quarterly*, 42: 276–303.

Bradenburger, A. and Stuart, G. 1996. Value based business strategy. *Journal of Economics & Management Strategy*, 5: 5–24.

Brickley, J.A. 1999. Incentive conflicts and contractual restraints: Evidence from franchising. *Journal of Law and Economics*, 42: 745–774.

Brickley, J.A., and Dark, F.H. 1987. The choice of the organizational form: The case of franchising. *Journal of Financial Economics*, 18: 401–420

Brickley, J.A., Dark, F., and Weisbach, M. 1991. An agency perspective on franchising. *Financial Management*, 20: 27–35.

Brockner, J. 1992. The escalation of commitment to a failing course of action: Toward a theoretical progress. *Academy of Management Review*, 17: 39–61.

Buaron, R. 1981. New-game strategies. *McKinsey Quarterly*, Spring, 24–40.

Burgelman, R.A., and Grove, A.S. 1996. Strategic dissonance. *California Management Review*, 38: 8–28.

Busby, J.S., and Pitts, C.G.C. 1997. Real options in practice: An explanatory survey of how finance officers deal with flexibility in capital appraisal. *Management Accounting Research*, 8: 169–186.

Carney, M., and Gedajlovic, E. 1991. Vertical integration in franchise systems: Agency theory and resource explanations. *Strategic Management Journal*, 12: 607–629.

Castanias, R.P., and Helfat, C.E. 1991. Managerial resources and rents. *Journal of Management*, 17: 155–171.

Castanias, R.P., and Helfat, C.E. 2001. The managerial rents model, theory and empirical analysis. *Journal of Management*, 27: 661–678.

Castrogiovanni, G.J., Combs, J. G., and Justis, R.T. 2006. Shifting imperatives: An integrated view of resource scarcity and agency reasons for franchising. *Entrepreneurship Theory and Practice*, 30: 23–40.

Caves, R.E., and Murphy, W.F. 1976. Franchising: Firms, markets, and intangible assets. *Southern Economic Journal*, 42: 572–586.

Chase, W.G., and Simon, H.A. 1973. Perception in chess. *Cognitive Psychology*, 4: 55–81.

Cohen, M.S., Freeman, J.T., and Wolf, S. 1996. Metrecognition in time-stressed decision making: Recognizing, critiquing, and correcting. *Human Factors*, 38: 206–219.

Combs, J.G., and Ketchen, D.J. 1999. Can capital scarcity help agency theory explain franchising? Revisiting the capital scarcity hypothesis. *Academy of Management Journal*, 42: 196–207.

Courtney, H., Kirkland, J., and Viguerie, P. 1997. Strategy under uncertainty. *Harvard Business Review*, November-December, Harvard Business School Publishing.

Covin, J.G., and Miles, M.P. 1999. Corporate entrepreneurship and the pursuit of competitive advantage. *Entrepreneurship Theory and Practice*, Spring, 47–63.

Cyert, R.M., and March, J.G. 1963. *A behavioral theory of the firm*. Englewood Cliffs, NJ: Prentice Hall.

D'Aveni, R. 1994. *Hypercompetition: Managing the dynamic of strategic maneuvering*. New York: Free Press.

Damos, D.L., and Wickens, C.D. 1980. The acquisition and transfer of time-sharing skills. *Acta Psychologica*, 6: 569–577.

Dant, R.P., and Kaufman, P.J. 2003. Structural and strategic dynamics in franchising. *Journal of Retailing*, 79, 63–75.

Dierickx, I., and Cool K. 1989. Asset stock accumulation and sustainability of competitive advantage. *Management Science*, 35: 1504–1513.

Dijksterhuis, A., and Aarts, H. 2010. Goals, attention, and (un)consciousness. *Annual Review of Psychology*, 61: 467–490.

Drucker, P.F. 1970. Entrepreneurship in business enterprise. *Journal of Business Policy*, 1: 3–12.

Drucker, P.F. 1985. Entrepreneurial strategies. *California Management Review*, 27: 9–25.

Drucker, P.F. 1994. The theory of the business. *Harvard Business Review*, September-October, Harvard Business School Publishing.

Drucker, P.F. 1998. The discipline of innovation. *Harvard Business Review*, November-December, Harvard Business School Publishing.

Dutton, J.E., and Jackson, S.E. 1987. Categorizing strategic issues: Links to organizational action. *Academy of Management Review*, 12: 76–90.

Eisenhardt, K., and Martin, J. 2000. Dynamic capabilities: What are they? *Strategic Management Journal*, 21: 1105–1121.

Eisenhardt, K.M. 1989. Making fast strategic decisions in high velocity environments. *Academy of Management Journal*, 32: 543–576.

Emery, F.E., and Trist, E.L. 1963. The causal texture of organizational environments. *Human Relations*, 21–32.

Endsley, M.R. 1988. *A construct and its measurement: The functioning and evaluation of pilot situation awareness.* Hawthorne, CA: Northorp Corporation.

Endsley, M.R. 1995. Toward a theory of situation awareness in dynamic systems. *Human Factors*, 37: 32–64.

Endsley, M.R., and Bolstad, C.A. 1994. Individual differences in pilot situation awareness. *International Journal of Aviation Psychology*, 4: 241–264.

Fine, C.H., Vardan, R., Pethick, R., and El-hout, J. 2002. Rapid-response capability in value-chain design. *MIT Sloan Management Review*, Winter, 69–75.

Fracker, M.L. 1988. A theory of situation assessment: Implications for measuring situation awareness. In *Proceedings of the Human Factors Society 32nd annual meeting*, 102–106, Human Factors and Ergonomics Society.

Fredrickson, J.W., Davis-Blake, A., and Sanders, W.M.G. 2010. Sharing the wealth: Social comparisons and pay dispersion in the CEO's top team. *Strategic Management Journal*, 31: 1031–1053.

Galbraith, J.R. 1973. *Designing complex organizations.* Reading, MA: Addison-Wesley.

Gallini, N.T., and Lutz, N.A. 1992. Dual distribution and royalty fees in franchising. *Journal of Law, Economics, & Organization*, 8: 471–501.

Garvin, D.A. 1993. Building a learning organization. *Harvard Business Review*, July-August, Harvard Business School Publishing.

Garvin, D.A., Edmondson, A.C., and Gino, F. 2008. Is yours a learning organization? *Harvard Business Review*, March, Harvard Business School Publishing.

Gavetti, G. 2012. Toward a behavioral theory of strategy. *Organization Science*, 23: 267–285.

Gavetti, G., and Levinthal, D. 2000. Looking forward and looking backward: Cognitive and experiential search. *Administrative Science Quarterly*, 45: 113–137.

Gavetti, G., Greve, H.R., Levinthal, D.A., and Ocasio, W. 2012. The behavioral theory of the firm. *Academy of Management Annals*, 6: 1–40.

Gazzaniga, M., Heatherton, T., and Halpern, D. 2010. *Psychological science.* New York: Norton.

Gentner, D. 2002. Psychology of mental models. In *International encyclopedia of the social and behavioral sciences*, 9683–9697, Amsterdam: Elsevier Science.

Ghemawat, P. 1991. *Commitment: The dynamic of strategy.* New York: Free Press.

Gibbons, R. 1998. Incentives in organizations. *Journal of Economic Perspectives*, 12: 115–132.

Gifford, S. 1992. Allocation of entrepreneurial attention. *Journal of Economic Behavior and Organization*, 19: 265–284.

Glassman, R. 1973. Persistence and loose coupling in living systems. *Behavioral Science*, 18: 83–98.

Grant, R. 1996. Toward a knowledge-based theory of the firm. *Strategic Management Journal*, 17: 109–122.

Grinyer, P.H., Mayes, D., and McKiernan, P. 1988. *Sharpbenders: The secrets of unleashing corporate potential.* Basil Blackwell.

Hambrick, D., and Mason, P. 1984. Upper echelons: The organization as a reflection of its top managers. *Academy of Management Review*, 9: 193–206.

Hamel, G., and Prahalad, C.K. 1994. Competing for the future. *Harvard Business Review*, July-August, Harvard Business School Publishing.

Hatsopoulos, G.N. 1995. How can big companies keep the entrepreneurial spirit alive? *Harvard Business Review*, November-December, Harvard Business School Publishing.

Heaton, J.B. 2002. Managerial optimism and corporate finance. *Financial Management*, Summer, 33–45.

Helfat, C.E., and Peteraf, M.A. 2015. Managerial cognitive capabilities and the microfoundations of dynamic capabilities. *Strategic Management Journal*, 36: 831–850.

Hodgkinson, G.P., and Healy, M.P. 2011. Psychological foundations of dynamic capabilities: Reflexion and reflection in strategic management. *Strategic Management Journal*, 32: 1500–1516.

Holland, J.H. 1992. *Adaptation in natural and artificial systems.* Ann Arbor: University of Michigan Press.

Holt, C.P. 1995. How can big companies keep the entrepreneurial spirit alive? *Harvard Business Review*, November-December, Harvard Business School Publishing.

Itami, H. 1987. *Mobilizing invisible assets.* Cambridge, MA: Harvard University Press.

Itami, H., and Nishimo, K. 2010. Killing two birds with one stone: Profit for now and learning for the future. *Long Range Planning*, 43: 364–369.

Jensen, M. 1986. Agency costs of free cash flow, corporate finance, and takeovers. *American Economic Review*, 76: 323–329.

Johnson, M.W., Christensen, C.M., and Kagermann, H. 2008. Reinventing your business model. *Harvard Business Review*, December, Harvard Business School Publishing.

Kahneman, D., and Tversky, A. 1979. Prospect theory: An analysis of decisions under risk. *Econometrica*, 47: 263–291.

Kaplan, R.S., and Norton, D.P. 1992. The balanced scorecard. *Harvard Business Review*, January-February, Harvard Business School Publishing.

Kauffman, S. 1993. *The origins of order.* New York: Oxford University Press.

Kauffman, S.A. 1991. The sciences of complexity and "origins of order." Working Paper, Santa Fe Institute.

Kauffman, S.A. 1995. Escaping the Red Queen effect. *McKinsey Quarterly*, 119–129.

Kelley, H.H. 1971. *Attribution in social interaction.* Morristown, NJ: General Learning Press.

Kiesler, C.A. 1971. *The psychology of commitment.* New York: Academic Press.

Kiesler, S., and Sproull, L. 1982. Managing response to changing environments: Perspectives on problem sensing from social cognition. *Administrative Science Quarterly*, 27: 548–570.

Kirzner, I.M. 1997. Entrepreneurial discovery and the competitive market process: An Austrian approach. *Journal of Economic Literature*, 35: 60–85.

Kogut, B., and zander, U. 1992. Knowledge of the firm, combinative capabilities, and the replication of technology. *Organization Science*, 3: 383–397.

Lafontaine, F. 1992. Agency theory and franchising: Some empirical results. *Rand Journal of Economics*, 23: 263–283.

Lafontaine, F. 1993. Contractual arrangements as signaling devices: Evidence from franchising. *Journal of Law, Economics, and Organization*, 9: 256–289.

Lafontaine, F., and Shaw, K.L. 1999. The dynamics of franchising contracting: Evidence from panel data. *Journal of Political Economy*, 107: 1041–1080.

Lafontaine, F., and Shaw, K.L. 2005. Targeting managerial control: Evidence from franchising. *Rand Journal of Economics*, 36: 131–150.

Lavie, D. 2006. Capability reconfiguration: An analysis of incumbent responses to technical change. *Academy of Management Review*, 31: 153–174.

Lazear, E.1989. Pay equality and industrial politics. *Journal of Political Economy*, 97: 561–580.

Lazear, E., and Rosen, S. 1981. Rank-order tournaments as optimum labor contracts. *Journal of Political Economy*, 89:841–864.

Leonard-Barton, D. 1992. Core capabilities and core rigidities: A paradox in managing new product development. *Strategic Management Journal*, 13: 111–125.

Levinthal, D.A., and March, J.G. 1993. The myopia of learning. *Strategic Management Journal*, 14: 95–112.

Levitt, T. 1966. Innovative imitation. *Harvard Business Review*, September-October, Harvard Business School Publishing.

Lippman, S., and Rumelt, R. 1982. Uncertain imitability: An analysis of interfirm differences in efficiency under competition. *Bell Journal of Economics*, 13: 418–438.

Louis, M., and Sutton, R. 1991. Switching cognitive gears: From habits of mind to active thinking. *Human Relations*, 44: 55–75.

Luehrman, T.A. 1998. Strategy as a portfolio of real options. *Harvard Business Review*, September-October, Harvard Business School Publishing.

MacDonald, G., and Ryall, M.D. 2004. How do value creation and competition determine whether a firm appropriates value? *Management Science*, 50: 1319–1333.

MacMillan, I.C. 1988. Controlling competitive dynamics by taking strategic initiative. *Academy of Management Executive*, 11: 111–118.

Martin, R.E. 1988. Franchising and risk management. *American Economic Review*, 78: 954–968.

Michael, S.C. 1996. To franchise or not to franchise: An analysis of decision rights and organizational form shares. *Journal of Business Venturing*, 11: 57–71.

Miles, R.E., and Snow, C.C. 2003. *Organizational strategy, structure, and process.* Stanford, CA: Stanford University Press.

Miller, D. 1983. The correlates of entrepreneurship in three types of firms. *Management Science*, 29: 770–791.

Miller, D.T., and Ross, M. 1975. Self-serving biases in the attribution of causality: Fact or fiction. *Psychological Bulletin*, 82: 213–225.

Minkler, A.P, and Park, T.A. 1994. Asset specificity and vertical integration. *Review of Industrial Organization*, 9: 409–423.

Minkler, A.P. 1992. Why firms franchise: A search cost theory. *Journal of Institutional and Theoretical Economics*, 148: 240–259.

Mishra, C.S. 2015. *Getting funded: Proof-of-concept, due diligence, risk and reward.* New York: Palgrave Macmillan.

Mishra, C.S., and Zachary, R.K. 2014. *The theory of entrepreneurship: Creating and sustaining entrepreneurial value.* New York: Palgrave Macmillan.

Mishra, C.S., and Zachary, R.K. 2015. The theory f entrepreneurship. *Entrepreneurship Research Journal*, 5: 251–268.

Mosier, K.L, and Chidester, T.R. 1991. Situation assessment and situation awareness in a team setting. In *Designing for Everyone*, 798–800, London: Taylor & Francis.

Myers, S.C. 1977. Determinants of corporate borrowing. *Journal of Financial Economics*, 5: 147–175.

Myers, S.C., and Majluf, N.S. 1984. Corporate financing and investment decisions when firms have information that investors do not have. *Journal of Financial Economics*, 13: 187–221.

Nonaka, I. 1994. A dynamic theory of organizational knowledge creation. *Organization Science*, 5: 14–37.

Norton, S.W. 1988. An empirical look at franchising as an organizational form. *Journal of Business*, 61: 197–218.

Ocasio, W. 1997. Towards an attention-based view of the firm. *Strategic Management Journal*, 18: 187–206.

Ocasio, W. 2011. Attention to attention. *Organization Science*, 22: 1286–1296.

Ocasio, W., and Joseph, J. 2005. An attention-based theory of strategy formulation: Linking micro- and macroperspectives in strategy processes. *Advances in Strategic Management*, 22: 39–61.

Orton, J.D., and Weick, K. 1990. Loosely coupled systems: A reconceptualization. *Academy of Management Review*, 15: 203–223.

Oxenfeldt, A.R., and Kelly, A.O. 1969. Will successful franchise systems ultimately become wholly-owned chains? *Journal of Retailing*, 44 (4): 69–83.

Pennington, N., and Hastie, R. 1993. The story model for juror decision making. In *Insie the juror: The psychology of juror decision making*, 192–221, New York: Cambridge University Press.

Penrose, E. 1959. *The theory of the growth of the firm*. New York: Wiley.

Peteraf, M.A. 1993. The cornerstones of competitive advantage: A resource-based view. *Strategic Management Journal*, 14: 179–191.

Polanyi, M. 1967. *The tacit dimension*. Garden City, NY: Anchor.

Porter, M. 1996. What is strategy? *Harvard Business Review*, November-December, Harvard Business School Publishing.

Porter, M.E. 1980. *Competitive strategy: Techniques for analyzing industries and competitors*. New York: Free Press.

Porter, M.E. 1985. *Competitive advantage: Creating and sustaining superior performance*. New York: Free Press.

Posner, M., and Petersen, S. 1990. The attention system of the human brain. *Annual Review of Neuroscience*, 13:25–42.

Prahalad, C.K., and Bettis, R.A. 1986. The dominant logic: A new linkage between diversity and performance. *Strategic Management Journal*, 7: 485–501.

Prahalad, C.K., and Hamel, G. 1990. The core competence of the corporation. *Harvard Business Review*, May-June, Harvard Business School Publishing.

Prendergast, C. 2002. The tenuous trade-off between risk and incentives. *Journal of Political Economy*, 110: 1071–1102.

Prokesh, S.E. 1997. Unleashing the power of learning: An interview with British Petroleum's John Browne. *Harvard Business Review*, September-October, Harvard Business School Publishing.

Rasmussen, J. 1979. *On the structure of Knowledge – A morphology of mental models in a man-machine system context*. Denmark: Riso Natural Laboratory.

Reed, R., and DeFillippi, R.J. 1990. Causal ambiguity, barriers to imitation, and sustainable competitive advantage. *Academy of Management Review*, 15: 88–102.

Rindova, V.P., and Kotha, S. 2001. Continuous "morphing": Competing through dynamic capabilities, form, and function. *Academy of Management Journal*, 44: 1263–1280.

Rouse, W.B., and Morris, N.M. 1986. On looking into the black box: Prospects and limits in the search for mental models. *Psychological Bulletin*, 100: 349–363.

Rubin, P.H. 1978. The theory of the firm and the structure of the franchise contract. *Journal of Law and Economics*, 21: 223–234.

Rumelt, R.P. 1984. Towards a strategic theory of the firm. In *competitive strategic management*, 556–570, Englewood Cliffs, NJ: Prentice Hall.

Sachs, W.M., and Meditz, M.L. 1979. A concept of active adaptation. *Human Relations*, 32: 1081–1093.

Sanchez, R. 1995. Strategic flexibility in product competition. *Strategic Management Journal*, 16: 135–160.

Sarasvathy, S.D. 2001. Causation and effectuation: Toward a theoretical shift from economic inevitability to entrepreneurial contingency. *Academy of Management Review*, 26: 243–288.

Sartar, N.B., and Woods, D.D. 1991. Situation awareness: A critical but ill-defined phenomenon. *International Journal of Aviation Psychology*, 1: 45–57.

Schumpeter, J.A. 1934. *The theory of economic development*. Cambridge: Harvard University Press.

Sen, K.C. 1993. The use of initial fees and royalties in business-format franchising. *Managerial and Decision Economics*, 14: 175–190.

Senge, P.M. 1992. Mental models. *Planning Review*, 20: 5–10.

Shane, S.A. 1996. Hybrid organizational arrangements and their implications for firm growth and survival: A study of new franchisors. *Academy of Management Journal*, 39: 216–234.

Simon, H.A. 1947. *Administrative behavior*. Chicago, IL: Macmillan.

Smith, K., and Hancock, P.A. 1995. Situation awareness is adaptive, externally directed consciousness. *Human Factors*, 37: 137–148.

Spender, J.C., and Grinyer, P.H. 1995. Organizational renewal: Top management's role in a loosely coupled system. *Human Relations*, 48: 909–926.

Staber, U., and Sydow, J. 2002. Organizational adaptive capacity. *Journal of Management Inquiry*, 11:408–424.

Staw, B.M., and Ross, J. 1989. Understanding behavior in escalation situations. *Science*, 246: 216–246.

Stevenson, H.H., and Gumpert, D.E. 1985. The heart of entrepreneurship. *Harvard Business Review*, March-April, Harvard Business School Publishing.

Stevenson, H.H., and Jarillo, J.C. 1990. A paradigm of entrepreneurship: Entrepreneurial management. *Strategic Management Journal*, 11: 17–27.

Stinchcombe, A.L. 1968. *Constructing social theories*. Chicago, IL: Chicago University Press.

Teece, D. 1986. Profiting from technological innovation: Implications for integration, collaboration, licensing and public policy. *Research Policy*, 15: 285–305.

Teece, D.J. 2007. Explicating dynamic capabilities: The nature and microfoundations of (sustainable) enterprise performance. *Strategic Management Journal*, 28: 1319–1350.

Teece, D.J., Pisano, G., and Shuen, A. 1997. Dynamic capabilities and strategic management. *Strategic Management Journal*, 18: 509–533.

Thompson, R.S. 1994. The franchise life cycle and the Penrose effect. *Journal of Economic Behavior and Organization*, 24: 207–218.

Tushman, M.I., and Anderson, P. 1986. Technological discontinuities and organizational environments. *Administrative Science Quarterly*, 31: 439–465.

Vecchiato, R. 2015. Creating value through foresight: First mover advantages and strategic agility. *Technological Forecasting and Social Change*, 101: 25–36.

Walsh, J.P. 1995. Managerial and organizational cognition: Notes from a trip down memory lane. *Organization Science*, 6: 280–321.

Wegner, D.M. 1986. Transactive memory: A contemporary analysis of the group mind. In *Theories of group behavior*, 185–208, New York: Springer-Verlag.

Weick, K. 1982. Management of organizational change among loosely coupled elements. In *Change in organizations*, 375–408, San Francisco: Jossey-Bass.

Weick, K.E. 1995. *Sensemaking in Organizations*. Thousand Oaks, CA: Sage.

Weistein, N. 1980. Unrealistic optimism about future life events. *Journal of Personality and Social Psychology*, 39: 806–820.

Wernerfelt, B. 1984. A resource-based view of the firm. *Strategic Management Journal*, 5: 171–180.

Wenerfelt, B., and Karnani, A. 1987. Competitive strategy under uncertainty. *Strategic Management Journal*, 8: 187–194.

Wickens, C.D. 1984. *Engineering psychology and human performance*. Columbus, OH: Merrill.

Williams, C., and Mitchell, W. 2004. Focusing firm evolution: The impact of information infrastructure on market entry by U.S. telecommunications companies, 1984–1998. *Management Science*, 50: 1561–1575.

Williamson, O.E. 1985. *The economic institutions of capitalism*. New York: Free Press.

Windsperger, J., and Dant, R.P. 2006. Contractability and ownership redirection in franchising: A property rights view. *Journal of Retailing*, 82: 259–272.

Zahra, S.A., and Covin. J.G. 1995. Contextual influences on the corporate entrepreneurship-performance relationship: A longitudinal analysis. *Journal of Business Venturing*, 10: 43–58.

Index

C.S. Mishra, *Creating and Sustaining Competitive Advantage*,
DOI 10.1007/978-3-319-54540-0

D

V

The manufacturer's authorised representative in the EU is Springer Nature Customer Service Centre GmbH, Europaplatz 3, 69115 Heidelberg, Germany. If you have any concerns regarding our products, please contact ProductSafety@springernature.com

Printed and bound by CPI Group (UK) Ltd, Croydon, CR0 4YY

25/09/2026

02222881-0001